Eve Kosofsky Sedgwick is one of the most original and influential thinkers in critical and gender theory. Her work includes such groundbreaking books as *Epistemology of the Closet* and *Between Men: English Literature and Homosocial Desire*, writings that have powerfully influenced ideas of the body, of literature, and of identities. *Regarding Sedgwick* brings together new essays by distinguished critics to provide a sustained critical engagement with Sedgwick's work. The volume includes an extensive interview with Sedgwick, in which she speaks of her work, and of the situation of queer studies, critical theory, and the academy at the turn of a millennium.

Stephen M. Barber is Assistant Professor of English at the University of Rhode Island. He has published on 1930s British and European culture, Virginia Woolf, Michel Foucault, and Gilles Deleuze.

David L. Clark is Professor in the Department of English at McMaster University where he teaches critical theory and Continental philosophy. He is co-editor of *Intersections: Nineteenth-Century Philosophy and Contemporary Theory* and *New Romanticisms: Theory and Critical Practice*.

Regarding Sedgwick
Essays on Queer Culture and Critical Theory

Edited by Stephen M. Barber and David L. Clark

Routledge
Taylor & Francis Group

NEW YORK AND LONDON

Published in 2002 by
Routledge
29 West 35th Street
New York, NY 10001
www.routledge-ny.com

Published in Great Britain by
Routledge
11 New Fetter Lane
London EC4P 4EE
www.routledge.co.uk

Routledge is an imprint of the Taylor & Francis Group.
Printed in the United States of America on acid-free paper.

10 9 8 7 6 5 4 3 2 1

Library of Congress Cataloging-in-Publication Data

Regarding Sedgwick : essays on queer culture and critical theory / edited by Stephen M. Barber
and David L. Clark
   p. cm.
   Includes bibliographical references and index.
     ISBN 0-415-92818-4 — ISBN 0-415-92819-2 (pbk.)
1. Sedgwick, Eve Kosofsky—Criticism and interpretation. 2. Homosexuality and literature—
History—20th century. 3. Gays' writings—History and criticism—Theory, etc. 4. Sedgwick, Eve
Kosofsky—Knowledge—Literature. 5. Lesbians in literature. I. Barber, Stephen M., 1965–
II. Clark, David L., 1955–

PS3569.E316 Z73   2002
809'.93353—dc21   2002075150

CONTENTS

Envois

INTRODUCTION

Queer Moments
The Performative Temporalities of Eve Kosofsky Sedgwick

Stephen M. Barber and David L. Clark

In 1980, if someone had prophesied
this rack of temporalities could come to us,
their knowledge would have seemed pure hate;
it would have seemed so, and have been so.
It still is so.

   Yet every morning
we have to gape the jaws of our unbelief
or belief, to knowing it.
—Eve Kosofsky Sedgwick, "Joy. He's Himself Today! He Knows Me!"

In 1995, Eve Kosofsky Sedgwick—"*primum mobile* of queer theory," it has been said[1]—remarked in an interview that "the historical links between the emergence of queer theory and the emergency of AIDS are very close." "For one thing," she continues, "theory is important with this disease, because the self-evident categories that we had before don't work about this virus. AIDS, among all of the tragedy and devastation, also makes a huge problem for thinking, and in AIDS activism the interpenetration of theory and activism is extensive and very productive." But, she adds, "it looks . . . as though gay politics right now is interested in forgetting about AIDS." The banishment of AIDS from memory "that's going on in a lot of mainstream gay culture, especially gay male culture and politics" is, Sedgwick notes, symptomatic of or concomitant with an "anti-intellectualism and re-naturalizing of identity categories. . . . The marginalization of critical thought about concepts and categories and the marginalization of a sense of urgency about the AIDS emergency really go together" (Kerr and O'Rourke, 7, 8). Five years after that interview, fourteen years into the story of the institutionalization of gay and lesbian studies, and two decades into the AIDS emergency, Sedgwick offers the following observation in her interview for the present volume: "AIDS issues are nowhere in the political programs of mainstream gay organizations." Taken together, these statements can be understood as Sedgwick's reply to her own conditional conjecture, posed in 1993 at a time when its audience could have read it as tentatively inauspicious: "In the short-shelf-life American marketplace of images, maybe the queer moment, if it's here today, will for that very reason be gone tomorrow" (1993, xii). Although Sedgwick's musing hints at a possible closure of the queer moment, the conditional embedded within it—"*if* it's here today"—importantly leaves open to question not only *what* "the queer moment" is, but also whether and *when* it is. These conjectures echo other hesitations in Sedgwick's writings regarding the presence of a queer moment. Thus, even the ingenuously jubilant claim from the same pages, "It was a QUEER time," comes to us by way of the past tense, and for all the mounted evidence *for* the queer moment offered in surrounding sentences, conclusive conviction is hedged by a prefatory supposition: "I suppose this must be called the moment of Queer" (xi–xii).

Sedgwick's reluctance in 1993 to affirm decisively that this *is* the queer moment, sustained even "when the wave of a broadly based public movement somehow overtakes and seems to amplify (amplifies by drowning it out?) the little, stubborn current of an individual narrative or obsession, an individual wellspring of narrow, desiring cathexis and cognition" (1993, xi), suggests that a problem about temporality may be for her a defining aspect of that moment. Sedgwick's speculation about its future initially seems to cast the span of "queer" within a recognizably temporal frame, but what remains evident in the forward to *Tendencies*, as across the entire body of her work, is another conception and unfolding of temporality, a specifically queer temporality that is at once indefinite and virtual but also forceful, resilient, and undeniable. This Sedgwick calls "an immemorial current" and "a continuing moment" (1993, xii), the sort of persistent present formulated by Gayatri Chakravorty Spivak, in another connection, as a "non-dimensional verbal mode" that signifies "not a future present but a persistent effortfulness that *makes* a 'present'" (Spivak, 156; emphasis added).[2] If in the vicinity and midst of Sedgwick's conditional suppositions we can discern a vigilance that is not simply an equivocation, it is because nobody more than Sedgwick herself has strained so purposely to give a body (of self, of works) to the queer moment and to use that body to demonstrate that, if "queer" exists at all, it can only be in the mode of an ongoing performativity: in a present created and sustained by the effortful acts— productions and interventions—that embody it.

In the fields of literary theory and cultural studies, and among those within and outside the academy concerned with the politics of sexuality, Sedgwick's work stands apart for its critical daring, conceptual originality, and, not least, for the power and scope of its impact. From *The Coherence of Gothic Conventions* (1980) and *Between Men: English Literature and Male Homosocial Desire* (1985) to *Epistemology of the Closet* (1990), *Tendencies* (1993), and beyond, her writings constitute a series of decisive though often controversial interventions, changing for a generation of scholars and activists—as this volume attests—how we think about the nexus of identities, desires, bodies, prohibitions, discourses, and the play of power. A crucial force in the emergence of gay and lesbian studies, *Between Men* provided a set of highly sophisticated intellectual itineraries and conceptual tools for analyzing the psychosocial complexities of male bonding in the British culture of 1750 to 1850. Just as eventfully, the talks, articles, and essays that would appear in the early 1990s as *Epistemology of the Closet* and *Tendencies* turned their attention—and ours—to the phenomenology and politics of twentieth-century Western male homosexuality and to the always problematic conceptualization of homosexuality more generally. In the opening paragraph of *Epistemology of the Closet*, Sedgwick memorably proposed that "an understanding of virtually any aspect of modern Western culture must be, not merely incomplete, but damaged in its central substance to the degree that it does not incorporate a critical analysis of modern homo/heterosexual definition" (1990, 1). While writing that book, she was simultaneously theorizing in its sister text, *Tendencies*, distinctly "queer" forms of self-fashioning and performance. The success of Sedgwick's comprehensive thought in altering intellectual itineraries across the disciplines has proven remarkable for any number of reasons, not the least of which has to do with the manner in which her writing "keeps faith"—to use her own phrase—with a difficult but vital ethical grounding.

This collection of essays reflects a general critical consciousness that it is now possible, after more than a decade into the emergence of queer theory, to begin to delineate Sedgwick's prodigious role in its formation and significance. Sedgwick says that Oscar Wilde was "hyper-indicative" of his age. Could this not justifiably be said of her with regard to our own time, as heterogeneous as that moment surely is? In her preface to *Between Men*, composed seven years after the work's initial publication, Sedgwick writes: "From the 1990s vantage of an elaborated and activist gay/lesbian studies scene in academia, a vocal and visible national gay/lesbian movement, and (for me and for many other women and men of various dissident sexualities) an emerging, highly productive queer community whose explicit basis is the criss-crossing of the lines of identification among genders, races, and sexual definitions, it's hard to remember what that distant country felt like" (1992, viii). Sedgwick is straining here to recall the distant country from within which she wrote *Between Men*—a country that was then inhabited by her but not yet, for the most part, by openly gay men. This was at a time when the queer community was still her barely-articulated utopian desire. "Rereading the book now," she observes, "I'm brought up short, often, with dismay at the thinness of the experience on which many of its analyses and generalizations are based. Yet I'm also relieved, and proud, that its main motives and imperatives still seem so recognizable" (viii). Perhaps, now, with that self-recognizability more fully in view, we can begin to pose these questions of Sedgwick and of her writings: Whence came those motivations and imperatives whose existence would prove so formative? To what moments in the history of queer thought do they belong? How are they aligned with that history? Might they also be, in some ways, at odds with it?

Given the close historical links between the emergency of AIDS, and the emergence of queer theory in the U.S., and following the recent and pervasive cultural amnesia of AIDS in mainstream gay culture, it is not especially surprising to hear that the survival of queer theory has been questioned or its possible "death" bruited, however questioningly. To raise that question is to already answer it from elsewhere than *queer*. For the question (in one recurrent form: "Is queer theory in decline, over, extinguished?" etc.) betrays not only a pre-comprehended reification of the queer moment as queer theory but also an apprehension of that moment as exclusively and indicatively a point in time: merely a passing "trend," a move that thereby enacts an unwitting complicity with the cultural amnesia of AIDS that Sedgwick observes. A restrictive grasp of "queer" misses or lets go the diverse temporalities that both hinge on the term and instantiate its distinctive intellectual and political force. These include the effortful present-making of the persistent recognition that the AIDS emergency necessitates, and that we find so searingly stated in the poem that serves as our epigraph: "Yet every morning / we have to gape the jaws of our unbelief / or belief, to *knowing* it" (emphasis added). Certainly collapsing the queer moment into queer theory removes the numinous scenes of supple temporality that both occasion Sedgwick's conditional conjecture ("maybe . . . , if it's here today . . . ") and render it forever undecidable. What is strange here is that Sedgwick's musing, as if on a dare, seems for an instant to entertain queer's finale. Even so, that conjectural end is profoundly at odds with Sedgwick's own thought, a thought that is hyper-indicative not only of queer theory per se but also — and this is what we would stress here — of a queer moment defined as much by its own non-temporality as by the twists it gives (on that "rack") to all other temporalities. For Sedgwick's "queer moment" is comprised of a plethora of phenomenologies organized around two axes: On the one hand, sexual, gendered, and racial deroutinizations, and, on the other hand, deroutinizations of a disorienting and unpredictably temporal kind. "If what is at work here," she writes of her own writing, "is an identification that falls across gender, it falls no less across sexualities, across 'perversions.'" "And," she adds hauntingly, "across the ontological crack between the living and the dead" (1993, 257).

One precise yet also productively indefinable version of this ontological crack finds expression in Sedgwick's recent work on Buddhism—a work which also fully comprises a Buddhist practice. Here Sedgwick meditates on what is referred to in the Tibetan tradition as the *bardo* (the transitional time/space) of dying or, as Sedgwick invites us to think of it, "the bardo that extends from diagnosis until death" ("Come As You Are," unpublished ms.).[3] Situating AIDS activism within this opaque temporality or nondimensional time/space (which nevertheless yields, she suggests, "a cultural space in the west in which to articulate the subjectivity of the dying") ("Pedagogy," unpublished ms.), Sedgwick finds in the idea of the *bardo* of dying not only "a sufficiently extensive space to invite a lot of elaboration, but also *political éclat*— think how much the impact of AIDS activism came from the stunning novelty of seeing people with a fatal disease who were nonetheless physically strong enough, and for a long time, to undertake the project of their own, forceful representation" ("Come As You Are," unpublished ms.). For Sedgwick, "queer" is this forceful representation, and its potency and revelations prove inextricable from both the phenomenology of the emergency of AIDS and from the temporal disorientations in which *queer* lives immemorially. If it seems important to investigate the queer temporalities that Sedgwick unfolds across her work, it is because we believe that attempt can help to demonstrate the felicitous impossibility of calculating a determinable span for the queer moment. As already indicated, the potency of "queer" as a political term is indebted to certain temporal disorientations. Without a sense of these other-than-punctual (or: -chronological; -sequential) temporalities, it would be difficult to assess how the term functions politically—or, for that matter, how it functions in any way.

Consider, for an initial example, Sedgwick's own account of the political effectivity of the term "queer." "If queer is a politically potent term, which it is, that's because, far from being capable of being detached from the childhood scene of shame, it cleaves to that scene as a near-inexhaustible source of transformational energy" (1995, 210). How is one to sketch responsibly *that* queer temporality whose political "now" is eventuated by the transformational energy that dissolves the difference, chronologically conceived, between the queer adult that one *is* and the queer child that one *was*?

Even to have survived queer childhood challenges the common notion of an itinerary whose end is a vouchsafed adulthood, since the arrival into adulthood that *this* survival signifies only opens onto yet other spaces, other times, *to be survived*. Thus when Sedgwick asserts that to be a queer adult in 1993 is "to have survived into a moment of unprecedented cultural richness, cohesion, and assertiveness for many lesbian and gay adults," we must be ready to hear the attendant qualification that disallows any easy approach to a time/space of postsurvival because, as she notes, "how permeable the identity 'survivor' must be to the undiminishing currents of risk, illness, mourning, and defiance" (1993, 3). After all, "[o]ne set of effects" she describes of "the profligate way this culture has of denying and despoiling queer energies and lives . . . turns up in the irreducible multilayeredness and multiphasedness of what queer survival means—since being a survivor on this scene is a matter of surviving *into* threat, stigma, the spiraling violence of gay- and lesbian-bashing, and (in the AIDS emergency) the omnipresence of somatic fear and wrenching loss" (1993, 1–3). When she considers her "adult friends and colleagues doing lesbian and gay work," Sedgwick indeed "feel[s] that the survival of each one is a miracle." That they, like herself, exist at all is an astonishing fact, but a fact no less overshadowed by the death one has escaped, and that so many others have not. "[E]veryone who does gay and lesbian studies is haunted by the suicides of [queer] adolescents" (1), she writes, recalling for us the near seamlessness that irreducibly obtains between the living and the dead.

The tableau that Sedgwick so often draws upon in her early work—"the tableau of two men chasing one another across a landscape [in which] . . . it is importantly undecidable . . . whether the two men represent two consciousnesses or only one" (1986, ix)—is eclipsed in her later writings by another tableau. This one, figured as a cleaving that crucially leaves undecidable where one subjectivity begins and the other ends, is paradigmatic not of the male paranoid plot of which the earlier one is representative, but rather of the similar inimitabilities that can be augured, that can obtain, between subjects who face one another in, precisely and paradoxically, disorienting temporal fissures. As in her allusions to scenes of shame, survival, and queer work, an important and recurring figure in the queer problematization of time in her writing assumes the intra-subjective form of an adult-child cleaving. The transformational energy in Sedgwick's examples of that cleaving draw specifically on both the affect shame and on the phenomenology of queer survival. As we shall see, there are in these examples other impulses, other engines, other intersubjective cleavings electric with comparable force. But the queer potency of the covenants that can obtain between adults and children remains singularly important. For if Sedgwick understands her writing to be the continuation of a kept promise made to herself as a child, it is also a promise kept to and for other queer children. About the latter promise, we have this stirring summons: "How to tell kids who are supposed never to learn this, that, farther along, the road widens and the air brightens; that in the big world there are worlds where it's plausible, our demand to *get used to it*" (1993, 2). So many promises to keep:

the promises by the queer adult borne of the queer child who made those promises. But also, always, one must keep the promises to the others, those for whom the air is still thin and the road narrow. Indeed this cluster of living promises, never punctually fulfilled as such, and therefore all the more necessary to make and keep, emerges as the condition of Sedgwick's oeuvre. After all, the figure of adult/child cleaving is not only the condition of her own writing but, if Sedgwick is right, of queer theory *tout court*: "I think many adults (and I am among them) are trying, in our work, to keep faith with vividly remembered promises made to ourselves in childhood: promises to make invisible possibilities and desires visible; to make the tacit things explicit; to smuggle queer representation in where it must be smuggled and, with the relative freedom of adulthood, to challenge queer eradicating impulses where they are to be so challenged" (1993, 3).

With these promises to challenge in mind, we re-open the foreword to *Tendencies* in order to re-encounter Sedgwick's conjecture (if, in the end, it can be called this) regarding the future of the queer moment: "maybe the queer moment, if it's here today, will for that very reason be gone tomorrow." We notice now that the paragraph within which this conjecture is embedded is also, in effect, initiated and energized by it. The paragraph begins teetering on the edge of a possible paralysis and perhaps cynicism; but, if it begins thus, it just as significantly and forcefully ends with two overturning and extraordinary claims: "The immemorial current that queer represents is antiseparatist as it is antiassimilationist. Keenly, it is relational and strange" (xii). The penultimate sentence posits an immemorial current as constitutive of queer even as that very current can be gleaned only in the representation that queer undertakes. That queer *undertakes*? Are we to understand "queer," then, to be a quasi-intentional agent? Perhaps. In any case, it is, Sedgwick tells us, a force, specifically a *relational* force, quite as "ethics" is for Michel Foucault.

Gilles Deleuze observes: "Foucault doesn't use the word *subject* [in his ethics] as though he's talking about a person or a form of identity, but talks about 'subjectification' as a process, and 'Self' as a relation (a relation to oneself). And what's he talking about? About a relation of force to itself (whereas power was a relation of a force to other forces), about a 'fold' of force. About establishing different ways of existing, depending on how you fold the line of forces, or inventing possibilities of life that depend on death too, on our relations to death: existing not as a subject but as a work of art. He's talking about inventing ways of existing, through optional rules, that can both resist power and elude knowledge, even if knowledge tries to penetrate them and power to appropriate them" (Deleuze, 92). Foucault, now: "To be 'gay,' I think, is not to identify with the psychological traits and the visible masks of a homosexual but to try to define and develop a way of life" (Foucault, 138). And, finally, Sedgwick: "'[G]ay' and 'lesbian' still present themselves (however delusively) as objective, empirical categories governed by empirical rules of evidence (however contested). 'Queer' seems to hinge much more radically and explicitly on a person's undertaking particular, performative acts of experimental self-perception and filiation. A hypothesis worth making explicit: that there are important senses in which 'queer' can signify only *when attached to the first person*. One possible corollary: that what it takes—all it takes—to make the description 'queer' a true one is the impulsion *to* use it in the first person" (1993, 9). If "queer" is a temporality, a "moment," it is also then a force; or rather, it is a crossing of temporality with force. "The *immemorial current* that queer represents" conveys a persistent present, "a continuing moment" (xii), in short, *temporal* force. Immemorial, crossed with current, or cleaved to it— the phrase is accomplishing a great deal. *Immemorial*, as defined by the *American Heritage Dictionary*: "Reaching beyond the limits of memory—or history"; *Current*: "Belonging to the present time; prevalent, esp. at the present time; a steady onward movement; flow, as in liquid, or electric charge." At the same time "the immemorial current that *queer represents*" conveys *critical* force: the current, a countercurrent, is also, Sedgwick writes, "a continuing movement," "recurrent, eddying, *troublant*" (xii). Foucault captures precisely the multivalent sense of this temporal and critical force in his portrayal of modernity as "an attitude rather than as a period of history." "And by 'attitude,'" he stresses, "I mean a mode of relating to contemporary reality; a voluntary choice made by certain people; in the end, a way of thinking and feeling; a way, too, of acting and behaving that at one and the same time marks a relation of belonging and presents itself as a task" (304). This attitude, "a philosophical ethos that could be described as a permanent critique of our historical era," requires, Foucault says, "permanent reactivation" (312). It seeks not "to understand the present on the basis of a totality or of a future achievement;" rather, it searches "for a difference: What difference does today introduce with respect to yesterday?" (305). What is one to make of this striking resonance between Foucault's "modernity" and Sedgwick's "queer"? Foucault follows a certain critical tradition that dates the Enlightenment as the beginning of modernity, but he also breaks from it inasmuch as "enlightenment" signifies for him not a historical epoch but an effortful and on-going attitude. Dare one think enlightenment as queer? This, in any case, seems to us an inexplicit argument made by a number of our contributors; it also strikes us as one moment among many during which Foucault and Sedgwick would appear to inhabit, and call others to inhabit, the same singular and indecipherable first person of that attitude: "I mean. . . ."

Sedgwick registers the critical force (eddying, troublant) of this queer current in the foreword to *Tendencies*—indeed, at the precise moment that she expresses her concern for a future queer present: "I mean the essays collected in this book to make, cumulatively, stubbornly, a counterclaim against that obsolescence: a claim that something about *queer* is inextinguishable" (1993, xii). "I mean" is not conventionally understood to be among classic instances of "performative utterances" (utterances, that is, that do what they say in or through the very saying of them). However, Sedgwick's project is not just to fill in the blanks of some preexisting performative convention in critical theory but rather (as she says of Fanny in *The Golden Bowl*) to move elaborately athwart it. "I mean," in this instance operates as a nonce performative, does what it says through its very saying: that is, it forestalls and displaces—without preventing—the eradicating, extinguishing impulses that at once threaten and condition its utterance.

Sedgwick has long been interested in, and has written extensively on, queer performativity in the forms, to name only a few, of "coming out," of "work around AIDS and other grave identity-implicating illnesses," and of "the self-labeled, transversely but urgently representational placarded body of demonstration" (1995, 207). The idea of a performativity beyond or at odds with referential meaning proves indispensable to her thinking inasmuch as it provides critical leverage for investigating "the obliquities among meaning, being, and doing." But as Sedgwick and Andrew Parker point out in their introduction to *Performativity and Performance*, the phase of critical theory that is of special pertinence to "queer" derives from a third generation of performance/performativity studies. Following, first, "the pre-Derridean project of definitively segregating constatation from performativity, and theatrical speech from 'ordinary language'" and, second, the more recent work in the field that Sedgwick and Parker characterize as predominantly *epistemologically* invested, this new critical phase is seen as "strikingly refrain[ing] from looking to performativity/performance for a demonstration of whether or not there are essential truths or identities, and how we could, or why we couldn't know them." More positively, they write: "As a certain stress has been lifted momentarily from the issues that surround *being something*, an excitingly charged and spacious stage seems to open up for explorations of that even older, even newer question, of how saying something can be doing something" (16).

Many readers have no doubt felt this kind of performativity at work in *Between Men*, although, to our knowledge, it has not been written about explicitly as such. In the pages of *Rolling Stone*, however, the book is referred to as "the text that ignited gay studies," and the *Village Voice Literary Supplement* is surely catching on to its performative aspect when it acknowledges *Between Men* as "in many ways the book that turned queer theory from a latent to a manifest discipline."[4] Indeed, among that text's numerous accomplishments perhaps most significant is the way in which a certain crucial invocation there functions as a performative. That invocation? It is of an audience: an audience created by being imagined and interpellated, which is also and more precisely to say, along with Sedgwick on Henry James, a queer audience that is desired. In a remarkable passage in her preface to the second edition of *Between Men*, Sedgwick retrospectively discusses her own passage on the train of invocation from relative naïveté to worldliness: "That there was something irrepressibly *provincial* about the young author of this book is manifest. But will it make sense if I describe that provinciality as not only a measure of her distance from the scenes of gay male creativity, whose utopian invocation tacitly motivates the book, but also a ground of her passionate, queer, and fairly uncanny identification with it?" (1992, ix) Sedgwick's avowed provinciality ceases to be opposed to the urbane and becomes instead its condition, the ground, as we see, of her passionate, queer, and uncanny identification with gay male creativity. (Of course, as a "deconstructive and very writerly close reader" [1992, vii], Sedgwick's take on binary oppositions proceeds with an awareness of any given term's implication in its other, so that the "metropolis [is] continually recruited and reconstituted by having folded into it the incredulous energies of the provincial. Or—I might better say— the provincial energies of incredulity itself" [1992, ix].) What we want to stress is that the utopian invocation of scenes of gay male creativity which, by her own account, impelled the writing of *Between Men* would itself, exactly by way of the book's accomplishment, become central to the formation of the scene of creativity—not exclusively gay or male—now known as queer theory. If with *Between Men*, Sedgwick understands herself to have been moved in part by a desire that took the form of a productive refusal of absence (or, as she insists, "The yearning makes the incredulity"), that desire in effect helped forge the "communities toward whose readership the book so palpably yearns" (1992, ix).

Sedgwick's oeuvre can itself be understood as "an excitingly charged and spacious stage," a promising proscenium. In the text of a talk originally given in 1991, Sedgwick examines the performative aspects of queer protest in explicitly political contexts. Here, answerability to the earlier child-adult promises takes the form of a projected body—Sedgwick's own body together with the collective body comprised of demonstrators from the Ad Hoc Coalition of Black Lesbians and Gays and from ACT UP-Triangle. The protest targeted the University of North Carolina's local public broadcasting station, which was refusing to air Marlon Riggs's *Tongues Untied*, "a stunning film," she explains, "on the genocidally underrepresented topic of black gay men in the U.S."

(1993b, 122). As her title, "Socratic Raptures, Socratic Ruptures: Notes Toward Queer Performativity," indicates, Sedgwick is concerned to elaborate something of the specificity of queer performativity, noting along the way "how arduous a thing it is any time a group of people try to project voices and bodies into a space of public protest that has continuously to be reinvented from scratch, even though (or because) the protest-*function* is so routinized and banalized by the state and media representations that enable it" (1993b, 122–23). Correspondingly, reinvention here takes the form of the *smuggling* that we saw augured by the ("vividly remembered") promises made to queer youth, and the various forms of representation that are its condition include the term that figures so centrally in Sedgwick's lexicon of queer performativity, namely, and again, *shaming*. "The uses we had for [the] news apparatus," she reflects of the demonstration, "as opposed to the uses it had for us, I condensed in my mind under the double formulation 'shaming and smuggling.' With the force of our words—referentially, that is—our object was to discredit the hollow pretense at 'representing' the public maintained by our local 'public' broadcasting station; to shame them into compliance or negotiation on the issue of airing this rare and important film. With the force of our bodies, however—and in that sense performatively—our object was not merely to demand representation, representation elsewhere, but ourselves to give, to *be* representation: somehow to smuggle onto the prohibitive airways some version of the apparently unrepresentably dangerous and endangered conjunction, *queer* and *black*" (1993b, 125).

That particular conjunction has been the object of Sedgwick's careful attention in many ways over many years. In 1996, for example, she both edited and brought to publication a collection of stories, poems, and selections from notebooks and journals by the gay African-American writer, Gary Fisher, who had been her graduate student ten years earlier. "It wasn't commonplace back then," she recalls in her afterword to that book, "at least it hadn't happened to me before, to hear from young people that the futures they look forward to are so modest in duration" (1996, 276). Fisher was not only, as Sedgwick discerned, a deeply talented writer ("To say someone has found an art: doesn't it mean that they have learned, not just to solve problems in the medium, but to formulate new problems in it—whether soluble or not—that would be worth solving?" [278]); he was also (and for the most part closetedly) HIV positive. He was, further, someone for whom "his own identification as black could hardly be a settled or simple thing. To see that unsettled and unsimple were constitutive conditions—rather than prohibitive ones— for thinking about race and racism was probably the single event that most galvanized the writing and perception of his last decade" (274–75). For Sedgwick, this had been no less true, if differently, of herself as "a woman [who has] been intimately formed by, among other things, the availability for my own identifications of men and of male 'perversion,' courage, care, loss, struggle, and creativity," along with, after 1991, the unsettled and unsimple constitutive condition of her living with a "very often fatal disease that makes its own demands of a new politics, a new identity-formation" (1993, 263).

It was in their exchange of "war stories"—of assaults of medication, of trauma, of the possibility of imminent death—in 1991, after her diagnosis with breast cancer and three years before Fisher's death from AIDS related complications, that Sedgwick experienced the dissolving force of "the particular awe or shyness that can separate the healthy from the ill" (1993, 280). "I remember," she recounts of a scene in a Castro bar, "I remember describing to Gary what I'd experienced as the over whelming trauma of half a year of chemotherapy-induced baldness." It was, she continues

> a narcissistic insult of no medical significance whatever, that had so completely flooded my psychic defenses that, for the whole duration of the treatment, almost every hour of consciousness had remained an exhausting task.
>
> Gary said, yes, this was what it felt like for him to have KS lesions on his arms. Nobody else ever saw them: he always wore long-sleeved shirts. But alone, he said, in his apartment, he would spend hours, sometimes whole days of months, paralyzed in front of his mirror, incredulous, unable—also unable to stop trying—to constitute there a recognizable self. Impaled by stigma.
>
> After Gary's death I recounted this conversation to one of his sisters. She said: I think that's how Gary experienced being black, too. (1993, 281)

What Sedgwick traces throughout Fisher's writing (despite the recurrent inability of its author to constitute a recognizable self in that mirror)—and what again and again she herself so movingly at once avails and presents—is a "giving-face." "And while for another person," she concludes, "or at another place or time, it might have been true that fatality played no very necessary role among these elements of a sexuality, for this person, at this time and place it was central, the need to give face—or many faces—to a fate" (1993, 284). To give face, or many faces, where the refractory mirror represents to its viewer the cleaving figure of two interminably indistinguishable *and* utterly other subjects: for Sedgwick, this represents an amplification of the self in its very dissolution or drowning when, again, "the wave of a broadly based . . . movement somehow overtakes and seems to amplify . . . the little stubborn current of an individual narrative or obsession, an individual wellspring of narrow, desiring cathexis and cognition." "The fierce beam of history that propelled Gary Fisher's sexual imagination," she echoes in another register, "was evidently less that of individual trauma than of a more collective violence and loss. All the more was it a trauma that he couldn't otherwise make present to himself, a violence that his culture offered him the most impoverished means for realizing and hence mourning" (1993, 284).

Only two years prior to Sedgwick's encounter with Fisher at Berkeley, another moment was beginning to take shape whose genesis in loss, mourning, trauma, and activism was being realized in, among other forms, that of a new discipline: "that early though startlingly recent moment in the institutionalization of gay/lesbian studies" (1993, 253). 1986: the year Sedgwick taught her first lesbian and gay critical theory class (it was in the English Department at Amherst College [she would move later to Duke University, and then to CUNY]), and significantly, the year when, as she notes in her "obituary" for Michael Lynch, "I, who didn't [then] personally know anyone with AIDS, met and fell in love with Michael Lynch" (1993, 253). "[A] long-time pioneer of gay studies," "a defining figure in the story of gay studies," Lynch had been, as Sedgwick writes, "somebody who catalyzed, crystallized, fecundated projects, institutions, and communities wherever he had been—wherever geographically, wherever institutionally, wherever in identity and experience" (1993, viii, 256, 253). The "I" who met that figure remains queerly indeterminate. Who cleaves to whom? She to him or he to her? "It was nobody simpler than the handsome and complicated poet and scholar I met in him." It was, she continues, "a queer but long-married young woman whose erotic and intellectual life were fiercely transitive, shaped by a thirst for knowledge and identifications that might cross the barriers of what seemed my identity. It was also someone who had it at heart to make decisive interventions on two scenes of identity that were supposed not to have to do with each other: the scene of feminism, where I 'identified' and which I knew well; and the scene of gay men's bonding, community, thought, and politics, a potent and numinous scene which at the experiential level was at that time almost totally unknown to me" (1993, 253).

At the time of their momentous encounter, Lynch was himself not only living with HIV but also facing the diagnosis of AIDS in his "ex-lover, housemate, best-loved friend, a medical researcher, Bill Lewis, who was to die suddenly the next fall" (1993, 253). Lynch's "availability to be identified with and loved," Sedgwick hypothesizes, "must have had everything to do with this moment"— this moment, that is to say, of loss: "The same loss, the same history of struggle and subtraction made Michael available to my identification and love, opaque to my knowledge" (1993, 253). That opacity of knowledge, figured in the cross-mirroring faces and forces of available identification, is the kind of disorienting refraction that Sedgwick sees as constitutive of a self, *her* self, the self that fecundates and is fecundated by inimitable similarities, similar inimitabilities. Unlike Fisher's mirror that could not avail to him the visage that would enable the constitution of a recognizable self (as it could so gorgeously to his readers), and unlike family mirrors in which Sedgwick sees offered up wounded visages to queer kids (the family mirrors that stigmatize their beholders), Sedgwick's mirrors disclose visages and visions that bear witness to a queer time, to a moment, that is to say, hitherto unseen.

Hitherto unseen? Not quite, for as we saw of *Between Men*, Sedgwick had herself already been acting as harbinger to that moment whose evolution she would continue to sustain and at whose instigation, as throughout its unfolding, powerfully figures Proust. "*A la recherche du temps perdu* has remained into the present the most vital center of the energies of gay literary high culture," she remarks, "as well as of many manifestations of modern literary high culture in general" (1990, 213). In *Epistemology of the Closet*, and again in the interview included in this volume, Sedgwick traces to Proust-reading at least one of her catalytic moments, and throughout her work he appears as a generative force as well as an abetting resource in her intellectual and emotional life in ways no doubt comparable to the cross-identifications between herself and Michael Lynch, Michael Moon (who, with Sedgwick, co-authored a number of essays, including "Divinity: A Dossier, A Performance Piece, A Little-Understood Emotion" from *Tendencies*) and Gary Fisher, not to mention a profusion of other queer people and literary figures (such as Oscar Wilde, Emily Dickinson, Henry James, and Willa Cather). Inasmuch as it spurred the writing that forged a moment, the potent and numinous scene of Proust-reading in question staged, she remembers, the actualization of a knowledge that was evidently otherwise experientially unknown to her. She notes: "During the writing of *Between Men*, I was very involved with lesbian-inflected feminist culture and critique, but I actually knew only one openly gay man" (1990, viii). The generative moment itself she describes this way:

> I was reading Proust for the first time during just the short stretch of years during which it occurred to me to have ambitions that were not exclusively under the aspect of eternity: to want to publish visibly, know people, make a go of it, get a run for my money. Oddly, of course, it was reading Proust that made me want these adventures and think I could find them. The interminable meditation on the vanity of human wishes was

a galvanizing failure for at least one reader: it was, if anything, the very sense of the transparency and predictability of worldly ambitions that gave me the nerve and skill to have worldly ambitions of my own. (1990, 240)

In a more recent essay, "Paranoid Reading and Reparative Reading," Sedgwick re-opens *A la recherche du temps perdu* in order to make salient the degree to which Proust's narrator's revelations are indebted to a specifically queer temporal disorientation. "Think," she enjoins us, "of the epiphanic, extravagantly reparative final volume of Proust, in which the narrator, after a long withdrawal from society, goes to a party where he at first thinks everyone is sporting elaborate costumes pretending to be ancient—then realizes that they *are* old, and so is he—and is then assailed, in half a dozen distinct mnemonic shocks, by a climactic series of joy-inducing 'truths' about the relation of writing to time" (1997, 26). Concerning these queer-spawned realizations about that relation of writing to time, Sedgwick points out that although "the narrator never says so[,] the complete temporal disorientation that initiates him into this revelatory space would have been impossible in a heterosexual *père de famille*, in one who had meanwhile been embodying, in the form of inexorably 'progressing' identities and roles, the regular arrival of children and grandchildren." The passage from Proust that Sedgwick has in mind is in any case worthy of full recitation, and here perhaps *especially* since it assists us in dramatizing the inimitability that similarly characterizes both Proust and Sedgwick. "And now I began to understand what old age was," Proust's narrator reflects:

—old age, which perhaps of all the realities is the one of which we preserve for longest in our life a purely abstract conception, looking at calendars, dating our letters, seeing our friends marry and then in their turn the children of our friends, and yet, either from fear or from sloth, not understanding what all this means, until the day when we behold an unknown silhouette—which teaches us that we are living in a new world; until the day when a grandson of a woman we once knew, a young man whom instinctively we treat as a contemporary of ours, smiles as though we were making fun of him because it seems that we are old enough to be his grandfather—and I began to understand too what death meant and love and the joys of the spiritual life, the usefulness of suffering, a vocation, etc. (Proust, qtd. in Sedgwick, 1997, 26)

With a delight that owes something to *laissez-faire* but probably more to the *hauteur* of indifference, Sedgwick and Andrew Parker announce in their co-

authored "Performativity and Performance" that *"Le marriage, c'est les autres"*
(1995, 11). But if the redeemability of the family is not pressingly or ostensibly
a question in the passage of Proust (it is a question to which Sedgwick offers
a complex response in "Tales of the Avunculate"—itself an *envoi*, in some
sense, to her friend Craig Owens, whose memorial she includes in *Tendencies*),
what certainly *is* at issue there, as in Sedgwick's work generally, are the revelations secured exactly by an infelicitous relation to one's—or simply *the*—
genealogical family. Thus in an earlier moment of her writing to which we
have already referred, Sedgwick turns to Balzac, in whose grand narrative of
the move from the provinces to the metropolis she finds a gloss (*avant la lettre*)
of the unfolding narrative that characterizes queer beginnings, queer life.
Although she makes autobiographical use of this narrative as well, it is to
Proust, as we have seen, that she returns in order to foreground the catalytic
queer moment of her own professional threshold: first Balzac, from whom all
roads begin, and then to Proust, to whom, if one's lucky, all roads lead. "The
more than Balzacian founding narrative of a certain modern identity for Euro-
American gay men," she writes, "vibrates along a chord that stretches from
provincial origins to metropolitan destinies. As each individual story begins in
the isolation of queer childhood, we compulsorily and excruciatingly *misrecognize* ourselves in the available mirror of the atomized, procreative, so-called
heterosexual pre- or ex-urban nuclear family of origin, whose bruisingly inap-
propriate interpellations may wound us—those resilient or lucky enough to
survive them—into life, life of a different kind. The site of that second family
and belated life, those newly constituted and denaturalized 'families,' those
tardy, wondering chances at transformed and transforming self- and other-
recognition, is the metropolis" (1992, ix).

The allusion to Balzac's narrative appears tellingly enough in Sedgwick's
preface to *Between Men*: Its appearance there proves significant because the
publication of that book in 1985 in effect shuttled its author, by her own
account, from the provinces to the metropolis, from ambitions directed merely
toward immortality ("under the aspect of eternity"), to more "worldly" ambitions whose scope encompassed, precisely, the world. As noted above, the revelations and impact of *Between Men* cleared the way for the beginning of the
institutionalization, one year later, of lesbian and gay studies. That its revelations owe to its author's queer survival from the life of the family into life of a
different kind suggests how early in her thought, when she was intending the
book as an intervention in feminist critique, she was remarking a shift in power
from the Name of the Father, to the Name of the Family, an observation and
articulation arguably as significant to critical theory as Foucault's not unrelated
analysis of the shift from disciplinary to bio-political power. In "Tales of the

Avunculate," Sedgwick suggests that "the precapitalist or early-capitalist func-tions of the Name of the Father [have] been substantially superseded, in a process accelerating over the last century and a half, very specifically by what may be termed the Name of the Family—that is, the name Family" (1992, 72). "Within this family," she continues, "the position of any father is by no means a given; there are important purposes, including feminist ones, for which the term 'familialism' may now usefully be substituted for 'patriarchy'." Elsewhere, Sedgwick asks that we begin to imagine a way of thinking athwart the episte-mology of the family ("an impacted social space" where countless identitarian dimensions "line up perfectly with each other"): a mode of thought or theo-rizing that could "valu[e] the ways in which meanings and institutions can be at loose ends with each other" (1993, 6). "What if," she supposes, "the richest junctures weren't the ones where *everything means the same thing?*" (6). It was an epistemology attached to that supposition that helped Sedgwick to articu-late what she refers to in the preface to *Between Men* as a "pointedly . . . com-plicating, antiseparatist, and antihomophobic contribution to a feminist move-ment" (1992, viii).

The feminist epistemology that Sedgwick found needy was one that evi-dently resonated for her with that epistemology of the family where everything lines up neatly to mean the same thing. The revelatory spaces opened by Sedg-wick's oeuvre are, in relevant ways, resonant with those in Proust, although hers appear to have been intuitive from the start whereas his, we recall, are repre-sented as only gradually reached ("I began to understand . . ."). What most cleaves their knowledges each to the other is a certain distance—cognitive, affective, somatic—from the family. In "Queer and Now," Sedgwick retro-spectively sees the consistency in her life exactly to have been "a ruling intu-ition . . . that the most productive strategy (intellectually, emotionally) might be, whenever possible, to *dis*articulate them one from another, to *dis*engage them—the bonds of blood, of law, of habituation, of privacy, of companionship and succor—from the lockstep of their unanimity in the system called 'family'" (1993, 6). Although she identified as a feminist (and still does) "fairly unprob-lematically" ("Not," she writes in her preface, "that I think the transferential poetics of identification and address are *ever* simple; they aren't"), and although she "was surprised, exultant, grateful to be lifted into the whirlwind of that moment of activist grand theory," she also "wanted" and "*needed*," she insists, "feminist scholarship to be different." "In particular," she recalls, "I found oppressive the hygienic way in which a variety of different institutional, con-ceptual, political, ethical, and emotional contingencies promised (threatened?) to line up together so neatly in the development of a feminocentric field of women's studies in which subjects, paradigms, and political thrust of research, as well as the researchers themselves, might all be identified with the female. Participating in each of these contingencies, I still needed to keep faith, as best I could, with an obstinate intuition that the loose ends and crossed ends of identity are more fecund than the places where identity, desire, analysis, and need can all be aligned and centered" (1993, vii–viii).

From those retrospectively scanned contingencies to the contingent party scene that spawns Proust's "joy-inducing 'truths'," Sedgwick finds herself returned to the scene of the present where she notes the "more recent and terrible contingency, in the brutal foreshortening of so many queer lifespans, [that] has deroutinized the temporality of so many of us in ways that only intensify this effect" (1997, 26). Sedgwick's allusion to AIDS reorients us to phenomenologies of temporal disorientation, to the fundamental unknowability of the queer moment, with its own joy-inducing truths, and just as surely to an uncertainty that envelops this moment. Referring to those living with HIV and AIDS and of herself with regard to her then-recent diagnosis of breast cancer, Sedgwick writes, as though already invoking the *bardo* of dying: "I still want to know more and more about how . . . people deal with this long moment, and about how I will. As whom, as what I may deal with it; out of what spaces I may speak of it, or be spoken for in these identities and struggles—I know these are not simply for me or even for my immediate communities to decide; yet I relish knowing that enough of us will be here to demonstrate that the answer can hardly be what anyone will have expected" (1993, 266). Though their outcome is cast into an unknowable future, this sense of demonstration and of the skills required to undertake it "could not have evolved," Sedgwick stresses, "outside the context of liberatory identity politics and AIDS activism." But their flavor is also, as she says of Lynch, similarly and inimitably her own.

"So much about how to be sick," Sedgwick writes, " —how to occupy most truthfully and powerfully, and at the same time constantly to question and deconstruct, the sick role, the identity role of the 'person living with life-threatening disease'—had long been embodied in [Michael Lynch], and performed by him, in ways which many of us, sick and well, have had reason to appreciate keenly" (1993, 261). For those of us who knew Michael Lynch, and for those of us who lived on to see other temporalities emerge and unfold within our long moment, how true all of this reads; and how powerfully true, too, for those who did and did not know Michael Lynch, Sedgwick's attribution of exemplarity to him rebounds on, signifies, *herself*. For it is Sedgwick who has manifested most visibly, in her writing, her art, and her self, the present that she sees given to her by Lynch: this exemplary present of "entrust[ing] as many people as one possibly can with one's actual body and its needs, one's stories about its fate, one's dreams and one's sources of information or hypothesis about disease, cure, con-solation, denial, and the state of institutional violence that are also invested in one's illness" (1993, 261). In "A Poem Is Being Written" Sedgwick describes her motivation for undertaking ventures in public *self*-representation as "a fantasy that readers or hearers would be variously—in anger, identification, pleasure, envy, 'permission,' exclusion—stimulated to write accounts 'like' this one (what-ever that means) of their own, and share those" (1993, 214). In "White Glasses," she extends this wish for a collective body of work to the "intellectual, emo-tional, bodily self as refracted through illness and as resistant to it": "It's as though there were transformative political work to be done just by being available to be identified with in the very grain of one's illness—being available for identifica-tion to friends, but as well to people who don't love one; even to people who may not like one at all nor even wish one well" (1993, 261).

Being available for identification where identification is anything but a pre-comprehended, felicitous, or familial term is the poetics and ethics of Sedg-wick's work. Who can forget the extraordinary ways that Sedgwick's "I" means—performatively, epistemologically, autobiographically, institutionally, politically—or how this "I" at once demands, gives, and *is* queer representa-tion? "Perhaps," she offers in her foreword to *Tendencies*, "it would be useful to say that the first person throughout represents neither the sense of a simple, set-tled congratulatory 'I,' on the one hand, nor on the other a fragmented post-modernist postindividual—never mind an unreliable narrator. No, 'I' is a heuristic; maybe a powerful one" (1993, xiv). The refusal to settle into a con-gratulatory comfort with regard to the queer moment; the refusal, too, to min-imize that immemorial current by reducing it to any one of its manifestations; the refusal, finally, to resign to an overwhelmingly present amnesia of the AIDS emergency: All these refusals, and so many affirmations besides, bespeak Sedgwick's "I" and the peculiar temporal disorientations within which that "I" abides. That her speculation of a time in the future for queer appears at all is ultimately less ironic than it is cautionary and mobilizing: at once a con-frontation with and meditation on the possible dissolution of the (punctual) queer moment, Sedgwick's conjecture is also the condition of and motivation for the projection and forceful representation, here and now, of the persistent present-tense ("I mean") that "queer" represents. This present tense, forwarded into an unknowable future, *remains*. "That's the wonderful thing about the printed word," she remarks in her interview with us: "it can't be updated instantly. It's allowed to remain anachronistic to the culture of the moment."

Even so, Sedgwick's 1993 evocation of a heuristic "I," that singular first per-son whose name seems a metonym of our moment, is taken up by her seven years later with an expressed (countercurrent?) wish to see this first person dissolved in ways that differ significantly from those discussed above. "There are psychological motivations, no doubt, behind the wish to do without the first person," she muses (replying here to our interview question—ultimately difficult to broach, this—on the complex ontological status of her use of the first person singular). "One of them—a fairly recent one, I guess—has to do with the consciousness of mortality that's gotten so sharp. I have an intense wish to be assured that the people and communities I'm leaving behind can take care of themselves—that they don't need 'me,' my thought, my labor of regenerating a first person to keep them going." Although she consigns this wish "to an insanely grandiose fantasy about my importance to others' lives," there can be no question as to the sanity of the realization of this importance. So when she earlier writes, "My own real dread has never been about dying young but losing the people who make me want to live" (1993, 264), that dread reverberates, understandably, beyond that self, with the wave of a larger critical movement and with a large collective sense of possibly *not wanting to give in* to Sedgwick's wish. Possibly? But, then, how to give in? How can one give in? This collective "not wanting" issues less from need than from love—or, more specifically, from what Sedgwick has portrayed as "falling in love":

> a matter of suddenly, globally, 'knowing' that another person represents your only access to some vitally
> > transmissible truth
> > or radiantly heightened
> > mode of perception
> and that if you lose the thread of this intimacy, both your soul and your whole world might subsist forever in some desert-like state of ontological impoverishment." (1999,168)

When Sedgwick lost the mortal thread of her intimacy with Gary Fisher, her response to his death from within that desert-like state of ontological impoverishment took an undecidable form of mourning. Her profound anxiety that North American mainstream gay culture is amnesing AIDS is by now a part of the *knowing* towards which she beckons us in the poem on Fisher that heads our introduction. The loss of Fisher to Sedgwick takes the form of a text, a published work of love, one that reflects for all of its opacity the *knowing* that queer life, like queer death, can signify. "If an idiom is like a syntax," Sedgwick writes in her afterword to *Gary In Your Pocket* "—at least, if it is for some people— then to be inhabited like this will be familiar to those who sometimes fall asleep reading, and then dream their own mental semantics into the sentence structure of the author. The time of immersion in this volume has brought me many such experiences. Almost every night of it I have dreamed, not *of* Gary, but *as* him—have moved through one and another world clothed in the restless, elastic skin of his beautiful idiom. I don't know whether this has been more a way of mourning or of failing to mourn; of growing steeped in, or of refusing the news of his death. One thing I couldn't doubt: For all its imposing reserve and however truncated, Gary's is an idiom that longs to traverse and be held in the minds of many people who never knew him in another form" (1996, 291). So, too, of Sedgwick's idiom. To traverse it, to be held by it, to inhabit it, to cleave to it: These experiences, for the collective that she desired, imagined, and has summoned into being, continue to evolve this moment of queer, this persistent *queer and now*.

As we have stressed throughout our introduction, and as the essays collected here attest, the evolution of this moment of queer is anything but predictable. We call the first section of the book *Sedgwick's Subjects and Others* in order to emphasize how the arguments gathered there respond to the charged crossing at which Sedgwick's theories of "the subject" and the subject of Sedgwick's "theory" intersect. We note that although these essays are to different degrees committed to outlining an aspect of Sedgwick's theory of the subject, often times and most interestingly an "other" (to that subject) appears in the form of the undertaken reading or critique: thus, Sedgwick's "*Others.*" When an other to Sedgwick's subject is explicitly suggested, that is to say when a decisive move away from her account of subjectivity is recommended, this tends strongly to be done in name of "politics."

Alone among the contributors to this collection, Douglas Crimp explicitly positions the work of queer theory within the time of AIDS. In other ways, however, his essay speaks pointedly to concerns raised elsewhere in the volume. For example, the antinormative politics towards which he beckons has as its primary resource the mobilizing energies of shame and shaming. The possibilities of shame that he sees at work in Warhol's cinema are manifestly different from another expressly political enterprise evoked in this volume, the one suggested by Lauren Berlant's essay. For Berlant, shame may figure a *too* psychically invested subject, when, to her own thinking, queer thought would do well to depart from the hegemony of the psychic "interior" and its affects. Something of an implicit and surprising difference between Crimp's and Berlant's essays may be gleaned from precisely the uses to which "shame" is put. Berlant describes Sedgwick's mode of reading as a project "to *deshame* fantasmatic attachment so as to encounter its operations as knowledge" (emphasis ours), an enterprise that wins Berlant's critical sympathy even as the sense of shame that she has in mind here would seem directly at odds with the ways that both

Sedgwick and Crimp might want it to signify. For Crimp and Sedgwick what may be most interesting about a given fantasmatic attachment is its psychic life *in* shame (a shame whose political efficacy knows virtually no end); as Crimp suggests, to "deshame" that investment would be tantamount to participating in normalizing rather than resistant politics. Even so, it is antinormative politics that Berlant also wishes to see queer thought addressing and activating when she asks in all urgency whether "the project of queerness [must] start 'inside' the subject and spread out from there?"

If Berlant takes a distance from what she perceives as the subject of interiority in Sedgwick's theory, Judith Butler returns to that very subject only to find in it a "capacity," "a specifically ethical practice" that, as Ross Chambers shows in an entire essay on the subject, at once reflects on and rehearses unpredictability in the form of a highly sophisticated incoherence. This incoherence may be, Butler suggests, the theoretical underpinning of Sedgwick's "subject," but that subject only dates, she argues, to *Epistemology of the Closet*, having replaced the otherwise more structurally-determinate subject of *Between Men*. Paul Kelleher also turns his eye to the subject of *Between Men* in his outline of the theoretical career of Sedgwick's "paranoid Gothic," although his account is concerned to mark the historical grounds for the manifestation of any one of Sedgwick's named "subjects": the (British male) subject of the homosocial triangle from about 1750 to 1850; the (Western male) subject of homo/heterosexual definition from about 1850 to the present. Like Butler, Deborah Britzman in her contribution looks to the psychic life of Sedgwick's subject, but she focuses her attention on "theory" *as* Sedgwick's subject. Resistance in her reading thus signifies less sociologically than psychically. Moreover, like Butler and Chambers, she attends to how ethical obligation quickens Sedgwick's work. To Berlant's pointed question about whether a queer project need necessarily begin within the subject Britzman would respond, and for ethical as well as political reasons, *where else?*

Kelleher's essay underscores the place of *literature* in the history of sexuality, noting its absence, in a sense, from Foucault's work and its on-going, vital presence in Sedgwick's. His emphasis on Sedgwick's literary interests anticipates the question raised in the volume's second assemblage, *Writing Ethics: Reading Cleaving*: namely, the ways in which the "literary" comes specifically to signify the "ethical" in Sedgwick's work. In the volume's first section, Butler distinguishes herself from Sedgwick by remarking upon her own formation as "a more conceptually linear philosopher" and Sedgwick's as "a passionate literary scholar." Certainly Butler sees Sedgwick's literary investments as fundamental to the innovative and responsible character of her theory; and beyond that, Butler happily concedes that her own work has been enriched by the encounter with literature that she finds so exemplarily capacious in Sedgwick. Indeed, like Berlant whose essay largely focuses on a novel, Butler turns to Henry James's *The Wings of the Dove* in the final move of her essay. But whereas Berlant analyzes a novel in order to make salient a different enterprise for queer thought, Butler finds in James' novel important parallels to Sedgwick's ethical practice. The first essay of *Writing Ethics: Reading Cleaving* makes an ever stronger effort to locate Sedgwick's work in an ethical, literary tradition: For Sedgwick's "ethics of inversion," Ross Chambers insists, partakes of a prestigious line in literary history that is "itself part of the history of homosexuality's modern emergence." Chambers reads as ethical Sedgwick's assertion that homosexuality should be understood as paradigmatic (rather than as an exception); and, like Butler, he characterizes Sedgwick's analyses of the general instabilities of identities, their incoherence, as *queer*. In this, Chambers concludes, Sedgwick counts among the most innovative and ethical theorists of "queer," her compatriots, it turns out, all literary figures ranging from Whitman, Proust, and James, to Colette and Wittig. To this august list we would add Woolf.

Kathryn Bond Stockton assents to this view by making Sedgwick not only ethically *comparable* to Henry James (Butler concludes by implying a similar resemblance), but also *indistinguishable* from him. Stockton reads James' novella, "The Pupil," as authored by Sedgwick, and she reads other texts by Sedgwick as though they were "literary" through and through. The "literary" again emerges as a synonym for the "ethical," just as do the reading practices "obliged" by Sedgwick's writing. Stockton forcefully writes that Sedgwick's work fosters queer kids, by which she also had in mind queer readers who themselves become writerly-readers and readerly-writers, each cleaving to the other.

Reading figures just as powerfully for Melissa Solomon as a site of the "ethical," in as much as reading Sedgwick opens capacious expanses for theorizing lesbian identity anew. After Sedgwick, Britzman evokes a space of intellectual and affective parturition whimsically called "theory kindergarten," and it is Sedgwick's oeuvre as a whole that Solomon visits precisely as a resource and enactment of such a transitional time/space—or what she names, also after Sedgwick, the *bardo*. In contrast to Berlant, who describes Sedgwick's work as issuing from a consciousness with a certain embodied past and a specific history of nurturing, Solomon describes Sedgwick's writing as an endless exposition of a consciousness in transition. Attentive to that consciousness, the acts of "writing" and "reading" themselves become transitional or, in a way, indistinguishable. For Sedgwick, to draw lines between "theory" and "poetry" is to err; no less, she argues, for "reading" and "writing," in a sense. Both Stockton and Solomon rehearse this sense in their self-set tasks of demonstrating the ethics of Sedgwick's thought.

Like Solomon, Nancy K. Miller reads Sedgwick's life-texts as *bardo*-inflected, and turns her eye from the written text to cloth figures. Even so, Miller says of the latter that they are "poetic forms;" they figure affective structures of their creator's phenomenology of illness "as surely as the graphic signs of the page." Miller is referring to Sedgwick's A *Dialogue on Love* which, although sister-text to the cloth figures, nevertheless, it must be admitted, is inexorably *other* to them. For all similarities aside, Miller asks, "What happens when the written text vanishes? What reactions are produced by the cloth figures and what sort of a response is possible?"

Perhaps in *Envois*, the concluding section of this volume, James Kincaid makes an attempt to answer just such questions, since as long as he writes, he suggests, Sedgwick's written text will never vanish: It will be reproduced, re-addressed to its initial sender, even if the envois purportedly is meant for the eyes of our readers. Kincaid may be right, but also and no doubt in ways unintended by him. For if Sedgwick's written text does not vanish, it is not merely at the level of echoes, incorporated sentences, thoughts, images, and words; Kincaid's essay also wonderfully embodies symptoms of the very processes described by Sedgwick in her theory of the homosocial. A point made by Kelleher is useful here; he finds in Sedgwick a Jamesian presence (not as in James Kincaid, but Henry James), describing her *Epistemology* as a "high-Jamesian love letter" addressed to the works of D. A. Miller. Kincaid also addresses D. A. Miller, but his words are hardly those one would find in an amatory epistle. Miller's work, he suggests, exemplifies the policing desires of what Sedgwick calls "paranoid" reading practice. But, in an essay as complicatedly affecting as Kincaid's, perhaps it should come as no surprise that this critical gesture also amounts to a kind of love: the one found in the homosocial triangular structures of desire that Sedgwick made famous. It could be argued that Kincaid raises Miller's name only passionately to refuse it, thereby buoying the possibility of an unrivaled approach to his avowed other, Eve Kosofsky Sedgwick.

We turn now to a reading of each of our contributor's essays.

> Fantasy yearns always and only for itself: we desire to desire, to fantasize, with the result that all amorous gazes are somehow voluptuous, regardless of who is looking at whom. As spectators, we erotically cathect with the longing, wide-eyed gaze. . . .
> —Alice Kuzniar, *The Queer German Cinema*

Queer Before Gay is the working title of the larger project from which Douglas Crimp draws his contribution to this volume. In that title, two worlds—two forms of the politics of desire—are adjoined by a preposition that registers both historical unfolding and an ethical compromise. Taking the cultural microclimate of New York City as an exemplary case, Crimp argues that "gay" today mostly signifies the normalization and desexualization of its queer antecedents. The blunting of queer's resistant particularities is perhaps no more evident than in the progressive historical narrative of gay and lesbian life that is emblematized by the Gay Pride phenomenon, a narrative for which Crimp hopes his and Sedgwick's respective work will function as a counter-memory. Gays are told and tell themselves that the years since the Stonewall riots have been ones of political advancement; but as Crimp suggests, this ameliorative tale of hard-won formal equalities is belied by the material ways in which the discipline and harassment of queer bodies have only increased. The city administration of New York continues to wage war on gay nightlife, for example, while the mayor participates in the Gay Pride parade in the light of day. This inverse switching between private surveillance and public exposure is no doubt enabled by the analogously telling incoherences that Crimp finds in the Gay Pride movement itself. With its showy emphasis on the making visible of lives that were once deemed to be unviewable, Gay Pride effectively performs the imagined crossing from a closeted and socially fragmentary state of repression to a mature and communally sanctioned condition of self-actualization. But this political spectacle, *this* "placarded body of demonstration" (1995, 207), is possible, Crimp insists, only at the heavy cost of conjuring away the irreducible differences that properly inhabit and energize whatever is or could be meant by "gay." Crimp is therefore heartened by counter-cultural 'zines like *Swallow Your Pride* that quickly respond to the homogenizing impetus of Gay Pride with pointed irreverence. As one related website puts it: "are you sick of the continual crackdown on queer visibility, on the streets, in the parks, and on surveillance cameras? are you tired of being targeted by capitalist union-busting corporations desperate for your gay dollars? then help to organize GAY SHAME 2000! an anti-assimilationist radical queer alternative to consumerist 'pride' celebrations."[5]

For Crimp, however, the pacification of queer is much more than a matter of aligning the desires of gays and lesbians with those of a presumptively heterosexual middle-class. *Shame* rather than bourgeois inoculation is the key to grasping why gay has, with such alacrity, come after queer, and why it is that queer will always come *before* gay for thinkers like Crimp and Sedgwick. Gay Pride is a movement whose solidarity is forged out of a sense of public and collective expiation, the shameless assertion of the end of shame. Yet as Crimp points out, putatively rectifying speech acts of this kind are compromised from the start because they rely upon, and spectacularly reproduce, conventionally moralistic understandings of the nature of shame, understandings that are coarsely bipolar: Either shame is the poisonous affect that disables the self-assertion at the heart of identity politics or it is the disciplining milieu in which immoral and criminal subjects are encouraged to come to their senses. (With the resurgence of interest in the execution of "public sentences" in the U.S., "shame" has increasingly become the theatrically performed sign that justice has been served . . . or is imagined to have been served.) In America, it seems, one is either too disgraced or not disgraced enough; the subject either of the violent interpellating query, "Have you no shame?," or of the commanding call to arms, "Have no shame!"

Sedgwick never speaks of "gay" and "queer" in the pointedly antithetical manner that we see in Crimp, although on the very few occasions when she does gather these terms together for comparison and contrast she proceeds in a manner that isn't entirely at odds with Crimp's position either. On the question of shame, however, the two thinkers are much more closely allied. As Sedgwick argues in a series of essays on the question of shame and performativity with which Crimp's unfolding *Queer Before Gay* project is in close conversation, there are powerful and identifiably queer ways of thinking about shame for which the available and authoritative models are all but irrelevant. In Sedgwick's hands, shame is a uniquely productive affect that vivifies and consolidates the subject in a moment of wincing isolation; it is the stubborn and performatively vivid way of being a subject at the instant that the circuit of recognition, of seeing that one is being seen and acknowledged by another, is broken or bent; it is where and how the subject turns when the light of that returned gaze flickers or goes out. To say that this embarrassed tropism is merely a turning *inward* is for Sedgwick to miss a vital point about the positivity of shame, namely its *demonstrative* character, the myriad ways in which— under certain conditions that await further analysis—it can and is put to creatively performative work. In this, Sedgwick's project intersects quite unexpectedly with that of Julia Kristeva, for whom *melancholy* (surely not unrelated to shame), far from the mute withdrawal from the social body, functions positively as a felt point of resistance to the incoherent demands of an oedipalized culture. We might add here that the reciprocating gaze whose delicate and supercharged sightlines form the shame matrix has always already *threatened* to collapse and deform, if not in fact then in principle, for the condition of the possibility of any circuit of recognition is that it can be breached. Ignominy is thus in a sense "older" than the subject, the estranging space of exposure in which a subject performatively occurs. But perhaps not just any subject, for both Sedgwick and Crimp tentatively suggest that while (transvalued) shame need not necessarily be identified as queer, queer experience remains a peculiarly privileged vantage point from which to consider its relationship with performativity, gender, and the politics of resistance. These connections remain far from obvious, though, and one senses in Sedgwick more than Crimp a reluctance to discuss them. At the conclusion of her inaugural essay on the question, for instance, her "gesture at . . . summing up" is conspicuous for its repeated denials (i.e., for describing what she doesn't know and isn't saying about the being-queer of either performativity or shame) (1995, 236). Still, clearly for both Crimp and Sedgwick, shame remains tantalizingly productive: What pleasures and pains flourish, what lives are possible when one is born into a world that is experienced aslant? What unpredictable futures await those for whom being shamed is a condition of personal and political efflorescence rather than emaciation and incarceration? What new optics will need to be created through which even to glimpse the fecund boundary zones, at once fierce and playful, of "shame-creativity"? How to look to the side of the white-out glare of other spectacles of visibility, Gay Pride, for example?

As Sedgwick also argues, what is extraordinary and undertheorized about shame is the complexity of its contagious nature; witnessing the shaming experience of another renders that witness vulnerable not so much to the other's shame but to the other's openness *to* shame, the sense of his or her answerability to the other's hopes, fears, and desires. Here Sedgwick executes a curious reversal of a move that is central to Butler's work on the performativity of gender (learned anew, she acknowledges, from Sedgwick), the very work that Sedgwick acknowledges is the dialectical ground for her own writings on the performativity of shame. Such are the dialectical complexities attending the convocation of these thinkers. For Butler, as Sedgwick characterizes her work, gender melancholia is "instituted by the loss, not of particular objects of desire, but of proscribed desires themselves." Shame, on the other hand, involves not the disavowal of desire but the spontaneous avowal of one's susceptibility to the disavowal of an other's desire; shame, we might say, is what it feels like to be the object of or witness to someone else's melancholic renunciation.

Sedgwick acknowledges that Silvan Tomkins's treatment of shame as the affective ground for the psyche is one of the very few available theoretical models that allow for its positivity. As such, it informs Sedgwick's argument at multiple levels. But it is worth suggesting that both Sedgwick's and Crimp's positions also evoke critical antecedents along startlingly different theoretical registers. Consider for example the work of Emmanuel Levinas (to whom Crimp in fact briefly alludes), notably his account of the ethical convocation that irrepressibly obtains between subjects who are as vulnerable as they are distinct. For Levinas, we are each held "hostage" to an other's alterity and mortality (Levinas 1996, 121–22); in Sedgwick, tellingly, this capture or obligation happens in less obviously wrenching ways, through a more oceanic experience of "suffusion" and "flooding." Yet both Levinas and Sedgwick turn to the "face" as a figure not only for the natal scene of the subject's singularity and exposure but also, perhaps most important, for the piercing irrefusability and extroversion of those mortal essences. This, we have suggested, is what Sedgwick's writing continuously performs: a giving-face. The summons of responsibility is a given, radically undeniable, *out*, so to speak, for both Levinas and Sedgwick because of the spectacular and inextinguishable fact of the face, blushing for example in the case of Sedgwick, hungry in the case of Levinas. (Could one rigorously show these urgent countenances to be unrelated and without analogy to each other?) Farther afield, we might also consider the faint but insistent Heideggerian resonances in Sedgwick's claim that non-normative shame names an alternative and fundamentally interrogative way of being in the world, a way that is all but forgotten amid the complacent everydayness of heterosexual self-identification. As Sedgwick says, queer shame is queer because it is "the place where the *question* of identity arises more originarily, and most relationally" (1995, 239). Compare this to Heidegger's concept of *Das Schuldigsein* or primal "guilt;" ostensibly emptied of its moralistic connotations, "guilt" describes the root milieu of belatedness and answerability in which Dasein's existence is not presumed but raised resolutely as a question (Heidegger, ¶58). To those many for whom the *being-there* of Dasein is not an undertaking, guilt remains, like conventionally understood shame, merely a condition of debilitation and delinquency. Heidegger's project is of course fundamentally ontological in nature, and so worlds away from Sedgwick's steadfastly ontic focus. "Dasein," Levinas once smartly said, "is never hungry" (Levinas 1969, 134)—to which we might add, neither does it blush nor feel shame. Yet reading Heidegger after Sedgwick helps to recover the affective remainder haunting his work, the curious undertow of embodied life that tugs at his abstractions and that prevents him ever from entirely spiriting richly emotive terms like "guilt" away from their origins in felt experience. Finally, Sedgwick's interest in thinking shame through pyschologistic models of the failure or continuation of the "gaze" (1995, 211) cannot help but recall the French reception of Hegel's *Phenomenology of Spirit*, with its emphasis on the formation of provisional identities amid the heady push and pull of reciprocally recognized and misdirected looks and desires. Butler's important account of the psychic life of Hegel's bondsman (initially published at about the same time as Sedgwick's inaugural essay on "Shame and Performativity") is uncannily apposite here. As Butler argues, the bondsman passes from servitude to a state of unhappy consciousness (that is, he comes into a condition of specifically human being) at the moment that he confronts the absolute lord, namely death (Butler 1997, 41). The bondsman is nothing less than mortified by death, shamed before its implacable and non-seeing gaze, its radical indifference to his life. It is Hegel's genius to have seen that this mortification means not the withering destruction of the subject, but the perilous means by which an agented consciousness emerges at all. Deprived of its former existence as the master's instrument, this flinching self-consciousness is now nothing but its "stubborn attachment" to itself (Butler 1997, 33, 42–43), the miraculous and chancy projection of itself into the wide world. Butler rightly focuses on the viscerality of this identity formation in Hegel, the subject "shattering" (*Psychic Life*, 41) into a kind of life at the moment of its most intense humiliation. It is hard not to think of Sedgwick's emphasis on the "flooding" of the subject by shame, its dilation and thickening, felt along the blood and "in the muscles and the capillaries of the face" (1995, 236). Hegel's unhappy consciousness, like Sedgwick's shamed subject, is as improbable as it is undeniable; both are paradigmatic cases of being, as she says, "way out there" (1995, 214).

"Unhappy consciousness" well describes the harassed subjects of the Warhol films to which Crimp attends in his essay for this volume. He suggests that a resistant rather than conformist or collaborative politics of shame and visibility has a long history in New York City, going back to the experimental cinema produced by The Factory in the 1960s. (Sedgwick's analysis of "a sexuality organized around shame" in Henry James's Prefaces to the New York Edition of his novels suggests the existence of a much longer history still.) The radical nature of Warhol's films, Crimp points out, lies not only in their gender-dissonant subjects but also in the complex cross-identifications viewing audiences are prompted to make with those subjects.[6] Shaming scenes are crucial to many of Warhol's films, a fact which has prompted some to criticize him for brutalizing his subjects, ambushing them in embarrassing ways that have since become the primary mise-en-scène of certain forms of telejournalism. In the specific case of *Screen Test #2*, the camera rolls while Mario Montez is coerced into stripping off his drag self to reveal his "true" sex, then forced to confront his fearful abjection as a Catholic that is so lapsed as to have dropped out of even God's vision. God may or may not see Montez for what he "really" is, but Warhol certainly does. Do these films then peer voyeuristically at their subjects, both feeding greedily off of their suffering and delighting in having apprehended their sexual or moral "truth"? Crimp emphatically claims that this is not the principle motivation or effect of Warhol's queer cinema. The viewer, Crimp argues, does not see these mortified subjects as through a looking-glass, coolly apprehending them from a normatively judgmental distance. To witness Montez's agony is rather to be imbued with a squirming sense of one's own radical jeopardy, one's own susceptibility to the gaze—as if Montez were the means by which Warhol turns his ridiculing camera on his audience, one member at a time. In Montez's sad eyes, each viewer sees himself or herself; but this is no mirror-stage, and Montez is hardly a transparent medium of reflection. Instead, it is his radical opacity, his blazoning singularity that turns the viewer's gaze back upon itself. Caught up in this shaming nexus, Montez's "difference is preserved," his embarrassed indignity broadcasting another and finer dignity that Crimp names "queer."

We are reminded of Sedgwick's remark about the meaning of "queer": "there's no way that any amount of affirmative reclamation is going to succeed in detaching the word from its associations with shame and with the terrifying powerlessness of gender-dissonant or otherwise stigmatized childhood" (1995, 210). Does the shaming scene in a film like *Screen Test #2* succeed in detaching itself from the normative humiliation it appears to inflict on Mario Montez? Montez seems to have been sacrificed to Warhol's queer art, *for shame*, indeed. We wonder whether—or to what degree—that "so-real" collateral damage justifies the shame-creativity it was designed to quicken in audiences. In other words, quite apart from what queer audiences do with shame in *Screen Test #2*, how did Montez experience Warhol's camera: as a scene of humiliation or as the queerly resistant citation of a scene of humiliation? Sedgwick's cautionary remark points out that the two things can never completely be separated. It is revealing to note, as Crimp does, that Warhol said he couldn't bear the sight of some of the scenes he was responsible for having created, but rather than stopping the film, he claimed simply to have left the room. By watching the film—in effect, *staying* in the room—does the viewer come fantasmatically to take the place of Warhol, bearing witness to his ambivalent abstention from this difficulty, his half-hearted leave-taking from the swirl of voyeuristic violence and productive shame?

Although taken up primarily with an extended reading of Mary Gaitskill's novel, *Two Girls, Fat and Thin*, Lauren Berlant's essay (of the same name) begins and ends by situating itself amid another experimental queer project that is proximate to—but nevertheless distinctly different from—Sedgwick's. From Sedgwick, we learn, Berlant received an education of the senses, a schooling in the ethical importance of affirming without shame the unruly surprise of desire, fantasy, and attachment. There is enormous knowledge to be had in pleasure, a lesson that Sedgwick's work teaches by example, not least in taking such palpable pleasure in knowledge. Berlant attributes this "unsurpassable" teaching to Sedgwick's "grandiosity," a term that evokes not only a certain "capaciousness" of thought (the quality that Butler, as we shall see, also sees in Sedgwick's work), but also an element of ironic, even showy publicity vis-à-vis desire and its (dis)contents. Identifying a certain splendor and largesse in Sedgwick's writings is important to the dialectic of Berlant's argument (a dialectic captured in its very title), since among the several aspects of queer work after Sedgwick that troubles her is its inherent valuation of the interior life of the queer subject, or rather the valuation of that subject as a kind of privileged interiority. Does the focus on the inward landscapes of queer desire unwittingly return us to the political detachment, the insularity of "the private tremulous body" with which Frances Barker identified the advent of modernity? Perhaps the cultivation of the subject's reparative competence in parsing its affective life and that of like-minded others blunts rather than galvanizes the radical possibilities of the queer project because it re-entrenches the principle interests and motivating anxieties of the bourgeois subject—the subject of possessive individualism whose most valuable commodity is itself as the proprietor of its own tendencies and capacities. For Berlant, queer theory and critical practice too closely resemble what might be called the new *Bildung*, part of a historical unfolding that, beginning in the eighteenth century, saw the emergence of a psychologizing rhetoric of the psychic life of affect and habit, and the identification of inward experiences and their exchangeable symbolic forms with a particular social and ethical authority. One troubling symptom of that return of the bourgeois repressed is the professionalization of queer studies. The creation of a "field with a jargon and things," as Berlant scathingly puts it, is less about advancing the political purposes of cultural critique and more about the training up of readers and writers who are proficient in being professionally queer. Mobilized around the signifier "Sedgwick," this field is the privileged social space in which the telling of heroic stories of *becoming possible* in a heteronormative world can stand in for the rather more banal experiences of *becoming academic*. Under such conditions, Berlant implies, what are the chances of a break-out, of real social and political intervention? Pierre Bourdieu and John Guillory have argued that the logic of professionalism organizes academic postmodernity,[7] and, if that is so, then these are conditions that neither Berlant, nor any other contributor to this volume, nor most of its readers, is in a position to escape. And Berlant's essay concedes as much, perhaps most obviously in the sometimes microscopic attention that it pays to Gaitskill's novel; whatever the radicalized content of Berlant's argument, its form as a close reading of a single text anchors its operation in the rule of literature.

Berlant remains suspicious about the angling of queer knowledge towards the "biographical," but she admits that there is pleasure to be found there too—indeed, pleasure of the best kind: the guilty kind. Although it is expressly against her own "inclination," as she says, Berlant cannot resist indulging in a brief moment of autobiographical writing, as if to innoculate her essay with the self-reflective impulse that she also resists. Berlant compares what she imagines to be Sedgwick's "public stories"—brimming with "loving family and friends"—to the relative scarcities of her own (im)personal critical genealogy, fraught with "disappointment, contempt, and threat." For Berlant, it comes down to two uses of "being fat," two allegories of insatiability: Sedgwick imagines enfolding those for whom she cares in her protecting embrace, while Berlant hallucinates about a man whose hungry passions expose him ceaselessly to the maddening absence of what he cannot have. It is impossible not to see a theory of politics staged here as a theory of the difference between inaugural personal settings, one reparative, leading to the filling in and gathering together of a unique "self," the other agonistic, born of the forces that leave the personality depleted, empty. But what history teaches, or at least what it teaches Berlant, is that the violence and deprivation she survives is *nothing personal*, not when what are sometimes deemed to be the most individual of experiences, one's indubitably hurtful and loving attachments, are in fact mediated and discursivized and impersonal through and through. For Berlant, desire is indeed always desire of the other (an *other's* desire), anonymous as it is precipitous, after which what is misrecognized as its subject inevitably arrives too late and hungrily looking for an explanation that will never come. But this belatedness, far from disabling or embarrassing, is both the space of a certain resolute freedom and the obscure well-spring of her political and intellectual ardor—an argument, we note, that is not entirely dissimilar, structurally speaking, from the one that Heidegger advances in *Being and Time*, where *Dasein*, that most fundamentally impersonal form of subjectivity, affirms its "possibilities" not in spite but because of its "throwness," its having been cast amid the inhuman structures that make it possible (¶58).

Where desire is, no personality shall be—only personality effects. How then to practice a queer politics that refuses the consolations of selfhood, and that passionately attaches to what Berlant calls "impersonality"? The thinness of the "thin girl" in her essay's title usefully stands as a visceral figure for this question, and for the infinitely voluptuous possibilities that inhere in its asceticism. We see why Gaitskill's novel is of such sustained and sustaining interest to Berlant, for its titular "girls" live ferocious lives (even their passivities are brutally intense), but they do so in ways that are at once stagy and compulsive, ironic and addictive, inhabiting a no-man's-land between, on the one hand, what they misrecognize as themselves, and, on the other, the roles they create, or stumble across, half-consciously saving themselves from being wholly swallowed up in those misrecognitions. "Dorothy Never" and "Justine Shade" impress Berlant because they are not so much characters as placeholders, depthless signs for subjectivity rather than subjects with interior lives set decisively against an exterior world. They live lives of corporeal agony and pleasure, to be sure, but theirs are bodies without organs, charged sites of desire and symbolic exchange that cannot unequivocally be attributed to personalities and yet are not simply machinic in nature. Via Gaitskill, Berlant rewrites the narrative of Sedgwick's "masturbating girl;" this time she is not confined to the intensely private spaces, the rural bedrooms of Austen's great houses, but living mad and bad in the Big Apple.

Writing and thinking impersonally is, as one might expect, very hard to do, and Berlant's prose responds to this difficulty in a variety of telling ways. For example, we notice her essay's shifting terms of address. Although Berlant begins by evoking someone named "Sedgwick," she shifts to the more intimate "Eve" and "the girl" at the moment she most decisively signals her allergy to the cult of personality organizing queer studies. The essay concludes with an ironically polite reference to "Professor Sedgwick," as if returning the discussion to the courteous encounters in impersonal airports in which she and Sedgwick are said primarily to have crossed paths in the flesh. Another formal detail worth considering in Berlant's essay is the long catalogue of food-stuffs to which readers are treated early on in her analysis of *Two Girls, Fat and Thin*. Although this is all fare avidly consumed by the novel's central characters, food as such happens not be the object of their desires. Instead, food is one of the principle means (along with sex) by which the characters *stage* their desires, so that rather than risking uncontrollable attachments to particular comestibles, they fix their passions on the impersonal forms by which those attachments are made meaningful to them. (One is reminded of Mark Twain's joke about people who are so brainily removed from the quotidian that when they go to a restaurant they eat the menu.) Berlant herself reproduces this queer split between the form and content of desire by compiling the list and folding it into her argument. The catalogue has an oddly disembodying or attenuating effect, replacing the work of criticism with the pleasure of collecting; we are reminded of the impersonality and anti-humanism of Alain Robbe-Grillet's *chosisme*, his radically "objective" narratives. At the same time, the objects making up the list are not simply objects (how could they be?), but scrumptious edibles, each of which returns different readers to the question of taste, which is the question of personality and individuality par excellence. Personality contaminates impersonality, just as the opacities of desire complicate any dream of zero degree writing. And vice versa. Towards the conclusion of her essay, Berlant makes a revealing gesture; the "two girls," she observes, "drink a soothing cup of tea and unclench into consoling positions, *much like the one I am in now toward you*" (emphasis ours). You, who? Sedgwick? Berlant's readers? Is this not a token of friendship and intimacy, a quiet unclenching of the strict demands of impersonality? It is tempting to say "yes, yes" to these questions. Yet one of the things that prevents us from rushing in to join Berlant's consoling *ménage* is that her words remember a trick performed in one of Keats' poems. In a lyric from his "Posthumous and Fugitive Pieces," Keats spooked his readers by holding out his "living hand": "See here it is—I hold it toward you" (438), he writes, knowing that it is almost impossible to refuse the attractions of what Walter Jackson Bate calls "empathy . . . focused on the physical functions of the body" (592). Yet refuse we must, or as best we can, for, as Keats knew, his gesture towards forging a sympathetic meeting of minds was spoiled from the start by the special form of impersonality a much later generation would call the death of the author. Like Berlant, he promises empathy and personality, but can only show it to us in a handful of signs.

In *Bodies that Matter* Judith Butler wryly remarks that "the promise of the phallus is always dissatisfying in some way" (57). On this deflationary point Sedgwick and Butler would no doubt agree, making the different ways in which they confront psychoanalysis all the more revealing. Sedgwick has often preferred to eschew it altogether, either by occupying its terms only cursorily, or, as has been the case in recent years, through *blocking* and *displacing* its considerable presence in the field by turning to alternative psychological models for which Freud or Lacan are deemed to be without significant interest or pertinence. Sedgwick's account of her psychotherapy in *A Dialogue on Love* and her revivification of the affect-theory of Silvan Tomkins are two striking cases in point. Butler, on the other hand, continues to work with psychoanalysis in close quarters, and has described her own writing "as a certain cultural engagement with psychoanalytic theory that belongs neither to the fields of psychology nor to psychoanalysis, but which nevertheless seeks to establish an intellectual relationship to those enterprises" (1997, 138). Just so for Butler's contribution to this volume, "Capacity," an essay that makes the following case: while psychoanalysis may have limited relevance to Sedgwick's work, that same work has considerable consequences for psychoanalysis. As Butler demonstrates, Sedgwick's writings bring out the difficulties with which Freud and Lacan acknowledge the circulation of bodies, pleasures, and identificatory positions that overrun a given notion of (hetero)sexual difference. Lacan, for example, treats the "phallus" as a social signifier in a zero-sum game whose presence in one location is predicated on its absence from another. But as Butler suggests, the dyadic nature of this calculus of sexual exchange is not capacious enough to register—much less ascribe value—to the excesses and irreducible remainders that necessarily and unpredictably attend the ebb and flow of desire. The "phallus" does indeed disappoint, and never more consequentially than in the inability or unwillingness of its theorization to answer two questions that matter greatly to Sedgwick, "Who loves whom? How would we ever know?" If desire is always desire of the other (as Lacan insists in his refashioning of Hyppolite's Hegel), the trajectories, motivations, and outcomes of desire cannot always be anticipated or normalized as such—and should not be, for as Butler concludes, Sedgwick's work is above all else exemplary for its call for "an ethics of capacity." A justifiable anxiety about psychoanalysis is not that it cannot account for the exorbitance of desire and the desire of exorbitance, but that it cannot abide by the possibility that there will never be such an accounting—not while desire is splayed out over time (rather than, say, fixed in the planar space of an imagined Oedipal triangle), and not while its senders and addressees remain flickeringly, ardently, half-known and half-knowable both to themselves and to each other.

How to do justice to desire, then? By way of an answer, Butler returns to the triangular formations of Sedgwick's *Between Men*, mimicking in her own argument Sedgwick's critical reproduction of the triangles of sexual exchange that had been the focus of René Girard and Claude Lévi-Strauss. In effect, reading the later Sedgwick back into the earlier, Butler points to the "unknown thought" that enlivens and unsettles the homosocial circuitry of these triangles. Sedgwick's argument had been that the homosociality of these triangles is not secured at the expense of heterosexuality but rather via the conduits of heterosexual exchange. Butler takes that argument one step further, demonstrating that the weaving of these passions means that their trajectories and outcomes will remain so unpredictable that one could never know ahead of time which desire was the conduit for the other, or to what degree that switching had itself become desirous. When Butler turns to Kimberley Pierce's film, *Boys Don't Cry*, the performative possibilities of this productive indeterminacy are allowed vivid expression. Although the film finally attempts to realign gender and sexuality according to the law of sexual difference (the working title of the film was, astoundingly, *Take It Like a Man!*[8]), the principle characters evoke the chance, as Butler says in another context, of "being elsewhere and otherwise" (1997, 130) than that law. By differently and self-differently desiring each other, the central characters, Brandon and Lana, create a thrillingly amorous space in which identifications proliferate and where nominally "homosexual" passions get played out in "heterosexual" settings and "heterosexual" passions get played out in "homosexual" settings. These are the sources of the characters' most exquisite and transgressive pleasures—pleasures not so much derived from object choice as from the supple movement between choosings. If Brandon is a "girl" "doing" a "boy" desiring a girl, that desire is made up of several components, including not only her/his desire for the girl but also the desire of the girl (who desires a boy as well as a boy being done by a girl). Under such fluid and florid conditions, desire and identification, usually treated as mutually exclusive psychic phenomena, cross over in ways that Pierce's film seems, for all of its complexity, barely able to embrace. (Sedgwick's interest in rendering indeterminable any defining differences between identity and desire appears most explicitly in her chapter on Wilde and Nietzsche in *Epistemology of the Closet*.) The pathos in Pierce's film derives from "the passion of non-knowledge" [*la passion du non-savoir*]—as Derrida would say (1991, 75)—with which Brandon's and Lana's desires are quickened, just as it does from the murderous foreclosure of that passion that forms the film's violently hyper-phallicized conclusion.

Again: "Who loves whom? How would we ever know?" The answers to Sedgwick's questions lie in the asking of them, for they bid Butler to tarry alongside the opacity and accident of our desirous lives. In a brief but telling discussion of the concluding scene of *The Golden Bowl*, Butler points to the unexpected openings created by the triangle between Maggie, the Prince, and the mutual object of their differing desires, Charlotte. What is remarkable for Butler is that this scene of parting lacks the recriminations and moralizations that the law of sexual difference might ordinarily require. These sorts of narrowing judgments appear to have withered away in the light not so much of the characters' self-knowledge, as in their dawning sense of the unknowability of their desires for each other, for others, for the others who are also themselves. "This is not a love based on repudiation," Butler pointedly says of James's characters, characters who model for their readers "an ethics of capacity rather than disavowal." One cannot miss the understated self-reference being made here, for of course the psychic landscapes of texts like *Bodies that Matter* and *Gender Trouble* are inhabited precisely by subjects who are at once riven and enlivened by the mournful forces of denegation and denial. Butler begins by telling us that it was Sedgwick who "moved her to think otherwise," and she concludes her essay by showing how.

> Perhaps some progress was made by Freud; but with such circumspection, such medical prudence, a scientific guarantee of innocuousness, and so many precautions in order to contain everything, with no fear of "overflow," in that safest and most discrete of spaces, between the couch and discourse: yet another round of whispering on a bed.
> —Michel Foucault, *The History of Sexuality: An Introduction*

Among the few points at which Sedgwick attends positively to psychoanalytic theory after Freud is in her introductory essay to *Novel Gazing*, where she acknowledges that "psychoanalytic thought offers richly divergent, heterogeneous tools for thinking about aspects of personhood, consciousness, affect . . . that, while relevant to the experience of gender and queerness, are often not centrally organized around 'sexual difference' at all" (1997, 11). Sedgwick includes Freud as part of this resistant strand of psychoanalysis, but she is thinking primarily of the later writings of Melanie Klein, whose distinction between the "depressive" (or "reparative") and "paranoid-schizoid" psychic positions she will subsequently adapt to a reading of the interpretive practices that produce and police contemporary theory. It seems worth saying here that there are regions of Sedgwick's work in which this sort of concession to psychoanalysis would be mostly inconceivable, psychoanalysis more normally forming the object of her exacting disinterest. The significance of that complex refusal will not have escaped Deborah P. Britzman, for whom strong psychoanalytic inquiry remains the central methodological framework for a series of groundbreaking essays on post-Freudian thought and the question of pedagogy—her contribution to this collection being one of her most recent interventions. Britzman distinguishes between what she ironically calls the "bad story" (19) of Freud and the psychoanalytic thought informing her own work, but not without also drawing attention to the psychical action that is palpably under way any time the objects of our intellectual desire are imagined to be either "good" or "bad." And, in a certain fashion, they are always being imagined in these sorts of contestatory affective terms, as anyone who has sat in on a departmental meeting or participated in a scholarly conference can well attest. As Britzman argues in the essay written for this volume, "Theory Kindergarten," a pressing question for the academic imaginary is therefore the exploration of "our adeptness at dismissing theories that run contrary, not just to prevailing conventions but, more significantly, to who we think and wish we and others might be in and for our theory." Essays like Sedgwick's "White Glasses" or "A Poem is Being Written" exemplify this critical (re)turn to the "theorist" within theory—a (re)turn that cannot be described simply as personalizing or psychologizing critical practice in the form of autobiography. The palpable presence of "Sedgwick" within her writing can be alienating for some, and quite the opposite for others—as essays in this volume by Solomon and Kincaid attest. Britzman would ask why writers express revulsion or enchantment in regard to particular modes of thinking and writing? Sedgwick's queer attraction to Silvan Tomkins's psychology of affect, or her use of Klein in "Paranoid Reading and Reparative Reading," are somewhat different cases in point, less obviously self-referential, yet similarly animated by the belief that the political unconscious is but one unconscious among many. As Britzman points out, Klein and Tomkins are difficult figures for the practice of antihomophobic inquiry, not least for dwelling differently on the instinctual forces molding the psyche that seem all but totally disconnected from projects of political and social change. But as Britzman argues, Sedgwick's engagement with contrary or unlikely bodies of thought is less about recuperating them for the purposes of doing good social work and more about the ways in which their stark inaccessibility to what currently constitutes that work throws into relief how and why some theories matter, and others do not.

For Britzman, Sedgwick's writings are valuable for their work as a "theory of theory." In her hands, a theory of theory does not have as its objective an authoritative meta-discourse; nor is its outcome a disabling plummet into an abyss of regression and abstraction (theories of theories of theories, etc . . .)—although there is no guarantee that in a moment it cannot and will not morph into either of these paradigmatically paranoid possibilities. Instead, Britzman treats a theory of theory as an always provisionally occupied critical posture that says something about the irreducible affective realities, the psychical *situatedness*, and the sheer *ordeal* of theories. What accounts for the passional investments and displacements of theory, its palpable identificatory and disidentificatory possibilities and intensities, its strange double-life as an allegory of knowledge and of something other than knowledge? To explore the resistances that make these questions as difficult as they are necessary, and to think about theory as a particularly telling form of resistance, Britzman reads Sedgwick alongside the work of Klein, whose reflections on the entanglements of thought in the archaic regions of affect, phantasy, and other discarded contents of the psyche offer up a counter-intuitive and useful language with which to consider where and why something like "theory" happens at all. For Klein, theory, like the theorist, begins amid a radical indeterminacy analogous to the zone of indecisiveness through which Kierkegaard once said all decision and judgment must pass for these future-making acts to be what they are. As Derrida points out, Kierkegaard called that zone "madness" (1995, 65; 1990, 967), and one could be forgiven for using the same psychologistic term to describe the terrifying inauguration of the subject described by Klein, in which cognition and affect, love and hate, aggression and helplessness, at once torture and constitute the psyche. In Klein's work, the subject's mental life springs indeterminately out of a setting that is somehow a scene of both a nativity and a crime, a collage of the psyche's violent rendering of the world and its fitful decision to make something meaningful, perhaps even loving, out of its supercharged fragments. The felt "memory" of that duplicity is for Klein shattering and anxious; but both Sedgwick and Britzman make a point of bringing out what tends to be understated in Klein's later work, and that is that the same primal confusion, traumatic though it is, is also the very opening of the chance of thought. That chance, that incalculability, is what quickens and exceeds and disputes theory. As Paul de Man once said in another context, "nothing can overcome the resistance to theory since theory *is itself this resistance* (de Man, 19). Or, to paraphrase Britzman, theory is always also a *working through* of theory, at once an instance and an allegory of its exorbitant and ongoing natal labor. What strikes Britzman about Sedgwick's writings is perhaps the naked way in which they bear that *Durcharbeitung* for all to see. This is not to return us to a primal scene as such, which remains entirely fantasmatic in nature; it is instead a return to the laborious work that is its trace in all other scenes and that renders those scenes other than themselves. Additionally, in that work, there are pleasures to be hazarded, acts of love to be initiated and experienced. These are all forms of reparative work with what remains—and something always does remain, if one has the eyes to see it and the ears to hear of it. Perhaps this accounts in part for the unique voice we sometimes perceive in Sedgwick, the robust and polished confidence of her Proustian sentences as well as writing that seems deliberately cast at "the most stretched and ragged edges of one's competence" (1997, 12). The obscure and rhythmically desirous body of "Sedgwick" that we are invited to observe in essays like "A Poem is Being Written" (a text to which Solomon also attends in this volume) is both an instance of that boundary-work and a figure for what surprising things can come of returning to what Britzman calls "theory kindergarten." The passionate but tentative travail of identification without identities that we see in Sedgwick's friendship with Lynch in "White Glasses," or the fragile truces and provisional reconciliations that Sedgwick forges in *A Dialogue on Love:* These are other cases in point, as fragile and important as the future. To the reparative work that forms the most moving points of Britzman's analysis we might add another labor of love, namely Sedgwick's recent and decisive foray into weaving, collages, sculpture, and printmaking. In her essay on paranoid and reparative reading practices, Sedgwick finds solace in the ability "to use one's own resources to assemble or 'repair' the murderous part—objects into something like a whole—though not . . . necessarily like any preexisting whole." "Once assembled to one's own specifications," she adds, "the more satisfying object is available both to be identified with and to offer one nourishment and comfort in turn" (1997, 8). Fingering those partly assembled and partly found textures in our own hands, we cannot but feel that these fragments make those words flesh.

"If Love Were All: Reading Sedgwick Sentimentally," Paul Kelleher's contribution to this volume, traces the theoretical career of the Gothic (first as an object of genre criticism, then as theoretical inquiry itself) across Sedgwick's writing and seeks to make more salient for queer theory the express need to embark upon—in opposition to re-enactments of the paranoid Gothic genre—a study of the relations between sentimentality and sexuality. Like Butler, Kelleher adopts terms and reading strategies drawn from Sedgwick's later work in order to reconsider positions that she originally took up in the earlier. Specifically, Kelleher turns to the Gothic as a means to speculate not on the discourses of homophobia but rather on the culture of homophilia. That culture, he stresses, is structured by the dialectic of the auto-affective and hetero-affective subject. Sentimentality, he argues, is in a privileged position to perform a work beyond the binary opposition of "the heterosexual" to "the homosexual" in part because it knows a prehistory of sexuality. Turning to the eighteenth-century Kelleher invokes subjects of passion who were also simultaneously subjects of manners, ethics, and affection. Shaftesbury's moral philosophy proves to exemplify a model of ethical normativity that knows no recourse to the either/or diagnosis of "homosexuality" and "heterosexuality;" instead it draws upon and renders manifest a "philanthropic calculus of the sentiments." By focusing attention on the traditions of sentimentalism Kelleher seeks to pry open further a space for queer theory wherein the critical reflection of its motives may be gleaned and enjoyed anew.

In "Strategic Constructivism? Sedgwick's Ethics of Inversion," Ross Chambers discerns in Sedgwick's *Epistemology of the Closet* an affirmative deconstruction that does not so much refuse the terms of the essentialist-constructivist debate as it alters them (by replacing their respective hermeneutic presuppositions with an interest in "minoritizing" and "universalizing" discourses) and, so doing, changes the subject. Chambers' claim that Sedgwick changes the subject is meant to extend beyond reference to the debate in question to an implicit and simultaneously ethical and pragmatic revaluation in Sedgwick's work—a minimal idealization—of "the homosexual." In so doing the latter itself becomes, as for Proust (who notably shares with Sedgwick what Chambers elegantly calls an "eminently tactful constructivism"), paradigmatic rather than merely minoritized, even as minoritization is, as Chambers points out, for Sedgwick the condition of possibility for universalization. While David Halperin finds in *Epistemology of the Closet* "the basic method of Foucauldian discourse analysis" (38), Chambers draws out from this same work a basic deconstructive position on the question of essentialism and/or logocentrism. In the closing pages of his argument, moreover, yet another tradition emerges, for if the intellectual itinerary of Sedgwick embraces an ethics of inversion (an ethics of reversal and unveiling), that ethics in turn embraces Sedgwick's itinerary: *on a touche au vers*, writes Mallarmé; and Sedgwick's writing, Chambers observes, participates in that ethical literary tradition, which runs from Wilde and Whitman to Wittig and beyond.

A number of our contributors choose to theorize Sedgwick by reading her works as literary texts. Kathryn Bond Stockton's essay, "Eve's Queer Child," is as illuminating a study of Henry James's "The Pupil" as it is of Sedgwick's work on queer childhood. Stockton shows that to distinguish between James's

novella and the "proto-gay child" conceived by Sedgwick is to betray an ignorance — but an ignorance which may be forgiven since until Stockton's discovery of Sedgwick's authorship, "The Pupil" was indisputably held to have
been penned by James. Of the many revelations offered by "Eve's Queer
Child" perhaps its disclosure of the true origin of "The Pupil" is the most surprising. Stockton begins her essay, rather indiscreetly we fear (although she
claims to break only an already-open secret), by outing Sedgwick not as a writer
in the guise of a theorist, but as the very author of the novella hitherto attributed to James. This is a scholarly find unmatched in recent years. Indeed, it
vies only with Wilde's discovery and disclosure of the "actual [male] beloved"
of Shakespeare's sonnets in his "Portrait of Mr. W. H." (If Stockton were not
already a distinguished theorist, she could rest her laurels on this discovery
alone — picked up, admittedly, from the disreputable source of a rumor mill
not far from the cloak-room of Grand Central Station.) Of her own writing
Sedgwick says in an interview that she "strongly resists seeing categorical differences in the kind of undertakings theory and poetry are. Even as a critic and
theorist, I see myself as a writer first; it keeps striking me how much formal
issues about critical and theoretical work are of the essence of what's being
accomplished in that area" (Kerr and O'Rourke, 3). If Sedgwick is a readerly-
writer, she is no less a writerly-reader. On the matter of her self-described "visceral near-identification with the writing I cared for, at the level of sentence
structure, metrical pattern, rhyme," she relevantly suggests that it "was [for her]
one way of trying to appropriate what seemed the numinous and resistant
power of the chosen objects. . . . For me, this strong formalist investment
didn't imply (as formalism is generally taken to imply) an evacuation of
interest from the passional, the imagistic, the ethical dimensions of texts, but
quite the contrary: the need I brought to books and poems was hardly to be cir-
cumscribed, and I felt I knew I would have to struggle to wrest from them sustaining news of the world, ideas, myself, and (in various senses) my kind"
(1993, 4).

The recognition that Sedgwick's writing can read "like" the writings of many
of her kind (Proust's, for example, as several of our contributors note with us in
one way or another) does not occasion in all of her readers a response of *joie de
lire*, of *joie delire* for such inimitable similarities. Indeed, as *The Norton Anthology of Theory and Criticism* intimates, often malicious charges against the density and abstraction of Sedgwick's "formalist" prose abound. Invariably, and it
seems to us inarguably, these issue out of distinctly anti-intellectual quarters.
In *Who Was That Man? A Present for Mr Oscar Wilde* (where the term "present" signifies in the same multiple ways we have described of Sedgwick's present), Neil Bartlett speculates on why queer discourse is so often richly layered

and complexly nuanced: "The need to talk among ourselves has made our language elaborate," he explains. "Not for us the literary 'realism' and simplicity of expression that is meant to characterize a confession or autobiography. At times we have talked in languages that no one else could understand. . . . In Wilde's exotic, allusive vocabulary, [for example,] high literature aspires to the status of slang" (Bartlett, 80). Just so (minus the incomprehensibility) with Stockton's dense and deft essay; the allusive vocabulary therein is indebted to an erudition characteristically mediated through a readerly-writing of a writerly-reading of literary and theoretical writings by among others, Sedgwick, James, Jane Austen, Wilde, Freud, and Deleuze. In Bartlett's *Present* it is also never easy to determine who is speaking: Wilde, a host of other contemporaneous gay men, or Bartlett "himself" ("himself," because Bartlett's "identity" is exactly — and this is his point — comprised of Wilde's, and of those other gay men, past and present). Who speaks in Stockton's essay? Stockton? Sedgwick? James? Eve's queer child? The authority to determine between these is joyfully undermined, so that perhaps after all James and not Sedgwick is the author of "The Pupil;" perhaps after all Sedgwick and not Stockton produces "Eve's Queer Child;" perhaps after all and in a sense Stockton is "The Pupil" or, for that matter, "Eve's Queer Child."

"The Pupil" emerges in Stockton's reading not as the autobiography of any identity, but rather as Sedgwick's "clever portrait of a masochistic pleasure she knew as a child: a rhythmic, syntactical rehearsal of shame that generates aesthetic forms;" in other words, "The Pupil" is a miniature, meta-self-portrait, a discourse by Sedgwick on the pleasure of her generative (and, make no mistake, queer) attachments to formalism. Facing Sedgwick, Stockton returns our attention to the tableau of adult/child cleaving where, once again, the beginning of one subjectivity and the end of another is impossible to differentiate — including and especially the selves in the portrait(-making). How to distinguish here between subjects (in its various senses) of portraits? For woven into the child/adult cleaving that is the subject of "Eve's Queer Child," Stockton discerns still others: James/Sedgwick; Sedgwick/Stockton; Stockton/James. "The Pupil," she suggests, concerns the queer relation between a boy and a young man; it also concerns Sedgwick "as" that boy and "as" that young man; it is about queer filiation, queer childhood, queer (re)production; further, it concerns Stockton herself as Sedgwick's "pupil," and as the very subject of "The Pupil." Stockton carries Sedgwick's queer child in the form of the essay in question. She is, in other words, Sedgwick's pupil, delivered as a kind of envoi to her teacher.

To attempt to disentangle Stockton's cleavings is only further to entangle them, and we are left with what may best be described not as Wilde's earnest infant (deposited at Grand Central Station), nor even Sedgwick's "Pupil" (left there for recovery by Moon), but rather an earlier form, an umbilical cord. That production (Stockton's essay) is a reproduction of a most queer kind — spawned in a two-fold embrace with Sedgwick ("mother to avuncular texts") and in the three-fold embrace of Stockton/Sedgwick/James. Stockton's essay, "Eve's Queer Child" is after all just that: *Eve's queer child*, given to Sedgwick by Stockton (no doubt impelled by shame-induced motives to make up for the original indiscretion), who discreetly but finally dissimulates the very fact of delivery. For she climactically comes out to say, "I am Eve's pupil and, *if asked*, will have her child." Here the consignment of an already-accomplished delivery (the production of the essay) to a conjectural future echoes a profound point rehearsed by Stockton in her development within this essay of a four-fold model of queer childhood: that one can never be a queer kid, one can only, retrospectively, have been a gay child. Thus, the delivery of "Eve's Queer Child" from Stockton to Sedgwick folds a (wished for) future ("if asked, [I] will have her child") into a present that can only be elegiacally rendered.

It is the cleaving of one's adulthood to one's former childhood that enables, sustains, and nurtures the kinds of reading practices engaged by Sedgwick and other queer theorists. "I think that for many of us in childhood," Sedgwick suggests, "the ability to attach intently to a few cultural objects, objects of high or popular culture or both, objects whose meaning seemed mysterious, excessive, or oblique in relation to the codes most readily available to us, became a prime resource for survival. We needed for there to be sites where the meanings didn't line up tidily with each other, and we learned to invest those sites with fascination and love. This can't help coloring the adult relation to cultural texts and objects; in fact, it's almost hard for me to imagine another way of coming to care enough about literature to give a lifetime to it" (1993, 3). Stockton turns both to Sedgwick's fetishism and masochism in order to lay bare the "more than rare notion of the masochistic child as the quintessential pupil": the pupil Sedgwick remembers herself as being, the pupil that Stockton schools herself in becoming, "The Pupil" that Stockton attributes to Sedgwick, and, finally, the pupil who wants to be "Eve's Queer Child," Stockton herself.

In "Flaming Iguanas, Dalai Pandas, and Other Lesbian Bardos (A few perimeter points)" Melissa Solomon extends Sedgwick's recent interest in the Tibetan Buddhist concept of the bardo to lesbian studies in order "to open pathways [there] previously hidden or blocked." Solomon's task is, as her metaphors suggest, an incendiary undertaking, an ethical venture, and in some respects a solitary one in lesbian studies. As she writes, "[Sedgwick's] books are (purported to be) solely about men and for men and the degree to which Sedgwick, herself, is perceived as a straight woman whose celebratory love for certain gay male writers and friends is (purportedly) a metaphor for the limited purview and relevance of her work to lesbian studies." Solomon's essay explodes that purview and opens it onto nothing less than a capacious bardo space: "This essay," she writes in a way that approximates Sedgwick's "I mean," "is a nascent experiment in providing lesbian studies [not only with Sedgwickian/Solomonian axioms, but also] with a different, Buddhist vocabulary (alternately, conceptual space or purchase) helpful for recognizing the bardo spaces in Sedgwick's writing pertinent to questions [not of lesbian epistemology but] of lesbian realization." The differences between epistemology and realization prove essential to the groundwork Solomon here bravely constructs, and mimes a move orchestrated by Sedgwick in her turn away from exclusive presumptions that link the performative to the epistemological. And again, this so as to keep open the stage of queer thought: to guard its originary spaciousness, its "capacity," as Butler calls it in another register. Solomon writes: "Because Sedgwick's work is so richly and indisputably relevant to lesbian studies, it is surprising to me—stupefying, actually—how willfully or vehemently that relevance has, in certain instances, been either denied or overlooked and, as a result, how little explored these riches, to this day, remain."

Like other contributors to this volume, Solomon turns to a novel not to "apply" Sedgwick with the intent of gathering the text's queer revelations but rather, in the other direction, to stage an encounter that yields surprising revelations about Sedgwick's work. The novel in question is Erika Lopez's *Flaming Iguanas*, whose temporal and spatial unfolding hinges on the kinds of time/spaces we touched upon in our introduction: Its protagonist is "a girl biker, whose performative, self-reinventing travels are insistently and resistantly never told as a 'developmental narrative,' nor even necessarily as a progressive or sequential one." Solomon's interest throughout, echoing Sedgwick's, is in "passages," passages in which she persuasively gleans the coming together of two terms: "lesbian" and "bardo." Her presumption in cleaving these two words is "not," she says, "that lesbian modifies bardo," but that "bardo, as a concept, may be useful for describing the transitional spaces between different and conflicting definitions of lesbian." She elaborates, "The concept 'bardo,' is in part defined by *absence* of epistemology, and so as a noun-partner to 'lesbian' the word is a lexical tool for remembering that both 'lesbian' and 'bardo' live in the same definitional non-state and yet both concern very much what is 'to come:' not in an anticipatory way, but in the way that periods of deep uncertainty— for a concept whose definition is so fraught—become the condition of possibility for new change." Solomon's essay is a landmark for exactly the kind of transformations she sees enabled by Sedgwick for lesbian studies. If Stockton implicitly attributes to her own intellectual succor Sedgwick's care for queer kids, and thereby delivers onto Sedgwick a pupil exquisitely fostered and queerly schooled, Solomon for similar reasons of vitality and generation draws on Sedgwick's opus not only to find the lesbian bardo but also to give, to represent, that bardo: "Sedgwick's opus if is full of lesbian bardos," she discerns. "For me," she tells us, "the 'lesbian bardo' is that Sedgwickian place (process? state? method?) I visit when I write from within [what Sedgwick calls] the 'stimulating' aether of the unnamed, the lived experiment."

No discussion of the complicating and capacious presence of "love" in Sedgwick's work is possible now without a close engagement with A Dialogue on Love. Nancy Miller's essay, "Reviewing Eve," demonstrates the importance of such a reading, and she begins by acknowledging an important paradox to be found in Dialogue: The very autobiographical text that by virtue of its genre promises intimate access to the author's identity inaugurates a new moment in its author's intellectual itinerary, "a reluctance to return to the familiar, narrow domain of the first person." But the essay in question from the outset implicitly problematizes the familiarity of the first person whose name is Sedgwick and thereby throws light on the degree to which any generic form undertaken by Sedgwick—love, no less—is transformed.

Among the meanings of queer is "trans" or "across," and it has functioned for Sedgwick as such especially when writing criticism in the first person. As Miller observes in her own identificatory reading of Sedgwick's therapy memoir or intellectual autobiography, Sedgwick's cross-identifications enact queer performativity rather than the work of the copula: Her love "with" gay men is also at times "as a gay man" (1993, 256). Sedgwick, who has written so forcefully on the emergence (sometime around the turn of the century: Wilde's Dorian Gray is a sign post) of the conflation of desire and identification, undertakes, so Miller argues, a new queer voyage—this one having to do with how to live on in the face of a life-threatening illness. Inarguably Sedgwick, by way of desire and identification, has been doing this all along: Writing gay affirmative criticism within a murderously homophobic culture, and rememorating the forces and lives that attach to AIDS. The new twist is in Sedgwick's practice of Buddhism and weaving, both of which suggest another disruption of the familiar first-person. This oddly serene and energetic manifestation of Sedgwick occasions yet two more re-viewings of her by Miller: first, of an exhibition of cloth figures, hung at the university where both teach, and of Sedgwick's presentation, "In the Bardo," that introduced this installation. If the "autobiography" in its account and performance of therapy occasions for Miller as reader self-identificatory possibilities (at once felicitous and infelicitous), the exhibition and its introduction compel in her a rather different, jarring, and ethical set of responses, the overarching sense of which is an unwillingness to attend Sedgwick on this new voyage. For this voyage is not the voyage out into queer, but a voyage whose new map reaches beyond life to its other, or to the in-between whose territory is always already queer. Miller's review presents itself as a rememoration of a work whose author Miller wants not to have to rememorate, a work that, nevertheless, already moves toward the in-between of a wildly defamiliarizing queer presence/absence.

> The lover's solitude is not a solitude of person (love confides, speaks, tells itself), it is a soli-
> tude of system: I am alone in making a system out of it (perhaps because I am ceaselessly
> flung back on the solipsism of my discourse). A difficult paradox: I can be understood by
> everyone (love comes from books, its dialect is a common one), but I can be heard
> (received 'prophetically') only by subjects who have *exactly and right now* the same lan-
> guage I have.
> —Roland Barthes, *A Lover's Discourse*

If Stockton imagines herself as Sedgwick's queer child or as producing her queer child, then James R. Kincaid frankly casts himself as her lover. His essay, "When Whippoorwills Call," is therefore appropriately delivered as a *lettre d'amour* to Sedgwick. To be sure, it is a love-letter with a twist, or rather several twists, one of which is that it begins speaking of the beloved in the third person but concludes in the second. On the way towards that intimate address, the essay is also an acerbic pronouncement on the state of academic discourse. Kincaid is palpably impatient with what he considers to be the pervasiveness and longevity of paranoid reading practices. In Sedgwick's work, reparative and paranoid styles of thought can be braided together in a lively if nonsymmetri-cal weave, the knots of the one being a source of the other's unravelling; in Kincaid's view, however, the fabric of recent intellectual life feels much coarser. For him, "the policing model" of criticism has handily won the day, relegating alternative modes of writing and reading, so it appears, to "marginal" locations—love-letters between like-minded friends of the notion of reparation, for example. Everywhere Kincaid turns he sees a fear of the future, an allergy to the *arrivant* and *non-savoir*; this dread of the unknown is perhaps most evi-dent in the witheringly normative stance that contemporary historicism takes toward the past. In this brave new world the university is structured mostly to reproduce its stranglehold on what was and what will be, breeding in graduate students the same sclerotic vision with which their professors, always already wary and eagle-eyed, produce knowledge and patrol knowing. We take Kin-caid's point, and remark that at the root of his broadly articulated fears is a finer passion for complicating and reconceiving pedagogy that we also see in

Berlant's contribution to this volume, and in Sedgwick's distrust of "infinitely doable teaching protocols of unveiling [that] have become the common currency of cultural and historicist studies" (1997, 21). Still, we are struck by the excoriating efficiency and panoptic perfection of academic postmodernity as Kincaid imagines it, not least because this picture seems somewhat at odds with the dailyness and unruliness of actual institutionalized intellectual life, and in particular with the myriad ways in which the classroom, in all of its manifestations, does not or does not only fit a carceral model of explanation and operation. Moreover, we wonder whether the subjection of graduate students and faculty to the orthopaedic designs of "intensive and continuous 'pastoral' care"—to recall a phrase from D.A. Miller that Sedgwick mulls over (1997, 19)—is a somewhat less pressing problem than other, more locally consequential disasters: Underfunded humanities programs, and the relegation of too much of the university's work to part-time status, to name two. (Of course, these are only of concern to those with the extreme good luck of possessing a university education in the first place.) In the interview that closes this volume, Sedgwick herself expresses pleasure that she has recently found in mingling with graduate students whose narratives of *becoming possible* are shaped by quite other imperatives and expectations than those of professionalization. Perhaps it is precisely because of Kincaid's happy situation within the contemporary American university that he is in a position to rail against its unhappy faith in the shaming powers of "knowingness," if only in a letter to his beloved.

Calling for a radical scepticism about the methods of the new literary histories, Kincaid reflects on the irreducible opacity of the objects of our critical desire, and on why it is, notwithstanding the latest technology, they remain complicatedly, coyly, and distressingly *other*—and thus so very much like the ones we love. And if love has got something to do with it, why paranoid theory's anxious refusal of that most cherished of affects? Worse, why the panic at the prospect of ever being found out as a secret sentimentalist? Wallace Stevens once said that sentimentality is the failure of the imagination, and if there is one thing anyone in literary studies doesn't want to be a failure at it is that. But is sentimentality always a sign of intellectual dereliction? Kincaid unabashedly folds into the texture of his prose gushing snippets of show tunes, and the maudlin lyrics—half-remembered and half-created—from barbershop quartets, as if daring his readers to find him hopelessly, helplessly lovesick, a sentimentalist so far out of the closet that it isn't funny.

We admit to being tempted to take that dare. Sentimentality could be considered the occupational hazard of the writers of love letters, if it weren't also their profession. Kincaid's essay is written as a correspondence between intimates where talking about what is wrong with the outside world is a way of confirming with his beloved what is right with the private one they two have created. "Us" against "them:" It is the basic plot of the most sentimental of love stories, although you would think from what Kincaid says that "us" sometimes feels so voluminous as to include "them." "[N]o one in love with Eve Sedgwick (all of us) can write about her," he begins, making the first of several deliriously hyperbolic claims. Claims of the kind, we might add, that the authors of *billet-deux* have been making about the subjects of their desire since Shakespeare mooned over his "Mr. W. H.," and with the same refined self-consciousness that comes of being madly in love, and knowing intensely that it is so. No one in love with Sedgwick can write about her, Kincaid claims; but perhaps one can write to her and with her. And so he does, thereby putting his readers in the curious position of over-hearing rather than hearing what he is saying, with all the risks of prurient excitement and banality that can come from such eavesdropping. As readers, we have in effect purloined Kincaid's letter, now left in plain view for those who have the eyes to see it or the money to buy this book. When Kincaid identifies in Sedgwick a capacity to write in a fashion that is "personal but not private, shyness issuing a come-on," we take it that he is also referring to the mannered inwardness with which his own essay is stylized. In this sense, Kincaid's essay is at cross-purposes with Berlant's, the latter of which understands itself to be dedicated to a project of impersonalism. Flaunting the scholarly conventions of intellectual property and propriety (all's fair in love and war), Kincaid claims, in Sedgwick's name, swathes of her words for himself: "Eve is the we of me," he proclaims. When Kincaid speaks in persona as Sedgwick (or is it Sedgwick speaking through Kincaid?), we are reminded of the weird combination of felt passion and campy improbability characterizing Flaubert's "*Madame Bovary, c'est moi!*" or Catherine's cry in *Wuthering Heights*, "I am Heathcliff." Kincaid's essay has many of the features that we would associate with *lettres d'amour*: the magical belief that the lovers share identical thoughts; the exquisite pleasures to be found in recollecting what they have said and done together as a couple; the jauntily colloquial rhetoric whose lightness of touch belies the weight of feeling in the absent presence of the beloved; the obscurities and lacunae whose significances only the lovers know, and perhaps not even them; the joyous and anxious hope for approval from the beloved; the need for her consent to be what he imagines her to be — here, her willingness to "do" "Sedgwick" for him; and finally, the longing to be together, felt so intensely that he imagines that he is with her, talking the same talk, walking the same walk. And yet of course he is not "Eve" and cannot be her, as Kincaid well knows. How else to explain the need for a love-letter that bears his signature? She may be the "we" of him, but is he the "we" of her? No one could answer that question unequivocally, not while there is a chance that a love-letter will not find its addressee. But there is pleasure to be found there too. "I was wishing I was hurrying / home toward you," concludes the little love poem by Everette Maddox whose title adorns Kincaid's essay, the speaker's heart skipping a beat at the thought of the hurrying and of the wishing to be hurrying rather than the prospect of arriving as such.

Such a writerly love, this, begging the very question Sedgwick and Adam Frank put so pointedly in their introduction to *Shame and Its Sisters*: "What does it mean to fall in love with a writer?" (1995, 23). Typically, it is a simple query with extraordinarily expansive motivations and consequences. It means: What is a "writer," and what must "love" be if it can be said to describe reading, or something like reading? And, more troublingly: To love a writer—how would one ever know? It is telling that Sedgwick and Frank broach these questions in the context of introducing work—the writings of Silvan Tomkins—that is methodologically alien to them, profoundly different conceptually and rhetorically from their own writings, and so what a certain reader might too quickly call "unlovable." Tomkins' editors have collected and selected his work, carefully reducing the body of his writings to a representative core as a way of preserving and indeed reanimating its significance. Surely this is an act of love, or the action of a melancholically incorporating fantasy that no one could rigorously show to be unrelated and without analogy to love. What then does it mean to fall in love with a writer? Fidelity, yes, but also a certain faithlessness, a turning from what is understood or felt to be, as Sedgwick and Frank quietly acknowledge, "a theoretical moment *not* one's own" (1995, 23). With this understated phrasing we are invited to dwell not only on the alterity of Tomkins' writings, but also on the sifting work of identification performed by the "not," that is, by the act of saying that that person's work, his "theoretical moment," is not mine. But what does it mean to determine what one is and has as a thinker, reader, writer, and lover on the basis of what one says no to, or believes that one is saying no to? And again the problem: How would one ever know that one had in fact experienced or at least suffered such a missed encounter, and thus had apprehended or punctually been in the presence of the *not-one's-own*? A certain melancholy attends the relationship that a reader shares with a "theoretical moment not one's own," an avowed disavowal that attaches the reader to those writings not in spite of that "not" but precisely because of it, through it as a kind of *via negativa*. From what imagined vantage point could a reader determine decisively that another's "moment" was not "one's own"? Could one properly and in all rigor claim that any theoretical moment in the symbolic order was or was not in one's possession? Like loving, reading extends along so many dimensions that aren't well described in terms of distinguishing decisively between object-choices, "*this* theoretical moment is mine, but *that* one is *hers*," and so on. In an elegant reading of the play of friendship and love in Kant, Jacques Derrida questions the German philosopher's distinction between friendship, which Kant identified with the virile maintenance of a respectful distance, and love, which for him always felt like drowning in someone else's thoughts and feelings. In Kant, heterosexual love unhealthily attracts, while homosocial friendship healthily repels. But as Derrida asks, "why would this distance be presented *as* repulsion? . . . Why would love be only the ardent force of an attraction tending towards fusion, union, and identification? Why would the infinite distance which opens respect up, and which Kant wishes to limit by love, not open love up as well" (1997, 255)? The essays in this volume speak in different ways to the very chances that Derrida evokes. No one in love with Sedgwick can write about her, Kincaid claims, taking it as axiomatic that love threatens to collapse the difference between lovers: "Who can find the distance or wants to?" he also asks. The case of Sedgwick's love for Tomkins points to other, less privative and confining possibilities, possibilities that are not unavailable in Kincaid's essay. "Love" in this instance (which we would argue is the paradigmatic rather than the exceptional instance in her work) is not a figure for fusion but for difference, and for the obligations that attend the immeasurable remoteness of the beloved from the lover. No one can find these distances because they have always already found us.

Many people have helped see this book into existence. We are indebted to William Germano at Routledge for his sustained support, as well as to Julian Devereux, Gilad Foss, Julie Ho, and Damian Treffs for helping shepherd the book through to completion. Thanks go to the University of Rhode Island for providing course release. Sarah Brophy, Jennifer Blair, and Sonal Nalkur each provided assistance when it was most needed. Naureen Hamidani helped in the preparation of the manuscript, and for her efforts we are appreciative, as we are to Jamie Carr for compiling the index. Partial funding for this project was provided by the Arts Research Board (with funds provided by the Social Sciences and Humanities Research Council of Canada), as well as by the Ontario Work Study Programme, in conjunction with the Office of Student Financial Aid at McMaster University. For making copies of Sedgwick's "Off My Chest" column available to us, we are grateful to Elsie Hsieh, Assistant Editor at *MAMM Magazine*. Portions of two essays in this volume have appeared previously and are reprinted here with kind permission of the editor or publisher: Judith Butler, "Longing for Recognition," *Studies in Gender and Sexuality* 1.3 (2000): 271–90; Nancy K. Miller, "All About Eve," *The Women's Review of Books* 17.2 (1999): 21–22. Mary Capello, Maxim Daamen, Mathilda Hills, and Jean Walton offered continuous encouragement. Melissa Solomon's suggestions were invaluable throughout the book's gestation. The contributors to this collection enriched our understanding of the provenances, arguments, and implications of Sedgwick's work and presence. For this, we are thankful. We are also very grateful to Barbara Herrnstein Smith for her incisive reading of the introduction's first part. Finally, we thank Eve Kosofsky Sedgwick for her time and efforts during the interview process, and for so much more.

Notes

1. We cite Simon Watney's book-cover endorsement to Sedgwick's *Tendencies*.
2. It cannot be without significance that both Spivak and Sedgwick, in different contexts, animate this persistent present in their work: Sedgwick as *primum mobile* of queer theory, and Spivak as *primum mobile* of postcolonial critique.
3. Sedgwick reports that her work on this terrain is significantly affected by Sogyal Rinpoche's *The Tibetan Book of Living and Dying*.
4. Both descriptions heralded the re-publication of *Between Men*, and appeared as blurbs for the book.
5. See GAY SHAME 2000. Fri, April 14, 2000. http://queer.tao.ca/qrg_org/ msg00110.html.
6. As it happens, this is also the thesis underwriting Alice Kuzniar's recent study of queer German cinema.
7. See, for example, "Part One" of Guillory's *Cultural Capital: The Problem of Literary Canon Formation*, and Bordieu's *Reproduction in Education, Society, and Culture*.
8. See Kevin Dreyfus. "Brandon Teena Story Gets Fictional Treatment." *IndieWIRE*. http://www.indiewire.com/film/production/pro_980925_HarrisTeena.html.

Works Cited

Barber, Stephen M., and David L. Clark. "This Piercing Bouquet: An Interview with Eve Kosofsky Sedgwick." In *Regarding Sedgwick: Essays on Queer Culture and Critical Theory*, eds. Stephen M. Barber and David L. Clark (New York: Routledge, 2002).

Barker, Frances. *The Private Tremulous Body: Essays on Subjection* (London and New York: Methuen, 1984).

Barthes, Roland. *A Lover's Discourse*, trans. Richard Howard (New York: Hill and Wang, 1978).

Bartlett, Neil. *Who Was That Man? A Present For Mr Oscar Wilde* (London: Serpent's Tail, 1986).

Bate, Walter Jackson. *John Keats* (Cambridge: Harvard University Press, 1963).

Bourdieu, Pierre. *Reproduction in Education, Society, and Culture*, trans. Richard Nice (London: Sage Publications, 1977).

Britzman, Deborah P. *Lost Subjects, Contested Objects: Toward a Psychoanalytic Inquiry of Learning* (Albany: State University of New York Press, 1998).

Butler, Judith. *Bodies that Matter: On the Discursive Limits of 'Sex'* (New York: Routledge, 1993).

———. *The Psychic Life of Power: Theories in Subjection* (Stanford: Stanford University Press, 1997).

De Man, Paul. *The Resistance to Theory*, foreword by Wlad Godzich (Minneapolis: University of Minnesota Press, 1986).

Deleuze, Gilles. *Negotiations: 1972–1990*, trans. Martin Joughin (New York: Columbia University Press, 1995).

Derrida, Jacques. *Cinders / Feu la cendre*, trans./ed. Ned Lukacher (Lincoln & London: University of Nebraska Press, 1991).

———. "Force of Law: The 'Mystical Foundation of Authority,'" trans. Mary Quaintance. *Cordoza Law Review* 2.5–6 (July/August 1990): 919–1045.

———. *Gift of Death*, trans. David Wills (Chicago: University of Chicago Press, 1995).

———. *Politics of Friendship*, trans. George Collins (London and New York: Verso, 1997).

Dreyfus, Kevin. "Brandon Teena Story Gets Fictional Treatment." *IndieWIRE*. http://www.indiewire.com/film/production/pro_980925_HarrisTeena.html.

Foucault, Michel. *The History of Sexuality: An Introduction: Volume 1*, trans. Robert Hurley (New York: Vintage Books, 1978).

———. "What is Enlightenment?" In *Ethics: Subjectivity and Truth*, edited by Paul Rabinow, trans. Robert Hurley et al. (New York: New Press, 1997), 303–319.

[QRG] GAY SHAME 2000. Fri, 14 Apr 2000. http://queer.tao.ca/qrg_org/msg00110.html.

Halperin, David. *Saint Foucault* (New York: Oxford University Press, 1995).

Heidegger, Martin. *Being and Time*, trans. John Macquarrie and Edward Robinson, (New York: Harper & Row, 1962).

Keats, John. *Poetical Works*, ed. H. W. Garrod (Oxford: Oxford University Press).

Kerr, Mark, and Kristen O'Rourke, "Sedgwick Sense and Sensibility: An Interview with Eve Kosofsky Sedgwick." http://www.smpcollege.com/litlinks/critical/sedgwick.html.

Kierkegaard, Søren. *Fear and Trembling and Repetition*, trans. H. Hong and E. Hong (Princeton: Princeton University Press, 1983).

Kuzniar, Alice. *The Queer German Cinema* (Stanford: Stanford University Press, 2000).

Leitch, Vincent B. *Norton Anthology of Theory and Criticism* (New York: Norton, 2001).

Levinas, Emmanuel. "Essence and Disinterestedness" in *Basic Philosophical Writings*, eds. Adriaan T. Peperzak et al. (Bloomington and Indianapolis: Indiana University Press, 1996), 109–127.

——. *Totality and Infinity: An Essay on Exteriority*, trans. Alphonso Lingis (Pittsburgh: Duquesne University Press, 1969).

Sedgwick, Eve Kosofsky. "After word," in *Gary in your pocket: Stories and Notebooks of Gary Fisher*, ed. Eve Kosofsky Sedgwick (Durham: Duke University Press, 1996), 273–91.

——. *Between Men: English Literature and Male Homosocial Desire* (with a new preface by the author) (New York: Columbia University Press, 1985, 1992).

——. *The Coherence of Gothic Conventions.* (with a new preface by the author) (New York: Methuen, 1976, 1986).

——. "Come As You Are." (Unpublished ms.).

——. *A Dialogue on Love* (Boston: Beacon Press, 1999).

——. *Fat Art, Thin Art* (Durham: Duke University Press, 1994).

——. *Epistemology of the Closet* (Berkeley: University of California Press, 1990).

——. "Introduction: Performativity and Performance," in *Performativity and Performance*, eds. Andrew Parker and Eve Kosofsky Sedgwick (New York: Routledge, 1995), 1–18.

——. "Paranoid Reading and Reparative Reading; or, You're so Paranoid, You Probably Think This Introduction is About You," in *Novel Gazing: Queer Reading in Fiction* (Durham: Duke University Press, 1997), 1–37.

——. "Pedagogy." (Unpublished ms.)

——. "Shame and Performativity: Henry James's *New York Edition* Prefaces," in *Henry James's New York Edition: The Construction of Authorship*, ed. David McWhirtes (Stanford: Stanford University Press, 1995), 206–239.

——. "Socratic Raptures, Socratic Ruptures: Notes Toward Queer Performativity," in *English Inside and Out: The Place of Literary Criticism*, eds. Susan Gubar and Jonathan Kamholtz (New York: Routledge, 1993), 122–36.

——. *Tendencies.* Durham: Duke University Press, 1993.

Spivak, Gayatri Chakravorty. *Outside in the Teaching Machine* (New York: Routledge, 1993).

⬭ **Sedgwick's Subjects and Others**

1

Mario Montez, For Shame

Douglas Crimp

From shame to shyness to shining—and, inevitably, back, and back again: the candor and cultural incisiveness of this itinerary seem to make Warhol an exemplary figure for a new project, an urgent one I think, of understanding how the dysphoric affect shame functions as a nexus of production: production, that is, of meaning, of personal presence, of politics, of performative and critical efficacy.[1]

Eve Sedgwick's intuition, indicated here in one of her essays on queer performativity, might be more unfailing than she knew, since at the time she wrote this sentence she would have seen very little of what most bears it out—Andy Warhol's vast film production from the mid-1960s.[2] I want in this essay to consider one instance of Warhol's mobilization of shame as production, and in doing so I want to specify the urgency Sedgwick imagines such a project might entail, an urgency that compels a project of my own.[3] I should qualify "my own" by adding that this project heeds Sedgwick's axiom for antihomophobic inquiry: "People are different from each other." This is, of course, Axiom 1 from the introduction to *Epistemology of the Closet*, but I take it to be much more thoroughly axiomatic for Sedgwick's writing generally and what I've learned most from it: the ethical necessity of developing ever finer tools for encountering, upholding, and valuing other's differences—or better, differences and singularities—nonce-taxonomies, as she wonderfully names such tools. In one of the many deeply moving moments in her work, Sedgwick characterizes this necessity in relation to the "pressure of loss in the AIDS years"—years in which we sadly still live—"that the piercing bouquet of a given friend's particularity be done some justice."[4]

"Poor Mario Montez," Warhol writes in *Popism*,

> Poor Mario Montez got his feelings hurt for real in his scene [in *Chelsea Girls*] where he found two boys in bed together and sang "They Say that Falling in Love Is Wonderful" for them. He was supposed to stay there in the room with them for ten minutes, but the boys on the bed insulted him so badly that he ran out in six and we couldn't persuade him to go back in to finish up. I kept directing him, "You were terrific, Mario. Get back in there—just pretend you forgot something, don't let *them* steal the scene, it's no good without you," etc., etc. But he just wouldn't go back in. He was too upset.[5]

Poor Mario. Even though Andy is full of praise for Mario's talents as a natural comedian, nearly every story he tells about him is a tale of woe:

> Mario was a very sympathetic person, very benign, although he did get furious at me once. We were watching a scene of his in a movie we called *The Fourteen-Year-Old Girl* [also known as *The Shoplifter* and *The Most Beautiful Woman in the World*, the film is now known as *Hedy*], and when he saw that I'd zoomed in and gotten a close-up of his arm with all the thick, dark masculine hair and veins showing, he got very upset and hurt and accused me in a proud Latin way, "I can see you were trying to bring out the worst in me."[6]

I call my project, provisionally, "Queer before Gay." It entails reclaiming aspects of New York City queer culture of the 1960s as a means of countering the current homogenizing, normalizing, and de-sexualizing of gay life. In an essay initiating the project, on Warhol's classic 1964 silent film *Blow Job*, I wanted to contest the facile charge of voyeurism so often leveled at Warhol's camera.[7] It seemed to me important to recognize that there can—indeed must—be ways of making queer differences and singularities visible without always entailing the charge of violation, making them visible in ways that we would call *ethical*. In that essay, titled "Face Value" both to suggest that I meant to pay attention to what was on the screen (in this case, as in so many others, a face) and to gesture toward Emmanuel Levinas's ethics, I contrasted the self-absorption of the subject of *Blow Job* to what seemed to me its comic opposite, the utter self-consciousness of Mario Montez as he performs mock fellatio on a banana in *Mario Banana*, a single 100-foot-reel Warhol film of the same year as *Blow Job*.[8] On this subject of Mario's self-consciousness, Warhol writes, "He adored dressing up like a female glamour queen, yet at the same time he was painfully embarrassed about being in drag (he got offended if you used that word—he called it 'going into costume')."[9]

How certain the violation, then, when Mario was subjected by Warhol in *Screen Test #2* to being shamed precisely for his gender illusionism, or perhaps his gender *illusions*. Warhol—with his uncanny ability to conceal dead-on insight in the bland, unknowing remark—writes of that film in a parenthetical aside in *Popism*, "*Screen Test* was Ronnie Tavel off-camera interviewing Mario Montez in drag—and finally getting him to admit he's a man. . . ."[10] I call this "insight" because, although it doesn't really describe what takes place in the film at all, it nevertheless gets right to the point of what is most affecting, most troubling, most memorable about it—that is, Mario's "exposure"—a word that Warhol used, in its plural form, as the name of his 1979 book of photographs,[11] and the word Stefan Brecht chose to characterize Warhol's filmic method:

> Warhol around 1965 discovered the addictive ingredient in stars. He found that not only are stars among the industrial commodities whose use-value is a product of consumer phantasy, a phantasy that publicity can addict to a given brand of product . . . , but that what addicts the consumer is the quality of stardom itself. . . . He set out to isolate this ingredient, succeeded, proceeded to market it under the brand name "Superstar,"—Warhol's Superstar. Superstar is star of extraordinary purity: there is nothing in it but glamor, a compound of vanity and arrogance, made from masochist self-contempt by a simple process of illusio-inversion. The commercial advantages of this product originated in its area of manufacture: the raw materials, any self-despising person, were cheap, and the industrial process simple: to make the trash just *know* he or she is a fabulous person envied to adoration. You didn't have to teach them anything. If the customers would take them for a star, they would be a star; if they were a star, the customers would take them for a star; if the customers would take them for a star the customers would be fascinated by them. Exposure would turn the trick. Here again Warhol's true genius for abstraction paid off: he invented a camera-technique that was nothing but exposure.[12]

Ostensibly just what its title says it is, *Screen Test #2* is the second of Warhol's screen test films of early 1965 in which Ronald Tavel, novelist, founding playwright of ridiculous theater,[13] and Warhol's scenarist from 1964 to 1967, interviews a superstar for a new part (*Screen Test #1*, which I haven't seen, stars Philip Fagan, Warhol's lover of the moment, who shared the screen with Mario in *Harlot*, Warhol's first sound film and the first in which Tavel participated.)[14] In the case of *Screen Test #2*, Mario Montez is ostensibly being tested for the role of Esmeralda in a remake of *The Hunchback of Notre Dame*. He is shown throughout in a slightly out-of-focus close-up on his face, wearing (and often nervously brushing) a cheap, ratty dark wig. He also wears dangling oversize earrings and long white evening gloves. For a long time at the film's beginning, he ties a silk scarf into his wig, using, it seems, the camera's lens as his mirror. After speaking the credits from off-screen, where he remains throughout the film, Tavel begins to intone, insinuate, cajole, prod, demand: "Now, Miss Montez, just relax . . . you're a lady of leisure, a grande dame. Please describe to me what you feel like right now."

"I feel," Mario begins his reply—and there follows rather too long a pause as he figures out what to say—"I feel like I'm in another world now, a fantasy . . . like a kingdom meant to be ruled by me, like I could give orders and suggest ideas."

Poor Mario. This kingdom is ruled by Ronald Tavel. It is he who gives orders and suggests ideas. At first, though, he indulges Mario's fantasy. He asks about his career to date, allowing Mario to boast of his debut as Delores Flores in Jack Smith's *Flaming Creatures*, his part as the handmaiden in Ron Rice's *Chumlum*, his starring role as the beautiful blonde mermaid in Smith's *Normal Love* and his small part as the ballet dancer wearing hot pink tights in the same film. Asked whether the critics were satisfied with his performances, he gives an answer fully worthy of his namesake in Jack Smith's famous paean, "The Perfect Filmic Appositeness of Maria Montez."[15] "It's a funny thing," Mario says with no guile whatsoever, "but no matter what I do, somehow it comes out right, even if it's meant to be a mistake. The most wonderful mistakes that I've done for the screen have turned out the most raging, fabulous performances."

Poor Mario. Now begins his humiliation. Tavel tells Mario to repeat after him, "For many years I have heard your name, but never did it sound so beautiful until I learned that you were a movie producer, Diarrhea." Mario is obliged to say "diarrhea" again and again, with various changes of inflection and emphasis. Then to lip sync as Tavel says it. "Mouth 'diarrhea' exactly as if it tasted of nectar," Tavel instructs. Mario obeys, blissfully unaware of where this game of pleasing a producer named Diarrhea will lead. He will gamely demonstrate his ecstatic response to "playing spin the bottle"—to masturbating, that is, by shoving a bottle up his ass (remember, though, we see only his face).[16] Mario will ferociously mime biting the head off a live chicken as he obeys Tavel's demand that he pretend he is a female geek. He will show how he'll manage, as Esmeralda, to seduce three different characters—captain, priest, Quasimodo—in *The Hunchback of Notre Dame*. He'll scream in terror and dance a gypsy dance with only his shoulders; he'll pout, sneer, and stick out his tongue; he'll cover the lower half of his face with a veil and show that he can be evil or sad using only his eyes. He'll repeat after Tavel, apparently as an exercise in stressing consonants, "I have just strangled my pet panther. Patricia, my pet panther, I have just strangled her, my poor pet. Yet I am not scratched, just a little fatigued."

Now and again Tavel gives encouragement: "That's fine, Miss Montez, thank you very much." "That was delightful, Miss Montez." "Thank you, Miss Montez, that was beautiful, that was perfect, and I think we are going to sign you on immediately for this role."

"How can I ever thank you?" Mario replies, so delighted as to make it obvious he's still hoodwinked. But the encouragement only sets Mario up for his fall, which comes near the end of the film's second thirty-three-minute reel. Mario has just cheerfully described the furniture in his apartment. Then it comes, as if out of nowhere.

"Now, Miss Montez, will you lift up your skirt?"

"What?" Mario asks, with a stunned look. He's clearly caught completely off guard.

"And unzipper your fly."

"That's impossible," Mario protests, shaken.

"Miss Montez," Tavel continues, "you've been in this business long enough to know that the furthering of your career depends on just such a gesture. Taking it out and putting it in, that sums up the movie business. There's nothing to worry about, the camera won't catch a thing. I just want the gesture with your hands. This is very important. Your contract depends on it." Following confused, helpless, silent stalling, Mario finally gives in, and the humiliation continues: "Look down, look down at it," he's commanded.

"I know what it looks like," is his petulant response.

"Zipper your fly half way up and leave it sticking out. That's good, that's good, good boy, good boy." When he refers to Mario this way, Tavel isn't calling attention to Mario's "true" gender; far worse than that, he's treating Mario like a dog. "Take a look at it, take a look at it please. What does it look like?"

Mario half-heartedly fights back, "What's it look like to you?"

"It looks fairly inviting, as good as any," Tavel answers, not with much conviction. "Will you forget about your hair for a moment. Miss Montez, you're not concentrating."

But Mario is defiant: "It's really senseless what you're asking me. I must brush my hair."

Mario finally seems able to put a stop to this couch-casting episode, and we breathe a sigh of relief. But Tavel has still one more ordeal in mind, and it's no doubt all the more painful for Mario because it follows upon the mockery of his cross-dressing. Remember that Warhol writes in *Popism* of Mario's embarrassment about doing drag. He goes on to explain that Mario "used to always say that he knew it was a sin to be in drag—he was Puerto Rican and a very religious Roman Catholic. The only spiritual comfort he allowed himself was the logic that even though God surely didn't *like* him for going into drag, that still, if He really hated him, He would have struck him dead."[17] So, resisted by Mario in making him expose his sex, the ever-inventive Tavel moves on to a new torment. Showing Mario how to take a supplicating pose, with eyes and hands turned heavenward, he instructs him to say, and repeat, and repeat again, "Oh Lord, I commend this spirit into Thy hands." Poor Mario looks alternately bewildered and terrified, as though he feels he might truly be struck dead for such irreverence. Finally, though, Tavel has little time left to taunt his superstar. As Mario begins to acquiesce in giving the camera the cockteaser look Tavel wants, the film runs out. Just how tense the experience of watching Warhol's films makes us is revealed to us from the release that comes when the reel comes to an end, a moment always entirely unanticipated but occurring with astonishingly perfect timing.

Many of Warhol's films include similar scenes of extraordinary cruelty that are met with disbelief on the part of the performers, most famously when Ondine, as the pope in *Chelsea Girls*, slaps Ronna Page. "It was so for real," Warhol writes, "that I got upset and had to leave the room—but I made sure I left the camera running."[18] The moment that I'd found most discomfiting, up to seeing Mario's shaming in *Screen Test #2*, is when Chuck Wein, who's been taunting Edie Sedgwick through the whole of *Beauty #2*, but who's rarely a match for her sparkling repartee, suddenly hits the raw nerve of her relationship with her father. She looks more stunned than if she'd been literally hit, like Ronna. It isn't merely a look of incredulity, it's one of utter betrayal, a look that both says, *Surely you didn't say that*, and pleads, *How could you possibly say that? How could you so turn our intimacy against me? Would you really do this for the sake of a film? I thought we were just play-acting.*

George Plimpton captures the feel of such moments when he describes *Beauty #2* in Jean Stein's devastating book *Edie*:

I remember [Chuck Wein's] voice—nagging and supercilious and quite grating. . . . A lot of the questions, rather searching and personal, were

about her family and her father. On the bed Edie was torn between react-
ing to the advances of the boy next to her and wanting to respond to these
questions and comments put to her by the man in the shadows. Sometimes her head would bend and she would nuzzle the boy or taste him
in a sort of distracted way. I remember one of the man's commands to her
was to taste "the brown sweat," but then her head would come up, like
an animal suddenly alert at the edge of a waterhole, and she'd stare across
the bed at her inquisitor in the shadows. I remember it as being very dramatic . . . and all the more so because it seemed so real, an actual slice
of life, which of course it *was*.[19]

How might we square these scenes of violation and shaming with what I'm
describing as an ethical project of giving visibility—and I want also to say dignity—to a queer world of differences and singularities in the 1960s? What does
the viewer's discomfiture at Warhol's techniques of exposure do to the usual
processes of spectator identification?

To answer these questions, I need to take a detour through the present,
whose sexual politics fuels my interest in this history in the first place.

Following New York's annual gay pride celebrations in 1999, the *New York
Times* editorialized:

When police harassed gay patrons of the Stonewall Inn in 1969, the
patrons stood their ground and touched off three nights of fierce civil dis-
obedience—prominently featuring men in drag. . . . The building that
once housed the Stonewall Inn on Christopher Street has earned a list-
ing in the National Register of Historic Places, becoming the first site in
the country to recognize the contributions that gay and lesbian Ameri-
cans have made to the national culture. This also marks the gay rights
movement's evolution from a fringe activity to a well-organized effort
with establishment affiliations and substantial political clout.

Noting that the gay pride parade included Mayor Rudolph Giuliani and Fire
Commissioner Thomas Von Essen, the *Times* concluded, "Things have come
a long way since those stormy summer nights in 1969."[20]

The *Times*' view marks the extent to which the various myths about
Stonewall and the progress of gay rights have now become commonplace and
official, even to the point of the newspaper's ritual nod to the prominence of
drag queens among the Stonewall rioters. But we might be inclined to skepticism toward this bland narrative of progress through its unremarked report of

the mayor's participation in the parade, because not since the days of Stonewall has queer nightlife in New York been so under attack by a city administration. Harassment and padlocking of gay clubs have again become commonplace in New York City. The response to this disjunction between the *New York Times'* sense of our having come a long way and the experience of many of us in New York has been for queers to organize, for the past several years, during the time of the gay pride celebrations, a counter-event devoted explicitly to shame. Gay Shame's annual zine is called *Swallow Your Pride.*

These may seem like no more than the usual exercises in camp humor aimed at normalizing, mainstream gay and lesbian politics. But given the place of shame in queer theory— and in earlier queer culture, if we can take what I've described in Warhol's *Screen Test #2* as in any sense representative of that culture—I think we would do well to take the idea seriously.

What's queer about shame, and why does it get posed against the supposedly shame-eradicating politics of gay pride?

For an answer, I turn to Eve Sedgwick's essay "Queer Performativity: Henry James's *The Art of the Novel.*"[21] Schematically, Sedgwick suggests that shame is what makes us queer, both in the sense of having a queer identity and in the sense that queerness is in a volatile relation to identity, destabilizing it even as it makes it. Sedgwick finds in shame the link between "performativity and— performativity" (1993, 6), that is, between the two senses of performativity operative in Judith Butler's enormously generative work *Gender Trouble.* Performativity 1: "the notion of performance in the defining instance theatrical," and Performativity 2: that of "speech-act theory and deconstruction," in which we find a "necessarily 'aberrant' relation" between a performative utterance and its meaning (1993, 2). In order to demonstrate this latter, Sedgwick departs from J. L. Austin's paradigmatic instance of the performative in *How to Do Things with Words,* that of the "I do," of "I do take thee to be my lawful wedded wife" (how ironic that this has become the very performative that the official gay and lesbian movement in the U.S. has expended all its recent energies and resources to be able to utter!). Sedgwick moves from Austin's "I do" to the more "perverse"—the "deformative," she also calls it (1993, 3)—"Shame on you." For which, I want to suggest, "for shame" works just the same, linguistically and performatively, excepting that, when written, it can also be read the way I'd like it to be read here: as advocating shame. I hope it will become clear as I proceed that favoring shame in the way I intend it is just the opposite of, say, conservative Catholic ideologue Andrew Sullivan's view that contemporary American society lacks sufficient shame. Sullivan's is a conventionally moralistic view of shame's function. Mine, I hope, is an ethico-political one.[22]

Shame, in Sedgwick's view, is equally and simultaneously identity-defining and identity-erasing; in Sedgwick's words, it "mantles the threshold between introversion and extroversion" (1993, 8). Moreover, shame appears to construct the singularity and isolation of one's identity through an affective connection to the shaming of another:

> One of the strangest features of shame (but, I would argue, the most theoretically significant) is the way bad treatment of someone else, bad treatment *by* someone else, someone else's embarrassment, stigma, debility, blame or pain, seemingly having nothing to do with me, can so readily flood me—assuming that I'm a shame-prone person—with this sensation whose very suffusiveness seems to delineate my precise, individual outlines in the most isolating way imaginable. (1993, 14)

I want to reiterate this passage, since I think it gets to the crux of the matter. In the act of taking on the shame that is properly someone else's, I simultaneously feel my utter separateness from even that person whose shame it initially was. I feel alone with my shame, singular in my susceptibility to being shamed for this stigma that has now become mine and mine alone. Thus, my shame is taken on in lieu of the other's shame. In taking on the shame, I do not share in the other's identity. I simply adopt the other's vulnerability to being shamed. In this operation, most importantly, the other's difference is preserved; it is not claimed as my own. In taking on or taking up his or her shame, I am not attempting to vanquish his or her otherness. I put myself in the place of the other only insofar as I recognize that I too am prone to shame.

But who is prone to shame? The answer, for Sedgwick, will necessarily be a bit tautological. A shame-prone person is a person who has been shamed. Sedgwick associates the susceptibility to shame with "the terrifying powerlessness of gender-dissonant or otherwise stigmatized childhood." And therefore, if "queer is a politically potent term . . . that's because, far from being capable of being detached from the childhood scene of shame, it cleaves to that scene as a near-inexhaustible source of transformational energy" (1993, 4).

In this power of transformation, performativity functions both theatrically and ethically. Just as shame is both productive and corrosive of queer identity, the switching point between stage fright and stage presence, between being a wall flower and being a diva, so too is it simultaneously productive and corrosive of queer revaluations of dignity and worth.

In his book about the banishment of sex from contemporary queer politics, *The Trouble with Normal*, Michael Warner argues that we need to "develop an ethical response to the problem of shame." "The difficult question is not: how do we get rid of our sexual shame?" Warner writes, "The question, rather, is

this: what will we do with our shame? And the usual response is: pin it on someone else."[23]

How does this work, performatively? Sedgwick explains:

> The absence of an explicit verb from "Shame on you" records the place
> in which an I, in conferring shame, has effaced itself and its own agency.
> Of course the desire for self-effacement is the defining trait of—what
> else?—shame. So the very grammatical truncation of "Shame on you"
> marks it as a product of a history out of which an I, now withdrawn, is *pro-
> jecting* shame—toward another I, an I deferred, that has yet and with dif-
> ficulty to come into being, if at all, in the place of the shamed second
> person. (1993, 4)

Saying "Shame on you" or "For shame," casts shame onto another that is both
felt to be one's own and, at the same time, disavowed as one's own. But in those
already shamed, the shame-prone, the shame is not so easily shed, so simply
projected: it manages also to persist as one's own. This can lend it the capacity
for articulating collectivities of the shamed. Warner explains,

> A relation to others [in queer contexts] begins in an acknowledgment of
> all that is most abject and least reputable in oneself. Shame is bedrock.
> Queers can be abusive, insulting, and vile toward one another, but
> because abjection is understood to be the shared condition they also
> know how to communicate through such comradery a moving and unex-
> pected form of generosity. No one is beneath its reach, not because it
> prides itself on generosity but because it prides itself on nothing. The rule
> is: get over yourself. Put a wig on before you judge. And the corollary is
> that you stand to learn most from the people you think are beneath you.
> At its best, this ethic cuts against every form of hierarchy you could bring
> into the room. Queer scenes are the true *salons des refusés*, where the
> most heterogeneous people are brought into great intimacy by their com-
> mon experience of being despised and rejected in a world of norms that
> they now recognize as false morality.[24]

The sad thing about the contemporary politics of gay and lesbian pride is that it
works in precisely the opposite way: It calls for a visibility predicated on homo-
geneity, and on excluding anyone who does not conform to norms that are taken
to be the very morality we should be happy to accept as the onus of our so-called
maturity. It thus sees shame as conventional indignity rather than the affective
substrate necessary to the transformation of one's distinctiveness into a queer

kind of dignity. This is why the queer culture of the 1960s, made visible in Warhol's films, is so necessary a reminder of what we need to know now.

So I'll return, in closing, to the shaming of Mario Montez in *Screen Test #2*. As I mentioned before, I wanted, in my earlier essay on *Blow Job* to contest the cliché of Warhol's filmic vision as voyeuristic. I argued there that formal features in Warhol's films—different formal features in different films, of course— worked to foreclose a knowingness about the people represented in them. Warhol found the means to make the people of his world visible to us without making them objects of our knowledge. The knowledge of a world that his films give us is not a knowledge of the other for the self. Rather what I see, when, say, I see Mario Montez in *Screen Test #2*, is a performer in the moment of being exposed such that he becomes, as Warhol said, "so for real." But unlike Warhol we don't leave the room (nor, for that matter, I'd bet, did Warhol). Rather we remain there with our disquiet—which is, after all, what? It is our encounter, on the one hand, with the absolute difference of another, his or her "so-for-realness," and, on the other hand, with the other's shame, both the shame that extracts his or her "so-for-realness" from the already for-real performativity of Warhol's performers, and the shame that we accept as also ours, but curiously also ours alone. I am thus not "like" Mario, but the distinctiveness that is revealed in Mario invades me— "floods me," to use Sedgwick's word— and my own distinctiveness is revealed simultaneously. I, too, feel exposed.

Ronald Tavel, the brilliant, ridiculous scenarist—brilliant, indeed, at ridicule[25]—seemed to provide just exactly what Warhol wanted. "I enjoyed working with him," Warhol wrote, "because he understood instantly when I'd say things like, 'I want it simple and plastic and white.' Not everyone can think in an abstract way, but Ronnie could."[26]

Tavel repays Warhol's compliment:

This operation-theatre he brings us to and in which we at first resentfully feel ourselves to be the patient, suddenly actualizes as the real and traditional theatre: we are audience as always, suddenly alive and watching, horrified after amused, scholarly after ennuied. And alarmed. The 'destructive' artist proves again the prophet and makes of his life a stunning cry, withal keeping his mask-distance of laughter and contempt. He emerges gentle from a warehouse of Brillo boxes, having stated his bleak vision, as social an artist as any 30s fiend could ask for.[27]

Tavel continues in the same essay, "The Banana Diary: The Story of Andy Warhol's 'Harlot,'"

The New American Cinema has taken the mask off rather than putting it on. . . . The souls of the beings we view are enlarged before us, even to the point of snapping out of character and blinking into the camera; an instant more and they would be waving at us. That these souls are wretched, which means our souls are wretched, has brought the accusation of brutality and sadism against the movement. Yet who among us, in his own life, escapes the complex of sado-masochistic chaos or finds his way about in a commodiousness less than brutal?[28]

It should be clear from this, I believe, that Tavel's purpose in *Screen Test #2* is to solicit from Mario exactly what we see: Mario's irresistible, resplendent vulnerability. We see his soul enlarged before us most conspicuously at those moments when Mario is overcome with shame, and when we become aware—painfully—of his shame as what Sedgwick calls a blazon. That blazon, which we share, might well proclaim a new slogan of queer politics: For Shame!

Notes

Thanks for inspiration, ideas, facts, and feedback to Callie Angell, Jonathan Flatley, Matthias Haase, Juliane Rebentisch, and Marc Siegel.

1. Sedgwick, Eve Kosofsky, "Queer Performativity, Warhol's Shyness, Warhol's Whiteness," in *Pop Out: Queer Warhol*, eds., Jennifer Doyle et al. (Durham: Duke University Press, 1996), 135.
2. Warhol withdrew his films from circulation in the beginning of the 1970s. After his agreement in 1982 to allow the Whitney Museum of American Art to research and present the films, the museum began showing them in installments, the first in 1988, the second in 1994. See *The Films of Andy Warhol: An Introduction* (New York: Whitney Museum of American Art, 1988), and Callie Angell, *The Films of Andy Warhol: Part II* (New York: Whitney Museum of American Art, 1994). *Screen Test #2*, the film discussed here, was restored in 1995 and screened in 1998.
3. The stakes of such a project comprise a portion of my argument in "Getting the Warhol We Deserve," *Social Text* 59 (Summer 1999), 49–66.
4. Sedgwick, Eve Kosofsky, *Epistemology of the Closet* (Berkeley: University of California Press, 1990), 23.
5. Warhol, Andy, and Pat Hackett, *Popism: The Warhol Sixties* (New York: Harcourt Brace & Company, 1980), 181.
6. Ibid, 91. Hedy Lamarr was notoriously litigious; thus, since Warhol's film, with a script by Ronald Tavel, was inspired by a real-life incident in 1966

in which Lamarr was charged with shoplifting (charges of which she was later cleared), the title was variously obfuscated. Lamarr was arrested at least twice more for shoplifting.

7. My work on Warhol's films owes an enormous debt to the careful work and intellectual generosity of Callie Angell, curator of the Warhol Film Project.

8. Crimp, Douglas, "Face Value," in *About Face: Andy Warhol Portraits*, ed. Nicholas Baume (Hartford: Wadsworth Atheneum, and Pittsburgh: Andy Warhol Museum, 1999), 110–25.

9. Warhol and Hackett, 91.

10. Ibid., 124.

11. Warhol, Andy, *Andy Warhol's Exposures* (New York: Andy Warhol Books/Grosset & Dunlap, 1979).

12. Brecht, Stefan, *Queer Theater* (New York: Methuen, 1986), 113–14.

13. "In 1965, Tavel was the Warhol dramatist in residence. He did the scenarios for what were, except for *Harlot* and *Drunk*, Warhol's first sound movies: *Screen Test Number One, Screen Test Number Two, Life of Juanita Castro, Vinyl, Suicide, Horse, Bitch, Kitchen*. His Warhol scripts, directed by John Vaccaro 1965–7, also became the first plays of the Playhouse of the Ridiculous" (Brecht, 107; see also the footnote on page 29).

14. There was no scenario for *Harlot*. The soundtrack consists of an off-screen conversation improvised on the spot by Tavel, Billy Name, and Harry Fainlight. The conversation is reproduced in Ronald Tavel, "The Banana Diary: The Story of Andy Warhol's 'Harlot,'" in *Andy Warhol: Film Factory*, ed., Michael O'Pray (London: British Film Institute, 1989), 86–92.

15. See *Wait for Me at the Bottom of the Pool: The Writings of Jack Smith*, eds. J. Hoberman and Edward Leffingwell (New York: Serpent's Tail, High Risk Books, 1997), 25–35. Originally published in *Film Culture* 27 (Winter 1962–63).

16. This moment of *Screen Test #2* suggests that the tour de force scene of Paul Morrissey's *Trash*—Holly Woodlawn's coke-bottle masturbation scene—was a reused Tavel idea. For all that Morrissey professed to find Warhol's early films self-indulgent, dull, and pretentious, he nevertheless made much use of them for his own film making.

17. Warhol and Hackett, 91.

18. Ibid., 181. Warhol writes that "Ondine slapped 'Pepper,'" remembering Angelina "Pepper" Davis in place of Ronna Page.

19. Stein, Jean, ed. with George Plimpton, *Edie: American Girl* (New York: Grove Press, 1994), 242.

20. "Stonewall, Then and Now," *New York Times*, 29 June 1999, A18.

21. Sedgwick, Eve Kosofsky, "Queer Performativity: Henry James's *The Art of the Novel*," GLQ 1, no. 1 (1993), 1–16. Hereafter page numbers cited in text.

22. "Readers who have paid attention to the recent, meteoric rise of shame to its present housewife-megastar status in the firmament of self-help and popular psychology . . . may be feeling a bit uneasy at this point. So, for that matter, may those used to reading about shame in the neo-conservative framework that treasures shame along with guilt as, precisely, an adjunct of repression and an enforcer of proper behavior. In the ways that I want to be thinking about shame, the widespread moral valuation of this powerful affect as *good* or *bad, to be mandated* or *to be excised*, according to how one plots it along a notional axis of prohibition/permission/requirement, seems distinctly beside the point" (Sedgwick, "Queer Performativity: Henry James's *The Art of the Novel*, 6).

23. Warner, Michael, *The Trouble with Normal: Sex, Politics, and the Ethics of Queer Life* (New York: Free Press, 1999), 3.

24. Ibid., 35–36.

25. ". . . the universal humiliation of all characters in this [ridiculous, queer] theatre gives it a repulsive air of viciousness, even cruelty, because it is absolute: the victims are accorded no basic dignity, no saving graces. We are not reassured of worthy or innocent motives of underlying rational seriousness. The characters are not just clownish or foolish but clowns and fools. They are not exactly funny. Isolated clown scenes, jokes and parodies that at first seem pure fun trouble us by their implications of profound ridiculousness. Some important, often protracted, actions are specifically and formally cruel humiliations: Bajazeth's enslavement in [*When*] *Queens* [*Collide*]/*Conquest* [*of the Universe*], the entire action of *Screen Test*, Lady Godiva's undressing (according to [John] Vacarro), in *Lady Godiva*, Victor's re-education in *Vinyl*. These humiliations bring this close to a theatre of the terrible. It takes a strong stomach to participate in their fun . . . " (Brecht, 36). *Screen Test* and *Vinyl* are both films by Warhol whose scenarios by Tavel became plays performed by the Playhouse of the Ridiculous.

26. Warhol and Hackett, 91.

27. Tavel, 77–78.

28. Ibid., 85.

Two Girls, Fat and Thin

Lauren Berlant

When You Wish upon a Star

History hurts, but not only. It also engenders optimism and disappointment, aggressions that respond to the oppressive presence of what dominates or is taken-for-granted. Both emotions are responses to prospects for change. It is not usual to think of critical theory as an optimistic genre, since it creates so much exhausting anxiety about the value of the pleasure of thinking even the "thinki-est" thought.[1] But the compulsion to repeat optimism, which is another defi-nition of desire, is a condition of possibility that also justifies the risk of having to survive, once again, disappointment and depression, the protracted sense that no-one, especially oneself, is teachable after all. All that work for what? Love isn't the half of it.

To be teachable is to be open for change. It is a tendency. It is to turn toward the story of what we have said in terms of phrases we hadn't yet noticed.[2] Eve Sedgwick's work has changed sexuality's history and destiny: She is a referent, and there is a professional field with a jargon and things, and articles and books that summarize it. For me, though, the luck of encountering her grandiosity, her belief that it is a good to disseminate the intelligent force of an attachment to a thing, a thought, a sensation, is of unsurpassable consequence. In the pleas-ure/knowledge economy of her work, the force of attachment has more right-eousness than anything intelligibly or objectively "true": She enables the refusal of cramped necessity by way of a poetics of misrecognition.

This is the process described by the concept of misrecognition. Misrecog-nition (*méconnaissance*) describes the psychic process by which fantasy recalibrates what we encounter so that we can imagine that something or someone can fulfill our desire. To misrecognize is not to err, but to project qualities onto something so that we can love, hate, and manipulate it for having those qualities—which it might or might not have.[3] A poetics of misrecognition may seem to risk collapsing the critical analysis of fantasy into fantasy. Maybe so, but such a risk is unavoidable. Fantasy is that which manages the ambivalence and itinerancy of attachment: It provides representations to make the subject appear intelligible to herself and to others throughout the career of desire's unruly attentiveness to new objects. That is, fantasy parses ambivalence in such a way that the subject is not defeated by it. To track fantasy across the scene of the subject in history, in this view, is to take seriously the magical thinking, or formalism, involved in seeing selves and worlds as continuous and whole.[4] This is a theory of being, and it is also a theory of reading.

As any reader of her work on Henry James would attest, Sedgwick's mode of reading is to deshame fantasmatic attachment so as to encounter its operations as knowledge.[5] For example, we may feel the violence of history as something "it" does to "us": But Sedgwick argues that the stories we tell about how subjectivity takes shape must also represent our involvement with the pain and error, the bad memory and mental lag, that also shape our desire's perverse, twisted, or, if you prefer, indirect routes toward pleasure and survival. To admit your surprising attachments, to trace your transformation over the course of a long (life) sentence, is sentience. That's what I've learned. The pain of paying attention pays me back in the form of eloquence: A sound pleasure.

Yet for a long time now, Sedgwick argues, skepticism has been deemed the only ethical position for the intellectual to take with respect to the subject's ordinary attachments. Even Adorno, the great belittler of the popular pleasures, can be aghast at the ease with which intellectuals shit on people who hold to a dream.[6] Dreams are seen as easy optimism, while failures seem complex. Sedgwick writes against the hermeneutics of suspicion on the grounds that it always finds the mirages and failures for which it looks: She finds critics overdedicated to a self-confirming scene of disappointment.[7] In this view the disappointed critic mistakes his act of negation for a performance of his seriousness; perhaps he also elevates his thought by disdaining anything that emanates a scent of therapy, reparation, or utopianism.

How does one go about defetishizing negation, while remaining critical? Begin with Freud's dictum that there is no negative in the unconscious. Sedgwick seeks to read every word the subject writes (she believes in the author) to establish the avowed and disavowed patterns of his/her desire, and then understands those repetitions in terms of a story about sexuality that does not exist yet as a convention or an identity. That aim is what makes her writing so optimistic.

In it the persistence of sexually anomalous attachment figures the social potential of queerness, in which what counts is not one's "object choice" as such but
rather one's sustaining attachments, which are only sometimes also one's social
relations. In this way repetition, heavily marked as a process of reading and
rereading, has a reparative effect on the subject of an impossible sexuality. The
queer tendency of this method is to put one's attachments back into play, into
pleasure, into knowledge, into worlds. It is to admit that they matter. In Sedgwick's work, desire's self-elaboration enables an aesthetic that is organized neither by the sublime nor the beautiful, the dramatic nor the banal, but by something vibratingly quiet. This would also be the erotic tonality struck by what she
calls "reparative criticism," her antidote to the hermeneutics of suspicion. Set
against the practice of deconstructing truth forms that she locates in literary theory of the 1970s, the aim of reparative criticism is to sustain the unfinished and
perhaps unthought thoughts about desire that are otherwise defeated by the roar
of conventionality or heteroculture.[8] Any writer's task, in this view, would be to
track desire's itinerary, not on behalf of confirming its hidden or suppressed
Truths but to elaborate its variety of attachments as sexuality, as lived life, and
as an unfinished history that confounds the hurts and the pleasures.

I love the idea of reparative reading insofar as it is a practice of meticulous
curiosity. But I also resist idealizing, even implicitly, any program of better
thought or reading. Those of us who think for a living are all too well-positioned
to characterize acts of thought as dramatically powerful, whether effective or
futile; we are set up to overestimate the clarity and destiny of an idea's effects.
This can produce strange distortions in the ways we stage agency as a mode of
heroic authorship, and vice versa. Thus the distinction I'm making here is
about an attitude toward what thinking (as *écriture*) can do. I'm suggesting that
the overvaluation of thought is both an occupational hazard and part of a larger
overvaluation of a certain mode of self-reflective personhood.

Elaine Hadley tells the long history of the liberal elevation of cultivated self-
reflection starting from its congealing image in Mill's *Autobiography*. Mill, she
argues, posits an identity between thought and interiority, such that his version
of the ethical subject takes on the shape of the intellectual who cultivates his
self-awareness — that is, his awareness of himself as a self.[9] More recently, there
was a seemingly antithetical moment — call it '68 — when a program of history
from and of the subject opposed the proprietary clarities of institutional and
bodily truth claims even, or even especially, in liberal capitalist/democratic
contexts that elevate mental abstraction over bodily labor. In this Anti-Oedipal
moment the subject's amalgam of knowledges — thoughts and practices —
became a generative ground for refiguring the normatively social, especially in
the domains of socialist and sexual politics. Bodies were elevated as, in a sense,

smarter and more knowing than minds, although ultimately the distinction heads toward exhaustion.

We are still in that epoch and need still to be, and yet there can be an uncanny confluence between the ideal of liberal abstraction or inner-directedness and the antiliberal orientation toward the subject. I often experience the radical project as having attenuated somewhat, as it is thematized in stories about exemplary individualities and individuals seen swimming or drowning amidst unjust forces. Like Eve, my desire is to angle knowledge toward and from the places where it is (and we are) impossible. But individuality, that monument of liberal fantasy, that site of commodity fetishism, that project of certain psychoanalytic desires, that sign of cultural and national modernity, is to me a contrary form, a form that needs interruption by a contrary. There is an orientation toward interiority in much queer theory that brings me up short, makes me wonder: Must the project of queerness start "inside" of the subject and spread out from there?

This distinction is not an opposition. Here is a biographical way of showing it, though in writing this way I am working against my own inclination. Eve's public stories about becoming possible — in *Fat Art/Thin Art*, *Tendencies*, and *A Dialogue on Love* — recount a crowded world of loving family and friends in which she thrives partly by living in the fold of her internal counter-narrative.[10] My story, if I wrote it, would locate its optimism in a crowded scene too, but mine was dominated by a general environment not of thriving but of disappointment, contempt, and threat. I salvaged my capacity to attach to persons by reconceiving of both their violence and their love as impersonal. *This isn't about me.* This has had some unpleasant effects, as you might imagine. But it was also a way to protect my optimism. Selves seemed like ruthless personalizers. In contrast, to think of the world as organized around the impersonality of the structures and practices that conventionalize desire, intimacy, and even one's own personhood was to realize how uninevitable the experience of being personal, of having personality, is. Out of this happy thought came an orientation toward passions of all sorts, including those intellectual and political.

Attachments are made not by will, after all, but by an intelligence after which we are always running. (It's not just "Hey, you!" but "Wait up!"[11]) This lagging and sagging relation to attachment threatens to make us feel vertiginously formless, except that normative conventions and our own creative repetitions are there along the way to quell the panic we might feel at the prospect of becoming exhausted or dead before we can make sense of ourselves.[12] In other words, the anxiety of formlessness makes us awfully teachable, for a minute. To the degree that the conventional forms of the social direct us to recognize only some of our attachments as the core of who we are and what we belong to, one's relation to attachment is impersonal. To belong to the normal world is to misrecognize only these modes of intelligibility as expressing one's true self. It brings out my queerness to think of living less as self-extension than as a process that interferes with the drama of the self. You will note that I am talking about impersonality not as the opposite of the personal—say, as "structure" or "power"—but as one of its conditions.

In this sense, my world operates according to a proximate, but different, fantasy of disappointment, optimism, and attachment than the one I attribute to Eve. I think of how I met the girl. We are both shy—who isn't? She gave a paper, and we talked about it. Years later, I gave one, and she listened to it. She wrote another book and I read it. There were meetings in airports and hotel dining rooms. We took walks, talked. Once, by accident, we took a small plane together. Reading is one place where the impersonality of intimacy can be transacted without harm to anyone: so are writing and paper-giving. There is no romance of the impersonal, no love plot for it. But there is optimism, a space across which to move.

Stupid optimism is the most disappointing thing of all. By "stupid" I mean the faith that adjustment to certain forms or practices of living and thinking will secure one's happiness: for example, the prospect of class mobility, romantic narrative, normalcy, nationality, or better sexual identity. Here is a stupidity of mine: "History is what hurts," that motto of *The Political Unconscious*, is a phrase that I love.[13] It resonates as truth; it performs a truth-effect in me. But because it is in the genre of the maxim I have never tried, I realize, to understand it. That is one project of this essay.

Did Somebody Say *Wish*?

Bodies and sexualities were in the wings of the previous section. Eve and I both write about fat because we identify as it, rightly or wrongly. She: "I used to have a superstition that / there was this use to being fat: no one I loved could come to harm / enfolded in my touch."[14] Me, writing about someone else, of course: "for him, it is a narrative in which the very compulsion to desire specific things . . . forces him to risk insatiability, a constant inadequacy to one's own desire."[15] My claim is that our relations to these modes of embodiment register our proximate approaches to the incorporative and impersonal strategies of queer/utopian thought.

Mary Gaitskill's novel, *Two Girls, Fat and Thin*, tells a story that comes close to encapsulating these dialectical impulses. All of her books try to make sense of the relation between painful history and the painful optimism of traumatized subjects trying to survive within that history, since they cannot put it behind them.[16] Trauma can never be let go of: it holds you. It locates you at the juncture of the personal and the impersonal, specifying you at the moment of least control over your own destiny and meaning. You become like a small pet that, when picked up, never stops moving its legs.

In *Two Girls, Fat and Thin*, Dorothy Never and Justine Shade—shades of *The Wizard of Oz*, *Pale Fire*, and *Justine*—come in contact because of their common interest in Anna Granite, an Ayn Rand-like figure. Like Rand, Granite intoxicates her audience with the promise that identification with one's sexual and intellectual power can produce happiness and fulfillment, achieving a victory over the deadening normal world.[17] Justine Shade has decided to write an article on Anna Granite and the people who follow her for *Urban Vision*, a hip paper like *The Village Voice*. She has learned of Granite at her day job in a doctor's office, where the promise they make to cure bodies in pain appears to her a false but necessary form of forestalling despair. When a young patient with heart disease tells her about Granite, the philosophy strikes Justine as both stupid and powerful.

Dorothy Never had once been a Granite acolyte, liberated by the thought of living and promoting the beauty of destructive passion. The two girls meet when Dorothy responds to a three by five card Justine posts on a Laundromat wall that asks for information about Granite. At the time of their meeting, neither Justine nor Dorothy has had a good conversation with anyone in many years: Each has long ago drawn a "cloak" around herself (Gaitskill 1991, 112, 158, 173) that acts as an "invisible shield" or "square of definition" (128, 129). Yet from the moment of their initial phone call they resonate with each other, a resonance that they take personally but which has, in a sense, nothing to do with the other except insofar as the other functions formally as an enigmatic opportunity for something transformative. "I invented possible scenarios daily," Dorothy thinks, "growing more and more excited by the impending intellectual adventure" (17). They convert into disembodied, vocal actors in each other's fantasy world: Dorothy is "lulled by the expressionless, melancholy quality" of Justine's voice (16), while Dorothy's "voice . . . stroked Justine on the inside of her skull in a way that both repelled and attracted her" (23). There is an attachment: yet the interlocutor factors in it not as a human, but as an opportunity for the possible emergence of something human. This paradox of the impersonality of attachment, that it circumvents the personal—the historical—on the way to enumerating their relation, organizes the women's mutual attraction/aversion throughout the novel. They feel taken over by it at the same time as they are taken up in it.

Likewise, during the studied formalism of the interview, they find themselves overwhelmed by a compulsion to historicize, to narrate their lives to each other. In part, this is a banal effect of the event, in which journalism takes on contemporary modes of therapeutic confessional storytelling. Any number of times in the novel the girls tell their life stories to a stranger who exchanges his/her own for it: such is the strange sociability of contemporary trauma talk. But the girls' mutual attachment goes well beyond the content of the phrase. Each woman becomes a "strange world" into which the other "unwittingly pitched" herself (11, 17). They register ambivalence and embarrassment toward the enormity of this impulse, which is not at all their usual practice.

When Dorothy meets Justine and intensity grows between them this dissonance arises first clothed in Dorothy's fierce desire to tell Justine about her childhood and then as an aversion to Justine for animating this wish to tell. Meeting Justine makes Dorothy want to burst open a long life of self-containment, a life in which she has hoarded her knowledge and made her body into a grotesque shield (39). Obesity and ugliness create a force field around her, seeming to neutralize what, in those "gatherings of the normally proportioned," might come from others—curiosity or attachment (169). In this way she is protected from saying what she knows, just as she is protected from the world's demand to know what she knows. "I preferred the elegance of distance," she notes (226). One might say that she shows, rather than tells. Yet she is also like a sadistic Sleeping Beauty, aggressively waiting for an opportunity to trust someone. On meeting Justine Dorothy begins to detach from her own defenses, but not from her own pleasures. Her mode of enfleshment stays the same, but she follows the trail of the voice, and she's not sure why.

Justine's response to Dorothy is at first like Dorothy's to her—a desire to tell a hard story to a stranger to whom she feels averse, and then confusion about that impulse lived as ambivalence toward the person who animates it. Far more impersonal than Dorothy, Justine has a slower emotional metabolism (yet Dorothy is the fat one, Justine the thin), but eventually she returns to Dorothy, sensing that Dorothy knows something that Justine cannot bear to know on her own. This meeting and return frame the book. Meanwhile, the body of the novel narrates the whole life stories of Justine and Dorothy, which they never fully tell to each other. We witness them growing up paralyzed by fear and at the same time launching into madnesses of thinking, reading, eating, masturbating, attaching, and fucking. A traumatic frenzy of interiority and impersonality constitutes a scene of being and embodiment that they both control and control not a whit. If she wants a good life, what's a girl, or two girls, to do? When does doing matter?

This question takes shape generically through the novel's proximity to the case study. Each girl knows she's a case, in many senses—it's no accident that Justine works for a doctor and Dorothy for a law firm. This proximity to the case is repeated aesthetically as well. Until the very end of the novel, each chapter has its own narrative voice, which is to say that it assigns each case its own norm of expertise. Dorothy tells her own story in the first person, while a narrator talks about Justine as "she." Each girl's mode of representation performs her relation to impersonality and self-cultivation, but not in a mimetic way: That is, Dorothy details how protecting her vigilant subjectivity requires strategies of social impersonality, while Justine's narrator tenderly registers the formation of Justine's dissociated intimacies. Yet their distinct lives mesh thematically in a hundred ways too, as though there were a certain generic rhythm to the traumatic tableau: peripatetic nuclear families, miserable fathers and mothers, childhood sexual abuse, never the right tone of voice or body. When the two girls are in their childhood families, they don't notice it that much. Their mothers give them enemas, their fathers overvalue them, whatever: They love whatever they can misrecognize as love. Distortion is the shape love takes.

Here is some of the case study content: A doctor friend of her doctor–father repeatedly and painfully masturbates Justine at the age of five. The awful "clawing" feeling of this event confirms something overwhelming she already knows without knowing it about the too intense emotional enclosure of her family: it involves them-against-the-world with an intensity of hermeticism that holds her close, but impersonally so. Justine participates in the economy of familial love by being "good": pretty and smart and submissive to the scene of parental aggression. At the same time she cultivates school as an alternative public for her badness. At seven years old, she gets a neighbor friend to tie her up and whip her; at eleven, she and her friends torture a fat and ugly girl with the nickname "Emotional"; at twelve she rapes a playmate with a toothbrush, masturbating to the memory later (99, 109–11). Later, the playmate asks for more, and Justine refuses her. During high school she develops a secret trashy wardrobe in which she can fit in with the popular girls who are marked by being *knowing*. They produce hierarchies of social value by trafficking in stereotype and mockery; they compete among themselves sexually to have the most "adult" experience.

In short, school is a world in which intimacies are always betrayed. But to Justine its viciousness offers a kind of confirming relief, for the explicit rule of cruelty feels truer to her than the familial amalgam of aggressive intimacy. She enters into adolescent heterosexuality by enacting the ambivalence of this scene repeatedly, but with herself as top and bottom, men being merely the instruments of violent relief from her "goodness." Perhaps her most telling act is to design a plot to lose her virginity violently at home. The scene to which she lures an indifferent boy is the rough floor of the family's "rec room," and its purpose is both to enact a fantasy of sexual surrender and to remain interesting to her closest female friend, Watley. The unpleasant hardness of the unfeeling fuck confirms something ruthless in Justine, and yet it marks her vulnerability too: After pretending that the experience was good high drama, she confides in her friend that it wasn't. Watley drops her and uses the story as capital to diminish Justine socially. Vulnerability makes you worthless: Survival depends on producing forms of hardened identity and closeting the soft remainders. On realizing that she has been outed as a sexual failure, Justine "walked with her arms around her middle feeling loneliness and humiliation coupled with the sensation that she was, at this moment, absolutely herself" (156). At the moment of that holding thought she is having, perhaps, the best sex of her life.

Dorothy also grows up with an angry father and a passive–aggressive mother, both of whom comment constantly on their daughter, whose value shifts according to the tempestuous parental mood. As a child she loves being at the center of this shifty scene, and yet like Justine she is hypervigilant—she can tell that something is off. "One of my first clear memories is having to deny the concrete truths of my life, of denying the clear pattern of them" (32). In particular, Dorothy shares with Justine a family that is weirdly self-enclosed, and she is likewise split from herself as a result. But Dorothy produces a different kind of split. Usually a "vision of my embattled father with my mother and me standing behind him" animates her. Like superhero partners she and her father "aimed for higher things; we had relinquished beauty and pleasure and turned our faces towards the harsh reality of the fight against cruelty and falsehood" (123).

At the same time, Dorothy begins to cultivate "beautiful and elaborate fantasies" about many things, including men and women whom she finds "unbearably beautiful" (117). She associates her drive for beauty with her mother's drive toward fictionalizing and femininity. Dorothy and her mother spend her youth drawing fantasy pictures together on construction paper in crayon. They tell each other "airy" stories about their visions, and then eat lavish desserts. At first, Dorothy draws countless Heavens "full of grinning winged children, candy bars, cake, ice cream, and toys" (81); then, on hearing her mother read aloud *Peter Pan*, Dorothy turns toward an addiction to Never-Never Land.

> Its very name made me feel a sadness like a big beautiful blanket I could wrap around myself. I tried to believe that Peter Pan might really come one night and fly me away; I was too old to believe this and I knew it, but I forced the bright polka-*dotted* canopy of this belief over my unhappy knowledge. (81; emphasis added)

At ten, Dorothy—nicknamed "Dottie," then—is already practiced at disavowing disquieting knowledge she barely senses with an optimistic absorption in beauty. But the anomalous style of her attachment both to her unthought thought and its compensations resonates unpleasantly throughout her life. She lets slip to an already sexualized friend that Never-Never Land is her favorite fantasy world, and the friend immediately betrays the immature fantasy, making Dorothy the "queer" pariah at school. When strangers speak to her she becomes "struck dumb by trying too hard to discover the correct response" (115). This result is, in part, a relief, however: It confirms something inchoate about Dorothy's hyper-orientation toward her family, and the family's toward itself. The alien eyes of her peers force Dorothy to disfigure her family romance and family romance in general. This is played out as her physical withdrawal from the machinery of familial narcissism.

During Dorothy's early adolescence she gets quiet, fat, and disgusting, without knowing why. When I say "disgusting," I am not interpreting: Dorothy characterizes herself as "gross and unhealthy." When she is fifteen, her father abjectly enters her room to tell her that his frustration with the unjust world causes him to act out on her, and in the jumble of love and apology he utters he begins to molest and to rape her. This is no surprise to Dorothy, really, for

> underneath the fear and shame, underneath the excitement, it seemed that what was happening now between my father and me was only the physical expression of what always happened between us, even when he verbally reviled me. Tears came to my eyes; it seemed that his cruel words had clothed these loving caresses all along. (126)

This relation lasts for many years. At night, he grunts while she fragments in silence. During the day, he denounces her furiously—because she no longer obeys her mother. Dorothy looks down at her plate and eats. Subsequently, whenever she experiences anxiety, it is as though her organs explode through her body, in ways recognizable from the literature on incest but also, here, resonant as the bodily ground of what Justine calls Dorothy's soft and graceful corpulence.

> [M]ost of the time I felt as if my body had been turned inside out, that I was a walking deformity hung with visible blood-purple organs, lungs, heart, bladder, kidneys, spleen, the full ugliness of a human stripped of its skin. (161)

She comments that "these bodily memories are so unevenly submerged and revealed, so distorted . . . that they may as well be completely invented" (44): this is not to say that the post-traumatic subject is doomed to false- or pseudo-memory but that memory is mediated by fantasies and misrecognitions so powerful and gratifying in their intensity that one must read them, and oneself, with distrust even when the affect that binds one to memory feels true. To create forms for managing the post-traumatic drives requires an acute visceral and intellectual sensorium that monitors at all times. Monitoring is more important than knowing. All of the girls' creativity is sucked up by the optimism of that patrolling activity, which enables self-deferral as well. But monitoring in itself assures no authenticity: It just keeps the subject close to the enigmatic representation.

In the language of case study rationality, both girls can be said to know negation as something productive, at once an expression of attachment and a cutting gesture that enables someone, usually the tormenter, to stop feeling overwhelmed. The older men teach the girls the value of the cut, and they spend their teens and twenties reproducing its cruelty where and whenever they feel the need to rise above the engulfing world of normal intimacy.[18] Yet the cruel cut is not merely dissociative, anti-intimate: It also binds the girls to optimistic projects of embodiment and attachment.[19] This is to say that the relation between impersonal formalism and the project of unique self-cultivation are all tied up in the novel. Self-protection and risk are indistinguishable here.

From a distance, the girls' nexus of self-abuse and pleasure produces formally antithetical sexualities. Justine loses and finds herself in S/M while Dorothy practices a kind of distance learning, a mode of monitoring characterized by psychological sadism and sexual idealization.[20] Yet to the extent that these sexualities control the flow of risk and desire, they are formally identical. The girls share other pleasure styles as well, featuring the consumption of food and the production of intense intellection. Each, like sex, is a process of absorption and a way of being in the world, a way of bringing it in, entering it, and averting it. While optimistic, these habituated modes of being are also techniques of self-annihilation and negation, ways of using the episodic relief of particular exchanges in order not, for a minute, to be that ordinary failed person with that history. Even if one risks self-negation through such tendencies, not to be that person is an amazing thing. Strongly ambivalent, then, these three powerful modes of repetition, negation, and optimism are associated with the cultivation of the senses as well: Food, thought, and sex are comforting as well as risky and raw-making modes of engagement and exchange.

So in one view, these repetitions can be read as establishing a regime of self-continuity that amounts to the constellation called "who I am." At the same time the girls' capacity not to inhabit the case study version of their story ("Hey you!") that marks everything as a continuous symptom of the cultivated self, suggests something else: a project of interference with "personality." Their negativity can be read as a *departure from* rather than an *assumption of* a way of being "who they are." For the greater part of this essay I will turn toward this set of pleasures which, I am arguing, interfere with negating rhythms of self-continuity. Responding to trauma's haunting plenitude not with ascesis but with a formalist abundance, the girls' tactic of counter-absorption marks their will to live otherwise ("Wait up!").

Pleasure #1: Food (for Thought)

Separately and together the girls "snack" constantly and "savagely" (15, 37, 81, 93, 241). Their mouths and their eyes consume potatoes, "a brown-bagged carton of milk;" "rum-flavored marzipan candies, each wrapped in bright red tinfoil bearing a picture of a mysterious brown-haired lady in décolletage, bottled spring water" (12); sweet and sour pork (30); egg roll (36); cheese curls, diet soda, chocolate cake, cookies, sandwiches, coffee, Gruyère broche, Mystic Mint cookies (15); dainty fried snacks (25); "tea . . . lumps of sugar and cream," "boiled dumpling"(28); "white bags of candy" (44); "cream and eggs" (45); chili, potatoes, beer, dry roasted peanuts (47); chili over spaghetti noodles, chocolate ice cream, ungnawable jawbreakers (48); cinnamon toast and hot chocolate (52); tuna sandwich (55); mucusy eggs (56); gum (62); "old tea bags and carrot peels" (66); blazing Popsicles (66); Cream of Wheat (74); "apple cores, old potato chip bags" (75); "ice cream and . . . chicken pot pie . . . . Almond Joys, Mallomars, Mellomints, and licorice ropes" (76); "cookies . . . gum" 78; eggs (80); "crackers and peanut butter . . . . candy bars, cake, ice cream . . . . cake and ice cream" (81); "orange and pink candy . . . Sloppy Joes . . . hot chocolate" (84); "cookies and tea" (86); cocoa (87); gum (91); ice cream (93); candy necklaces (94); eggs (98); "alcohol mixed with Coca-Cola" (105); "ice cream and vanilla wafers" (107); "Choco Chunk bars and French fries" (114); "meat . . .potatoes . . . . iced tea" (118); sugar (119); "salad . . . . scalloped potatoes . . . . orange corn curls" (120); "potato chips and beer . . . bite-sized Heath Bars" (123); "pork chops and green beans . . . boxed lemon chiffon pie" (124); "carrots . . . potatoes" (128); "lime sherbet" (130); muffins (137); "gristle, . . . milkshake" (141); "coffee with three spoons of sugar" (146); "a box of chocolates, some of which had ladies' faces painted on them" (154); "a chocolate . . . another chocolate" (155); ice cream sandwiches (160); "a box of donuts and bag of potato chips" (161); "a bag of burgers, fries, and orange drink . . . French toast" (168); "two chocolate donuts wrapped in cellophane" (174); "mushroom fried rice with green peas and lurid red spare ribs" (175); "lumpy potatoes" (177); "cookies and coffee" (179); "salads . . . . water" (185); "coffee . . . . pizza . . . . diet root beer" (193); "take-out salad" (195; 233); "cheese sandwich, potato chips, and candy . . . milkshake and double fries"

(205); "lemon meringue pie" (206); "malteds and potato chips, jelly beans and roast beef sandwiches dripping gravy" (211); French toast (214); "can of soup . . . bread" (215); "wonderfully gooey apple pie" (221); "champagne with our omelettes" (225); "hot coffee and a bag of sugars, stirrers, and petroleum milk substitutes" (229); "muffins . . . bag of cookies" (232); "a bag of cashews, a bag of marzipan, and an apple" (234); cookies (238); grilled cheese sandwich (241); misshapen bran muffin (242); "a bag of potato chips and a bag of candy" (244); "a plate of jewel-like sushi and shiny purple seaweed . . . . sake" (248); cookies (258); "pastries and puddings" (260); cakes (261); chocolate cake (264); "bags of potato chips and cookies" (272); martinis (281); "little mints and chewy candies" (290); chamomile tea (309).

Forget the fat and calories: To live for one's snack is to live by the rhythm of one's own impulse for pleasure, as in creating "a paradise of trips to the grocery and take-out dinners" (76). "In this time of anorexic cuties" being a foodie is a way of both being and not being in the world, giving the girls leverage to engage in exchange and to withdraw from sharing anything with just anyone (95). Eating is *their* time. It's their *time*. When either woman travels, she marks time by eating. When she waits, she eats. When she thinks, she eats. She eats before and after sex. In response to the overwhelming feeling of "sickening boundlessness" or endless absorbing interiority, food shapes a space of time for her, an episode of alterity to herself that is nonetheless self-confirming (160). It provides and defeats structure. It makes consciousness (pleasure memory) and its opposite (inarticulateness) too.[21] That is to say the girls' relation to eating is a scene, not a symptom: among other things, the practice of eating provides a way to negotiate one's incoherence while nonetheless refusing to organize a personality to compensate for it.

Dorothy never feels full when she's on her own. Then, she can eat any spread infinitely. Only when she is absorbed in unoriginal acts—proofreading the law's text on Wall Street each night or transcribing the debates that take place in Granite's inner circle—does she feel something like satiety. To be unoriginal is thereby to gain a reprieve from desire's self-articulating pressure: Accordingly, the more intense the desire, the emptier the body feels. To empty out one's emptiness through work is something like negating the negation, at least for a minute, because work is absorbing, like eating. But Dorothy also shows that one cannot help but be original or to desire.

It was in Ohio that I developed what my mother came to call my "unattractive habits." First, I stopped brushing my teeth, except on rare occasions. All at once, I hated putting the paste-laden brush into my nice warm mouth and scraping the intriguing texture of food from my teeth, annihilating the rich stew of flavors, the culinary history of my day, and replacing it with the vacuous mint-flavored aftertaste, the empty cavern of impersonal ivory. . . . In addition, I began giving in to gross and unhealthy cravings: candy bars, ice cream, cookies, sugar in wet spoonfuls from the bowl, Hershey's syrup drunk in gulps from the can, Reddi-Wip shot down my throat, icing in huge fingerfuls from other people's pieces of cake. (64)

Dorothy shifts between the name brand particularity of her attachment and the formless inner world of taste that she also creates. Her body is a kitchen in which the things of exchange become *thingness*, sensory knowledge, and material for a counter-temporality ("the culinary history of my day") that enables her to "chop up and organize [her] life to lessen the impact of the outside world" (112). The violence of the chopping is accompanied by the pleasures of the result, which she appreciates with all the pride of an author. "It was never enough," she notes (64). Frequently, she reads when she eats. In the factory of Dorothy's abundant counter-sensorium, then, the personal is produced as a formally continuous but constantly mutating scene of gratifying repetition. The subtlety of her incremental attachment to tastes is strictly her property, her inalienable hoard. At the same time, auto-pollution is not just a victory over something: In school and in her family Dorothy is a stray, a "deject," an outsider. It is not enough to say she embraces her negativity, because she doesn't.[22] The pain of inassimilability is unbearable while also remediated through the modes of self-care I have been describing. Eating cuts a swath in the anhedonia she experiences in the normal world by liberating her from the time and space of her sociability, where she is only inadequate. Devouring, and its plangent after-affects, engender an endless present. Collaborating with her body makes it a gift that keeps giving, but it only gives to her, meanwhile confirming its social negation with bodily grossness. That two negatives do not make a positive here means that the rhythm of this process sets up an alternative way of relating to the formalism of negation. Dorothy's misery is central to the system, and her social abjection seals her off from the shame of wanting to be normal after all. Yet her will-to-absorption is a drive toward self-annihilation that seeks, at the same time, to be topped by its optimism for pleasure. She associates the annihilated self with the subjected, abjected, and therefore impersonal one, whereas her grandiosity is a creative force that thrives as long her enfleshment becomes separated into flavors, tastes, and smells.

Justine lives according to a similar scale of culinary plenitude, but its place in her sexual economy takes on quite a different shape, one involving cultivated objectification, rather than the subjective spreading we see in Dorothy's case.

In one moment the world of Justine, "alone under the covers with her own smells, her fingers at her wet crotch, was now the world of the mall filled with fat, ugly people walking around eating and staring" (93). To have sexuality even in private is to be exposed to her own hypercritical gaze. An object of her own disgust exposed as *having had* desire, Justine's desire is further degraded because of its banality; after all, in the mall as in masturbation she seeks to stimulate desire while minimizing surprise. Yet when Justine actually eats rather than fantasizes about it, the world seems manageable and pleasant: "When Justine left work she bought a bag of cookies and rode home on the subway eating them with queenly elation" (22). Justine's pleasure at public eating envelops her in a protective bubble: eating in public is better even than masturbating, because the outside is an anonymous space that enables episodic abandonment of the hurt self. While Dorothy's saturation by the taste of her uniqueness constitutes a kind of homeopathic aggression at her stereotypically enfleshed identity, Justine's mode of survival involves generating a pleasure in the repeated gesture rather than in any sensual or visual specificity. When it works, each woman is relieved of herself in the act of taking in what she can bear to have of what she wants. The processual nature of Dorothy's sensual ingestion paradoxically enables her to shape the external body as a blockage while the sensual intellectual zone allows infinitely hoarded internal self-elaboration. In contrast, for Justine eating is a formalist strategy of impersonality, of time- and space-making, whether or not it appears "really" to be creativity oriented toward the self. They share a formalism of the invented gesture, organized for survival: What differs between them are the ways their compulsion to eat negotiates the economy of the personal and the impersonal.

It would be too grand to call any of these moments of food exchange "agency" in any transformative sense. In *Two Girls, Fat and Thin* any individual's sustained emancipation from the hurt of history is unimaginable. History is what hurts because that which repeats in consciousness, that which gives the pleasure at least of self-continuity, is what the subject deems her history. She is what she continues to have been. Traumatically-identified people in this sense take a technical pleasure in their histories, insofar as their histories are what they have, their personal property. But this is not to say that the history that hurts is destiny, a gothic repetition. Optimistic compulsion in *Two Girls, Fat and Thin* produces a counter-temporality that provides not narrative continuity but something more like the deep red areas on an infrared image. It involves attempts to experience moments of negative density.[23] Inhabiting such dense moments of sensuality stops time, makes time, saturates the lived, imagined, and not-yet-imagined world. The impossible act the girls seek to repeat, for which food and eating serve to substitute, merges will and repetition to produce something not uncomplicated or amnesiac, but something that as yet has no content, just inclination. What they achieve is not nothing; nor is it readable. Paying attention to what's absorbing marks a direction for the will to take. At one point Justine thinks, "The hell of it was, the fat woman was obviously very tough in some way" (195): then, "a man in an Armani suit . . . wildly waved a broken bottle and yelled 'I love you! I love you! I want to eat your shit and drink your piss!'" (196).

Pleasure #2: (History Is What) Smarts

I have suggested that, for the girls, eating is a technique for pulling the world in and pushing it away according to their own terms and sense of pacing. It is neither an act of conscious intentional Agency nor a manifestation of unconscious symptoms in any objective sense, although the narrative center of the novel, which tells the girls' stories one episode at a time, does use eating to establish the girls' way of participating in ordinary life. Yet along with making sense of their lives in the usual way, the novel shows another mode of organizing knowledge about persons. Technically it provides a sense that pleasure—a reiteration that makes a form, not necessarily something that feels good—also captures a way of being a *something* unbound to an identity that circulates, or that can be tracked to personality. Christopher Bollas calls this the "unthought known," and argues that knowledge forms before it is experienced idiomatically, in terms of the subject's own patterning.[24] This suggests another way that traumatic repetition might generate knowledge beyond itself despite the manifestation of repetition as a kind of paralysis. The pedagogy of repetition involves a shift of the relation of content (the scene to which one returns) to form (the pacing and placement of one's attachment).

In *Caravaggio's Secrets*, Leo Bersani and Ulysse Dutoit describe the intricate relation between desire and form as the enigma of sexuality itself.[25] The enigmatic quality that allures derives from the sense that one's attachments are at best only symbolized in their objects, and that the objects are so charged by our regard for them that they remain enigmatic to us at the same time as they are never fully known. Bersani and Dutoit focus on the ways that sexual attachment is constituted by the risk of becoming open to the scene of unpredictable change that the misrecognition involved in erotic attachment brings. In their view, *jouissance* is a counter-traumatic shapelessness that shatters the ego, pleasing the subject's desire to be overwhelmed while marking a limit to what it can know. Nonetheless, attachment taps into a desire not-to-know as well, an aversion that has many simultaneous functions: preserving the object's enigmatic quality protects one from becoming bored with, alienated from, or overwhelmed by the object. At the same time the seriality of repetition protects the subject from experiencing the unbearable pull of her own ambivalence toward what she has attached to. In the world of *Two Girls, Fat and Thin*, this is why it is safer to open oneself up to reiterated forms rather than to persons or fetishes. The reliable rhythm of the girls' impulse to eat neutralizes the pressure of the pleasure motives it serves: eating is a way of admitting desire without having to "know" that its sensual enactment stands for anything but itself. It is an attachment to a process, not an object, with diverging implications for each of the girls. In both cases, though, having a masticating habit does not amount to an attempt to become null, numb, or stupid. These girls are sharp cookies. Here as everywhere in this novel, the visceral quality of attachment to a practice inevitably involves a kind of acute awareness as well.

The intellectual referent of the word "smart" derives from its root in physical pain. Smartness is what hurts, or to say that something smarts is to say that it hurts—it's sharp, it stings, and it's ruthless. It is as though to be smart is to pose a threat of impending acuteness (L. *acutus*—sharp). In this sense smartness is the opposite of eating, which foregrounds the pleasure of self-absorption, not its sting. In *Two Girls, Fat and Thin*, the fear of and attachment to that sting has multiple functions. As defense: hypervigilance enables pleasure in judging and explaining, including explaining away one's own contradictions; and it aims to ward off traumatic surprise. As libidinal drive: its constant activity works as well to find scenes for controlled acting out. For like eating, monitoring appears to control the shape and pacing of exchange. Hyperactively speaking, therefore, the counter-traumatic functions of smartness are almost indistinguishable from its traumatic effects. Mediated to people as a zone of personal perception and will, smartness can just as easily be seen as the site for grandiosity and dissimulation.

Both girls' hypervigilant minds munch the storied scenery of memory by reoccupying it optimistically with ideas. In itself, a new idea does not reeducate the mind, erasing or sublimating its knowledge. Rather, it organizes the opportunity to identify with *pursuit*, with the raw energy of desire. As children they read with the voracious need to inhabit parallel worlds that operate, as Justine says, according to better rules. In this sense even the aesthetic is an instrument for providing a better idea than the one that governs actual living: All novels are utopian, by definition. Definitism too appears to be an intellectual source for emancipatory optimism, but likewise, in the end, its content is irrelevant. For the girls, the pursuit of the ideal form is the pursuit of alterity. Risk, transformation, denegation, and beyond: a yet unenumerated possible destiny. Perhaps this is why Justine can only bear to get "ideas at the rate of about one a year" (18): It is still more risky to interfere with the reproduction of the life you know than to follow an instinct toward something.

Intellection thus appears in the novel as content—philosophy and plot—on the one hand and as a hunger for a kind or form of freedom on the other. That is, the emancipatory form does not require a particular content but instead the capacity to be both surprised and confirmed by an attachment of which one knows little. For both girls the word for this unthought form is "beauty," in its spectacularly alien capacity to absorb a person, to take her out of her old way of being whether or not she finds a place elsewhere. The most thematic but not least dramatic instance of this double movement is in Dorothy's encounter with Anna Granite. Dorothy:

> She showed me that human beings can live in strength and honor. And that sex is actually part of that strength and honor, not oppositional to it. And she was the first writer to do that, ever. To show that sex is not only loving but empowering and enlarging. Not only for men but for women. As you can imagine, this was a big revelation to me. And then the rest was just . . . the sheer beauty of her ideas. (27)

In this domain of Definitist thought, thinking and sex are modes of power that women and men wield with equal force. The couplet "thinking and sex" constitutes a utopianism whose violence and rage is embraced right up front as central to attachment and intimacy: Granite elicits a "muted snarl of urgency and need" from her followers (12).

Dorothy and Justine both see that Granite's followers are as likely to be nerds and strays as they are to be authoritarian masters. The rhetoric of greatness Granite speaks, for example, seems to be experienced by many of her followers as a kind of soft Nietzscheanism that rejects the emasculating proprieties of normative middle-class order. Dorothy's embrace of Definitism strikes a similar, but not identical chord. She attaches to a vision of sexual emancipation that is far more iconoclastic and risky, embodying a will of intelligence beyond intention and rationality, a will afraid of nothing, neither death, nor what's scarier, living. What she calls the "beauty" of this possibility makes her weep with anger and gratitude. For Definitism is the first philosophy of living that accommodates the range of Dorothy's responses to the world—her softness (desire for intimacy) and her hardness (rage and intelligence). Only in this domain are they continuous attitudes and positive values rather than evidence of monstrous vulnerability that requires hiding. For Dorothy, to develop a self that can exist powerfully, not in compensation for abject objective powerlessness but in affirmation of her power, is to denegate the aspersions of her family, her father, and the taxonomizing cruelty of the normal world. Then again, Dorothy is not actually transformed by Definitism. The beautiful idea turns out not to rehardwire the girl's capacity to navigate worldliness: When we meet her she has regressed to her adolescent bubble of sadistic thought and culinary self-consolation. What, then, is the value of the ideational event?

That's the beauty of it. On an impulse, Dorothy decides to leave college to join the Definitist Movement. "I could allow [Granite] to penetrate the tiny but vibrant internal Never-Never Land I'd lived in when there was no other place for me," she thinks, understanding that "the intimacy and understanding that I fantasized was such that it would rip my skin off" (167). To do that, though, she has to imagine that Granite will make that space beautiful, as she makes all others. "Beauty is part of what makes life livable" (133), Dorothy says, especially "strong, contemptuous beauty indifferent to anything but itself and its own growth" (132). Granite legitimates Dorothy's ruthlessness as a form not of monstrosity but beauty—in the abstract. Alas, when they meet, the girl struggles, feeling "disappointment, a dark wave under my need to worship"(169), for here was Granite "looking like a middle-aged housewife in a Chanel dress. No, no, she didn't look like that. I don't want that recorded. . . . She had beautiful lids and eyes," a "beautiful black cape," a "beautiful tan" (28–29). "Then the light caught the necklace she wore, the deep blue hunks of precious stone that encircled her, and in a flash, I saw her haloed by the brilliant wattage of blue, the air about her ululating with an iridescent current of energy. . . . My fantasy mightily puffed out its sails" (170). As was the case in her fantasy of Peter Pan, Dorothy here cannot bear to be disappointed (again): her desire for the beautiful idea to saturate both the abstract and concrete zones of survival compels her to project beauty onto the smallest screen. The novel makes clear that Definitism requires such a commitment to misrecognizing impossibility as the beautiful: Evaluating Bernard, another follower, Justine notes that "he arranged his perception into fantasies of beauty and strength, glory and striving, fantasies he nursed deep within himself. . . . Through this armor his deformed sensitivity strained to find the thundering abstracts of beauty and heroism that consoled it" (177). This is the compulsion to repeat optimism. Later, encountering Justine, Dorothy repeats this pattern. Paragraph by paragraph she judges her friend's physical, psychological, and intellectual adequacy to the beautiful idea and its transformative promise.

At the same time that she meets Granite, Dorothy renames herself. "Dotty Footie" becomes "Dorothy Never," a fantasy pseudonym borrowed from *Peter Pan*, a renaming that negates her family, marks her historical anonymity and stakes out her attachment to a transformational harmony of desire and will through the idea. Granite asks Dorothy to tell the story of her life and then hires her to be a secretary and a scribe for the conversations held in the circle of philosophers that Granite convenes. Dorothy's job is not to comprehend the beautiful ideas that whirl around her, but to take them down as dictation—as sound, not as meaning.

> The experience was so charged, so heady that I lived those days in my head, my breath high and quivering on the pinnacle of my deserted body. . . . After the first hours had passed, my frayed perception forked into two—one navigating the landscape of words, phrases, and ideas, the other absorbing the sounds, inflections, and tonal habits of the voices. This secondary perception transmuted words and phrases into sounds that took on shapes of gentleness, aggression, hardness, softness, pride and happiness, shapes that moved through the room, changing and reacting to one another, swelling and shrinking, nosing against the furniture, filling the apartment with their mobile, invisible, contradicting vibrancy, then fading away." (203, 209)

"Fortunately I went emotionally blank," Dorothy thinks (207), appreciating her post-traumatic capacity to dissociate in order not to interfere with the soundtrack she absorbs uncomprehendingly. This absorption marks another entry into the archive of beautiful forms she has amassed, and not surprisingly this time, as the sound fills her body no longer needs its protective cover of fat, and she loses piles of weight. It is as though the sound substitutes for food, and as though the rhythmic pleasure of talk sublimates the solitary pleasure of eating. "All loneliness is a pinnacle," Granite pronounces (163). It is not loneliness as abandonment but as the impersonality of intellectual intimacy that frees Dorothy from the compensatory body she had developed as ballast against annihilation. Fat, the congealed form of history that hurts: As though it were indeed true that "the body remembers everything" the loss of fat reveals a new Dorothy. She begins to shop, to cultivate her now striking looks, and to fall in love with a musculature she hasn't seen since she was struggling and fifteen. She also begins to have sexual feeling.

Characteristically, smartness for Justine provides a scene of optimism and absorption much like Dorothy's, but for Justine smartness is far less personalized and embodied, less oriented toward savior-heroes in their magnificent iconicity. Instead, to identify with intellectual absorption is to develop an internal aesthetic that serves as an index for the feeling she can imagine having in a better life. That is, smartness is not utopian in the productive sense, but marks a yet unembodied affective relation toward which she directs herself. Arguing for "the beauty of loneliness" and "the intrinsic value of beauty in writing," she does not make the connection explicit: and yet the isolation of writing constitutes for her a space of grandiosity without violence, a space of possibility (175,

235). "Stark" beauty is her chosen mode of public impersonality: Through writing she passes as normal by withholding her perversity. No one can see and therefore touch her plenitude: The hell of abandonment to herself is thereby safeguarded from further trauma.

Face to face, Dorothy experiences Justine as retiring and dutiful, marked by "methodical reserve," and otherwise "insubstantial" and tentatively alive (27–29, 12). But in her head, Justine is otherwise: gloriously judgmental like Dorothy, just less dramatic and vocal about it. She believes in her judgments, her pity, her contempt, her aversion, her ambivalence, and on the rare occasions when she has it, her approval. But it is difficult to inhabit this grandiosity in public: and in this sense she and Dorothy are grotesque inversions, each producing an impersonal body for the deterrence of others through strategies of hyperbole and litotes, hyper- and hyporepresentation. But the impersonality of the socialized flesh does not suggest that anyone's true personhood lies beneath. Their bodies are the condition of possibility for the truth-function: They provide a space for navigating the risk of *knowing*. They provide for the girls the time and space to judge freely, angrily and bemusedly; to seek the experience of big feeling and the protection from exposure. Impersonalizing bodies facilitate escape from the very monitoring intelligence that the girls also cherish.

In this regard, their overvaluation of the idea is akin to the pleasure of critical negation. The idea enables the girls to hold themselves, to embrace their own bodies at the pinnacle of their greatest humiliations. Their embodied cloaks of loneliness protect a cherished sense of bitter superiority and abjection. But, more cherished than the relation between contemptuous defensive knowledge and the libidinal stimulation of intellectual comfort are these forms of distance—of interference with the rhythm of the post-traumatic shuttle—that they have developed with an instinct toward surviving. The differences between them matter here, but as content more than form: Dorothy cultivates the idea as though it were an actual world *for her*, while Justine experiences in the alterity of thought a relief from the too intimate alterity of the world she lives in. For both girls, though, being mental provides almost a rhythmic relief from being reactive that protects what they know (without knowing it) about the possibility of a better or less bad relation to enfleshment, epistemology, fantasy, and intimacy.

It is with such strategies in mind, no doubt, that Adam Phillips titles his essay on intellectual subjectivity, "On Composure."[26] Phillips wants to understand why some people come to identify with their minds: not the mind as the true self but as an appendage that does things, that can be trained and cultivated for the self's benefit. The image of a judge watching him/herself judge, for example, and taking pleasure as though the judging organ were elsewhere. Phillips argues that children with unstable caretaking environments will sometimes turn to the mind as the better mother. It holds you, it maps the world for you, and perhaps most important, it produces a space of composure between you and the world, so that you amount to more than a reactive impulse ("Hey, you!"). The space of time that composure produces enables you to set the scene of your entrance and makes the world come to you when you want it ("My close-up, Mr. DeMille!") to some degree or another.

A number of consequences can be distilled from this structure. Phillips argues that the precociously mind-oriented child (read "intellectual") enters the world with "diffuse resentment," a certain self-confirming and sadistic thrill at the scene of optimism and disappointment.[27] Why is this, though? In part, disappointment can be channeled as though it were a judgment rather than a feeling, supporting the mytheme that the solitary and independent life of the brain precedes and is superior to the simple attachments of intimate proxim- ity. On the other hand, no one experiences abandonment as a pleasure that simply feels good. Dorothy: "I clawed backward into the past and found no comfort in anything there unless "comfort" could be had in the excruciating site of brute, ignorant love, cowed and trapped, exposed by the wildly panning camera of my memory" (162). My argument so far has been that this recogni- tion precisely brings the comfort or pleasure of recognition itself: but that this cannot be confused, say, with happiness. The mind enables alternative means of self-production without ever necessarily cultivating them. It is a camera that pans where it must, but also where you will it—not that the will is smarter or more creative than the unconscious (far from it!), but that one identifies one- self with its action. Usually, as Dorothy notes, there is "an awful thematic same- ness under the deceptive novelty of the experience" (160). As composure approaches the posture of impersonality, it protects the subject's sensorial capacity to impoverish threatening objects while animating new ones and, more importantly, animates animation itself, spurring new processes of *paying attention*.[28] At least this is the counter-traumatic structure of mindfulness in *Two Girls, Fat and Thin*.

Psychoanalysis always raises anxieties for critics about its tendency to uni- versalize individuality and normalize conventions of, say, individuation and autonomy as ideals of health that should be cultivated and always intelligible. Working between Winnicott and Lacan, Phillips articulates a different view, disidentifying health with the appearance of successful anything. Thinking about the form of the subject as related to his/her capacity to be composed, Phillips rethinks Freudian disease categories, pointing out that the pervert plays with his composure, the hysteric with its absence, and so on. In other words the idea of composure tells us that the symptom lies. When the pervert gives form to perversion, this is his/her performance of composure, a private way of keeping the world at bay until she/he is ready. What looks like an absence of composure might well constitute its presence at the level of form, not representation. The subject who identifies with thought might be able to disavow her/his dependency and disappointment through the appearance of composure, and s/he can act as an autonomous author of the salient terms of accountability, judgment, and value with which s/he and the world shall be measured. Or, disappointed in the world's unhomeliness, the subject might experience the contingency of autonomy in a way that either impoverishes or overvalues the boundaries made by intellectual will. Composure then might feel desperate, like the drag of melancholy or the push of mania. Or, perhaps the subject absorbs unhomeliness as a just desert for being unlovable. Composure then might be experienced not as a condition of action but of dark affectlessness or simple neutrality. From this perspective, one cannot predict how and when— with intellection as the guardian of the bruised and disappointed self— someone will move toward any number of possible identifications. Composure is the formalist protector of fantasy, the subject's medium for misrecognizing what it takes to make some sense.

Pleasure #3: Sex

Sex negates composure, except when it doesn't. We have seen that, throughout the novel, all forms—all patterns that can be misrecognized as objects— are managerial habits that orchestrate the subject's cadence of optimism and disappointment while minimizing her/his risk of unwanted exposure or discomposure. A complex relation of fantasy to self-understanding ensues: Even though I wish to remain myself, I want to experience discomposure, yet only the discomposure I can imagine, and how can I bear the risk of experiencing anything but it? And so on. What counts as composure might be a conventional style of instability rather than an instability that actually threatens the subject's core patterning. These questions of the seeming and being of exposure and instability are central to the scene of sex in practice. Both confirming and interfering with intelligibility, sex's threat is objectively indistinguishable from its capacity to confirm. How do you know whether a change is a change or the confirmation of a (conscious or unconscious) expectation?

A sex event technically interferes with the ordinary self, the self who mostly is not having sex, who spends time mostly not risking the pleasure of a momentarily different body/mind relation that predictably overwhelms. Tellingly, when the girls imbue ordinary acts of eating and thinking with qualities like "queenly elation," they are valuing the sense of mental uniqueness that they are able to project into the acts, which remain ordinary even as they open up into the extraordinary. It may look ordinary to eat a cookie or to be fat, but mentally, an infinite domain of optimism opens up directed toward an enigmatic somewhere. In contrast, what the girls value most about sex is its unoriginality. The more mental work involved, the more dangerous it is.

For instance, the orgasm seems to make you shatteringly different than your ego was a minute ago, but in another minute you are likely to be doing something utterly intelligible, like pissing, shmoozing, looking away, or walking into the kitchen and opening the refrigerator door. Is it not possible that the very unoriginality of the sexual experience, its banality, also makes it worth cherishing? This is not a rhetorical question, but one that argues methodologically against the transparency of bodily response. Shattering is not always shattering, just as shame is only one way of coding sexual aversion; sentimentality, say, might be a much bigger threat to someone's defenses than any sexual event is, *pace* normative ideology.[29]

When people consent to inhabiting the potential for change that sexual events require they are mainly consenting to enter a space whose potentially surprising consequences are kept to a minimum. The only requirement is that sexual subjects be able to manage any anxiety emerging from their failure—always possible—to be the *something* that they need or want to be. Such instability can have its comforts, nonetheless, if the subject can successfully control the degree of unwanted uniqueness engendered in the event. Bound optimistically to the impersonality of sex, s/he does not have to take personally *its* failure or *her* failure to do everything it is meant to do, in whatever context. So when Justine makes "what she hoped were attractive moaning noises" as a lover undresses her (149), and Dorothy describes "the mystery of masculine tenderness that enveloped me like the wings of a swan" (222), the girls perform rhetorically the comforting conventionality of sexual mimesis and the freeing impersonality of sexual sociability in general. There are phrases about sex that one can say; there are sounds that one can make; there are things one does and one doesn't do; there is what one can imagine. When one occupies the domain of those desires one is using fantasy norms to shape what feeling sexual is, in advance. Sex events might be expressive of one's true feelings or not, and they might be exciting, overwhelming, painful, and/or boring. One can never be sure, though, whether one will be confirmed or threatened by the negativity or positivity that one attaches to the event. The struggle to master the implications of the impersonality of sex is central to the novel, at least, if not to living: For the girls in particular, I have suggested, this is a fundamentally aesthetic question, a question of training the senses for building possible and beautiful worlds out of impossible ones.

Sex is the culminating counter-traumatic pleasure of *Two Girls, Fat and Thin*, then, because its challenge to the girls' composure is the greatest, even greater than the adrenaline rush that comes from a good thought or piece of cake. Adrenaline is the addictive booty in this novel: its experience always involves tapping into one's creativity, even if the scene of stimulation repeats the most unpleasant or disappointing urges of need and desire. An idea, a possibility, takes over the girls. Suddenly as though they are all nerve endings, they turn and return toward mania, compelled to be compelled to repeat. "Justine was morbidly attracted to obsessions" (21); Dorothy attaches to scenarios with "wildest invention . . . growing more and more excited" (17). Romance narrative and violent sex are twins here the ways the girls, fat and thin, are also nominally twins. These genres of the viscera use heightened adrenaline (from longing and fear) to play out a threat to the subject's attachment to formalism itself.

All genres produce drama from their moments of potential failure. (What, the romance might not pan out, or its failure might not affirm the beauty of the elusive ideal? The hero might not survive, or the rule of law that his survival affirms might not be affirmed by his death?) Just as thinking and eating turn out to be ways of managing the risk of sociability formally, sex works dialectically in this novel. It wears its ordinary dress as the site in which the subject's structuring drama is repeated, and it functions as well as a site of metacommentary about traumatic repetition and what it takes not to negate it, but to break its stride.

I have described the girls' attachment to reading as a space for detaching from the normative world while cultivating a parallel sensorium from it. By the time they become readers, both girls are hot for the dual historical functions of romance: as the site of grandiose alternative worlds and of recognizable intimate intensities. We cannot underestimate the gendered divisions that subject the girls to the thought that love plots, intellectual and sexual, will emancipate them from the deadening space of their own worlds. They read about suffering in Victorian literature, absorbed by its dramas of subordination. Further, like many middle-class American girls during the 1960s, they read Anne Frank's *Diary* and other Nazi and survivor tales from World War II, savoring and expanding these images of adolescent girl heroism.

This pedagogy of feminine suffering teaches many things. The girls learn to savor the story of bodily submission. They cultivate all sorts of scenes that repeat this submission and interfere with it too, by living the full range of their sensuality more fully as intellectuals than they do as social persons. As adolescents and adults, they read everything as romance, amalgamating the big passion of utopianism to the big passion of heterosexual lust. Even though one girl looks normal and the other grotesque from the perspective of white, middle class suburban femininity, these forms of survival render the public body more impersonal to them than the mental body is. They end up in New York City, where the relief and pain of that impersonality is a fact of life. Thereby the power of the idea merges into sexuality.

One would think that Anna Granite's ideology of conscienceless power might not appeal to girls so femininely trained and so post-traumatic. But, and crucially, Anna Granite disseminates her ideology through romance novels. In effect, she turns all readers into adolescent girls. A utopia of the ruthless drives uses the genre of the ruthless drives: how to tell them apart? Which is the tenor and which, the vehicle? Granite's novels, *The Bulwark, The Last Woman Alive,* and *The Gods Disdained,* are repeatedly characterized as trashy and preachy pornography. They are all about "the struggle of a few isolated, superior people to ward off the attacks of the mean-spirited majority as they created all the beautiful important things in the world while having incredible sex with each other" (163). This clearly ironic sentence is not ironic to Dorothy. Reading that the beautiful (fictional) Solitaire D'Anconti experiences trauma that forces "the hot anger of her pain into the icy steel of her intellect" makes Dorothy feel "possible," like a beautiful person whose social banishment is not fitting but the effect of a vicious and mendacious world (163–64). That Granite's plots feature women who submit and men who benefit from that submission is not supposed to be interesting: Dorothy scorns Justine for suggesting as much, arguing that the power to submit without fear of loss is the pinnacle of anyone's individuality—if they can bear the beauty of it. We have seen that Dorothy cannot bear the ugliness of it when Granite turns out to be, after all, a bad practitioner of her theory. When turned down sexually by a younger man, Granite banishes that man publicly from the cadre, wrecking the ideals for which Dorothy needs her idol to stand. Granite's belief in the ruthlessness of desire turns out to mean mainly her desire and not everyone's. To Dorothy, this threatens to make Granite's philosophy merely an individual's sexual alibi, not a way to retool the world for emancipated sexual personhood.

What would emancipated sexual personhood look like if she did encounter it? A cultivated individuality that merges inner ruthlessness with the beautiful form of desire in practice feels liberating to Dorothy in her intellectually organized affects. When she experiences it, however, the rhetorical archive for this fantasy is a romance novel, a vehicle central to the reproduction of feminine ideology in the first place. In *Two Girls, Fat and Thin,* the one relation involving sex that Dorothy seeks is with Knight Ludlow, "a wealthy New York financier" and colleague of Granite's. Engaged to someone else, Ludlow looks at Dorothy in a way so thrilling that her life changes overnight. She moves from her shabby apartment to a nice one, from shapeless clothes to shaped ones, and from exorbitant fat-eating to moderation. As they move toward becoming lovers, the language of her chapters takes up the song of romance: sparks fly and "streams of colored light" sway between them (218). "The ricocheting chatter in my mind became inaudible, the zipping comets of quasi thought slowed to melting putty. Rivulets of liquid gold, swollen with nodules of heat, spanned my limbs. A glimmering flower of blood and fire bloomed between my legs, its petals spanned my thighs" (222).

This ratcheted up, rhetorical blast crashes the moment Ludlow moves toward Dorothy's vagina. She turns to ice and then dissolves in tears. As she does, her traumatic story leaks out, but this enhances their romance. Knight holds her, tells her his hard stories, and they sleep together for days until they make love happily. At this point the language of the soft and warm flowering vagina reblossoms. Afterwards they eat a big champagne breakfast, and he leaves to rejoin his fiancée. Dorothy is happy: she has been idealized. That's the end of sex for her. The memory stays perfect, before it fades.

Justine's history of painful sex takes on much the same trajectory as Dorothy's romantic one. "This memory [of sexual violence], with its ugly eroticism, was not in the least arousing; however she recognized something compelling in it, a compulsion akin to that of a starving lab animal which will keep pressing the button that once supplied it with food, even though the button now jolts its poor small body with increasing doses of electric shock" (235–36). The story of the starving lab animal suggests the bare relevance of content to what drives a being toward what negates him: the unlivable experience of infinite need. The "poor small body" wants food, gets shocked, and is compelled to return to the place of pain by the possibility that shock will again turn to food. Or, the rat is compelled to return because returning is what the rat now knows how to do. All the rat might know is reduced to that one habit of living. The smarting rat is not using his smarts: it has no smarts. It is compelled to create a form of living through repetitions that do not gratify him. But they do gratify him too, in the sense that this is a scene he recognizes. Recognizing oneself when one has survived shock provides a foundation for a mode of survival that is more than just a failure to die.

Heterosexual conventionality is, exactly, a painful maze for Justine—given her history, a perverse desire. Like loneliness, S/M performs the unnaturalness of normal intimacy for her by eroticizing form and boundary. It takes up the aspects of grandiose suffering she already associates with love and rescue plots. Her femininity is all tied up with training in the excellence of survival against the odds, the uninevitability of happiness, the pain of bodily pleasure. In this sense sexual trauma only slightly exacerbates ordinary sexuality. Thus on the one hand, it is not surprising that she turns toward a formalist mode of sex that foregrounds and replays the unfailing merger of violence and pleasure. On the other, and like Dorothy, when Justine meets Bryan, an artist and an ad man who accosts her in a bar, the defensive impersonal version of Justine's social self develops a softer, more feminine persona than we or she has seen. Bryan immediately gets Justine's persona as the gamine/terrorizer she has been. She responds to his percipience by recounting to him a sexually violent experience with a lover who "penetrated" and "opened" her up in a way that she could neither control nor wanted to control.[30] He takes her up on the promise of that story, frightening her with an image of "people being tied up and beaten, women getting fucked by dozens of guys" (201); they proceed to a whirl of soft romance and hard sex. Their relation feels *normal*, reciprocal—confusing. Bryan's surprising penetration discomposes the intellectual in Justine, shredding the "cloak" of loneliness that has protected her as well as emotionally repeating the surprise of intense childhood sexualization. It gives her pleasure to return to this complex tableau, although her narrator makes it clear that she still must shift positions constantly to get the responses from him she wants. But that Bryan knows how to be human in the context of heterosexual and S/M formalism opens Justine up to new and destabilizing practices.

What's stunning is that each woman gets exactly what she wants out of consensual sex. She gets to be other than her default self. She gets to be impersonal by virtue of the imitative quality of the sex, its conventionality or formalism. At the same time, she can identify with that impersonality and see it as an opening up of something that may or may not lead to something else. Finally, each girl gets to experience a simple feeling with another person. For Dorothy, this is a scene in which she can socially experience ownership of unimpeded "beautiful" femininity, while for Justine this is a scene in which vulnerability and defense recombine into a personality that can be recognized and desired.

These enacted desires for simplicity, flow, and normalcy, in short, are gratifying to the girls. Formally these brief relationships repeat the girls' impulse to become other than who they are historically, but they repeat this desire with a change, in that a certain conventional feminine rhetoric and sensorium is let in the door. Is this irony, or is it destiny?

The end of the novel asks as much. Meeting Justine reclaims for Dorothy the desire for belonging that she once associated with Definitism. The energy released by these memories now attaches to Justine, not to the memories. This is why Dorothy sees their relation as "mind-boggling" (17): Justine becomes her newest object, her next opportunity to idealize and to become idealized by another human. Sex seems to interfere with idealization: but sex is only one route to love. As the novel closes, Bryan has just whipped Justine. At first, this is at her direction, but then it escalates beyond her consent (310). Meanwhile,

Dorothy is acting violent and crazy in public, sputtering curses and wild accusations aloud on the New York City subway while reading Justine's article on Anna Granite in *Urban Vision*. Dorothy feels both accurately depicted and "raped" by the article. She marches up to Justine's apartment furiously, and enters the room enraged. But seeing the scrawny, naked Justine tied to her bed all bloody, scarred, and fatigued, Dorothy takes up like a super hero, beating Bryan up and ejecting him from the room naked. Justine and Dorothy talk a little, but, exhausted by this show of violence and release, Justine falls asleep in Dorothy's arms. This is not a lesbian ending, exactly, since exhaustion is not sexuality. On the other hand, this mutual fall into bed is not nothing. It's something else.

Coda: Melotrauma

This is what we come to: the exhaustion of a repetition. What does it mean to turn an exhausted something into something other than itself—a lesson learned?

It may be that any commentary violates the spirit of the novel's ending, to the degree that the image of the two women hovers there as what it is. They need no longer to monitor. In contrast to us, they no longer shuttle between the traumatic and the critical. It is our task to catch up to them, to find out what happened: wait up! Were we to take on the tactic that sustained them throughout their struggles we would return to their desire for beauty, for absorption in the emancipating image or sound. We would have no choice but to be gratified that, finally, these two hypervigilant minds have come to rest in their bodies without being dead or crazy. It may be that the beauty of writing of love in the post-post-traumatic scene requires the risk of acknowledging, even coveting, the possibility of such simplicity.

This beauty is born of simple violence, too. Literally iconoclastic, it has beaten up on the heteroimago that has for so long provided the content for girlish fantasy. Now the girls are literally beyond biography. Not only that, but the door has been closed on boys. A newly sensible scene prevails to attach to that desire for an attachment to repeat. At least it amounts to a less bad world for anomalous women and sexuality, if not for sex. Perhaps it also sets forth a new lexicon for memory, and those lesbians and gay men Justine and Dorothy encounter suddenly become characters to whom they have paid too little attention (72, 116). We can extrapolate from this a practice of intimacy that does not refer to the birth or childhood family, property, or inheritance. Nor does it require the bodily and sensual cultivation of alternative worlds inside individuals who exchange stories about them without changing their actual lives. *If,* that is, we want to read Dorothy as beneficent, as something other than a monitoring top who now both rescues and fondles the adult, but diminutive, Justine Shade. Her father eerily haunts that structure. So does another subject: the young Dorothy. Earlier in the novel Dorothy reads *The Little Match Girl* the way she will later read of other suffering protagonists. She imagines rescuing the poor little girl, feeding her Cream of Wheat, and then sleeping with her, "her bony back pressed against my front, my arm wrapped around her waist" (74). At the end of the novel Justine *faces* Dorothy and falls asleep in her arms (312). Now Dorothy experiences "white flowers" blooming in her heart, and the erotic luminaries of Definitist romance who have "for so long" absorbed her libidinal energy suddenly dissolve. We know nothing about how Justine is feeling—the poor girl sleeps, impersonal as ever, but more relaxed. In other words, the novel can be read as Dorothy's voice-over, a sound loop, and the story of a mind-boggling tenderness that she loonily projects. As with so many voice-over narratives in which things happen outside of the writer's experience, the decision as to whether this is true testimony or a troubled scene is a matter of trust or transference (desire). In this case, the ordinary narrative questions are compounded by Dorothy's particular habit of idealization for emancipation from herself.

No matter, the novel's closing scene enables a *something* to be constructed in the present, from where the people are. We can even read this scene as the foundation for an actually feminist queer theory, if we can imagine Justine waking up rested and content. This would involve following sexuality along all of the perverse paths it will travel—the traumatic, the conventionally romantic, the experimental, the meaningless, the hysterical—paying less moral attention to visceral content and paying more respect to the simple imperative to fight for women where the urgencies are. Because it can seem so trivial, private, self-referential, and minor in the "big picture" of things, feminists have paid a big cost for attending to sex, the elaborate economies built around it, and their impact on women. Some have left feminism behind as white, heterosexual; a bourgeois tic. *Two Girls, Fat and Thin* provides a good case for both arguments.

The problem is most acutely staged in the terms of that other emancipating promise suggested in the sleepy ending: that of a post-psychological world, a world where people are defined in their actions and where the monitoring subject is not deemed closer to the truth about living. *Two Girls, Fat and Thin* associates psychological interiority with the traumatic incapacity to disavow: Trauma confounds the subject's censor, substituting its own wild aesthetic of distortion and repetition, and at the same time provides a counter-traumatic grandiosity for the now impossible subject. This novel provides for us an easy way to recognize trauma: it happens through sex. But the girls know it is more than this. Their families are traumatized and traumatic. I do not mean that all families are traumatic and traumaticized, but these particular families in their historical milieu were incited to attach to a good life that was not very good for anyone in it. The structuring "unthought known" of their lives is that the sexuality of the family, its amalgamated intimate and financial economy, is already a terrible context for the cultivation of anything. Sexual trauma shapes knowledge the girls already have, rather than being the event that merely structures subsequent consciousness.[31]

I have told a psychological story here about the two girls' will to attach, suggesting the convolutions of repetition in the traumas of femininity. I tell it this way because this is how the novel explains the mental involution and bodily expression of the two girls, and I wanted to spin out for you a concept of impersonality that both marks any ordinary subject and presents strategies for interfering with particular toxic intimacies. But, as Carolyn Steedman reminds us, typically only some people — the middle classes — get to have (complex) psychology, while others — on the economic bottom — are deemed as mere (simple) effects of social and material crises of survival.[32]

Justine and Dorothy are saturated by the mass cultural signs of the United States from the late '60s through the '80s. Like virtually every recent film about the '60s *Two Girls, Fat and Thin* locates the girls historically by depicting them listening to pop music, buying pop style, eating pop food, and watching pop TV. On television they witness the civil rights actions of 1963, Martin Luther King, and metropolitan rioting. Their parents pronounce lots of historically predictable softly liberal opinions from their perch at a safe distance. In short, the two girls are not exemplary traumatic subjects, or children, or women, or any kind of exemplary Subject of History, whether of nations, capitalism, or sexuality. They are two middle class white American girls, enclosed in nuclear families that live in communities so white that "the Jew" and "the Spic" are easy to spot from a distance. Economically more than comfortable, the girls nonetheless have virtually no resources but themselves and books with which to escape the given world. It is entirely predictable that they would end up addressing the problem of living by diving inside their bodies and feelings. Partly, this is training, as during adolescence, their parents send them to uncomprehending therapists. But even if this were not the case, the girls' isolation and involution are to be expected of children of the professional classes. Their interiority is the product, the cost, and the benefit of seeing themselves, in the terms of bourgeois universalism, as autonomous individuals who demand some attention and independence, parental affirmation and private space. What if the girls had inhabited worlds in which the burden to make happiness was not indexed according to power at work and harmony at home and by the achievement of a family so complete it needs nothing else but itself? They would not be who they are. In this sense too, what is personal about them is also impersonal. Not strategically, but analytically and historically speaking.

In short, even if we could agree on the meaning of the girls' final binding moment, their particular story can be only a part-object, involving the exhaustion or discomposure of heterocultural trauma stories as the destiny for certain sectors of the professional and metropolitan elite. When I say this I may sound accusatory: aha! But I mean not to sound that way, just to name the particular location out of which their drama comes. I also realize that there is nothing "beautiful" in this explanation of the repetitive modalities of optimism and disappointment, will and transformation that I have been tracking. Such a poetic seems so connected to the cultivation of selves, will, and desire that it feels like clunkification to say anything but "as sexualization is the problem so too will its better cultivation make the solution." But this has not been my argument.

Further, we are trained to read the end of a novel as though it provides a solution to a problem or a diagnosis of a case study subject. All the details meld into a shape, and finally a moment comes when it all makes sense. But Justine and Dorothy are not finding sexual truth when they finally get some rest from working the relations of trauma and absorption, history and fantasy, will and misrecognition, flesh and abstraction, form and content. The concept of the *two-as-one* as a solution to individual isolation is conventionally recognized as a requirement for happiness, but as such it nonetheless produces the kinds of hermeticism that marked the girls out in the first place as likely to misrecognize their story as personal trauma. Dorothy's movement toward Definitism demonstrates this paradoxically, as it requires a new style of risky collective identification and deprivatization in order to promote the legitimacy of all individual will. The "Two Girls'" twinning in the novel's title therefore suggests to me a different thought.

The novel's epigraph from Nabokov reads, "All one could do was to glimpse, amid the haze and chimeras, something real ahead." The closing image of Dorothy and Justine's attachment might testify to something real. We can also read the conclusion as the new present from which we cannot predict, but only intuit, futures. History is what has hurt and it continues to make shadowlines, and we are always in the haze of the present, sensing new repetitions-to-be, some of which can be willed, others of which remain enigmatic. We are still unlearning the transparency of repetitive representation, and still therefore improvising how else we might know to pay attention.

We are also given a little help toward this reading. When Dorothy provides that image of their final bodily intimacy, she produces it as a soundtrack. "Her body against me was like a phrase of music" (313). The soundtrack is not accompanied by dialogue: It is as though we have returned to the melodramatic stage where the smallest bodily gesture communicates so much about the ineloquence of the language we have. A musical phrase is powerful because it repeats: As we become attached to it, it helps us find a place before the plot tells what it means and where that place is. Melodrama is trauma's perfect vehicle in that regard, the unspeakable meeting the unsaid, all the while music bypassing the order of composure to make contact with the audience's affective intelligence. Melodrama is associated historically with the breakdown of political regimes (of class, of government, of family). These dissolutions release energies for social organization into the public that had been siphoned off into institutions. The transparency of melodramatic emotion responds directly to the enigma of a present no longer capable of being understood in terms of inheritance and its institutions—law, property, religion, family—whose oppressive histories have hurt but have also organized life consequentially. We can make a claim that the emphasis of melodrama shifts slightly in contemporary melotrauma. The former consoles its audience with an aesthetic of transparent embodiment and affect that produces continuity with the very past that is dissolving, while the latter humbles the viewer with the enigmatic quality of institutions, affects, and bodies in the present. Melotrauma is a fundamentally temporal form, focusing on the urgency to wrest the present both from the forms we know—the burden of inheritance, of personality, of normativity—and from the ones we can only imagine in the futures to which the claims of the present are always oppressively deferred.

So, the urgency to not take the present for granted as a rest stop between the enduring past and the momentous future provides another reason to conclude this essay with neither ringing optimism nor disappointment. To interfere with the work of trauma means to refuse its temporality. Singly, the girls countertemporalize constantly through fantasy and habit in the ways I have described. Together, they break the time-stunting frame of girlhood by finally relaxing in each other's presence. No longer living within the mania of intellectual and erotic attachment, they drink a soothing cup of tea and unclench into consoling positions, much like the one I am in now toward you. To lean into the body of an intimate is a most personal thing. But what's personal about it is like the deep anonymity of sleepers finally disburdened of the weight of bearing themselves.

Our Professor Sedgwick, whose beautiful and acute thought teaches me how to read the meaningful stammering of repetition, has elsewhere instructed us not to think that feelings are constructed, and I have no doubt that she is right that the body responds to stimulus as it will.[33] My angle on the question is slightly different. To me the evidence suggests a distinction between the moment of affect and what we call that affect. I may feel overwhelmed, I may feel composure: my panic might look like a stony silence, and my composure like a manic will to control. In one decade, what looks like a shamed response may look like an angry one in another. Subalterns seem always to have tone of voice problems. All babies smile, but it might be gas. One decides these things according to one's education in tracking repetition, form and norm. In contrast, an aesthetic that values the beauty of fantasy because it produces pleasures we can feel and not feel too overwhelmed by can believe too much in the thingness or idea of the representation, and can believe paradoxically that the viscera are hardwired as to motive and aim. This is a paradox because the motive and aim of the aesthetic education is to train the viscera. The aspect I love most about a poetics of misrecognition is that it teaches us that our viscera are teachable, if anything is. This view is also central to why I find impersonality such an optimistic concept for interfering with the march of individualities toward liberal freedoms.

I have tried to suggest, then, something quite different here. First, no model of subordination can rely on the view that emotions are transparent if the critic wants to interfere with the reproduction of normative claims about that which should organize optimism and disappointment. On this basis I have argued that pleasure does not always feel good, and that understanding the binding of subjects both to their negation and incoherence is key to rewiring the ways we think about what binds people to harmful conventions of personhood. Second, emotions have content and form (the repetitions—of word, lyric, music, or sound). They are not species of pre-ideological clarity, but quite the opposite: they are taught ("Hey, you!") and barely known ("Wait up!"). *Two Girls, Fat and Thin* articulates this haze of clarity and incoherence around emotions, as do the three zones of absorption the girls invent to interfere with the subordinations that feel inevitable. Third, the novel's conclusion tells us nothing conclusive about how not to be a case study subject, since all it represents is a fantasy that someday the self-consuming negotiation of ambivalence will stop and we can rest. I think of the relation of composition and composure. I am hoping it has something to do with a political claim on the present, but that might be just me. The novel presents eating as creativity and self-annihilation; language as meaning and sound; the intellect as weapon and cushion. These clusters of image and pulsions of attachment might mean anything or be meaningless. The test is a broadly historical one, which wonderfully unsettles what's personal and impersonal about being and having a history.

Notes

1. Sedgwick, Eve Kosofsky, *Fat Art, Thin Art* (Durham: Duke University Press, 1994), 160.
2. By "phrase" I refer both to *The 18ᵗʰ Brumaire of Napoleon Bonaparte* [in *The Marx-Engels Reader,* ed. Robert C. Tucker, 2ⁿᵈ ed. (New York: Norton, 1978), 594–617) and Jean-Francois Lyotard's *The Differend: Phrases in Dispute* (Minneapolis: University of Minnesota Press, 1988), where the concept of the phrase resonates musically—a form generated through repetition that comes to seem like the origin and limit of meaning, rather than a scene of it. The *differend* is what goes beyond the phrase; it is what, in Marx, the bourgeoisie cannot afford to avow and which, therefore, is everywhere enacted in the tawdry pleasure and violence of ordinary discipline and taboo.
3. See the keyword "Phantasy," in *The Language of Psychoanalysis,* eds. Jean Laplanche and J. B. Pontalis, and trans. Donald Nicholson-Smith (New York: W. W. Norton, 1973), 314–19.
4. On this question, see generally the work of Leo Bersani, Teresa DeLauretis, Laplanche and Pontalis, Jacqueline Rose, and Slavoj Zizek.
5. See "The Beast in the Closet: James and the Writing of Homosexual Panic," *Epistemology of the Closet* (Berkeley: University of California Press, 1990), and "Queer Performativity: Henry James's *The Art of the Novel,*" *GLQ* 1.1(1993): 1–16.
6. See Adorno, Theodor, "On Television," in *Critical Theory.*
7. Sedgwick, Eve Kosofsky, "Paranoid Reading and Reparative Reading; or, You're So Paranoid, You Probably Think This Introduction is About You," in *Novel Gazing: Queer Readings in Fiction,* ed. Eve Kosofsky Sedgwick (Durham: Duke University Press, 1997), 1–37.
8. Christopher Bollas puts forth the phrase "unthought known" for those knowledges one has inarticulately or unarticulated, and which one expresses in practices of being rather than in language. See *The Shadow of the Object: Psychoanalysis of the Unthought Known* (New York: Columbia University Press, 1987).
9. I learned to recognize the overvaluation of this mode of self-reflective, self-elaborating personhood as a major effect of the liberal project, dating from John Stuart Mill, from Elaine Hadley. See also David Lloyd and Paul Taylor, *Culture and the State* (New York: Routledge, 1998).
10. See Eve Kosofsky Sedgwick, *Tendencies* (Durham: Duke University Press, 1993), *A Dialogue on Love* (Boston: Beacon Press, 1999), and *Fat Art, Thin Art* (Durham: Duke University Press, 1994).

11. In the end, of course, it's a dialectic between the Althusserian "Hey, you!" and "Wait up!" but these locutions are not antitheses either, because they each mark the subject's lag (*Nachtraglichkeit*) with respect to the meanings and desires that organize her.

12. On repetition and convention as antidotes to the formlessness of subjects, see Bollas, Christopher, *The Shadow of the Object: Psychoanalysis of the Unthought Known* (New York: Columbia University Press, 1989), and Sedgwick, *Epistemology of the Closet*. See also Bersani, Leo, *The Freudian Body: Psychoanalysis and Art* (New York: Columbia University Press, 1986).

13. Jameson, Fredric, *The Political Unconscious: Narrative as a Socially Symbolic Act* (Ithaca: Cornell University Press, 1981).

14. Sedgwick, "The Use of Being Fat," *Fat Art, Thin Art*, 15.

15. Berlant, Lauren, *The Queen of America Goes to Washington City: Essays on Sex and Citizenship* (Durham: Duke University Press, 1997), 92.

16. Gaitskill, Mary, *Because They Wanted To* (New York: Scribner, 1997); *Two Girls, Fat and Thin* (New York: Vintage, 1991). All subsequent references to Gaitskill's novel will be cited in the body of the essay; *Bad Behavior* (New York: Vintage, 1988). Uncollected stories include "Suntan," in *Word* (12 July 1999):http://new.word.com./habit/suntan/story.html; with Peter Trachtenberg, "Walt and Beth: A Love Story," in *Word* (7 July 1999): http://www.word.com.features99/walt_and_beth/; "Veronica" in *POZ* (August 1998): http://www.thebody.com/poz/culture/8_98/fiction_gaitskill.html; "Folksong," in *Nerve* (1999): http://www.nerve.com/Gaitskill/folkSong/.

17. Thanks to Howard Helsinger for the *Pale Fire* reminder. The literary history whose repetition pulsates in this novel requires a story of its own.

18. On "normal intimacy," see Berlant, Lauren, "Introduction," in *Intimacy* (Chicago: University of Chicago Press, 2000). On case study normative intimacy see, in the same volume, Candace Vogler, "Sex and Talk." Vogler's procedures for tracking the contradictions between the ideology of more intimacy and the seemingly actual need for less of it is central to this essay's conceptualization of impersonality.

19. Freud's essay on "Femininity" argues that female masochism emerges from the lack of sanction for women's justified anger in and at the world. Much contemporary feminist theory follows through this line, although not Gilles Deleuze's "Coldness and Cruelty" [*Masochism* (New York: Zone Books, 1989)], which mainly forgets to remember women.

20. I refer to Freud's description of the child's desire to master the relation of control to loss of control in the *fort/da* game. The child's "loss" and "recov-

ery" of the top is read generally as the bargaining any subject does to retain a notion that her/his intelligibility or continuity in the world is a function of her/his will. However, the capacity of the ego to respond to contingency via a principle of form should not imply that the subject "really" is contingent and only masterful in a compensatory way. Each position, repeated countless times, is its own pleasure.

21. In *Kafka: Toward a Minor Literature*, trans. Dana Polan (Minneapolis: University of Minnesota Press, 1986), Gilles Deleuze and Felix Guattari comment that cultural minoritization—a relation of displacement within a hegemonic frame, a non-position of internal exteriority to ideal collective norms—is reenacted in the displacement of speech and writing by eating. Eating performs a displacement that is already a social fact: it stuffs the mouth that cannot be heard anyway, except as a distortion.

22. In Kristeva's version of abjection the abjected subject becomes a thing—a stray, a deject. One cannot, in my reading of this text, embrace one's abjection, because that would imply a capacity to disavow one's expulsion from normal personhood. That's the difference between a notion of subordination as subjectifying (I am an "x" kind of person) and desubjectifying (I am not a person, I have no form, I am a negative). I have suggested throughout this essay that these positions are inassimilable but proximate, articulated in the relation between a psychologically-oriented subjectivity and an impersonal one, at least in *Two Girls, Fat and Thin*, and perhaps beyond. See Julia Kristeva, *Powers of Horror: An Essay on Abjection* (New York: Columbia University Press, 1982).

23. See Stewart, Kathleen, *A Space on the Side of the Road* (Princeton: Princeton University Press, 1996).

24. See *The Shadow of the Object*, 4.

25. Bersani, Leo, and Ulysse Dutoit, eds., *Caravaggio's Secrets* (Cambridge, Mass.: MIT Press, 1998).

26. Phillips, Adam, "On Composure," in *On Kissing, Tickling, and Being Bored: Essays on the Uncommitted Life* (Cambridge: Harvard University Press, 1993), 42–46.

27. Ibid., 44.

28. Ibid., "First Hates," 24.

29. Here I allude to a longer argument I make elsewhere against the presumption of shame as the primary sexual affect (recognizable by queers). While I agree with Sedgwick that subjects' responses may well be hardwired as such, I maintain the importance of reading the gap between an affect and its coding. That gap is an historical and political one, one which is part of what's at stake in sexual politics. See Frank, Adam, and Eve

Kosofsky Sedgwick, *Shame and Its Sisters: A Silvan Tomkins Reader* (Durham: Duke University Press, 1995), and Warner, Michael, *The Trouble With Normal: Sex, Politics, and the Ethics of Queer Life* (New York: Free Press, 1999).

30. This story, of the lover who introduces a female protagonist to emancipating sexual violence (to which she becomes classically ambivalent), is a staple of Gaitskill's oeuvre since her first book, *Bad Behavior*.

31. Traditionally the Freudian *après coup* is structured by a primary trauma that finds form in a latter repetition (such as a childhood molestation that generates symptoms later on in life, after what looks like an irrational phobic symptom appears). Often in this novel, I am suggesting, the inverse relation applies.

32. Steedman, Carolyn, *Landscape for a Good Woman* (New Brunswick: Rutgers University Press, 1987). Sometimes this distribution happens because critics make it so, but it is also the case that the explanations of therapy culture are *very* class articulated.

33. See Frank, Adam, and Eve Kosofsky Sedgwick, eds. *Shame and Her Sisters: A Silvan Tomkins Reader* (Durham: Duke University Press, 1995), and Sedgwick, Eve Kosofsky, "A Poem is Being Written," in *Tendencies* (Durham: Duke University Press, 1993), 177–214.

3

Capacity

Judith Butler

I'd like to take the opportunity of this essay to say something about the experience of having one's thought remade on the occasion of reading Eve Kosofsky Sedgwick. I think that the first time I read her, I certainly had a dawning realization about how heterosexual triangles are framed and what sorts of homosociality they occlude and contain. That was no minor realization. But then of course I heard her (first in 1986) and read her again, and each time I was being asked to think differently than I usually do. Our sensibilities are in some ways profoundly different. She is a passionate literary scholar and innovative theorist, and my own formation is as a more conceptually linear philosopher, for better or worse. But I have needed the encounter with literature again and again in order to nudge me out from the tight grip of my conceptual threads. And this possibility for a kind of thinking that moves against the strictures of the rigorously logical has been part of the challenge of Sedgwick's work for me. And, of course, this is made all the more interesting by virtue of the fact that she is profoundly conceptual, although the concepts are very often staged in a certain relation to one another that produces dissonance and insight. They are also, almost always, inextricable from figures, from tone, from a form of political lyricism. Reading her has made me more capacious rather than less, and for that I am grateful. Let me recount my instances for you. I hope you will see the ways in which I have been moved to think otherwise by virtue of reading and teaching Sedgwick, and how in every instance it has demanded that I think in a way that I did not know thought could do—and still remain thought.

My trajectory will not be exhaustive, but let me give you three instances. The first has to do with the contribution that Sedgwick made to the Levi-Straussian notion of the exchange of women. Although she has preferred other sorts of psychology to psychoanalysis, I have wondered whether a specifically Sedgwickian reformulation of triangulation in *Between Men* does not entail rather significant consequences for the rewriting of the psychoanalysis of sexual exchange. Second, I had the opportunity to teach *Epistemology of the Closet* with Janet Halley at the Stanford Law School a few years ago, and I learned something through Halley about Sedgwick which moved me, once again, from a narrower to a more capacious logic in my thinking. Lastly, I read Henry James' *The Golden Bowl* and realized that the non-closure of that novel not only sustained important parallels to Sedgwick's own way of mapping conceptual dissonances, but that it also constituted a specifically ethical practice, one that maintains and provokes capacity.

Chapter One of *Between Men* is a very brief discussion of feminist theory, Jacques Lacan, Sigmund Freud, and René Girard. But it makes a point that was not made in quite this way before. She rewrites Girard to make the following insight: "in any erotic rivalry, the bond that links the two rivals is as intense and potent as the bond that links either of the rivals to the beloved: . . . the bonds of 'rivalry' and 'love,' differently as they are experienced, are equally powerful and in many senses equivalent" (21). Sedgwick is writing this text at a time in which the structuralist paradigm and its permutations prevail in feminist theory. So she considers this Girardian thesis in light of the Levi-Straussian postulation of the "exchange of women" as fundamental to culture itself. And because her interest in this book is male homosociality, the Levi-Straussian paradigm prompts her to make the following kinds of claims: "in any male-dominated society, there is a special relationship between male homosocial (including homosexual) desire and the structures of maintaining and transmitting patriarchal power . . ."(25). Thus the relationship with women within the structures is always tacitly structured by the relationship to other men. Sedgwick argues, "Levi-Strauss's normative man uses a woman as a 'conduit of a relationship' in which the true partner is a man."

It is, wonderfully, 1985 when Sedgwick publishes this text, and it was no doubt much easier then to posit true objects of desire. Indeed, Sedgwick's work in the last decade has not centered on triangles, and I suspect she might now bracket the question of "truth" in favor of more erotic possibilities for interpretation. I cannot imagine that she would necessarily accept a logic of noncontradiction for desire, in which one either desires a man or a woman, but not both, and not both at the same time. In fact, she has helped a generation to formulate a wider compass for desire. I wonder whether her triangles might not be

appropriated for another use. If we consider that the thesis of monolithic patriarchal power no longer holds unambiguously, then the triangles need not always
take the form in which men relate to other men through women in this way.
Indeed, where there is this homosocial triangulation of desire, it may well have
other meanings than those that are possible within the Levi-Straussian model.

When Jean Hyppolite introduces the notion of "desire of desire" in his commentary on Hegel's *Phenomenology of Spirit* (66), he means to suggest not only
that desire seeks its own renewal (a Spinozistic claim), but that it also seeks to
be the object of desire for the Other.[1] When Lacan rephrases this formulation
of Hyppolite's, he enters the genitive in order to produce an equivocation:
"desire is the desire *of* the Other" (my emphasis). What does *desire* desire? It
clearly still continues to desire itself; indeed, it is not clear that the desire which
desires is different from the desire that is desired. They are homonymically
linked, at a minimum, but what this means is that desire redoubles itself; it
seeks its own renewal, but in order to achieve its own renewal, it must redupli-
cate itself and so become something other to what it has been. It does not stay
in place as a single desire, but becomes other to itself, taking a form that is outside of itself. Moreover, what desire wants is the Other, where the Other is
understood as its generalized object. What desire always wants is the Other's
desire, where the Other is conceived as a subject of desire. This last formulation involves the grammar of the genitive, and it suggests that the Other's desire
becomes the model for the subject's desire.[2] It is not that I want the Other to
want me, but I want to the extent that I have taken on the desire of the Other
and modeled my desire after the Other's desire. This is, of course, only one perspective within what is arguably a kaleidoscope of perspectives. Among other
readings of this formulation, for example, there is the Oedipal one: I desire
what the Other desires (a third object), but that object belongs to the Other,
and not to me; this lack, instituted through prohibition, is the foundation of my
desire. Another Oedipal reading is the following: I want the Other to want me
rather than the sanctioned object of its desire: I want no longer to be the prohibited object of desire. Or then there is the inverse of the last formulation: I
want to be free to desire the one who is prohibited to me and, so, to take the
Other away from the Other and, in this sense, have the Other's desire.

   Lacan's way of formulating this position is, of course, derived in part from
Levi-Strauss's theory of the exchange of women. Male clan members exchange
women in order to establish symbolic relations with other male clan members.
The women are "wanted" precisely because they are wanted by the Other.
Their value is thus constituted as an exchange value, though one that is not
reducible to Marx's understanding of that term. Sedgwick came along in

Between Men, as we know, and asked who was desiring whom in such a scene. Her point was to show that what first appears to be relation of a man who desires a woman turns out to be implicitly a homosocial bond between two men. Her argument was not to claim, in line with the "Phallus" affiliates, that the homosocial bond comes at the expense of the heterosexual, but that the homosocial (distinct from the homosexual) is articulated precisely through the heterosexual. This argument has had far-reaching consequences for the thinking of both heterosexuality and homosexuality, as well as for thinking the symbolic nature of the homosocial bond (and, hence, by implication, all of the Lacanian symbolic). For the point is not that the phallus is had by one and not by another, but that it is circulated along a heterosexual and homosexual circuit at once, thus confounding the identificatory positions for every "actor" in the scene. The man who seeks to send the woman to another man sends some aspect of himself, and the man who receives her, receives him as well. She circuits, but is she finally wanted, or does she merely exemplify a value by becoming the representative of both men's desire, the place where those desires meet, and where they fail to meet, a place where that potentially homosexual encounter is relayed, suspended, and contained?

I raise this issue because it seems to me that it is not possible to read the profound and perhaps inescapable ways that heterosexuality and homosexuality are defined through one another. For instance, to what extent is heterosexual jealousy often compounded by an inability to avow same-sex desire? A man's woman lover wants another man, and even "has" him, and this is experienced by the first man to be at his own expense. But what precisely is the price that the first man has to pay? When, in this scene, he desires the desire of the Other, is it his lover's desire (let us imagine that it is), or is it also the prerogative that his lover has to take another man as her lover (let us imagine that it also is)? When he rages against her for her infidelity, does he rage because she refuses to make the sacrifice that he has already made? And even though such reading might suggest that he identifies with her in the scene, it is unclear how he identifies, or whether it is, finally, a "feminine" identification. He may want her imagined position in the scene, but what does he imagine her position to be? It cannot be presumed that he takes her position to be feminine, even if he imagines her in a receptive response to the other man. If that is his receptivity that he finds relocated there at the heart of his own jealous fantasy, then perhaps it is more appropriate to claim that he imagines her in a position of passive male homosexuality. Is it, finally, really possible to distinguish in such a case between a heterosexual and homosexual passion? After all, he has lost her, and that enrages him, and she has acted the aim he cannot or will not act, and that enrages him.

There seems to be more between the two of them than any dyadic account of desire could account for. But the third term, clearly, is also not reducible to the "phallus." Note here that the queer theoretical redescription of the "exchange of women" does not return to the Lacanian feminist insistence on the primacy of the phallus. It is not that one wants the desire of the Other because that desire will mimetically reflect one's own position as having the phallus. Nor does one want what other men want in order to more fully identify as a man. Indeed, as the triangulation begins in which heterosexuality is transmuted into homosociality, the identifications proliferate with precisely the complexity that the usual Lacanian positions either rule out or describe as pathology. Where desire and identification are played out as mutually exclusive possibilities against the inescapable background of a (presumptively heterosexual) sexual difference, the actors in the scene I describe can be understood only as trying to occupy positions in vain, warring with the symbolic that has already arranged in advance for their defeat. Thus, the man is trying to "refuse" sexual difference in imagining himself in his lover's position with another man, and so the moralizing relegation of desire to pathology takes place once again within the preorchestrated drama of sexual difference.

So let's complicate the scene again by rethinking it from the woman's point of view. Let's imagine that "she" is bisexual and has sought to have a relationship with man number one, putting off for a while her desires for women which tend to be desires to be a bottom. But instead of finding a woman as the "third," she finds a man, and "tops" him. Let's say, for argument's sake, that man number one would rather die than be "topped" by his girlfriend, since that would be too "queer" for him. So he knows that she is topping another man, possibly penetrating him anally, and he is furious for several reasons. For what is she after? If she is bisexual, she is a bisexual who happens to be "doing" a few men right now. But perhaps she is also staging a scene in which the outbreak of jealousy puts the relation at risk. Perhaps she does this in order to break from the relationship in order to be free to pursue "none of the above." Would it be possible to see her intensification of heterosexual activity at this moment as a way of (a) seeing her first lover's jealousy, and goading him toward greater possessiveness; (b) topping her second lover, and gratifying the desire that is off limits to her with the first; (c) setting the two men against one another in order to make room for the possibility of a lesbian relationship in which she is not a top at all; and (d) intensifying her heterosexuality in order to ward off psychic dangers she associates with being a lesbian bottom? Note that it may be that the one desire is not in the service of another, such that we might be able to say which one is the real and authentic one, and which is simply a camouflage or deflection. Indeed, it may be that this particular character can't find a "real" desire that supersedes the sequence that she undergoes, and that what is real is the sequence itself. But it may be that the affair with number two becomes, indirectly, the venue for the convergence of these passions, their momentary "constellation" and that to understand her, one must accept something of their simultaneous and dissonant claims on truth. Surely, the pattern in which a man and woman heterosexually involved both amicably break their relationship in order to pursue homosexual desires is not uncommon in urban centers in the last three decades. I don't claim to know what happens here, or what happens when a gay male and a lesbian who are friends start to sleep with one another. But it seems fair to assume that a certain crossing of homosexual and heterosexual passions takes place such that these are not two distinct strands of a braid, but simultaneous vehicles for one another.

I think that this comes out most distinctly in recent years when issues of transgender are discussed. It becomes difficult to say whether the sexuality of the transgendered person is homosexual or heterosexual. The term "queer" gained currency a decade ago precisely to address such moments of productive undecidability, but we have not yet seen a psychoanalytic attempt to take account of these cultural formations in which certain vacillating notions of sexual orientation are constitutive. This becomes most clear when we think about transsexuals who are in transition, where identity is in the process of being achieved, but is not yet there. Or, most emphatically, for those transsexuals who understand transition to be a permanent process. If we cannot refer unambiguously to gender in such cases, do we have the point of reference for making claims about sexuality? In the case of transgender, where transsexualism does not come into play, there are various ways of crossing that cannot be understood as stable achievements, where the gender crossing constitutes, in part, the condition of eroticization itself. In the film *Boys Don't Cry* (1999), it seems that transgender is about a girl both identifying as a boy and wanting a girl, so a crossing over from being a girl to being a heterosexual boy. She identifies as a heterosexual boy, but we see several moments of disidentification as well, where the fantasy breaks down: a tampon has to be located, used, then discarded with no trace. Her identification thus recommences, has to be re-orchestrated in a daily way as a credible fantasy, one that compels belief. The girl lover seems not to know, but this is the not-knowing of fetishism, an uncertain ground of eroticization. It remains unclear whether she knows even when she claims to know. Indeed, one of the most thrilling moments of the film is when the girlfriend, knowing, fully re-engages the fantasy. And one of the most brittle moments takes place when the girlfriend, knowing, seems no longer to be able to enter the fantasy fully. The disavowal not only makes the fantasy possible, but strengthens it, and on occasion strengthens it to the point of being able to survive avowal.

Similarly, it would be possible to say that Brandon's body stays out of the picture, and that this occlusion makes the fantasy possible, since it does enter the picture, but only through the terms that the fantasy instates. This is not a simple "denial" of anatomy, but the erotic deployment of the body, its covering, its prosthetic extension for the purposes of a reciprocal erotic fantasy. There are lips and hands and eyes, the strength of Brandon's body on and in Lana, her girlfriend, arms, weight, and thrust. So, hardly a simple picture of "disembodiment," and hardly "sad." When s/he desires her girlfriend's desire, what is it that s/he wants? Brandon occupies the place of the subject of desire, but s/he does not roll on his/her back in the light and ask the girl to suck off her/his dildo. Perhaps that would be too "queer," but perhaps as well it would kill the very conditions that make the fantasy possible for them. S/he works the dildo in the dark so that the fantasy can emerge in full force, so that its condition of disavowal is fulfilled. S/he occupies that place, to be sure, and suffers the persecution and the rape from the boys in the film precisely because s/he has occupied it too well. But do we say that Brandon is a lesbian or a boy? Surely, the question itself defines Brandon's predicament in some way, even as Brandon consistently answers the predicament by doing himself as a boy. And it will not work to say that because Brandon must do himself as a boy that this is a sign that Brandon is a lesbian. For boys surely do themselves as boys, and no anatomy enters gender without being "done" in some way.

Would it be any easier for us if we were to ask whether the lesbian who only makes love using her dildo to penetrate her girlfriend, whose sexuality is so fully scripted by apparent heterosexuality that no other relation is possible, is a boy or a "boy"? If she says that she can only make love as a "boy," she is, we might say, transgendered in bed, if not in the street. Brandon's crossing involves a constant dare posed to the public norms of the culture, and so occupies a more public site on the continuum of transgender. It is not simply about being able to have sex in a certain way; it is also about appearing as a masculine gender. So, in this sense, Brandon is no lesbian, despite the fact that the film, caving in, wants to return him to that status after the rape, implying, in fact, that the return to (achievement of?) lesbianism is somehow facilitated by that rape, returning Brandon, as the rapists sought to do, to a "true" identity that "comes to terms" with anatomy. This "coming to terms" means only that anatomy is instrumentalized according to acceptable cultural norms, producing a "woman" as the effect of that instrumentalization, normalizing gender even as it allows for desire to be queer. One could conjecture that Brandon only wants to be a public boy in order to gain the legitimate right to have sexual relations as he does, but such an explanation assumes that gender is merely instrumental to sexuality. But gender has its own pleasures for Brandon, and serves its own purposes. These pleasures of identification exceed those of desire, and, in that sense, Brandon is not only or easily a lesbian.

And, of course, all this brings me to Sedgwick's quite consequential formulation of gender and sexuality in *The Epistemology of the Closet*. For there, she makes clear that "dissonant" relations between gender and sexuality have to be assumed, that no structural or causal link between them can or ought to be posited, and that the vacillations between the two are precisely what need to be read by readers of sexuality. I've made clear what my problems with this approach are on other occasions, but this time I'd like to suggest something of what I've learned from it. And what I've learned has more to do with how theory is staged than with whether or not an argument is right. Notice the way the pattern works: "Axiom 2: The study of sexuality is not coextensive with the study of gender; correspondingly, antihomophobic inquiry is not coextensive with feminist inquiry. But we can't know in advance how they will be different" (27). The distinctions are made. The terms are not coextensive with one another. But even this is not an absolute distinction. They may line up in certain ways with one another, but they will not line up exactly with one another and, in that sense, they will not line up along the same border. So they are not matched up exactly, but neither are they absolutely separated. Indeed, the ways they will come together—and this formulation suggests that they invariably will—will not be fully predictable in advance. What will the unpredictable alliances be?

When Sedgwick gives us the relation between minoritizing and universalizing understandings of same-sex relations, we have to work even harder to make sure we don't fall into a reductive logic. She writes, "The most potent effects of modern homo/heterosexual definition tend to spring precisely from the inexplicitness or denial of the gaps *between* long-coexisting minoritizing and universalizing, or gender-transitive and gender-intransitive, understandings of same-sex relations" (47). Later on that same page, she makes clear that whether we are talking about conceptions of same-sex desire that insist upon particularity (minoritizing positions) or which insist that homosexuality is everywhere and, implicitly, in everyone (universalizing positions), we need to understand how these positions are staged in relation to one another, how they give us something like a "constellation"—in Walter Benjamin's sense—of homosexual positioning for our time. This historical perspective keeps Sedgwick's distinctions from being purely logical operators; indeed, the logical operator suffers a certain deconstruction here. She writes, "The project of the present book will be to show how issues of modern homo/heterosexual definition are structured, not by the supersession of one model and the consequent withering away of another, but instead by the relations enabled by the unrationalized coexistence of different models during the times they do exist"(47).³ Interestingly, she accepts the notion that a single subject may entertain these unreconciled positions simultaneously and, indeed, may be historically compelled to do so. So it is not the case that for every subject there is a single point of view, since the subject will be no less risen and mobilized by these incongruent positions as its historical time.

This approach to how positions coexist in "unrationalized" form is reiterated when Sedgwick turns to the way both essentialist and nonessentialist positions are held at once. She refers to an understanding that she believes most of us share during this time which is "organized around a radical and irreducible incoherence. It holds the minoritizing view that there is a distinct population of persons who "really" are gay; at the same time, it holds the universalizing views that sexual desire is an unpredictably powerful solvent of stable identities; that apparently heterosexual persons and object choices are strongly marked by same-sex influences and desires, and vice versa for apparently homosexual ones . . ." (85). Structuralist triangles have surely given way to a historically conditioned understanding of divergent positions that are held simultaneously and with incoherence. Or perhaps we should say: "incoherence" only within a certain principle or ordering whereby a logic of noncontradiction holds. Sedgwick takes us beyond that logic and opens up what I want to affirm as a certain ethics of thinking, one that postpones the question of logical incoherence in the name of historical possibilities that emerge when no single schema turns out to exhaust the epistemological field. Who can hold these schemas together without wanting to take sides, decide which is true, close down the unrationalized and the "incoherent." We are, it seems, structured by incompatible desires, but they come into relation with one another in ways that we cannot fully predict at this time, which are, we might say, a function and sign of our time.

In a sense, Sedgwick models for us a certain ethical embrace of the incongruent, one that proves to be intrinsic to the epistemology of modernity. The triangle no longer quite suffices to explain the dissonance at work here, but there is something that occurred in those early triangles that remains: The man's desire for the woman is at once his desire for the man, and the two desires, while not the same, nevertheless coexist in a strange simultaneity, the one functioning partially as the conduit for the other, but not, for that reason, having its own desirability reduced to a merely instrumental status. Who loves whom? And how will we ever know? These are the questions that Sedgwick prompts us to ask time and again. But the point will be to note how the question, to be answered, must trace a trajectory of desire that will remain ambiguous. "Homo/heterosexual": the term challenges us to think of a sequestered immanence in desire, one that does not obviate the need for identity claims, but makes us unknowingly capacious as we make them.

Consider the end of *The Golden Bowl* when Maggie reflects on the departure of Charlotte, her rival, and lights upon the ultimate value of her rival: "she felt her sincerity absolutely sound—she gave it for all it might mean. 'Because Charlotte, dear, you know,' she said, 'is incomparable.' It took thirty seconds, but she was to feel when these were over that she had pronounced one of the happiest words of her life." And as her father, Charlotte's husband, departs, leaving her daughter to confront the betrayal that her husband, the Prince, has committed with Charlotte, Maggie reflects on the strange occasion of this departure: " 'She's beautiful, beautiful!' Her sensibility reported to her the shade of new note. It was all she might have wished, for it was, with a kind of speaking competence, the note of possession and control; and yet it conveyed to her as nothing till now had done the reality of their parting. They were parting, in the light of it, absolutely on Charlotte's *value*" (577). We know that Maggie's attachment to her father must be attenuated, and we know that Maggie's love of the Prince is genuine, if distracted and somewhat abstract. But what do we know of Maggie's passion for Charlotte? And when Maggie and the Prince finally come to the realization of what has happened between them, there is no possibility of righteousness on either side. For each has desires that were more complicated than anyone could have known, and it is, significantly, at the moment that they find a common name for their desire—"Charlotte"— that the two are returned to one another:

> "Isn't she too splendid?" she simply said, offering it to explain and to finish.
> "Oh splendid!" With which he came over to her. (579)

That is not a love based on repudiation, for even though Charlotte must go, she remains between them, the token by which exchange is opened, the basis of their new bond. One waits through this long novel for the moment in which recriminations will be hurled, when the betrayal will be named or depicted in some way, when the Prince and Charlotte will have to confess. But that is not the moral vernacular at work in these pages, for what emerges is a constellation of desire and positioning that incongruously moves forward with its grief and its possibilities. An ethical affirmation of the middle terms that hover in partial shade between any two lovers. It is an ethics of capacity rather than of disavowal.

Sedgwick, like Michael Moon, is an assiduous reader of James, and I would not have found James if it were not for the readings of those two. Could it be that Sedgwick has brought into theoretical regions precisely that ethically capacious sensibility which affirms the necessity of the incongruous, and where the trajectory of desire requires a detour from the logic of either/or in order to thrive and—in whatever way—become known?

Notes

1. The following section of this paper (enclosed by line spaces) was published as part of a review essay on Jessica Benjamin entitled "Longing for Recognition," *Studies in Gender and Sexuality* 1.3 (2000).
2. For a critique and radicalization of the Lacanian formulation of this account of the mimetic formation of desire, see Mikkel Borsch-Jacobsen.
3. I take it that this insight has formed a certain methodological basis for the important work on law and sexuality written by Janet Halley.

Works Cited

Borsch-Jacobsen, Mikkel, *The Freudian Subject* (Stanford: Stanford University Press, 1988).

Boys Don't Cry. Dir. Kimberly Peirce. Twentieth Century Fox, 1999.

Freud, Sigmund, *The Standard Edition of the Complete Works of Sigmund Freud, Volume XVIII*, trans. James Strachey (London: The Hogarth Press and the Institute for Psychoanalysis, 1953–74).

Hyppolite, Jean, *Genesis and Structure in Hegel's* Phenomenology of Spirit, trans. Samuel Cherniak and John Heckman (Evanston, Ill.: Northwestern University Press, 1974).

James, Henry, *The Golden Bowl* (London: Penguin, 1984).

Sedgwick, Eve Kosofsky, *Between Men: English Literature and Homosocial Desire* (New York: Columbia University Press, 1985).

———. *Epistemology of the Closet* (Berkeley: University of California Press, 1990).

Theory Kindergarten[1]

Deborah P. Britzman

Eve Kosofsky Sedgwick and Adam Frank's (1995) introduction to the writings of psychologist Silvan Tomkins invites readers back into the transitional space of "theory kindergarten." Not coincidently, the thought of this archaic space can only be proposed by way of a theory of psychology. And, true to its dissonant spirit, their first use works with the force of something like a swipe. They write: "You don't have to be long out of theory kindergarten to make mincemeat of, let's say a psychology that depends on the separate existence of eight (only sometimes it's nine) distinct affects hardwired into the human biological system" (2). We are returned to our earliest forms of orality, a rather frightening place. Perhaps we must make mincemeat of a psychology that appears to make mincemeat of us. Here then is just the beginning of theory kindergarten: Everything is personified and knowledge is felt either as friend or foe. If theory never leaves kindergarten, neither does kindergarten ever leave theory.

To be wrenched back into theory kindergarten is *Unheimlich*, a strange reminder of what is utterly familiar, something we already know but rarely, if ever, can bear to admit. Christopher Bollas calls this *not quite* experience "an unthought known" (1987, 4). He refers not so much to the protective gestures of disavowal, undoing, or the other ego defenses, but rather to the difficulty of thinking: how the work of the ego structures both itself and the object and how even if the ego understands the known in terms of its conventions, rules, and traditions, for instance, the ego is not yet prepared to encounter its own thoughts. Within the unthought known, there is a sense of an inaugural confusion: no distinction can be made between the passion for knowledge and the passion for ignorance. This is the beginning of affect and in trying to account for whether Tomkins can be taken seriously by those who do not normally consider instinctual forces, Sedgwick and Frank offer to us not so much a justification for *why Tomkins*, but rather raise for theory another sort of dilemma: *why not Tomkins?* Their introduction inspires the question of how we reside in theory from the inside-out, that is, through a theory of affect. What are the stakes for theory when the problem of psychological significance can exaggerate or foreclose the fault lines of knowledge?

We do know what holds theory back from its own precocious curiosity. One trouble is resistance, not in the sociological sense of escaping power, but in the psychological sense of refusing to know, of not attending to psychic significance. Part of what is refused when theories of affect are refused is the startling and irrational reach of psychic reality through the transference: the ways that affects, ideas, and objects cannot quite be thought of as a quarrel and then, cannot quite justify their reasons for arguing. The other trouble is the theorist in theory. It is painful to entertain the possibility that, however one tries to pin down meanings by way of such stabilizing concepts as ideology, experience, identity, or culture, for instance, one is still not in control of intentions, of the symbolic reach of representation, and of course, the unconscious. That one's own knowledge begins in the failure of projection and in the embarrassment of acting out is such a difficult and painful admission that it is subject to forgetting. Resistance, too, is a sticky affair: deny it and it's proved; accuse someone of it and you may be characterizing yourself.

These passionate refusals are close to how Sedgwick (1993, 25) characterizes ignorance: not so much an absence of knowledge but its constitutive and organizing modality. No one is immune, which may be why, at least in theory, we try to keep our affects under wraps. In this way, theory has the capacity to work as an ego defense, warding off uncertainty and surprise, splitting good and bad objects, and managing to put its anxiety into knowledge while protecting its illusion of omnipotence. Sedgwick offers us a very different theory about theory in her considerations of what holds it together and what makes it fall apart. And, in much of her work it is the contingent figure of a child—indeed, a *"question-child"*—that ushers the problem of theory and its work of reparation into language.[2] This approach to the story of knowledge and ignorance has strong resonances with the object relations theory of Melanie Klein, who also tests her knowledge against what the child could not say but nonetheless felt. Klein terms this relation—between the urge and the word, and between the child and its objects—phantasy, a quality in relating made from the primal distress of anxiety, a painful combination of fears of annihilation, of not knowing, and yet, of still needing to know. Surely theory is entangled here.

Over the course of this essay, I explore more closely the workings of phantasy and how it wavers between aggression and reparation for, in much of what Sedgwick offers to us, this double movement of thought and so, of theory, is crucial for her method of taking the side of the discarded content, repairing the splitting made severe and grotesque through the exclusionary processes of binary operations, and even for reconfiguring the psychological significance of our work in theory kindergarten. Theory kindergarten wavers between discarding content and re-finding something of its significance. Such work requires that we encounter some difficult figures: for Sedgwick it is at first Tomkins, for me it is Sedgwick and Klein. If we never leave theory kindergarten, it is not because our inadequate knowledge somehow keeps us prisoners of illusion. Kindergarten, after all, is also a fun fair of experiments, thrilling surprises, mis-recognitions, near-missed encounters, and phantasies that lead, in the strangest directions, our games of "let's pretend." This spirit of bravely or even brazenly entering new kinds of symbolization, of allowing phantasy to become more generous and surprising, are part of its elaborate and illusive stakes. If, in the first instance, we must destroy knowledge before it destroys us, we are also able to make second thoughts and allow our thinking to figure something of its own repair. To imagine all of this requires not so much that we suspend our disbelief, but that we come to believe something incredible about our own suspense.

Like Tomkins, Klein is a difficult figure for theory. *And, why not Klein?* She, too, takes the side of the discarded content and the infant's anxiety; she places in parenthesis explanations for misery like the outside world, culture, and identity; she begins with the problem of persecutory anxiety and the phantasies that shatter and make object relations; she separates the goals of analysis from education in ways that put to rest the Kantian *Aufklärung* and the idealizations that secure knowledge to the side of enlightenment; she offers a theory of reading that emerges from primal anxiety and thus refuses to draw the line between symbolization and terror; and, she insists upon negativity as necessary for creativity, reparation, and gratitude. Klein, particularly after 1935, centers in her theories entanglements of love and hate, positing anxiety as the beginning of development, and seeing—within negativity—both potential and inhibition. For all of these reasons it is very difficult to recuperate Klein for projects of social transformation, particularly if what is meant by this plan is settling the trouble of thinking.[3] In fact, Klein gives us a view of the constitutive difficulty, indeed, the shock of learning, by taking us back to our earliest theory kindergarten, reminding us of its forgotten significance, then and now.

Klein is also difficult to work with for another reason, particularly in an essay that thinks with the writing of Eve Kosofsky Sedgwick, who noticed this as well:

Klein's theories of sexual difference and her discussions on object choice, cannot be of service to an anti-homophobic inquiry, which is, for Sedgwick, an ethical obligation.[4] The figure of the homosexual in Klein's work is pathetically unsurprising, a sexual failure who, having fled from the laws of heterosexual development, cannot sustain the good object. It is precisely at this point that her theory prohibits its own urge for reparation. There is no reparative urge in the Kleinian sense of the term: the object cannot be seen as whole, the debt to the other cannot be acknowledged, mourning will be interrupted, the goodness of the object will not be tolerated, the confusion of good and bad will persist, and the sense that the ego has the potential to do great damage cannot be acknowledged. If theory cannot face its own psychic reality, its own phantasies of love and hate, then the anxiety that inaugurates what Klein calls the depressive position—itself the grounds for reparation—cannot be worked through.

And yet, even this acknowledgment, that theory can be made from or lose the urge for reparation, is indebted to Klein. And so it must be from another vantage—the place where theory fails—that Kleinian thought might contribute to an ethical reading of how affects, as expressions of both aggression and love, can be creatively thought. Many of her concepts do reside in the urge to make reparation and better integrate dynamics of love and hate, feelings of loneliness and loss, and the development of gratitude made from the capacity to bear guilt. Her discussions on phantasy, psychic positions in object relations, symbolism and thinking, and on defenses such as splitting, projective identification, and confusion, offer insight into why binary splitting and the hostility of fragmentation that is made from it—what Sedgwick (1990) writes of as the contradictions between universalizing and minoritizing homo/hetero definitions— is still so prevalent, not just within the judicial/social/political ethos of our times but also, more intimately, within our own everyday anxieties over what constitutes and shatters the ground of our theory. One could, after all, read our categories of thought as saying something difficult about working through psychic reality. And both Sedgwick and Klein do just that work in their respective explorations of what inhibits the capacity to love and what allows love to do its work.

Phantasies, for Klein, structure knowledge of both the inside and the outside world. Precisely because they are there from the beginning of life, the material is made from a terrible and persecutory anxiety. The baby can neither ask nor answer the adult question, from where does anxiety come? Juliet Mitchell (1998) offers one of the more compelling definitions of the productive reach of Kleinian phantasy:

> In Klein's concept, phantasy emanates from within and imagines what
> is without, it offers an unconscious commentary on instinctual life and

links feelings to objects and creates a new amalgam: the world of imagination. Through its ability to phantasize, the baby tests out, 'primitively,'
thinks about it, its experiences of inside and outside. External reality can
gradually affect and modify the crude hypothesis phantasy sets up. Phantasy is both the activity and its products. (23)

As an unconscious commentary, phantasies are inchoate, pre-verbal and fragmentary. They represent the baby's premature attempt to master bodily anxiety, an anxiety that, in Klein's view (1946), is angry, terrifying, aggressive, and
subject to turning back against the self. Klein will come to call this painful constellation the paranoid-schizoid position, where phantasies of destruction,
including the worry that the ego will fall into bits, are projected into the
mother's body. All these bad injuring objects banished to the outside threaten
to return to have their revenge.[5]

Describing primitive unconscious processes brings Klein (1957) to the limits of language and hence to the limits of consciousness itself. In a footnote she
writes: "All this is felt by the infant in much more primitive ways than language
can express. When these pre-verbal emotions and phantasies are revived in the
transference situation, they appear as 'memories in feelings', as I would call
them, and are reconstructed and put into words with the help of the analyst"
(180). It is almost as if Klein tried to answer that childlike question, why do we
have language at all? However negative—and, indeed, for Klein there is a kernel of negativity within psychical life—phantasies are the conditions from
which identification and symbolization emerge. From the beginning, the baby
equates her or his bodily anxiety with objects in the world. Through the infant's
projection of her or his bodily sensations into that first other, "meanings" of
hate and love are confused. For Klein, psychic reality makes cognitive processes
possible even if the beginning must be traumatic. Cognition, the capacity to
find newer and newer ideas that can be unmoored from the frightening qualities of concrete symbolization, gradually comes into dialogue with phantasy.
Klein (1935) views this dialogue as a more complex anxiety—the depressive
position—where thinking is poignant, where the ambivalence made from both
loving and hating the same object does not devastate, and where there is concern for the other as a separate being.[6] And while thinking is never fully able
to escape the shadow of this first terror, it can come to tolerate, in very creative
ways, the anxiety that sets it to work.[7] This is what Klein means by learning and
perhaps what Sedgwick (1997) means by reparative reading.

These very difficult dynamics and the tender patience necessary to work
them through are the heart of Sedgwick's (1993) extraordinarily complex essay,
"A Poem is Being Written." She projects into the primal scene of writing, not

only the questions of a nine year old child, although these questions do test the limits of what we feel in poetry. But, also, readers are offered the heart-wrenching work of what else is being written as a poem is being written, when theory is being written. Sedgwick offers us some very Kleinian moves here, warning readers of the minefield of misrecognitions our own desires are apt to set off:

> The lyric poem, known to the child as such by its beat and by a principle of severe economy (the exactitude with which the frame held the figure)—the lyric poem was both the spanked body, my own body or another one like it for me to watch or punish, and at the same time the very spanking, the rhythmic hand whether hard or subtle of authority itself. What child wouldn't be ravenous for dominion in this place? Among the powers to be won was the power to be brazen, to conceal, to savage, to adorn, or to abstract the body of one's own humiliation; or perhaps most wonderful, to *identify with* it, creating with painful love and care, but in a temporality miraculously compressed by the elegancies of language, the distance across which this body in punishment could be endowed with an aura of meaning and attraction—across which, in short, the *compelled* body could be *chosen*. (184)

Where Sedgwick ends and the poem begins, where the reader ends and the writing takes over, where the language thrills and then stops one cold, and where being accrues and having overwhelms, how finely frayed are these lines? Indeed, it is a delicate work to choose to identify with the side of the discarded content, with the farthest outpost of the symbol's frontier, with the free association, and with the depressive position. We might also observe that the stakes are not with the familiar reversal of hierarchy, for that would place us in the realm of projective identifications, still dependent upon fragmenting the object relation in order to relieve our dependence from it. To work through these rather anxious defenses, to work the defense until it has no more use, demands, as well, a prior question: What holds the reader back? *Surely, what theory wouldn't be ravenous for dominion in this place?*

Sedgwick (1993) recognizes that in trying to make from the compelled body something chosen, the passion for ignorance must confuse itself with the passion for knowledge. She writes of the difficulties of what happens to the reader while reading: "There are psychological operations of shame, denial, projection around 'ignorance' that make it an especially propulsive category in the individual reader" (25). Ignorance, for Sedgwick inaugurates not just resistance, but also a confusion of its own time: "The energies of ignorance always make an appeal to, and thus require the expulsion of, a *time before*, a moment of developmental time . . . I don't know in trying to summon up an image of these energies whether it will be more effective to evoke in academic readers the time before we became literate or the time before we became expert at interpreting the signs associated with sexuality" (47). We might wonder, with Sedgwick, how such a distinction can be made for there is a great deal of mixup: Our learning of expertise is embroiled with our first theoretical attempts to know sexuality and these first attempts occur before we have language.[8] That "time before" is the time of phantasy, but then, to return to Klein, expelling something does not make it go away.

In our academia, can we ready ourselves to observe how the urge to expel ignorance produces rigid knowledge and more of an unthought known? Shall we admit our adeptness at dismissing theories that run contrary, not just to prevailing conventions but, more significantly, to who we think and wish we and others might be in and for our theory? Certainly affect threatens the omnipotence to which theory in silence aspires. And these affective tensions can exaggerate the space between what we know and what we want, between what we find and what we create, and between what we hold and what we destroy. Another sort of unthought known can also be observed here: Our internal conflicts structure what can be noticed in the world and held in theory. This may be why discussing Tomkins is of some use and Sedgwick and Frank's introduction returns us to arguments over the status of the subject and whether its qualities are essentially there or socially induced, over the material of human nature and how this stuff fuels and stalls emotional life, and over how affects become hallucination, perception, judgment, and yes, even theory. If theory kindergarten returns us to a certain sort of involuntary origin, a time before literacy, that begins in a debate between good and bad, love and hate, and that inaugurates our earliest object relations, can our sense of knowledge and our capacity to think from that which resists knowledge, namely the unthought known, ignorance, and phantasy, ever escape this first terrible sense of making something from nothing?

That theory kindergarten may serve as a metaphor for object relations, as a psychoanalytic commentary on both the "activity and products" of knowledge in psychic time, and as movement between the play of phantasy and reality, self and other, hide and seek, and aggression and reparation, means, among other things, that using knowledge is one way to make selves and to secure and undo our first projected boundaries.[9] Yet this process is precarious, subject to its own flaws and reversals, dependent not upon possessing the proper knowledge, for at least, in psychoanalytic views and also in much of what Sedgwick writes, knowledge must remain a paradox whether it is partial, split, or integrated. Robert Young's (1999) discussion of post-Kleinian thought also gets this dilemma: "One of the illuminating distinctions that post-Kleinian psycho-analysis has given us is that between knowing and knowing about. In psycho-analysis, knowing about something often operates as a defence against know-ing it in a deeper, emotional sense" (65). Sedgwick begins in the emotional sense of this confusion when she records "the energies of ignorance" as appeal-ing to "*a time before.*" Our uses of knowledge as deflection and substitution, as condensation, idealization, and as wish fulfillment, as the means to ward off and create new anxieties, and as the basis of what must be worked through, are part of theory's work. And these dynamics are also comparable to the work that goes on in psychoanalysis, where we learn that theory may well be a retro-spective reconstruction of what is felt before it can be known. Theory, precisely because of this trajectory, is always vulnerable to its own flawed dream work.

For these reasons and more, we must return to theory kindergarten for our work there may remind us of our first uses of objects we try to possess and dis-card, love and hate, diminish and idealize, split and integrate. Hannah Segal (1997) suggests this performance stages "the grammar of object relations" that comes to represent the underlying logic of affect (79). Object relations are not just a story of how we use objects but rather how, through relating, we begin to inaugurate and structure our very capacity to position ourselves in reality and phantasy and so, to the very work of thinking. From this view, what also goes on in theory kindergarten is akin to what Sedgwick (1997) imagines when she notices a certain precocious young reader

> who is reading for important news about herself, without knowing what form that news will take; with only the patchiest familiarity with its codes; without, even, more than hungrily hypothesizing to what questions this news may proffer an answer. The model of such reading is hardly the state of complacent adequacy . . . but a much more speculative, super-stitious, and methodologically adventurous state where recognitions, pleasures, and discoveries seep in only from the most stretched and ragged edges of one's competence. (3)

If we read for important news about ourselves, how this news becomes thought of as important, is, as Sedgwick suggests, just on the precipitate of knowledge. Here is another sort of loneliness made, by way of an old Jewish joke, when one cannot receive news of oneself: A person had spent a long time stranded on a desert island. Finally, rescuers arrived and found the person but also noticed that this person had spent time building three synagogues. The res-cuers asked, "But aren't you alone on this island?" "Yes, of course!" the person exclaimed. "So, why are there three synagogues?" "Well," the person responded, pointing to each building in turn: "This one I usually go to, this one I sometimes go to, and this one I would never step foot in." In theory kindergarten, our objects have more than one use: we have theories we always use, theories we sometimes use, and theories we would never step foot in, even though we must use these in order to disclaim them. Sedgwick's work spins this joke differently; she invites us into theories we might never step foot in but, once there, may learn something that startles the theories we always use and the theories we sometimes use. If we each must build at least three places in order to know where we are, if it takes three theories to make one theory, the joke may well be on us: Where exactly are we when we make theories we never step foot in? What makes theory important news? Why do we have theory at all?

I

One of the startling assertions of psychoanalytic thought is that one can mean something far away from what one says. From this unmooring of meaning comes the theoretical force of the transference: We must act out our meanings before they can be known. With the insistence that there is something of a disagreement between affect and idea comes another shock: it is the affect that makes the idea and not the other way around.[10] We have theory because we have aggression. Theory is not just a substitution for that elusive first object, and it is not just a sublimation, one far away expression of sexuality. More pointedly, it is a product and the activity of phantasy. Winnicott (1990) also notices our first uses of knowledge: they begin in aggressiveness, ruthlessness, the wish for omnipotence, and anti-concern. If the knowledge and the self can survive this first attack and not retaliate, it will then be deemed as worthy for our use. For Winnicott, creativity is made somewhere between destruction of knowledge and the illusion that knowledge matters. It is a precarious balance, where omnipotence is both sustained and destroyed, and where the knowledge at stake can tolerate its breakdowns without ruining something else. This is learning in its most rigorous and demanding sense because paradoxically the learning comes from outside, from the other. Whereas Klein offers us the figure of the analyst who helps through the offering of new words, for Winnicott it is the figure of the "good enough mother" whose work contains the abstract qualities of reparative theory: a good enough theory can survive the theorist's aggression, move beyond her need to sustain anxiety through manic defenses, and attempt, from this doubt, a capacity for concern and agony. Klein (1957) would call such concern for the other the desire for or urge to make reparation and gratitude. It is a debt to the other that is never fully paid.

If we can somehow move from primal anxiety to aggression, to depression, and to reparation, the timing at stake is not developmental, at least in terms of how development is normally exposed, for at least four significant reasons.[11] Developmentalism resides in the terrible confines of normal psychology, where stages are linear and chronological and thus thought to be mastered and transcended. In developmental models, experience is discrete, not continuous, immune from more elaborate editions of older conflicts. Theories of developmentalism posit that anxiety becomes less and less prevalent because reality testing becomes more and more adequate. For Klein, anxiety both allows and inhibits thought. The second reason has to do with how the ego itself feels about its own development, and what it means to learn from experience. According to Wilfred Bion (1994), there is a hatred of development, of having to learn, and this must be overcome. These implicit difficulties are expelled from developmentalism. The work of the ego is not developmental for a third reason: its work emanates from unconscious phantasies and these forces belong neither to chronological time, nor to the pressures of logic and convention. From the vantage of Klein and Winnicott, it is development that makes experience, not the other way around. And for both, anxiety does not just inhibit. Instead, in its uses of anxiety, the ego vacillates between the paranoid-schizoid and the depressive positions that are made from clusters or complexes of phantasies, defenses, and object relations. The fourth reason why Kleinian theory cannot be developmental is that each of these positions is necessary for the other and there is no absolute boundary between them. The ego cannot evacuate itself from these positions because these positions are, in a sense, constitutive of the ego. In Klein's view, the ego's use of knowledge and hence, theory, occurs not just along the lines of object relations but because of object relations.

In those first relations with objects, both phantasized and actual—and indeed, in the beginning, thanks to projective identification, or the means by which the ego rids itself of unbearable anxiety and yet continues to identify with it—there is and can be no distinction between phantasy and reality, between the inside and the outside. This may well be the condition for any poem to be written, where the question child, the poem, the writer, and the reader, must rework the very boundaries of affect and thought. "From the beginning," writes Klein (1957), "all emotions attach themselves to the first object" (234). Even the terms of good and bad are unstable and subject to confusion. Because object relations occur before the infant has any access to a knowledge of them, their foundation is essentially made from unconscious phantasy, that in turn requires the elaboration of psychical positions: the paranoid-schizoid and the depressive. These positions are where the ego elaborates itself as it struggles with the nature of reality and phantasy, as well as with possessing and with letting go. Even to think such positions requires an imaginative practice akin to what Sedgwick (1990, 1997) calls "risking the obvious" and, in her discussion of Klein, "reparative reading practices."

Part of what must be imagined is the destructive beginnings of our judgments, our earliest forms of theory kindergarten. This is what Sigmund Freud (1925), in his essay "On Negation," suggests as our earliest experiences with judging good and bad, with introjection and projection, and with taking the side of "no." In Freud's words, "Expressed in the language of the oldest—the oral—instinctual impulses, the judgement is: 'I should like to eat this', or 'I should like to spit it out'; and put more generally: 'I should like to take this into myself and to keep that out.' That is to say: 'It shall be inside me' or 'it shall be outside me'" (237). However elegantly wrapped, our intellectual judgement may also be saying something difficult. As Freud says, "This is something I should prefer to repress" (236). Or, in the case of the joke, another negation: "this is a place I will never step foot in, even if I built it."

Whereas for Freud the sentence that tries to make itself into a judgment is one of splitting, "I shall spit this out and I shall eat this," for Klein, the sentence is convulsive, bellicose, belligerent, and frightened, more along the lines of a preemptive paranoid talisman principal: "this is eating me because I have killed it and so I shall kill it before it returns to eat me again." This rather vicious cycle, where cause and effect are confused through projection, is one Joan Riviere (1952) also tries to put into words: "You don't come and help, and you hate me, because I am angry and devour you; yet I *must* hate you and devour you in order to make you help" (47). Put as simply as possible, at the level of phantasy (and phantasy is where Klein plays), there is no boundary between symbolization and terror. This is another sort of theory kindergarten: We must make mincemeat of knowledge before it makes mincemeat of us.

If we can never be free of negation, if negation is one of those sticky ego defenses that protects the ego from that which it cannot bear to know and yet still taunts thought, if, even in what we discard, there is still preserved an attraction and a wish to keep this hidden, it still takes a theory of affect to understand something deep about the subtleties of not choosing to notice psychic reality. Klein seems to step back from Freud's description, focusing on what comes before the spitting out, namely the taking in or, the introjection of the object. This primary activity when it is akin to nourishment, served as a nascent model for Klein's views on reparation. She returns to the work of introjecting the good object not from the viewpoint of phantasies of invasion but from the position of curiosity and of containing. Sedgwick (1997) sees something of this loving work in her description of the work of reading: "to read from a reparative posi-

tion is to surrender the knowing, anxious paranoid determination that no horror, however apparently unthinkable, shall ever come to the reader *as new*: to
a reparatively positioned reader, it can seem realistic and necessary to experience surprise" (24). Reparative readings offer us a very different sense of reality testing, not so much that of Freudian ego, where what is tested is the verac-
ity of the object in terms of its re-finding. Rather a reparative position tests the
ethicality of one's own theory, one's own phantasy of encountering the world.
Surely, we are back to "a *question-child*," Sedgwick's young reader who loves
"the most stretched and ragged edges of [her] competence."

Sometimes, there can be no surprise because the theory itself forecloses
reparative readings and because there is a hatred of development that severs
theory from its own imagination. And when this occurs, there is no existence
for the "question-child." Sedgwick (1993) analyses these painful moves in,
"How to bring your kids up gay," an essay that considers one devastating form
of homophobia in psychiatry. Perhaps it takes the loving reparation of the figure of the child's queer body, who catches, without reason, the shadow of the
mother's femininity or the father's masculinity, even if these were not the first
shadings of gender offered, to remind one of the chances nature can take. The
figures of the sissy boy, the he–she girl, and the so-called gender disorder, are
lovingly held by Sedgwick and are no longer poster children for pathology. One
can look upon psychiatric theories of gender as saying something about our
own stalled academic arguments on the status of nature and culture in our theories. Sedgwick restages these debates, now along the lines of Kleinian positions. Like the paranoid-schizoid position which cannot recognize its own
potential, or indeed, its need to injure, the anxiety that collapses gender with
sexuality must foreclose the relation of sexuality to curiosity. There is, in these
psychiatric theories, a terrible confusion of hatred, helplessness, and not knowing. Sedgwick strongly urges psychiatry and gay activists toward a reparative
reading practice that does not settle the nature/culture debates, since no theory can do that. She asks for a theory that does not find itself securing its own
presumptive ontology but rather welcomes gay children:

> In this unstable balance of assumptions between nature and culture, at
> any rate, under the overarching, relatively unchallenged aegis of a cul-
> ture's desire that gay people *not be*, there is no unthreatened, unthreat-
> ening theoretical home for a concept of gay and lesbian origins . . . in
> the absence of a strong, explicit, *erotically invested* affirmation of some
> people's felt desire or need that there be gay people in the immediate
> world. (164)

Eros can make of ontology, after all, something improper. In her introduction to *Novel Gazing*, where finally the figures of Tomkins and Klein meet tentatively, Sedgwick raises for the nature/culture debates more dilemmas: Is there something within the human that is in excess of ontology and its knowledge-representatives? And then, is there a knowledge that can represent its own blind spots, indeed, that tries to make reparation for its first destructive moment of knowing? What is it to welcome Eros from this design? Surely more questions can be raised here, but one of the more interesting, because it harkens back to a moment in theory kindergarten where the preoccupation with being treated fairly was excruciatingly insisted upon, is asked by Adam Phillips (1999): "how does one take justice seriously if one takes nature seriously?" (10). Sedgwick offers us a variation: How does one take reading seriously if one takes psychic reality seriously?

II

One of the great originators of the idea of theory kindergarten and the story of how knowledge develops for the child was, of course, Freud who calls children "little sex researchers" (1905, 194). His second essay on infantile sexuality suggests that because we have sexuality from the beginning of life, we have curiosity. And because curiosity comes before knowledge, our earliest theories of sexuality must run from the ridiculous to the magical and from the paranoid to the sublime. These sexual theories are, for Freud, representative of not just the instinct for pleasure but also of that other instinct, our drive to know, or the instinct to master. Klein's early analytic theories began with that principal—what she called "the epistemophilic instinct"—but she stretched it to its limits by heightening not instinct but phantasy, not mastery but anxiety, and not real angst but that which comes before it: the aggressive and sadistic defenses that collapse knowing with possessing. For Freud, the instinct to master was a part of one's curiosity toward the outside world and toward what other bodies looked like. Klein, however, directs curiosity back upon itself, to its own inside. She argues that the desire to know does not reside in rendering the visible as intelligible but, instead, curiosity's preoccupation is with trying to make sense of the invisible, with what the baby cannot see. It is the empty space within, that the curiosity aims to fill, and for the Kleinian baby, the empty space that must be filled with phantasies is the interior of the mother's belly. In Klein's strange words: "In the earliest reality of the child it is no exaggeration to say that the world is a breast and a belly which is filled with dangerous objects, dangerous because of the child's own impulse to attack them" (1930, 233). At least initially, knowledge is equated with possession and not having knowledge feels as if something was stolen. And yet, having knowledge is also filled with danger, for at the level of phantasy, possessing is the same as injuring and stealing. And these injured objects do not, at least in phantasy, take being destroyed lightly.

Another way Klein describes the epistemophilic instinct is in the awkward phrase, "the highest flowering of sadism" or sadism at its height (Petot, 187). It was her first attempt to convey the idea that the aim of sadism is, in phantasy, to annihilate the object that the phantasy has already injured. For both Klein and Freud, the instinct to master was tied to the ambivalent desire to both destroy and control and thus preserve the object. And yet, this work of preservation defies mastery, for at least in the Kleinian view, the injured object returns to retaliate and to persecute. The desire to know, then, is traumatic and painful, entangled in primal helplessness and paranoia, and occurs too early to be clarified by language. In Klein's view, "One of the most bitter grievances which we come upon in the unconscious is that these many overwhelming questions, which are apparently only partly conscious and even when conscious cannot yet be expressed in words, remain unanswered . . . In analysis these grievances give rise to an extraordinary amount of hate" (1928, 188). Klein's understanding of ignorance then, particularly because it can be noticed only retrospectively, is extremely difficult to bear and even the knowledge that attempts to assuage our having to learn is linked, by Klein, with the confusion made from a strange combination of affect: love and hate, traumatic frustration, the dread of injury, and with helplessness.

The painfulness of learning is what Klein sketches through her positions and in a late essay on the problem of thinking, Klein insists that this painfulness is there from the beginning: "I recognized, in watching the constant struggle in the young infant's mental process between an irrepressible urge to destroy as well as save himself, to attack his objects and to preserve them, that primordial forces struggling with each other were at work . . . I had already come to the conclusion that under the impact of the struggle between the two instincts [life and death], one of the ego's main functions—the mastery of anxiety—is brought into operation from the very beginning of life" (1958, 236). Although Klein would later abandon her concept of "epistemophilic instinct" in order to move closer to that which she saw as inaugurating and shattering the uses of knowledge, namely positions within anxiety, she preserves a kernel of its force with her life long question of "what holds the child back?" and, with the question of how the ego comes to tolerate its own constitution (Pontalis, 95).

Klein makes some very startling and, for some, outrageous claims about where knowledge comes from and about what comes before we have the tenacity to engage something like it. She claims to think with infants, finding negativity at the heart of their phantasy life, constructing a very different version of theory kindergarten and a very different position for the theorist. "Let's note," observes Jacqueline Rose, "that the genesis of the persecutory object in Klein-ian thinking casts a shadow over interpretation, since, according to the logic of negation, interpretation comes as a stranger from the outside. And let's note too that if Klein makes of the analyst a fool and a fantast, it is from this place that the analyst has to try to speak . . . between the baby ignorant of the exter-nal world and the scientist aware of nothing else" (169–70). Sedgwick, too, would occupy this very difficult space, not just in her artful use of lists, but also in her offering to readers fantastic returns to the shadowy world of literature and sharp analyses of how the external world tries to foreclose imagination. Is this the space where the urge for reparation is lost and found?

III

Surely it would be a terrible place if all that happened in theory kindergarten was learning how to defend oneself against the most violent and recursive attacks of anxiety. In her introduction to *Novel Gazing*, Sedgwick thoughtfully calls this mode of internal persecution, "a position of terrible alertness" (1997, 8). She was speaking again about theory, but this time as a problem of paranoia, an intellectual example of Klein's paranoid/schizoid position. The position is one of preemptive retaliation, made from phantasies, or better, from an unbear-able sense of not knowing and not being able to stand it. For Klein, we all begin in anxiety and this difficult beginning inaugurates a second way to think, what Klein calls reparation. This is the desire to save the object from destruction, to consider the object not just from the vantage of introjection and projection of part objects, but to allow simultaneously both the object to be whole and the self to care, to mourn, and to give gratitude. In the strange calculus of Melanie Klein, we split in order to attempt integration. In the strange calculus of Eve Kosofsky Sedgwick, we write and read in order to surprise ourselves, and to move thinking closer to the question of love: "The desire of a reparative impulse . . . is additive and accretive. Its fear, a realistic one, is that the culture surrounding it is inadequate or inimical to its nurture; it wants to assemble and confer plenitude on an object that will then have resources to offer an inchoate self" (1997, 27–28).

Here are some resources we might use. Sedgwick's haunting essay, "White Glasses" offers us a story of how identifications work against all odds:

> Now, I know I don't "look much like" Michael Lynch . . . Nobody knows
> more fully, more fatalistically than a fat woman how unbridgeable the

gap is between the self we see and the self as whom we are seen . . . and
no one can appreciate more fervently the act of magical faith by which
it may be possible, at last, to assert and believe, against every social possibility, that the self we see can be made visible as if through our own eyes
to the people who see us. (1993, 256)

There is, in this essay, a desire to honor the invisible and the contents of our
own belly. Putting on these glasses, one offers homage to a vision of loving the
self and the other, and feels gratitude for the passionate work of identifications.
And the choice made, which is to say, the allowance for the free association of
phantasy, is to set loose identification from the agonies of ontology. It is, simply put, to choose to love and to make of that work a certain relation that can
take its residence, in the words of Sedgwick, "across the ontological crack
between the living and the dead" (1993, 257).

But to take residence, to be addressed by one's own phantasies, and to risk
the work of loving, is also, at some intimate level, very lonely. It would not be
until the end of her life that Klein would take on an experience that her work
hinted at all along, namely feelings of loneliness. "On the Sense of Loneliness"
is, for me, one of her most poignant and suggestive essays. As in many of her
essays, she reviews her key theoretical efforts, but what seems to set this essay
apart from others is the poignancy of her own thinking and a certain grace. In
ways that may not be so apparent in her earlier work, Klein here acknowledges
the difficulties and the sadness that the ego incurs when it tries to accept the
work of integration. In staying with the ego's own feelings about itself, Klein
brings the desire for reparation back to the self who not only has the capacity
to destroy the object, but who also knows that doing so would mean destroying
the self as well. Leaving this vicious circle, Klein admits, is very painful for the
ego: "The coming together of destructive and loving impulses, and of the good
and bad aspects of the object, arouses the anxiety that destructive feelings may
overwhelm the loving feelings and endanger the good object" (1963, 301). The
pain of integration also makes one lonely, for in accepting the good and the
bad, omnipotence must be given up. And, without the illusion of omnipotence,
a certain sense of hope is also lost. What makes the work of integration so difficult, Klein suggests, is that it is also, paradoxically, a work of mourning. And
yet, there will still be enjoyment:

The capacity for enjoyment is also the precondition for a measure of resignation which allows for pleasure in what is available without too much
greed for inaccessible gratifications and without excessive resentment
about frustration. Such adaptation can already be observed in some

young infants. Resignation is bound up with tolerance and with the feeling that destructive impulses will not overwhelm love, and that therefore goodness and life may be preserved. (310)

We can, I think, glimpse the painful work of integration in Sedgwick's record of her own analysis, the beautiful gift, *A Dialogue on Love*. There is no need to argue for the currency of affect nor even to protect theory from that which makes it fall apart. And surely we can understand that we take reading seriously precisely because we take psychic life seriously. If we are to work our identifications and not our points of view, if the resources that the other offers are what allows one and the other's reparative urges to deepen, then *A Dialogue on Love* is one place to learn this again. Still, what the careful reader might grasp is neither a better knowledge of Sedgwick nor even an understanding of the transitional space of that other theory kindergarten—analysis. More pertinent, more surprising, more intimate, more reparative, the reader might read for important news about herself, for noticing that her own destructive readings will not overwhelm the very new work of theory that Sedgwick proposes: The work of love.

Notes

1. This work was supported by the Social Science and Humanities Research Council of Canada, under the auspicious of "The Difficult Knowledge of Teaching and Learning in the University: A Psychoanalytic Inquiry," Grant #410-98-1028. The views expressed here do not represent the Council.
2. The figure of "the question-child" belongs to Pontalis and his discussion of how Melanie Klein's work with children transformed her understanding of Freud and her difference from Anna Freud's didactic and moralistic views on the psycho-analysis of children. Pontalis's characterization of Klein's own theoretical transformation gets at the status of "the question-child":
    > If in her first text, Melanie Klein's attention was held above all by the child's inhibitions, it was because they assumed an exemplary value for her: the child had more to say for himself than what he actually said. . . . She therefore chose not to define the conditions which should be fulfilled by child analysis, but to submit psychoanalytic theory and methods to the disconcerting test of the child's speech . . . a matter of coming to meet the child's psychic reality and measuring adult knowledge against it "in the spirit of free and unprejudiced research." (95–96)
3. For a very thoughtful discussion on the uses of Kleinian theory as offering

new ways to work through contemporary debates between modernity and postmodernity, see Steuerman.

4. This dilemma is one Sedgwick acknowledges when she considers the teaming up of psychoanalysis with queer theory. She raises the question of which psychoanalysis and then answers, not the one that posits sexual difference as an ontological exclamation. In Sedgwick's (1997) view: "From such often tautological work, it would be hard to learn that—from Freud onward, including for example the later writings of Klein—the history of psychoanalytic thought offers richly divergent, heterogeneous tools for thinking about aspects of personhood, consciousness, affect, filiation, social dynamics, and sexuality that, while relevant to the experience of gender and queerness, are not centrally organized around 'sexual difference' at all" (11). Sedgwick goes on to observe that while psychoanalytic categories are certainly not immune from the history of psychoanalysis, the desire for a purely (innocent) theory that can somehow "guarantee nonprejudicial . . . beginning" (12) may well be a symptom of paranoid defense against the capacity to be surprised. From another vantage, this wish for a pure theory may also be a symptom of the desire for omnipotence, surely a force in theory kindergarten.

5. The paranoid-schizoid position is an outcome of what, for Klein, is a primal struggle that inaugurates the ego's capacity to feel itself: the fight between the death drive and the life drive. What the infant projects is this struggle, that is, fragments of her or his internal world. But this process of projection, felt as capable of invading the body of the mother, also splits the ego into fragments and so the ego's fear of annihilation, made from its own death drive, is sustained in the very attempt to console itself. Here is Klein's (1946) description: "I hold that anxiety arises from the operation of the death instinct within the organism, is felt as fear of annihilation (death) and takes the form of fear of persecution. The fear of the destructive impulse seems to attach itself at once to an object—or rather it is experienced as the fear of an uncontrollable overpowering object. . . . Even if these objects are felt to be external, they become through introjection internal persecutors and thus reinforce the fear of the destructive impulse within" (4–5).

6. In the depressive position, the ego is able to feel distressed about its phantasies. Klein (1935) has a very lovely description of this first poignant attempt to think about the other: "The ego then finds itself confronted with the psychic reality that its loved objects are in a state of dissolution—in bits—and the despair, remorse and anxiety deriving from this recognition are at the bottom of numerous anxiety situations. To quote only a few

of them: there is anxiety how to put the bits together in the right way and at the right time; how to pick out the good bits and do away with the bad ones; how to bring the object to life when it has been put together; and there is the anxiety of being interfered with in this task by bad objects and by one's own hatred, etc." (269)

7. This distinction between the symbol and what it represents is discussed by Hannah Segal (1988) who extends Klein's (1930) discussion on the failure to symbolize, where the ego cannot distinguish, cannot gain any perspective on phantasy and reality and instead collapses the symbol with the original object. Segal offers the example of the man who could not play the violin in public because he equated this activity with masturbation. The representation and the feeling could not be thought. This activity is emblematic of the paranoid-schizoid position, where, "the concept of absence hardly exists," (164) and where the depressive position becomes foreclosed. In her summary of Ernest Jones's work in the area of symbolization, Segal offers a cogent observation on the painful efforts that symbolization attempts to assuage: "one might say that when a desire has to be given up because of conflict and repressed, it may express itself in a symbolical way, and the object of the desire which had to be given up can be replaced by a symbol" (162). And yet precisely because the symbol is a substitution, it is also tied to the work of mourning and to the working through of the depressive position.

8. Julia Kristeva, in working with the early theories of Freud, makes the point that we have sexuality before we have language. Even in learning language, what the young baby learns is the love of and erotic tonality of communication. Sedgwick's "A Poem is Being Written" makes this point as well. Yet putting our sexuality into language will always be an insufficient project because there is a constitutive conflict between sexuality and language. Kristeva puts the dilemma this way: "The particularity of our species, immature at birth, with an initial linguistic incapacity, carves out the asymptote between the sexual and the verbal and prevents the gap between them from one day being filled" (32–33).

9. For a thoughtful discussion of how the dynamics of "hide and seek" play out in educational spheres, see Pitt.

10. The counter-intuitive view that affect allows for the possibility of the idea is drawn from the work of Wilfred Bion (1994) and his notion that it is thought that makes the thinker: "The problem is simplified if 'thoughts' are regarded as epistemologically prior to thinking and that thinking has to be developed as a method or apparatus for dealing with 'thoughts.' If this is the case then much will depend on whether the 'thoughts' are to be

evaded or modified or used as part of an attempt to evade or modify something else" (83).

11. For a discussion of Kleinian understandings of "development" see Hinshelwood (1991). He notes six interactive aspects: "(1) physiological maturation; (2) phases of the libido; (3) the reality principle; (4) the development of object-relations; (5) development of the ego; and (6) the sequence of anxiety-situations" (277).

Works Cited

Bion, Wilfred, *Learning from Experience* (Northvale, NJ: Jason Aronson Inc., 1994).

Bollas, Christopher, *The Shadow of the Object: Psychoanalysis of the Unthought Known* (New York: Columbia University Press, 1987).

Freud, Sigmund, *The Standard Edition of the Complete Psychological Works of Sigmund Freud*, ed. and trans. James Strachey, in collaboration with Anna Freud, assisted by Alix Strachey and Alan Tyson. 24 vols. (London: Hogarth Press and Institute for Psychoanalysis, 1953–74).

———. "On negation." 1925. Standard Edition 19. 235–42.

———. "Three essays on sexuality." 1905. Standard Edition 7. 125–243.

Hinshelwood, R. D., *A Dictionary of Kleinian Thought* (London: Free Association Books, 1991).

Klein, Melanie, *Envy and Gratitude and other works, 1946–1963* (N.p.: Delcorte Press/Seymour Lawrence, 1975).

———. *Love, Guilt and Reparation and other works 1921–1945.* (London: Hogarth Press, 1975).

———. "The psychotherapy of the psychoses" (1930). In *Love, Guilt and Reparation* (London: Hogarth Press, 1975) 233–35.

———. "On the Sense of Loneliness" (1963). *Envy and Gratitude and other works, 1946–1963* (N.p.: Delcorte Press/ Seymour Lawrence, 1975) 300–314.

———. "On the development of mental functioning" (1958). *Envy and Gratitude and other works, 1946–1963* (N.p.: Delcorte Press/ Seymour Lawrence, 1975) 236–46.

———. "Envy and Gratitude" (1957). *Envy and Gratitude and other works, 1946–1963* (N.p: Delcorte Press/Seymour Lawrence, 1975) 176–235.

———. "Notes on Some Schizoid Mechanisms" (1946). *Envy and Gratitude and other works, 1946–1963* (N.p.: Delcorte Press/Seymour Lawrence, 1975) 1–24.

———. "A Contribution to the Psychogenesis of Manic-Depressive States," in *Love, Guilt and Reparation* (London: Hogarth Press, 1935) 262–89.

———. "Early stages of the oedipus conflict," (1928). In *Love, Guilt and Reparation* (London: Hogarth Press, 1975) 186–98.

Kristeva, Julia, *The Sense and Non-Sense of Revolt: The Power and Limits of Psychoanalysis*, trans. Jeanine Herman (New York: Columbia University Press, 2000).

Mitchell, Juliet, "Introduction to Klein." in *Reading Klein*, ed. John Phillips and Lyndsey Stonebridge (New York: Routledge, 1998) 11–31.

Petot, Jean-Michel, *Klein: First Discoveries and First System, 1919–1932, Vol. I*, trans. Christine Trollope (Madison: International Universities Press, 1990).

Phillips, Adam, *Darwin's Worms* (London: Farber and Farber, 1999).

Pitt, Alice J., "Hide and Seek: The Play of the Personal in Education," *Changing English* 7.1(2000): 65–74.

Pontalis, J. B., "Between Knowledge and Fantasy." *Frontiers in Psychoanalysis: Between the Dream and Psychic Pain*, trans. Catherine Cullen and Philip Cullen (New York: International Universities Press, 1981) 95–111.

Riviere, Joan, "On the Genesis of Psychical Conflict in Earliest Infancy," *Developments in Psycho-Analysis*, ed. Joan Riviere, (London: Hogarth Press and The Institute of Psycho-Analysis, 1952) 37–66.

Rose, Jacqueline, "Negativity in the Work of Klein," *Why War? — Psychoanalysis, Politics, and the Return to Klein* (Oxford: Blackwell Press, 1993) 137–90.

Sedgwick, Eve Kosofsky, *A Dialogue on Love*. Boston: Beacon Press, 1999.

———. "Paranoid reading and reparative reading; or, you're so paranoid, you probably think this introduction is about you," *Novel Gazing: Queer Reading in Fiction*, ed. E. K. Sedgwick (Durham: Duke University Press, 1997) 1–40.

———. *Tendencies* (Durham: Duke University Press, 1993).

———. *Epistemology of the Closet* (Berkeley: University of California Press, 1990).

Sedgwick, Eve Kosofsky, and Adam Frank, "Shame in the Cybernetic Fold: Reading Silvan Thompkins." *Shame and Its Sisters: A Silvan Thomkins Reader*, ed. E. K. Sedgwick and A. Frank (Durham: Duke University Press, 1995) 1–28.

Segal, Hannah, "Phantasy and Reality," *The Contemporary Kleinians of London*, ed. Roy Schafer (Madison: International Universities Press, 1997) 75–96.

———. "Notes on Symbol Formation," *Klein Today: Developments in Theory and Practice, Volume I: Mainly Theory*, ed. Elizabeth Bott Spillius (London: Routledge, 1988) 160–78.

Steuerman, Emilia, *The Bounds of Reason: Habermas, Lyotard and Klein on Rationality* (London: Routledge, 2000).

Young, Robert, "Phantasy and Psychotic Anxieties," *The Klein-Lacan Dialogues*, ed. Bernard Burgoyne and Mary Sullivan (New York: The Other Press, 1999) 65–82.

Winnicott, D. W., "Aggression, Guilt, and Reparation," *Home is Where We Start From* (New York: Norton Press, 1990) 80–89.

5

If Love Were All: Reading Sedgwick Sentimentally

Paul Kelleher

Everyone will understand that X has "huge problems" with his sexuality; but no one will
be interested in those Y may have with his sentimentality: love is obscene precisely in that
it puts the sentimental in place of the sexual.
—Roland Barthes, A Lover's Discourse

I *was* a morbid
sentimental kid, I'm sure
of that . . .
—Eve Kosofsky Sedgwick, A Dialogue on Love

The readings Eve Kosofsky Sedgwick has produced over the past twenty years
have given us a keener, queerer sense of literature's place in the history of sexuality. Indeed, Sedgwick's distinctive rendering of the literary history of sexuality teaches us how the intimate communications between reader and writer,
writer and text, text and canon, are no less eventful than the dramatic crossings
among sexes, genders, and sexualities. One can hardly think of a moment in
Sedgwick's work when she doesn't gesture simultaneously to the theory and
practice of *both* sexuality and literature. Neither sexuality in the light of literature, nor literature in the light of sexuality: Sedgwick does justice to both,
rather, by reawakening our sense of what sexuality and literature *do*—together,
for one another, to one another. And perhaps most importantly, Sedgwick
brings out scenes in which only by habit could we discern sexuality and literature as two, distinct figures, so interchangeable are their profiles, so wonderfully mistakable are they for one another.

Given the influence of her writings on literature, and their currency as models for adventuresome styles of queer thought and expression, an inquiry into
Sedgwick's configuration of literary history seems necessary—specifically, an
inquiry into how Sedgwick's literary-historical orientation implicitly authorizes
and de-authorizes different forms of theoretical practice. An overstatement may
be as good a beginning as any for such a demanding task. Let me offer two: first,
Sedgwick's numerous and not-easily-classifiable theoretical interventions may
be read *as if* they were reducible to one, sustained, nearly (and until recently)

unvarying thought—a meditation, namely, on the Gothic novel (or, following her terms, the "male paranoid Gothic"). Second, queer theory has yet to articulate fully the intimate, if often only implicit or indirect, relations between sentimentality and sexuality (whether "normal" or dissident)—which bespeaks not a failure of critical imagination or intelligence, but rather the success of queer readings and reenactments of the Gothic genre and its attendant forms of paranoid subjectivity and social relation. The cohabitations of sentimentality and sexuality, however, have not gone unfelt; in fact, the simplest intuition of the pages that follow is that quite the opposite is the case.

As this essay hopes to make clear (though it warrants emphasizing from the start), the "sentimentality" I have in mind draws not only, or even largely, on its current usage: the unbecoming "sentimentality" attributed to figures, scenes, or texts whose first motive appears to be a kind of "unearned" or "manipulative" emotionalism. I will speak instead of another sentimentality: the affective practices—ethical, political, aesthetic, and erotic—that, from Restoration England to the contemporary United States, have underwritten what gets called "a self," "a subject," "a sexuality," "a life." *Sentimentalism* is no one thing, but rather points us toward a rich, heterogeneous history "tied in with the civil war in seventeenth-century England, with theological debates, and with evolving discourses about the nervous system" (Johnson 12). In literature, sentimentalism informs (and not always in obvious or predictable ways) the work of Richardson, Fielding, Wollstonecraft, Wordsworth, Mary Shelley, Carlyle, Dickens, George Eliot, Wilde, and James, and in philosophy, Locke, Shaftesbury, Hutcheson, Hume, Smith, Burke, Bentham, and Mill.[1] An "interdisciplinarity" before its time, sentimentalism is a theory of the sublime (authority, power, freedom, desire) as well as the ridiculous (feelings, bodies, dependence, desire again).

I. The Gothic Becomes You

Sedgwick's gravitation toward the Gothic, at least in published form, begins with *The Coherence of Gothic Conventions* (1980), which offers an expanded version of the dissertation she completed earlier at Yale. Sedgwick's aim in this work is to render a more critically acute understanding of "the Gothic": "I want to make it easier for the reader of 'respectable' nineteenth-century novels to write 'Gothic' in the margin next to certain especially interesting passages, and to make that notation with a sense of linking specific elements in the passage with specific elements in the constellation of Gothic conventions" (4). The Gothic, Sedgwick argues, enacts a double strategy of figuration and stylization. First, "when an individual fictional 'self' is the subject of one of these conventions . . . [i]t is the position of the self to be massively blocked off from some-thing to which it ought normally to have access. . . . The self and whatever it is that is outside have a proper, natural, necessary connection to each other, but one that the self is suddenly incapable of making" (12, 13). Second, "both the identification of center with self and the programmatic symmetry of the inside–outside relation are finally undermined in the same texts" (13). The "self" discovered in the confines of the Gothic is intensely relational precisely when this self appears most withdrawn or barred from "normal" forms of social relation. By Sedgwick's account, the Gothic novel does not reveal the interior, or repressed, of the Enlightenment mind, but rather, formalizes a powerful set of techniques for imagining and recognizing a "self." The Gothic, she writes, "enforces boundaries with a proscriptive energy in direct proportion to their arbitrariness. . . . 'X within and X without' or 'an X within an X' are the guiding structures of these conventions: a story within a story, a secret held by one char-acter and the same secret held by another, a prison from which there is escape into another prison, a dream from which one wakens to find it true. For char-acters within these conventions, to be active is either to impose an arbitrary bar-rier or to breach one, a breach that is transgressive and attended by violence at the threshold" (34). At one and the same time, the Gothic conventions fix and undo the self—commit the self, in other words, to a permanently vulnerable mode of cognition and embodiment.

In a wry, self-critical preface that opens the 1986 edition of *Coherence*, Sedg-wick records the uncanny prescience of her early writing: "Epicycles of the *unheimlich*—refusals and more transgressive onsets of mutual self-recogni-tion—would make for the plot and the thrills of this encounter; its conclusion, whether in wracking reunification or in sheer exhaustion, would nevertheless leave newly rationalized and strengthened a certain, fatally symmetrical, carceral sublime of representation, of the body, and potentially history and pol-itics as well" (v). Having already sharpened her sense of the Gothic's modus operandi in subsequent writings, the preface to *Coherence* both recognizes and departs from the argument, as well as the attitude, of this earlier work. Sedg-wick self-reflexively records the accounts left unsettled (or worse) by this first essay into the Gothic: "A certain early-deconstructive insouciance, in this study, about the exact boundaries or meaning of a 'self,' has, it is now clear, been paid for in the increased and ultimately legitimized charge given, in the self-embodiments it evokes, to the Gothic-inherited values of symmetry (through 'the double'), of privacy (through the manichean treatment of the speakable and unspeakable), and of heterosexual presumption" (vi). The pro-gression from *The Coherence of Gothic Conventions* to *Between Men* (1985) and the essay "The Beast in the Closet: James and the Writing of Homosexual

Panic" (1986) carries through what already had been evidenced in the earlier work: in Sedgwick's words, "the usable thoroughness with which [*Coherence*] performs as much as it thematizes certain Gothic gestures" (v–vi). More to the point, the "heroics of embodiment" (vi) entailed in reading and writing the Gothic demonstrate the tendency for Gothic material to reemerge as theoretical method.

The charge *Between Men* imparted to subsequent work on gender and sexuality followed, in large part, from the audacious reach of Sedgwick's central thesis: namely, that the generic dispensation of the male paranoid Gothic determines—and, for those who read against its grain, diagnoses—modernity's remodeled version of patriarchy: the continuum of male homosocial desire (ranging from outright hate to forthright love) and the homophobia always close to its heart. No less than the men who are plotted across its landscape, homosocial desire captivates Woman, holds her captive to the imperative that in order to pass as something other than the "homosexual" as such, desire between men must be mediated through Woman, and thus, given the more becoming and more socially useful complexion of masculine aggression, jealousy, and rivalry. The male paranoid Gothic electrifies the relations between men by imagining a kind of worst-case scenario for homosocial relations, counseling its readers that, at a moment's notice, the boundaries between self and other may be travestied and replaced by the bonds of a morbid, exploitative intersubjectivity. In what Sedgwick elsewhere christens the "Age of Frankenstein," male homosocial relations fall under the shadow of "the absolute omnipresence of [the] homophobic, paranoid tableau" of "two men chasing one another across a landscape" (*Coherence*, x, ix). "[T]he single, repeated image of that reversible chase, culminating in various versions of the anal rape of one man by another man," by Sedgwick's account, represents both the crudest image of "homosexual possibility" and the embodiment of "primal human essence or originary truth" (ix–x). In good deconstructive form, Sedgwick suggests that the thematic excesses of a "minority" literature, such as the Gothic, illuminate—or more precisely, constitute from within, only to be disavowed by—the everyday social commerce of the male "majority."

One of the surprises offered by *Between Men* is the counterintuitive claim that the male "homosexual panic" underwritten by the Gothic novel may, in fact, have preceded anything resembling a modern conception of "homosexuality." By setting aside the repressive hypothesis that homophobia operated on an already constituted homosexual minority, Sedgwick suggests that homophobia worked *in the absence of* a fully articulated homosexual subculture, and may have required, or at least capitalized on, this absence. Homophobia, paradoxically enough, anticipates and solicits the homosexual embodiment it ostensibly wishes left unconceived. In Sedgwick's words, "even motifs that might ex post facto look like homosexual thematics (the Unspeakable, the anal), even when presented in a context of intensities between men, nevertheless have as their *first* referent the psychology and sociology of prohibition and control. That is to say, the fact that it is about what we would today call 'homosexual panic' means that the paranoid Gothic is specifically not about homosexuals or the homosexual; instead, heterosexuality is by definition its subject" (*Between*, 116, emphasis original). In a chapter on James Hogg's novel, *Private Memoirs and Confessions of a Justified Sinner*, Sedgwick remarks that the conspicuous prioritization of homophobic over homophilic thematics, in this novel and beyond, may support her claim that the long moment of homophobia rendered up much of what looks and feels like male heterosexual identity.

> From this apparent disruption of order between homophilic and homo-phobic thematics, we can learn two things. First, we should be reminded by it that however radically the terms of the homosocial spectrum, and the meanings of homosexual identity, were changing in the two centuries after the Restoration, the thematics and the ideological bases of homo-phobia were probably the most stable and temporally backward-looking elements of the entire complex. . . . [Second,] the priority in this novel— in this period—of homophobic over homophilic thematics . . . under-writ[es] our speculation about a main function of homophobia in its modern, psychologized form. (114)

What is true of Robert, in Hogg's novel, is true of the generic male susceptible to homosexual panic: homophobia does "not in the first place . . . [repress] a pre-existent genital desire within him toward men, but . . . mak[es] him an excruciatingly *responsive* creature and instrument of class, economic, and gen-der struggles that long antedate his birth" (114; emphasis original). It will be useful to recall here that *The Coherence of Gothic Conventions* traces the simul-taneous isolation and undermining of the "self," the various forms of "violated separation" (99) that give rise and shape to the Gothic subject. *Between Men* subsequently redescribes the Gothic conventions of "violated separation" as the homophobic/homosocial conditions of male heterosexual identity and enti-tlement: "For a man to be a man's man is separated only by an invisible, care-fully blurred, always-already-crossed line from being 'interested in men'" (89).

With *Epistemology of the Closet*, Sedgwick advances further still the theo-retical career of the Gothic; here, the Gothic functions as a kind of generic unconscious that subtends not only the modern regime of homo/hetero defi-nition, but also the entire Western tradition of epistemological opposition, subordination, and exclusion. The germinal essay of the book, "The Beast in the Closet: James and the Writing of Homosexual Panic," performs a virtuoso reading of James, and along the way, extends forward in time the hypotheses of *Between Men* without diminishing an investment in the Gothic protocols of perversity, secrecy, and exposure. Whereas the subject of *Between Men* is male heterosexuality in the absence of a felt homosexual presence, the subject of *Epistemology of the Closet*, it may be said, is male heterosexuality in the presence of a felt homosexual absence. The crux of Sedgwick's reading of James' "The Beast in the Jungle" registers quite clearly this shift in theoretical orientation: "This is how it happens that the outer secret, the secret of having a secret, functions, in Marcher's life, precisely as *the closet*. It is not a closet in which there is a homosexual man, for Marcher is not a homosexual man. Instead, it is the closet of, simply, the homosexual secret—the closet of imagining *a* homosexual secret. Yet it is unmistakable that Marcher lives as one who is *in the closet*" (*Epistemology*, 205; emphases original).

To be sure, a critical sensibility responsive to the paranoid Gothic could have found no stronger excitation than D. A. Miller's essay, "Secret Subjects, Open Secrets" (*Novel*, 192–220), which inspires, and manifestly accelerates and emboldens, the protocols of reading and writing Sedgwick introduces in *Epistemology of the Closet*. "[P]aranoia is a form of love" (*Coherence*, xi): with *Epistemology*, Sedgwick delivers a high-Jamesian love letter to the paranoid intelligence of "Secret Subjects, Open Secrets," but, at the same time, manifestly redirects its address. While Miller's meditation on the "open secret" demonstrates the centrality of secrecy in captivating the modern liberal subject, Sedgwick raises the stakes by foregrounding the particular relation between the open secret and homo/heterosexual definition. In a word, Sedgwick *homosexualizes* the function of the "open secret": consequently, *Epistemology of the Closet* argues from the defining premise that "same-sex desire is . . . structured by its distinctive public/private status, at once marginal and central, as *the* open secret" (22; emphasis original).[2]

In 1986 Sedgwick looked forward to "[s]ome other year, soon one hopes, [when] it may be easier than it is right now to generalize with detachment about and then move on from the relation between Gothic paranoid homophobia and nineteenth- and twentieth-century structures of knowledge" (*Coherence*, xii). With the publication of her 1997 essay, "Paranoid Reading and Reparative Reading; or, You're So Paranoid, You Probably Think This Introduction Is about You," Sedgwick traces, as well as performs, an ethic of "reparative" writing—not, importantly, from a new-found position of "detachment," but rather through a recalibrated sense of theoretical attachment and investment.[3] The brilliance of Sedgwick's engagement with reparative reading lies in its heartening claim (or rather, its reminder) that knowing something to be "true," "powerful," or "efficient" doesn't necessarily entail our feeling, acceding to, or acting on its truth, power, or efficiency. Sedgwick closes the essay with these words:

> The vocabulary for articulating any reader's reparative motive toward a text or a culture has long been so sappy, aestheticizing, defensive, anti-intellectual, or reactionary that it's no wonder few critics are willing to describe their acquaintance with such motives. The prohibitive problem, however, has been in the limitations of present theoretical vocabularies rather than in the reparative motive itself. No less acute than a paranoid position, no less realistic, no less attached to a project of survival, and neither less nor more delusional or fantasmatic, the reparative reading position undertakes a different range of affects, ambitions, and risks. What we can best learn from such practices are, perhaps, the many ways in which selves and communities succeed in extracting sustenance from the objects of a culture — even of a culture whose avowed desire has often been not to sustain them. (35)

The impulse to turn away from paranoid reading indicates a form of theoretical longing, a need to account for the experiences left unrecorded, underdescribed, or misread by a reading practice schooled in the rhythms of the paranoid Gothic. To move from paranoid reading to reparative reading means, among other things, extricating oneself from the "structures of knowledge" upheld by the paranoid Gothic, in order to register how paranoia leaves us cold to what looks and feels (doesn't it?) like another world. However undernourished they are by the streamlining imperatives of paranoid structures of knowledge, *structures of feeling* nonetheless determine our reading and writing, living and loving, without being reducible in each and every instance to the stuff of cognition, much less paranoia. The Gothic tableau of two men in paranoid pursuit, which casts a long shadow over the male homosocial spectrum, no doubt gives some ground to other encounters, other scenes. Indeed, what seems to have been elided in the promulgation of the "open secret" as *the* structure for organizing homo/hetero definition, is the role of noncognitive aspects of sexuality. The queer-theoretical appropriation of paranoia as a way to apprehend the secret subject of modern sexuality overlooks constituents, such as emotion, affect, and drive, that are not exclusively, or even largely, cognitively based: what gets occluded, then, is the affective subject of sensibility.

II. Reanimating the Sentimental

Though Sedgwick doesn't (and, I suspect, wouldn't) characterize her recent thinking as such, to my mind the desire for an ethic of reparative reading signals a *sentimental turn* for queer criticism.[4] Some of the risks of bringing the "sentimental" to bear on queer reading have been broached by Sedgwick in *Epistemology of the Closet*. As she notes, in the course of a reading of Wilde, Nietzsche, and the "sentimental relations of the male body," "[t]he ballistic force of the attribution of 'sentimentality' is so intense today that I've found it amazingly difficult to think about any analytic or revaluative project involving it that wouldn't culminate its rehabilitative readings with some yet more damning unmasking of the 'true,' and far more dangerous, sentimentality of an author not previously associated with the term. This would be congruent with a certain difficult-to-avoid trajectory of universalizing understandings of homo/heterosexual definition . . . according to which authoritarian regimes or homophobic masculinist culture may be damned on grounds of being *even more homosexual* than gay male culture" (154; emphasis original). As the scare quotes around "sentimentality" in this passage and the next suggest, some explanations are in order before sentimentalism can be admitted into the domain of critical thought. "It would be hard to overestimate the importance of vicariousness in defining the sentimental. The strange career of 'sentimentality' . . . is a career that displays few easily articulable consistencies; and those few are not . . . consistencies of subject matter. Rather, they seem to inhere in the nature of the investment by a viewer *in* a subject matter" (150; emphasis original). *Epistemology of the Closet*, in fact, discusses "sentimentality" as if it were *already and irremediably* structured as another form of paranoia — that is, "the sentimental as the *insincere*, the *manipulative*, the *vicarious*, the *morbid*, the *knowing*, the *kitschy*, the *arch*" (143; emphases original). According to the terms of this analysis, sentimentality merely embodies a paranoia by proxy, a paranoia cunning enough to realize that the labor of discipline and punishment is all the more efficiently performed by its being delegated to the sentimental.

One approach for engaging "sentimentality" in nonallergic *and* critical fashion involves side-stepping a certain nominalist fallacy that would have us look for concrete practices of sentimentalism only in the vicinity of their discursive attribution and derogation. Comprehending the cultural career of sentimentalism means elaborating a theoretical protocol that identifies the residues of sentimentalism in neighborhoods that are not explicitly sign-posted, "sentimentality." Another approach, allied with the latter, would be to historicize the question of sentimentality. What gets bracketed as a resource for theory in Sedgwick's rendition of the literary history of sexuality is the literature and philosophy of sentimentalism. Whereas Gothicism, as we've seen, begins as an object of genre criticism only to grow into theoretical inquiry itself, sentimentalism fails to advance beyond anything other than a subject matter immune to even the most energetic attempts at critical reclamation. A chapter in *Between Men* is indeed devoted to Sterne's *A Sentimental Journey*; however, were one looking for a brilliant exposition of the ways in which literary genre and cultural form interrelate, one would be more rewarded by the following chapter, "Toward the Gothic: Terrorism and Homosexual Panic." Is it too banal to observe that "form" recapitulates "content"? "Toward the Gothic" cleaves *Between Men* nearly in two, much as the paranoia of homosexual panic cleaves—in both senses: divides and joins—the "male homosocial spectrum" with a "gaping and unbridgeable homophobic rift" (201). Sedgwick's provocative excursus on the Gothic enjoins its own effects: wherever we are in cultural or literary history, we implicitly are moving "toward" or "from" the paranoid Gothic—much as in Foucault's introductory volume to *The History of Sexuality*, we find ourselves either moving in a steady current "toward" homosexual nomination, circa 1870, or struggling in the historical wake it leaves behind.

By returning to the literary-historical context of sentimentalism—which overlaps with, yet predates, the rise of the Gothic novel—we discover that what looks and feels like normative affection or "sexuality" is not reducible only to the opposition between "hetero" and "homo." In other words, normative figurations of mind, body, and social relation may not be strictly synonymous with heterosexuality as such, and the equation of heterosexuality with normativity—through a shorthand term such as "heteronormativity" (Warner "Introduction" 1991)—necessarily entails a historical and theoretical remainder.[5] Sentimentalism, I suggest, enables us to account for this remainder. The eighteenth century's literature and culture of sentimentalism (as well as its nineteenth-century installments) offer exemplary sites for investigating not only the historical and cultural residues of heterosexual becoming, but also the *other* ways in which normativity has rendered our feelings, our selves. If "the paranoid Gothic is specifically not about homosexuals or the homosexual" but rather, "heterosexuality is by definition its subject" (Sedgwick *Between*, 116)—what, or who, is the subject of sentimentality? If the male paranoid Gothic generically presides over the formation of a homophobically-oriented male heterosexuality, and proleptically incriminates and "homosexualizes" epistemological relations between men, what specific claims are to be made in reference to the various genres of sentimentality?

Without contesting Sedgwick's analysis of modern-day homophobia (in truth, it remains second to none), we might, on the one hand, inquire into the literary and cultural career of *homophilia*, and postulate, in advance, that it cannot simply or adequately be described as the far end—the kinder, gentler pole—of the male homosocial continuum. On the other hand, and to my mind more promisingly, we might bracket the conceptual opposition between "homo" and "hetero" (which the term *homophilia* unavoidably recirculates), and begin to develop a broader, more theoretically experimental understanding of *philanthropy* (understood in its root sense, the love of the human). Before being impressed into the oscillations between "homo" and "hetero," the "same" and the "different," how do we become attached to, or oriented toward, anything or anyone at all? How do we discriminate and choose among goods—be they pleasures, bodies, ideas, or identities?[6] In a word, how do we learn to love—or for that matter, live?[7] By pulling back for a moment from our theoretical and everyday absorption in the hetero/homo divide, we comprehend anew the stretches of experience that respond to normative configurations. The binary opposition between the "heterosexual" and the "homosexual" fails to do justice, for instance, to the figures of the child and the adult, or the living and the dead, around whom collect *distributions*, not *oppositions*, of affect, investment, and value. Like the Gothic tableau of male paranoid pursuit, the homo/hetero binary renders a synchronically elegant profile of social being; but this analytic precision comes at the expense of being able to account for the less sensational, more mundane practices that shape "normal" and dissident lives, practices that bear, at best, an oblique relation to sexual desire, fantasy, or activity.

III. Foucault's Sensibility: We "Other Sentimentalists"

By separating questions of "normativity" from questions of "homosexuality" and "heterosexuality"—not definitionally, but tactically—we keep open the possibility of identifying different, not always-already converging, genealogies of the "straight male modern" subject (Brenkman).[8] My invocation of the critical term *normativity* intends to turn our attention to Foucault, but before going further, I want to offer a hypothesis regarding Foucault and literary history—not regarding Foucauldian redefinitions of the literary, but rather, the dividends of bringing literary history to bear on Foucault's writing. While Foucault traces the various manifestations of power, pleasure, and knowledge with an irresistible virtuosity, nearly every social form seems fully present and accounted for in his analysis *except* the domain of literary and artistic representation. A fact noticed before,[9] but one that still should prompt us to ask whether Foucault's unforgettable critical performance requires a certain readerly failure to fully comprehend the manner in which the history of sexuality gets told.[10] Rather than hold Foucault apart from literary history, it seems right to place one of the most stylized of theoreticians in the company of other, no less inventive, writers. One consequence of not reading Foucault against a literary background is the "common sense" of using Foucauldian theory to read Gothic and later, Gothic-influenced texts, without pausing to wonder whether the Gothic genre, in some measure, made a Foucauldian sensibility plausible, or even possible, in the first place. The repeated, and rarely successful, call to let "literature read theory" might begin by reading Foucault himself as a latter-day Gothic author, whose pages unfold "the fragment of darkness that we each carry within us: a general signification, a universal secret, an omnipresent cause, a fear that never ends" (*History*, 69).

Or, much less obviously, we might read Foucault as a latter-day philosopher of sensibility. In this regard, there might still be something left to extract from the often quoted, and quarreled over, passage in the first volume of Foucault's *History of Sexuality*, in which he offers a dramatic account of the discursive shift "from" the *sodomite* "to" the *homosexual*: "As defined by the ancient civil or canonical codes, sodomy was a category of forbidden acts; their perpetrator was nothing more than the juridical subject of them. The nineteenth-century homosexual became a personage, a past, a case history, and a childhood, in addition to being a type of life, a life form, and a morphology, with an indiscreet anatomy and possibly a mysterious physiology. . . . The sodomite had been a temporary aberration; the homosexual was now a species" (43). What interests me more is Foucault's intervening admonition that "[w]e must not forget that the psychological, psychiatric, medical category of homosexuality was constituted from the moment it was characterized—Westphal's famous article of 1870 on 'contrary sexual sensations' [*conträren Sexualempfindungen*] can stand as its date of birth—less by a type of sexual relations than by *a certain quality of sexual sensibility*, a certain way of inverting the masculine and the feminine in oneself. Homosexuality appeared as one of the forms of sexuality when it was transposed from the practice of sodomy onto a kind of interior androgyny, a hermaphrodism of the soul" (43; emphasis added). Foucault's reference to the *conträren Sexualempfindungen*, which may be rendered also as "contrary sexual feelings," suggests that the history of sexuality bears a striking resemblance to another domain: the "culture of sensibility."[11]

The Foucauldian history of sexuality, I would argue, recasts the history of sensibility. The historical parameters of *The History of Sexuality* (chiefly, the eighteenth and nineteenth centuries) are strongly congruent, if not almost identical, with the period in literary history that was densely populated with representations of characters preoccupied and transported by feeling, affect, the senses. The subject of sex and the subject of sensibility undoubtedly share more than just time on a common historical stage. No less than the workings of "power," the vicissitudes of sensibility directly implicated the individual, the family, the body politic, and the nation/state (including its history, politics, and forms of governance). The affective rituals of sentimentalism, and their grounding in the bodies of sensible subjects, no doubt figure in the "affirmation of self" (123) that Foucault argues was instrumental for the deployment of sexuality. However, Foucault's analyses—most particularly his deployment of the analytic category, "sexuality"—retroactively streamline, and misleadingly simplify, the messier, more unsystematized world of bodily and affective practices that obtained in a culture of sensibility. The advent of sexuality's regime, in other words, replaces the homosocial and heterosocial culture of sensibility with its "simple abstractions": "homosexuality" and "heterosexuality."[12] According to Foucault, the late eighteenth century witnessed the emergence of "a completely new technology of sex" (116), a "bio-power" (143), in which the convergence of "the disciplines of the body" and "the regulation of populations" (145) appropriated the question of life itself. How does this chapter in the history of sexuality collate with the culture of sensibility, particularly the late-eighteenth-century literature of sentimentalism? By what means was the affective subject of sensibility refigured as the amorous subject of, exclusively, "heterosexual" desire, and more, the normal subject of life itself?[13]

In order to develop a more diverse sense of heterosexuality's historical office, we might recall some episodes from the "prehistory" of the history of sexuality. Rather than subjects of "heterosexual" desire (first and last), the eighteenth century brings before our eyes individuals who imagined themselves, and others, as subjects of passion, certainly, but no less, subjects of manners, ethics, conversation, politeness, and affection. A strong sense of this world awaits the reader of *Characteristicks of Men, Manners, Opinions, Times* (1711), the collected writings of the third earl of Shaftesbury, who arguably was the first theorist of sentimentalism (Barker-Benfield 105–19). As Shaftesbury writes in his essay, "Sensus Communis," "All Politeness is owing to Liberty. We polish one another, and rub off our Corners and rough Sides by a sort of *amicable Collision*. To restrain this, is inevitably to bring a Rust upon Mens Understandings. 'Tis a destroying of Civility, Good Breeding, and even Charity it-self, under pretence of maintaining it" (1:39–40; emphasis original). The subject of Shaftesbury's thought was also the objective of his writing: the description and embodiment of the cultivated "man of feeling" (in 1771, Mackenzie's novel, *The Man of Feeling*, officially names this figure). At the head of a century in which the man of feeling would preside over the ethics and politics of sentiment, Shaftesbury authorizes an investment in sentiment, according to which matters of social being and belonging depended not solely on what one knew, but how one felt. Epistemology, then, follows the lead of the affections: "How wretched must it be, therefore, for MAN, of all other Creatures, to lose that *Sense*, and *Feeling*, which is proper to him *as a* MAN, and sutable [*sic*] to his Character, and Genius?" (1:255; emphases original).

More familiar to our eyes is Shaftesbury's discussion, in his essay "An Inquiry Concerning Virtue," of a strain of "unnatural affection" in the man whose "Disposition . . . render'd him averse to any Commerce with Womankind, and of consequence unfitted him thro *Illness of Temper* (and not merely thro *a Defect of Constitution*) for the Propagation of his Species or Kind" (1:200; emphases original). Importantly, though, Shaftesbury's diagnosis of unbecoming feelings in a male is not installed as the paranoid-epistemological fulcrum for homosocial relations; instead, this instance of "unnatural affection" takes its place in a broad catalogue of other, differently valued sentiments, whose common substrate is not a homophobically charged knowledge, but an ethically complex body of private and public affections. This structure is perhaps most discernible in his essay, "An Inquiry Concerning Virtue," where Shaftesbury traces the productive antinomy between affections directed toward the "private good" (the "self-affections") and those directed toward the "common good" (the "natural affections"). Affection, in itself, is neither good nor bad; rather, it is the degree, not the kind, of affection that warrants discussion and, if necessary, remediation. This moment in the essay is representative of many: "But if the Affection [for the private good] be then only injurious to the Society, when it is immoderate, and not so when it is moderate, duly temper'd, and allay'd; then is the *immoderate* degree of the Affection truly vicious, but not *the moderate*" (1:200; emphases original).

Were one to identify the lesson Shaftesbury most forcefully emphasizes in "An Inquiry Concerning Virtue," it would be that an unmodified "self-love" stands behind the majority of our "unnatural," or "unsocial," affections. Self-love signifies a withdrawal, or withholding, from ameliorating intercourse of whatever kind, be it with woman or man. The question of gender, interestingly enough, does not thoroughly engross Shaftesbury's vision of "heterosociality" — that is, by his terms, *any* other potentially qualifies as "the other" of mutually enriching and transformative affection.[14] This is not to say that Shaftesbury recommends himself as an unacknowledged precursor for queer or gender theory, as the following passage will make clear. What makes Shaftesbury a promising candidate for queer counterreading is not his conception of "heterosexuality" per se (sex between men and women is a given here), but rather his philosophical advocacy of the man of feeling as an individual characteristically predisposed to invest his affections in the question of life itself—its biological reproduction, but no less, the sentimental reproduction of its conditions of possibility.

[I]n the Passions and Affections of particular Creatures, there is a constant relation to the Interest of *a Species*, or *common Nature*. This has been demonstrated in the case of *natural Affection*, parental Kindness, Zeal for Posterity, Concern for the Propagation and Nurture of the Young, Love of Fellowship and Company, Compassion, mutual Succour, and the rest of this kind. . . . There being allow'd therefore in a Creature such Affections as these towards *the common Nature*, or *System of the Kind*, together with those other which regard *the private Nature*, or *self-System*; it will appear that in following the *first* of these Affections, the Creature must on many Occasions contradict and go against *the latter*. How else shou'd the Species be preserv'd? Or what wou'd signify that implanted *natural Affection*, by which a Creature thro [sic] so many Difficultys [sic] and Hazards preserves its Offspring, and supports its Kind? (1:227, 228; emphases original)

Shaftesbury's moral philosophy, as we see, does not rely on the homophobic protocols of paranoid knowledge; what does unfold in his pages, though, is a *philanthropic* calculus of the sentiments that understands the individual as subject, first and last, to the bonds of affective investment, obligation, and duty. Without recourse to the either/or diagnosis of "homosexuality" and "heterosexuality," Shaftesbury's vision of ethical normativity brings to our eyes a range of social being that too often falls outside queer theory's purview: the affiliations of father and friend, son and lover, which obtained before, and were in no sense superseded by, the advent of the so-called homosexual role.

In other words, before the installation of homo/heterosexual identity and its saturation of the epistemological field, the subject of sensibility navigated another dispensation of social being: the antinomy between the auto-affective and the hetero-affective subject. Whereas Shaftesbury multiplies the numbers and kinds of attachments that merit a positive valuation, the eighteenth-century culture of sensibility increasingly will adopt a worldview in which culture and custom are (imagined to be) sustained by the amorous rituals specifically shared by men and women. Heterosexuality, "as we know it," emerges within the historical process that more and more came to understand sexual desire between men and women as *the* affective virtue par excellence. Consequently, the range and mobility of the man of feeling's attachments eventually will settle into the libidinal monogamy of "heterosexual" desire. It remains for us to explain how the "virtue" of "heterosexual" desire became necessity, how the endpoint of the culture of sensibility became the proposition that life as such is strictly synonymous with, and wholly reliant on, the romance of an amorous heterosexuality.

An argument on behalf of a queer engagement with sentimentalism does not entail wishing that Sedgwick had written otherwise. Indeed, if Sedgwick's meditation on the male paranoid Gothic, and the Gothic's promotion of a homophobia-cum-epistemology, has deferred a dialectical encounter between the Gothic and the sentimental, that deferral cannot be regretted, for it has made us unquestionably queerer readers of the literary history of sexuality. Attending, for instance, to a figure such as the "man of feeling," we begin to see how the ethical norms of individual feeling and social relation—as theorized by British moral philosophy, and practiced by sentimental literature—might inform and redirect our current understandings of sexuality and normativity. Does "sexuality" absorb the sentiments, or rather, do the sentiments preserve different understandings of self and other, literature and culture, society and history? Does moral philosophy prefigure the advent of "sexuality," or permanently exceed its imperatives? In short, what's love got to do with "sexuality"? A queer engagement with the literary and philosophical traditions of sentimentalism will articulate, more explicitly, what I take to be the often diffuse or "ashamed" motives of queer theory: for instance, childhood, kinship, friendship, companionate intimacy, and social belonging. In this regard, hasn't Sedgwick been preparing us, all along, for a dialogue on love?

Notes

For their wonderfully careful and encouraging readings of this essay, I thank Julie Barmazel, Sarah Churchwell, Joan Dayan, Diana Fuss, Claudia L. Johnson, Andrew Krull, Jeff Nunokawa, Yaakov Perry, and Erwin Rosinberg. Special thanks go to Daniel Novak—best reader, best listener, best friend. Stephen Barber gave this essay its first push, and its last—and throughout, was a characteristically perfect host. At Duke, years ago, Eve Kosofsky Sedgwick instructed my undergraduate self in queer thought, and read, with incomparable encouragement, its earliest essays into queer writing. This one, also, is for her.

1. The scope of sentimentalism exceeds the national borders of England and America. In the interest of symmetry, and to avoid needlessly assimilating other national traditions, this essay shares the parameters of Sedgwick's work, namely, the Anglo-American context.
2. Perhaps it would be useful to recall here a work contemporary to both *The Novel and the Police* and *Epistemology of the Closet*. In *Desire and Domestic Fiction*, Nancy Armstrong argues from these premises: "first, that sexuality is a cultural construct and as such has a history; second, that written

representations of the self allowed the modern individual to become an economic and psychological reality; and third, that the modern individual was first and foremost a woman" (8). If we were to bring together the theses of Miller, Sedgwick, and Armstrong, a rather unexpected composite of the modern liberal subject emerges: "the modern individual was first and foremost" a composite subject, the fantasmatic union of "woman" and always-potentially-"homosexual" homophobic man.

3. While a steady acquaintance with this essay—at least for this reader—fails to diminish its *sui generis* theoretical feel, its premises are intimated in two earlier essays: "Queer Performativity: Henry James's *The Art of the Novel*" (1993) and "Shame in the Cybernetic Fold: Reading Silvan Tomkins" (1995).

4. It should be said that Sedgwick is not alone in turning to sentimentalism for critical inspiration or renewal. The protocols she gathers under the banner of reparative reading already are unmistakably operative in recent queer inquiries that unapologetically theorize in a sentimental key: these include, most notably, Koestenbaum; Miller, *Bringing Out Roland Barthes* and *Place for Us: Essay on the Broadway Musical*. For other recent studies that have offered illuminating treatments of gender, sexuality, and sentimentalism, see the following: Berlant; Burgett; Chapman and Hendler; Clarke; Cvetkovich; Ellison; Haggerty; Johnson; and Stern.

5. Warner's theorizing around the term *heteronormativity* has sharpened our sense of how social and cultural forms ideologically rhyme with the heterosexual couple form, and importantly, how and where this rhyme may be interrupted. My concern is with the critical/professional uptake of the term *heteronormativity*: recourse to the term, in print or discussion, functions too often as theoretical instant gratification, whereby remarking the "heteronormativity" of "x" is tantamount to self-evidently radicalizing and troubling the question of "x." For a demonstration of how *not* to diminish the leverage offered by the term *heteronormativity*, see Berlant and Warner's coauthored essay, "What Does Queer Theory Teach Us about X?" My remarks here take their cue from Sedgwick, "Shame in the Cybernetic Fold," in which she unsettles the theoretical self-evidence that routinizes and banalizes critiques of "biologism."

6. See Guillory for a suggestive discussion of ethics in Foucault's later work, and its implications for (re)orienting our relations to the ethical, the moral, and the aesthetic. I echo here Guillory's characterization of Foucault's understanding of "ethics": "Ethics was by contrast [to modernity's codes of "morality"] a realm in which one chose *between goods*, not between good

and evil, and a mode of action distinguished by possibilities of pleasure rather than a sense of obligation" (36; emphasis original).

7. On ethics as the predicament of one's having "to learn to live," see Derrida, xvii–xx.

8. We also keep open the possibility of more fully articulating a genealogy of normativity, one which would account for the points of contact and divergence between normative ethics and disciplinary norms.

9. Miller notes, in *The Novel and the Police*, that "perhaps the most notable reticence in Foucault's work concerns precisely the reading of literary texts and literary institutions, which, though often and suggestively cited in passing, are never given a role to play within the disciplinary processes under consideration" (viii n. 1). Miller quotes an interview, in which Foucault observes: "On every occasion I made literature the object of a report, not of an analysis and not of a reduction to, or an integration into, the very field of analysis" (viii n. 1). This interview is available in Foucault, *Foucault Live: Collected Interviews*, 150–53.

10. In a close reading of Foucault's *History of Sexuality: An Introduction*, Sedgwick characterizes the book's theoretical provocation as largely dependent on its performative force: "In the unmentioned, only slightly displaced continuity between what the book *says* and what it seems to *make happen*, readers can register the gap of unrationalized rhetorical force that the author has already thematized in the distance between what the repressive hypothesis says (sex is forbidden) and the almost hilarious proliferation of sexualized discourses that it in fact effects" ("Gender Criticism," 280–81; emphases original). According to Sedgwick, "The metonym for *sexuality* that *The History of Sexuality* effectually installs is *homosexuality*" (281; emphases original). Building on Sedgwick's reading of Foucault, I would suggest the following: if *The History of Sexuality* performatively installs homosexuality as the metonym for sexuality, this rhetorical act takes place, and is taken up, in a discursive context shaped by another, even more "unmentioned" and "unrationalized" element in this work: the vast history of literary theme, form, production, and reception. In short, the event called "Foucault" names an event in, and of, *literature*.

11. For a comprehensive study of this topic, see Barker-Benfield. See also Brissenden; Mullan; Todd.

12. In his invaluable study, *The Origins of the English Novel*, McKeon appropriates Marx's notion of "simple abstraction" (in the *Grundrisse*) in his dialectical account of the establishment of the genre, the "novel." "The origins of the English novel," McKeon writes, "occur at the end point of a

long history of 'novelistic usage'—at the moment when this usage has become sufficiently complex to permit a generalizing 'indifference' to the specificity of usages and an abstraction of the category whose integrity is presupposed by that indifference" (19). While this essay cannot offer a full development of this point, I would suggest that McKeon's lesson regarding the novel as "simple abstraction" can offer, mutatis mutandis, a dialectical model for tracing how the generic individuals, "homosexual" and "heterosexual," were historically and culturally consolidated and circulated—not least, I should add, in and through "the novel." See also McKeon, "Historicizing Patriarchy."

13. I am indebted to Jeff Nunokawa and Michael Warner for turning my attention—in two seminars (1996 and 1998, respectively)—to the question of how life and sexuality are mutually figured. For groundbreaking work on how sexuality and the life course are narrated and normalized, see Warner, "Irving's Posterity."

14. Shaftesbury's *Characteristicks* provides an opportunity to begin answering one question posed in Warner's essay, "Homo-Narcissism; or, Heterosexuality": "Why should gender amount to alterity *tout court?*" (193).

Works Cited

Armstrong, Nancy, *Desire and Domestic Fiction: A Political History of the Novel* (New York: Oxford University Press, 1987).

Barker-Benfield, G. J., *The Culture of Sensibility: Sex and Society in Eighteenth-Century Britain* (Chicago: University of Chicago Press, 1992).

Barthes, Roland, *A Lover's Discourse: Fragments,* trans. Richard Howard (New York: Hill and Wang, 1978).

Berlant, Lauren, *The Queen of America Goes to Washington City: Essays on Sex and Citizenship* (Durham: Duke University Press, 1997).

Berlant, Lauren, and Michael Warner, "What Does Queer Theory Teach Us about X?" *PMLA* 110.3 (May 1995): 343–49.

Brenkman, John, *Straight Male Modern: A Cultural Critique of Psychoanalysis* (New York: Routledge, 1993).

Brissenden, R. F., *Virtue in Distress: Studies in the Novel of Sentiment from Richardson to Sade* (London: Macmillan, 1974).

Burgett, Bruce, *Sentimental Bodies: Sex, Gender, and Citizenship in the Early Republic* (Princeton: Princeton University Press, 1998).

Chapman, Mary, and Glenn Hendler, eds., *Sentimental Men: Masculinity and the Politics of Affect in American Culture* (Berkeley: University of California Press, 1999).

Clarke, Eric O., *Virtuous Vice: Homoeroticism and the Public Sphere* (Durham: Duke University Press, 2000).

Cvetkovich, Ann, *Mixed Feelings: Feminism, Mass Culture, and Victorian Sensationalism* (New Brunswick, NJ: Rutgers University Press, 1992).

Derrida, Jacques, *Specters of Marx: The State of the Debt, the Work of Mourning, and the New International*, trans. Peggy Kamuf (New York: Routledge, 1994).

Ellison, Julie, *Cato's Tears and the Making of Anglo-American Emotion* (Chicago: University of Chicago Press, 1999).

Foucault, Michel, *Foucault Live: Collected Interviews, 1961–1984*, ed. Sylvère Lotringer, trans. Lysa Hochroth and John Johnston (New York: Semiotext[e], 1989).

———. *The History of Sexuality: An Introduction*, trans. Robert Hurley (1978) (New York: Vintage, 1990).

Guillory, John, "The Ethical Practice of Modernity: The Example of Reading," in *The Turn to Ethics*, ed. Marjorie Garber, et al. (New York: Routledge, 2000) 29–46.

Haggerty, George E., *Men in Love: Masculinity and Sexuality in the Eighteenth Century* (New York: Columbia University Press, 1999).

Johnson, Claudia L., *Equivocal Beings: Politics, Gender, and Sentimentality in the 1790s—Wollstonecraft, Radcliffe, Burney, Austen* (Chicago: University of Chicago Press, 1995).

Koestenbaum, Wayne, *The Queen's Throat: Opera, Homosexuality, and the Mystery of Desire* (New York: Poseidon Press, 1993).

McKeon, Michael, "Historicizing Patriarchy: The Emergence of Gender Difference in England, 1660–1760," *Eighteenth-Century Studies* 28.3 (1995): 295–322.

———. *The Origins of the English Novel, 1600–1740* (Baltimore: Johns Hopkins University Press, 1987).

Miller, D. A., *Bringing Out Roland Barthes* (Berkeley: University of California Press, 1992).

———. *The Novel and the Police* (Berkeley: University of California Press, 1988).

———. *Place for Us: Essay on the Broadway Musical* (Cambridge: Harvard University Press, 1998).

Mullan, John, *Sentiment and Sociability: The Language of Feeling in the Eighteenth Century* (Oxford: Clarendon Press, 1988).

Sedgwick, Eve Kosofsky, "The Beast in the Closet: James and the Writing of Homosexual Panic," in *Sex, Politics, and Science in the Nineteenth-Century Novel*, ed. Ruth Bernard Yeazell (Baltimore: Johns Hopkins University Press, 1986) 148–86.

———. *Between Men: English Literature and Male Homosocial Desire* (New York: Columbia University Press, 1985).

———. *The Coherence of Gothic Conventions*, 2nd ed. (New York: Methuen, 1986).

———. *A Dialogue on Love* (Boston: Beacon Press, 1999).

———. *Epistemology of the Closet* (Berkeley: University of California Press, 1990).

———. "Gender Criticism," in *Redrawing the Boundaries: The Transformation of English and American Literary Studies*, ed. Stephen Greenblatt and Giles Gunn (New York: Modern Language Association of America, 1992) 271–302.

———. "Paranoid Reading and Reparative Reading; or, You're So Paranoid, You Probably Think This Introduction Is about You," in *Novel Gazing: Queer Readings in Fiction*, ed. Eve Kosofsky Sedgwick (Durham: Duke University Press, 1997) 1–37.

———. "Queer Performativity: Henry James's *The Art of the Novel*." *GLQ: A Journal of Lesbian and Gay Studies* 1.1(1993): 1–16.

———. "Shame in the Cybernetic Fold: Reading Silvan Tomkins," in *Shame and Its Sisters: A Silvan Tomkins Reader*, ed. Eve Kosofsky Sedgwick and Adam Frank (Durham: Duke University Press, 1995) 1–28.

———. *Tendencies* (Durham: Duke University Press, 1993).

Shaftesbury (Anthony Ashley Cooper, 3rd Earl of Shaftesbury), *Characteristicks of Men, Manners, Opinions, Times*, 2 vols., ed. Philip Ayres (Oxford: Clarendon Press, 1999).

Stern, Julia, *The Plight of Feeling: Sympathy and Dissent in the Early American Novel* (Chicago: University of Chicago Press, 1997).

Todd, Janet, *Sensibility: An Introduction* (London and New York: Methuen, 1986).

Warner, Michael, "Homo-Narcissism; or, Heterosexuality," in *Engendering Men: The Question of Male Feminist Criticism*, ed. Joseph A. Boone and Michael Cadden (New York: Routledge, 1990) 190–206.

———. "Introduction," *Fear of a Queer Planet: Queer Politics and Social Theory*, ed. Michael Warner (Minneapolis: University of Minnesota Press, 1993) vii–xxxi. An earlier, slightly different version appears as Warner, "Introduction: Fear of a Queer Planet." *Social Text* 29 (1991): 3–17.

———. "Irving's Posterity," *ELH* 67.3 (2000): 773–99.

○ **Writing Ethics: Reading Cleaving**

$$\binom{6}{}$$

Strategic Constructivism? Sedgwick's Ethics of Inversion

Ross Chambers

In the late 1980s, when Eve Kosofsky Sedgwick was writing *Epistemology of the Closet*, gay and lesbian studies in the United States (particularly the gay part) were riven by a debate that had become acrimonious and unproductive. This was the debate between essentialists, who held that homosexuality is a human universal (like laughing) and as such a constant, independent of cultural and/or historical variations, and constructivists, who held that, like everything else in human culture, homosexuality is a product of the differential relations that constitute discourse, so that its signification varies historically and in different cultural contexts, and what is now called homosexuality is a purely modern phenomenon. Not quite grasping the constructivist position's grounding in structuralist and post-structuralist assumptions and hypotheses, essentialists took it for a nominalism and compared it with "labelling" theory in sociology; they also feared that, since it seemed somehow to imply that homosexuality wasn't really real ("just" a construction), constructivism would give comfort to the homophobic delusions of the right, always ready to view homosexuality as a perverse "lifestyle" that might be chosen, or not chosen, at will. To essentialists, homosexuality could not claim to be real (and hence legitimate) unless there was evidence, in the form of its universal self-sameness, that it was, so to speak, hard-wired into human biology and hence a natural phenomenon. No one seemed to notice that the two positions, essentialist and culturalist, were not necessarily incompatible; and compromise positions tended to rely on words-versus-things talk about supposedly meaning-free sexual-behavior, on the one hand, and what the behavior meant, on the other.

This was the background to a move that Sedgwick makes, in the early pages (40–42) of *Epistemology*, a move that has long intrigued me because it seems simultaneously pragmatic and ethical and the stakes of which I'll try to make a little more explicit in this essay. Acknowledging that, at the time of the book's writing, there was no way the constructivist/essentialist debate could be eluded, Sedgwick nevertheless proceeds to shift the terms of that debate, deftly substituting for the constructivism/essentialism binarism another binary pair, which—although she does not quite say so—actually itself presupposes a constructivist position. This is the minoritizing/universalizing pair, which has proven extremely influential: without quite putting an end to the essentialist/constructivist debate, Sedgwick's move has effectively backgrounded it, and allowed an ongoing conversation to bracket it out by, as it were, changing the subject.

She makes this substitutive move, Sedgwick explains, for pragmatic reasons: "it would seem to me that gay-affirmative work does well when it aims to minimize its reliance on any particular account of the origin of sexual preference and identity in individuals" (41). She means that, in a homophobic environment, it is difficult to argue a constructivist position without its being misinterpreted as implying the possibility of "choice," and appropriated therefore as support for "the overarching, hygienic Western fantasy of a world without any more homosexuals in it" (42). That Sedgwick's move is an example of what might be called strategic constructivism—a constructivism that disallows the question of how homosexuality comes about in order to concentrate on the issue of what it means and what social "work" it does—will be a small part of my argument in this essay. But I want principally to suggest that the stakes of Sedgwick's shift of emphasis and change of terms are not exhausted by the pragmatic advantages she claims for her move.

The terms "minoritizing" and "universalizing" that she prefers because they displace the unproductive and counterproductive essentialist/constructivist debate are not understood by Sedgwick, as the terms "essentialist" and "constructivist" seem largely to have been understood by the protagonists in that debate, as mutually exclusive alternatives one to the other, constituting an either/or proposition. Instead, Sedgwick asserts (and goes on to demonstrate), "minoritizing" and "universalizing" describe views that are subscribed to simultaneously, in modern culture, as definitions of homosexuality. In twentieth century culture's understanding of homosexuality there is thus a definitional "incoherence," and it is this incoherence in turn—given a homophobic general culture—that accounts both for the dynamics of the institution of the closet and for the energy with which the closet is policed.

Most moderately to well-educated Western people . . . seem to share a similar understanding of homosexual definition. . . . [This understanding] is organized around a radical and irreducible incoherence. It holds the minoritizing view that there is a distinct population of persons who "really are" gay; at the same time, it holds the universalizing views [sic] that sexual desire is an unpredictable solvent of stable identities; and that at least a male homosexual identity and modern masculinist culture may require for their maintenance the scape-goating crystallization of a same-sex male desire that is widespread and in the first place internal. (85)

The closet, that is, is a device to deny the incoherence by policing the separateness of the "really gay" from the general instability of identities, and which thus, when read symptomatologically, reveals that general instability. This argument is presented as an *"alternative* (although not equivalent)" (40) to the essentialist versus constructivist question. As such, it has the advantage that it "can do some of the same analytic work as the latter binarism" (40), but without leading to the pitfalls that arise when constructivism is misconstrued as implying choice. Such an "alternative," then, is not an either/or proposition; it is another way (possibly one among several) of getting antihomophobic work done.

To my mind something is being both acknowledged and backgrounded here. I mean that the analysis of the closet as an institution that arises from the incoherence of twentieth century perceptions of homosexuality that are simultaneously minoritizing and universalizing is an analysis that can only be made on constructivist (not essentialist) assumptions, something that Sedgwick neither denies nor affirms—she simply does not specify it. My own argument will make this point clearer, because I want to claim, and will try to show, that the minoritizing/universalizing binary is only apparently incoherent because it arises as a predictable consequence of *any* social taxonomy (such as the hetero/homosexual taxonomy) that attempts to sort people, for social purposes, into "classes" or "kinds"—a clearly cultural, hence constructivist position. Sorting of this kind, which occurs in every society, inevitably creates supposedly discrete categories out of what is arguably a continuum of differences; the categories, though, are actually in differential relation and so, being part of a single signifying system (or structure)—in the case of hetero/homosexuality a simple binary—can never be fully distinct one from the other. As a consequence, any such category will be minoritizing (or, noticing that some social categories, such as the class of straight, white males in Western society are minorities only in a numerical sense, one might prefer to say localizing) because its members will have been selected, contrastively, from a larger, global pool. But the membership of such a category (say "straight," but also "gay") will also be potentially universal, to the extent that, in a signifying system such as the hetero/homosexual binarism, each unit of signification harbors what Jacques Derrida calls the "trace" of the whole system, and so is inseparable from the rest of the system. No straightness without gayness and no gayness without straightness means, logically (by deconstruction 101) that both gay and straight are potentially universalizing categories, even though, "on the ground," one such category claims universality for itself and, by minoritizing the other (the prime function of the closet), denies it its potential universality.

Another approach to this constructivist conundrum would be to say, again with Derrida, that it is the "law of genre" that there be no occurrences that are not generic (they necessarily partake of the genre system) but also that no occurrence "belongs" exclusively to any given genre; there will be an overflow, and the overflow is a consequence of the logic of difference that governs the relation between genres. So if the signifying system offers the categories (genres) gay/straight (or, to complexify a bit, gay/bisexual/straight), then every individual will be assignable to one of those categories in a minoritizing, localizing way, while each of the categories, in a universalizing or globalizing way, will be capable of embracing the members of other categories, who overflow genre limits to the extent that, partaking of the same genre system, all genres harbor traces of all the others.

So if the incoherence that Sedgwick discerns in the twentieth-century understanding of homosexuality is, as she says, "irreducible," it is because such incoherence is a consequence of the cultural practice of sorting people into kinds that are in differential relation one with the other. The same kind of incoherence prevails in all other such classificatory systems (those of gender and of race, for example). My purpose, though, is not to *out* Sedgwick as a closet Derridean, although her move could certainly be described as substituting a certain deconstructive constructivism for the Foucault version of constructivist theory that was espoused, or rejected, in the essentialist/constructivist debate. There is no real point in outing Sedgwick's constructivism because she makes it clear from the start that her book's interpretations "may privilege constructivist over essentialist, universalizing over minoritizing, and gender-transitive over separatist understandings" (13). More interesting to me, and more to my present purpose, is the fact that she goes on to assert, in the same long sentence, that "nevertheless the space of permission for this work and the depth of the intellectual landscape in which it might have a contribution to make owe everything to the wealth of essentialist, minoritizing and separatist gay thought and struggle" (13). What this wonderfully even-handed and generous sentence reveals is that, although Sedgwick's positions may be constructivist (etc.), she does not regard constructivist, universalizing, gender-transitive thought as incompatible with essentialist, minoritizing and separatist thinking. Rather she presents the one (essentialism) as the condition of the other (constructivism)—this being, of course, a standard deconstructionist position on the question of essentialism and/or logocentrism. Essentialism and constructivism are interdependent: not the same as each other but not fully separate either—alternatives without being equivalent.

But in the same way and the same sense, as I've already suggested, the incoherence of the co-occurring twentieth-century definitions of homosexuality as both minoritizing and universalizing does not imply their incompatibility, but only reflects the logic of difference. "Minoritizing" homosexuality is itself a form of essentialism (it reifies a category); "universalizing" homosexuality, on the other hand, is a form of constructivism (it acknowledges that categories are caught up in systems of signification); but both (the essentialism of) minoritizing and (the constructivism of) universalizing definitions (alias constructions) are *allowed for*, therefore, as incoherent but not incompatible consequences of the logic of difference; they go together, alternatives that can't be fully disentangled from each other. And as it happens, in Sedgwick's analysis, the closet itself turns out to participate in the same minoritizing-universalizing, constructivist/essentialist, alternative-but-not-equivalent incoherence, since it simultaneously scapegoats a group (minoritizing it) and universalizes the situation of that group by proving to be, as Sedgwick demonstrates at length, "centrally representative of [the culture's] motivating passions and contradictions." The closet is thus, as she says, a "curious space that is both internal and marginal to the culture" (56). This curious space, which is also the minoritizing/universalizing space of homosexuality in modern culture (like the closet, "representative . . . even while marginalized by [cultural] orthodoxies" [57]), is the space reserved, I'll propose, for that which has the status of the paradigmatic. It is the paradigmatic, in my view, that produces an incoherence but not an incompatibility, an alternativity without equivalence, between localizing essentialism and a constructivism that is globalizing in its effect. And it is therefore because Sedgwick adopts a paradigmatic perspective on homosexuality, as an alternative to the essentialist/constructivist debate, that she is able to see it as generating a minoritizing/universalizing incoherence in modern culture—an incoherence that, although she does not point it out, just happens to be reflected in the essentialist (minoritizing)/constructivist (universalizing) debate itself. A debate in which, therefore, her book is itself obviously, inescapably and incoherently, participating.

I know you may be feeling dizzy. You also have the right to expect me to elaborate on my understanding of the paradigmatic, since the term is mine, not Sedgwick's. But let me first recapitulate a bit. I'm claiming that Sedgwick is well described as a paradigmatic thinker, whose book discusses the status of homosexuality in twentieth-century culture as a paradigmatic social "kind," in the way that the epistemology of the closet explores the structure and dynamics of the closet as likewise paradigmatic—that is, as both representative and marginal, or minoritized—within that same culture. The paradigmatic category (homosexuality) or phenomenon (the closet) is one that is, without real paradox, simultaneously particular and characteristic, representative of a generality; and that is so because it plays out a consequence of the logic of difference, which is that identity can only exist in, and as an effect of, a structure of differences that makes "identity" something that cannot be self-identical. In this respect, the book represents a genuine intervention in the essentialist/constructivist debate, showing the sense in which the two opposed sides are actually talking, from different angles, about the same issue: the paradigmatic character of homosexuality. But at the same time, it constructively shifts the terms of the debate (forgive the pun) in the direction of a question—the question I define as that of the paradigmatic—that is claimed to be both pragmatically less hazardous and epistemologically more cogent, because it eschews the vexed (and perhaps insoluble) question of origins in favor of what can be known: the meaning and value of homosexuality in modern Western culture.

Now, beyond these epistemological and pragmatic claims, there is another motive in Sedgwick's paradigmatizing move, which is the one I most want to stress because I understand it as ethical. For, as I've already hinted, it matters whether a social category, and the minoritizing/universalizing dynamics such a category is capable of generating, is regarded as *exceptional* in relation to a norm or a canon—a single "measuring stick"—or whether, instead, the category is regarded as one paradigm (a paradigm, if you will, of the human) in relation to other categories that are held to be equally—neither more nor less—paradigmatic. In the first instance, which can be illustrated by the case of homosexuality (regarded ideologically as a deviance from what Michael Warner has taught us to call heteronormativity), the category is subject to scapegoating, for example in the form of the closet. The function of the closet as a scapegoating institution is to police the dominant social status of the category or categories that, being held to constitute the norm, abrogate to themselves not only a paradigmatic character but also the status of unique paradigm. They claim to be *the* paradigm of the human, uniquely and exclusively the paradigm of the human, as opposed to being *a* paradigm (among others) of the human. The scapegoating functions to freeze, or essentialize, the minoritized category into the status of the exceptional or the abnormal, or even the abject, with the result that the universalizing potential of the minoritized category goes unrecognized in favor of the dominant class, which is not wrong in claiming to be paradigmatic but unjust in claiming to be uniquely and exclusively so.

In introducing the terms minoritizing and universalizing, then, Sedgwick was implying (without, I think, using the term) the paradigmatic status of homosexuality as a social kind, while arguing rather more explicitly for the paradigmatic status of the closet, as that which enacts, with respect to homosexuality, the peculiarly incoherent structure of social kinds in general, both "representative" and minoritized. Her ethical move, in *Epistemology*, consists, then, of asserting that homosexuality should not be understood as an exception, and hence as abnormal or pathological, in relation to a putative norm, but as paradigmatic, a concept that short-circuits ideas of normalcy and abnormality because paradigms exist, delusions of uniquely paradigmatic classes aside, *only* in relation to other paradigms, as members of a set. (If this were not the case, we would not need the word paradigm at all.) In this, she is thus reversing the value[1] assigned ideologically to homosexuality by according it the same kind of status, as an object of knowledge, as is enjoyed by those social kinds whose paradigmatic status is taken for granted and is not thought to generate an incoherence, in the way that, for example, the paradigmatic status of heterosexuality is assumed and constitutes heteronormativity. For if it is possible for straight people, as a social kind, to be generally understood as models of the human, without their being coextensive with the human population (which includes gay people), then it is possible, by the logic of the paradigm, to reverse the status of exceptionality assigned to homosexuality by showing the sense in which gay people, as a kind, are also definable in the same way. This is exactly what Sedgwick shows twentieth-century definitions of homosexuality perform. Because they are simultaneously minoritizing and universalizing, they point, as it were in spite of themselves, to the paradigmatic status of homosexuality.

The move Sedgwick makes, in showing that the marginalized is a misrecognized "norm," is like the solidarity she assumes between essentialism and constructivism, in that it is a characteristically deconstructive move. However it also has much in common, I'll suggest, with what has been a modern tradition in gay and lesbian writing itself, a tradition I'll refer to, for the sake of another cheap pun, as that of the ethics of inversion. This ethical move consists of taking what is regarded, in dominant ideologies, as minor, secondary, marginal, accidental, or abject (e.g., women, bodies, sexuality, criminality, colonial people) and showing it, instead, to be paradigmatic, in the sense that it is not only particular but also universalizing, both an "identity" and a model of the human. The explicit work Sedgwick's epistemology performs, its reversal of the positional value of the closet (not just a device particular to the oppression of homosexual people but one that can also be perceived as a model, and hence definitional, social institution in modern culture), is emblematic of that move, which has as its immediate corollary the similar reversal of position and value, from "exceptional" deviancy to paradigmatic status, that she foreshadows in pointing to homosexuality's "incoherent" modern status.

Paradigm is one of those messy words (like *subject*) that require definition whenever they are used. When I say *paradigm*, some will think of the verb paradigms they had to learn when acquiring a foreign language, or indeed of grammatical categories themselves (which are also a set of morphological forms). Others will think of Thomas Kuhn's use of the term in *The Structure of Scientific Revolutions* to refer to a general model or matrix within which certain hypotheses are conceivable while others that might be conceivable under a different paradigm are excluded. The definitional difficulty, I think, derives precisely from the minoritizing/universalizing "incoherence" brilliantly identified by Sedgwick as characteristic of homosexual definition in the twentieth century and which I am suggesting, more generally, is the definitional marker of paradigm status. A paradigm functions differently, I suggest, according as one considers it in relation to the population it defines or in relation to the set of paradigms of which it is itself a member.

In relation to its own membership, a paradigm has a *templating* function; it selects a factor of equivalence that makes its members interchangeable. Verbs, I was taught in grade school, are "doing words"; this hypothesis, a Kuhnian might say, fits the paradigm, that doesn't. Thus any member of the paradigm can substitute for any other, and the membership can be enumerated as in a list. This is the minoritizing function of the paradigm (indeed, it is in essence a stereotyping function). For example, in the sentence "I love apple pie," I can substitute "like" or "hate" or "want" for "love" (they are all verbs); and for "apple pie" I can substitute "ice cream" or "Mary" or "Jim" (they are all nouns). I can even substitute "love" for "apple pie," (i.e., "I love love"), since the same group of phonemes that is spelled love happens to be a member of the paradigm of nouns as well as of the paradigm of verbs. On the other hand, to say "I apple pie you, darling" would be more problematic. But population shifts from paradigm to paradigm *do* occur quite easily, and in fact it is common practice among English-speakers to verb a noun or noun a verb in this way. It is easy to imagine a context in which "I apple-pie you" might occur (pet language between lovers, for example). These phenomena, of shared ("love") and shifting ("apple pie") membership between and among paradigms—phenomena, that is, of categorical instability—arise because paradigms relate differently to their set than they do to their membership, and consequently have a universalizing or *modeling* function in addition to their minoritizing, templating function.

The relation of the paradigm to the other paradigms with which it forms a total set is not one of equivalence but of alternativity. It is not that one paradigm substitutes for another but that it presents itself as an alternative—but alternative within a totality that gives all the paradigms constituting the set a "family" resemblance. They are not aliens to one another, but related differentially. Thus the paradigm of verbs differs from the paradigm of nouns, but shares with it the quality of grammaticality; and a scientific paradigm can be replaced by an alternative paradigm only to the extent that the latter is also scientific. In the same way, homosexuality and heterosexuality are alternative ways of being sexual. . . . Thus, any paradigm has a universalizing potential with respect to the set, of which it is representative—a potential limited, however, by the universalizing potential of every other paradigm in the set, since all paradigms are likewise representative with respect to that set. The function of the paradigm, in this case, is not to template a membership but to model the whole set of paradigms, which does not consist therefore of a number of listable items but constitutes a structure of differences. When Sedgwick defines minoritizing/universalizing as an "*alternative* (although not equivalent)" (40) to essentialist/constructivist, she is in effect describing each of these pairs as the definition of an epistemological paradigm, and hence as being in structural (differential) relation to the other. They are not members of the same paradigm (in which case they would be interchangeable). Rather, she is defining her own move as effecting what Kuhn would call a paradigm *shift*—a shift made possible by the relation of difference-but-sameness, of alternativity but not equivalence, that prevails among paradigms that are members of a common set.

In the structure of differences that is a set of paradigms, the positional value of each paradigm is determined as a function of the negative relation it has to the other paradigm(s) in the set: *gay* signifies "not straight," and *straight* signifies "not gay"; similarly in the set of racial paradigms, black is "not white, not yellow," white is "not yellow, not black," and so forth. Whereas it is possible, internally to a given paradigm, to rehearse more or less successfully the criteria of equivalence that apply to members of that paradigm, the differential relation between and among paradigms is signaled by the evidence, often misrecognized because it is in the form of "traces," that negative elements (that which the paradigm is not) are a positive component of any given paradigm's definition (since it is not a paradigm except under the condition of there being other paradigms in a set). Gay traits show up in straight people and straight traits in gay people; black traits show up in white people and white traits in black; verbs are "nounable" and nouns "verbable." Or constructivism shows up in the minoritizing/universalizing epistemological paradigm, which is not an equivalent, but an alternative, as we saw above, of the essentialist/constructivist paradigm. And so on. In a structure there are only relations of difference; no element of the structure has an essence that would be proper to it, but instead a value that is determined, relationally, by the play of differences that constitute the structure; thus, shifts can occur. In its minoritizing role, the paradigm seems compatible with essentialist thinking, because it fixes its members into templates and describes them as equivalent; but in its universalizing aspect— as a model, not a template—it is compatible only with constructivist thinking, because its modeling is a matter of positionality and the logic of difference.

That shifts can occur is one thing, however; that they tend not to occur, or to occur only infrequently and partially, is another. The relative stability of sets of paradigms and of the identities they construct arises because they are so frequently subject, like structures in general, to the phenomenon of centralization, to which Derrida pointed in his early essay "Structure, Sign and Play," perhaps his best known piece. The practice of power results in one structural element (for present purposes, one paradigm in a set) being promoted, by a kind of coup de force, to a position of centrality, even though, as a purely formal entity, a structure does not and cannot have a center. The effect of this social phenomenon of centralization is to inhibit the "play" (Derrida's word) of differences, and thus to hold the value of all the remaining, ex-centric elements of the structure in place, a place *now* defined, in relation to the central element, as secondary, derived, inessential, inferior, and so on.

This is the move of normativity; it consists of raising straightness, whiteness or maleness, for example, to the status of a unique and exclusive measuring stick (or canon) against which nonstraightness, nonwhiteness and nonmaleness are found wanting. The strict policing of category membership by institutions such as the closet—the imposition of an identity—is part and parcel of this effort to maintain the conventional values of what is, in effect, now a hierarchical "system" rather than a structure; it does so by inhibiting the transferability between and among categories that is the sign of their differential relationality as elements of a structure and promotes an understanding of identity as paradigmatic. And it is in this context of centralization as a power-laden phenomenon that queerness can be understood. Queerness is, exactly, the evidence of continuity that nevertheless persists, occluded as it may be in such a regime, between or among paradigms that are supposed, for hegemonic purposes, to be separate, distinct and unbudging. As the manifestation of instability in a supposedly firm system, queerness is what Sedgwick describes, referring to the universalizing definition of homosexual desire, as an "unpredictable sol-vent of stable identities" (85). And we can identify her own term, *incoherence*—designating the minoritizing/universalizing dynamic of the paradigm—as a syn-onym, therefore, of what, since her book was written, many of us have taken to calling queerness.

But it is queerness, then—that is, the usually misrecognized or denied and so spectral "presence" of the equivalence-traits of a given paradigm in the other paradigm(s) of a set—that makes it possible to see, in any given paradigm, *a* model, as opposed to *the* model or norm, of the total population that is defined by a set of paradigms; queerness, that is, that destabilizes and unseats the hege-mony exercised by centralized norms. And the closet, in Sedgwick's episte-mology, is a quintessentially queer institution. Designed as a way of policing a minoritizing (and essentializing) of homosexuality, it inevitably *leaks*—having the structure of an open secret, in which (because "it takes one to know one") everyone shares—and in so doing produces a phenomenon of universalizing that demonstrates homosexuality's paradigmatic, not exceptional, status. Such queerness, then, or in Sedgwick's lexicon such incoherence, is what makes pos-sible the ethical reversal as a consequence of which the supposedly exceptional and abnormal (e.g., the closet as the marker of the stigmatization of homosex-uality) comes to be reclassified as representative or paradigmatic. And as a result of this reversal, the canonical (i.e., the ideological promotion of one par-adigm to a position of centrality as the unique and exclusive measuring stick) is unseated from its position of centrality to the extent that its own membership turns out to be not discontinuous with the membership of supposedly marginal categories and hence to be inseparable from that population. Or indeed, as Sedgwick gleefully points out, in the case of the Western literary canon and homosexuality, the two can be virtually indistinguishable; the canon is queer.

Has there ever been a gay Socrates?
Has there ever been a gay Shakespeare?
Has there ever been a gay Proust?
Does the Pope wear a dress? If these questions startle, it is not least as tau-tologies. A short answer, though a very incomplete one, might be that not only have there been a gay Socrates, Shakespeare and Proust, but that their names are Socrates, Shakespeare and Proust; and, beyond that, legion—dozens, or hundreds of the most *centrally* canonic figures in what the monoculturalists are pleased to consider "our" culture, as indeed, always in different forms and sense, in every other. (52, empha-sis added)

Thus the unseating of the canon is at the same time a promotion of homosexuality, from the status of exceptionality to that of being itself a paradigm (and hence, potentially, a canon). That it remains paradigmatic only, however, despite its near indistinguishability from the canon, is indicated by Sedgwick's immediate relativizing of that (Western) canon, as only one among several, as soon as she has made her point by pointing out that its population is massively homosexual. Even more interestingly, the move that simultaneously promotes homosexuality and demotes the canon to the same status (that of the paradigmatic) takes the form of an *unveiling of the obvious*: the questions are tautologies, the Pope does indeed wear a dress. That is, the paradigmatic status of a category whose exceptionality had been constructed as an effect of another category, also paradigmatic, passing itself off as a norm — "the" canon — is presented as something that was always already known, but misrecognized.

And this is the move that is executed too, although with less brio and more rhetorical caution, when Sedgwick offers minoritizing/universalizing — the definition of paradigmatic status — as "an *alternative* (though not equivalent)" to essentialist/structuralist, that is as an other paradigm, capable of "doing some of the same analytic work" (40). Her paradigm shift could be described by Nietzsche's word, *Umwertung*, the reversal of values (one model is unseated from a position of centrality while another candidate is raised to the status of model). But what the move does is to restore to its recognizably legitimate place (that of another paradigm) something that had been, inappropriately, misperceived, marginalized, occulted or forgotten, the question of homosexuality's origin, in this case, having been given a position of near exclusivity in gay-affirmative work while other questions, or at least one other question, equally legitimate and not unrelated but more "telling" (40), languished in darkness. A paradigm shift always consists, in this way, of promoting to paradigm status an element — already present in (as "trace") or implied by, an existing, dominant paradigm — that was thought to be nonparadigmatic; and so it brings with it a blinding sense of self-evidence. The response among interested parties tends to be "Aha!" (surprised recognition) and/or a certain ruefulness: "Why didn't I see that?"

This is the effect of unveiling (*a-letheia*; from *lethe*, oblivion) that is aimed at, I think, by the various turnarounds and reversals of value (*Umwertungen*) that have been essayed in the already quite long history of the ethics of inversion, which is itself part of the history of homosexuality's modern emergence. The project is always to show that a certain taken-for-granted social hierarchization, a centralization of focus and interest, a hypertrophy of normalcy and consequently an uncritical naturalization of corollary concepts like deviancy and exceptionality, have obscured the evidence of an "alternative" truth (aletheia), and inhibited possibilities of flexibility and fluidity that are inherent

in uncenteredness. Let me use Proust here as a marker for that ethical tradition; Proust who strategically occupies the final chapter of *Epistemology*, after
the readings of the book's other heroes: Melville, Nietzsche, Wilde, and James.
Thus, there is symmetry and an implied equivalence between Sedgwick's strin-
gent and strenuous reading of *A la Recherche du temps perdu* and her virtuoso
introduction, from which I have so far been drawing. Proust's novel begins in
a world—the world of Combray—in which both homosexuality and what
Proust calls sadism exist, but only marginally; and gets gradually taken over by
the figure of Charlus, in whom, as Sedgwick puts it (and the emphasis is hers),
Proust presents *"the spectacle of the closet as the truth of the homosexual"* (321)
and—I will add—the truth of the homosexual as a truth about the instability
of the social universe (to which Proust wishes to contrast the extratemporal
essences of the aesthetic). More particularly, it is a truth about the instability
of a strictly hierarchized social universe, policed most notably by snobbery; it
is in this supposedly firm system that homosexuality, policed by the closet, plays
its universalizing role of "unpredictable solvent of stable identities" (85).

But it is not just that, in *La Recherche*, the "race maudite"—analogously to
all the bands and "petits clans" in the novel—turns out to be virtually everywhere by the time the novel ends; it is also that, as Sedgwick shows, the novel
makes the act of reading it an exemplification of the dynamics of inversion by
turning the scapegoating "spectacle" of the closet into a universalizing phenomenon, in an enactment of the axiom that "it takes one to know one." The
scapegoat is a figure charged with the "sins" of a collectivity so that the collectivity can divest itself of those sins, (i.e., normalize itself, by banishing the scapegoat). To reverse the direction of this dynamic, as Proust's novel does, is thus to
charge scapegoating readers with the very stigma (in this case homosexuality)
that the scapegoating identifies. The pleasure that "we" take, like the narrator,
in reading homosexuality out of Charlus's comportment, also designates *us* as
members of Charlus's tribe. From being exceptional (and hence scapegoated),
Charlus comes to exert in this way the universalizing, as well as the minoritizing, function of the paradigmatic (not for nothing does the narrator refer to
other figures as "un Charlus"). And he is paradigmatic in a particularly economic and telling sense, since the readability that is responsible for his minoritization, by making his closetedness a spectacle, simultaneously universalizes
both his homosexuality *and* his closetedness. A society that closets homosexuality, in other words, is a closeted society; it occults a truth about itself.

All of which is confirmed, a contrario—although I am certainly betraying
here the complexity of Sedgwick's own scrupulous argument—by the opacity
of Albertine, whom neither the narrator, to his anguish, nor the reader can
read: "the crossing of an axis of sexual desire by an axis of gender-definition

has . . . the effect of guaranteeing . . . the availability of hidden bolt-holes for the coverture of meaning, intention, regard" (239). It is as if Albertine, cast in the role of love object, quits the domain of social observation altogether and consequently cannot be available to be read paradigmatically (of no one is it said that she is "une Albertine"). For the same reason, she is unavailable also — lesbian though she may be — for the function, enacted by Charlus, of outing the reader as the one whom it takes to know one.[2]

For lack of space, I invite my readers, at this point, to construct in their own mind the lineaments of the ethical tradition of reversal and unveiling that I call the ethics of inversion, the tradition for which I have used Proust as a marker and in which I place Eve Sedgwick herself. Some names to consider, in addition to those, from Melville to Sedgwick, that have already come up: Whitman, Gide, Colette, Cocteau, Forster, Ackerley, Stein, Barnes, Genet, Wittig, Hocquenguem. It is not necessary to be gay, however, in order to participate in this tradition, in the way that it is not necessary to be a woman to produce *écriture féminine*, although the evidence is that some personal affinity with queerdom in one or other of its manifold forms is a big help. And that said, there is a recognizably lesbian emphasis (having to do with women, sexuality, and the body) as well as a male emphasis (often entangled with questions of coloniality and postcolonialism). There is also, inevitably, a minoritizing or localizing emphasis (e.g., Wittig or Hocquenguem) and a universalizing emphasis of the kind we have just glanced at in Proust. To me it is not obvious that the inversion of values that is the project of this tradition necessarily entails an actual paradigm shift of the kind whose implications I have been exploring in *Epistemology*; but it does always entail the simultaneous promotion and demotion, to paradigmatic status, of, respectively, categories dismissed as exceptional, abnormal, abject (or at best secondary, marginal, and ex-centric), and categories held to be central, normal, canonical, and hence uniquely representative.

Which means finally that it is also, inevitably if often purely intuitively, a tradition of strategic constructivism — that is, of *constructivism* because it takes a philosophy of difference and relationality, rather than one of self-identity and essence, in order to unsettle (if not unseat) the power invested in centrality, normality, and hierarchy, policed by scapegoating; but of *strategic* constructivism because, as Sedgwick saw, constructivism that straightforwardly shows its constructivist hand is always subject to essentialist misinterpretation, and gets read as a philosophy of inauthenticity. Better, by a kind of feint, to conduct a metaphorical guerilla war that can be enacted novelistically, for example, rather than theoretically (we are disappointed by *Corydon* or Proust's "Race maudite" chapter, but delighted by *Les Faux-Monnayeurs* [The Counterfeiters] and *La*

Recherche), or through a barrage of epigrams and paradoxes (in the style of Wilde), or various performances of impertinence (à la Cocteau at one end of the scale, à la Genet at the other, with someone like Ackerley, perhaps, more or less in-between). It is only relatively recently that in some quarters and in certain societies critical work has itself begun, as Sedgwick and others demonstrate, to exercise the kind of solvent function that the ethics of inversion has always taken as its project. But it too, as perhaps the foregoing take on *Epistemology* will have suggested, prefers to make moves and to work pragmatically and on the terrain—that is, to strategize—rather than to lay down its theoretical cards (as I have done), and to make itself vulnerable, in a hostile universe, by slowing down the pace, occupying an uncompromising position, and holding forth, peremptorily and authoritatively, in the manner of a Master.

For perhaps the most salient feature of strategic constructivism, in the end, is that its strategy is modest: more tactical than it is strategic. Strategy, in Michel de Certeau's often-quoted definition, is grounded in mastery of a certain terrain (the military consequence of centrality); tactics are made possible, and simultaneously required, by the circumstance of ungroundedness that is brought about, for the tactician, by the other's strategic or masterful possession of the terrain. Strategic (tactical) constructivism consists of drawing the consequences of structural ungroundedness for systemic groundedness—for example, the incoherence of the closet as an institution of heteronormative society, and hence the paradigmatic character of homosexuality—but without seeming to acknowledge the ungroundedness one also assumes, that is, the actually tactical character of what "passes" (I use the term advisedly) as a strategy. A paradigm shift is the perfect exemplification of such a maneuver, since paradigms can only shift for structural reasons (i.e., the paradigm is itself a constructivist concept), yet the shift functions, not as something that looks like a dodgy move acknowledging its own inauthenticity, but as the strategic unveiling of an alternative truth. Strategic constructivists understand (and exploit) the vulnerability entailed by "mastery of a certain terrain"; they take advantage of it, but they do so without either making themselves vulnerable in turn to the ideological maneuvers of mastery (which declare constructivism illusory and/or inauthentic) or making concessions of their own to mastery's own attractions (by seeking, in turn, a position of authority, centrality, canonicity or groundedness, which would entail claiming to be in possession of "the" truth).

It is in this latter respect that strategic constructivism differs from its close cousin, strategic essentialism, which—although it is a constructivist tactic—mimes essentialist positions as the particular guerilla move, the feint that it favors. By contrast, *Epistemology of the Closet* fails spectacularly to take essentialist positions. At the same time, though, it refuses essentialist/constructivist debate, so that its actual constructivism is more enacted than it is claimed, and yet is *not disclaimed* either. (Indeed, as we saw, Sedgwick explicitly assumes it, as a constructivism that understands its debt to essentialism.) To be a strategic *constructivist* is to understand that essentialist constructions—including hierarchical, centralized, normative, social formations—can be outmaneuvered without being essentialist oneself (whether strategically or otherwise). But that also means *without reifying constructivism*, that is, without essentializing it as masterful possession of the terrain of truth. Strategic constructivism is thus not only tactical but also in some cases—notably that of Proust or Sedgwick—eminently tactful. In other cases (e.g., Genet) its self-questioning mode of questioning can take the form of a performance of impertinence. So although in my title there is a question-mark, it does not mean I'm dubious about the existence of such a thing as strategic constructivism, or its definition, or even about Sedgwick's practice of it, although I can always expect to be proven wrong. It does mean that I wanted to indicate that strategic constructivism is a self-questioning practice of dubiety, whether tactful or impertinent or somewhere in-between. It comes, so to speak, with its own (self-addressed) question-mark attached. A question-mark that keeps it honest.

Notes

1. I am using the term *value* both in the word's common meaning (as a synonym of worth) and, more technically, to refer to effects of positioning within a structure (English vowels, for example, vary in value as their phonetic environment varies).
2. This paragraph defines reading as the discovery and exploration of the paradigmatic character of the other, and hence of one's own self-otherness.

Works Cited

Derrida, Jacques, "Structure, Sign and Play in the Discourse of the Human Sciences," in *Writing and Difference*, trans. Alan Bass (Chicago: University of Chicago Press, 1978).
———. "The Law of Genre," trans. Avital Ronell, *Glyph* 7(1980): 176–232; reprinted *Critical Inquiry* 7.1: 55-81.
Sedgwick, Eve Kosofsky. *Epistemology of the Closet* (Berkeley: University of California Press, 1990).
Warner, Michael, ed., *Fear of a Queer Planet* (Minneapolis: University of Minnesota Press, 1993).

7

Eve's Queer Child

Kathryn Bond Stockton

I am going to break a secret.

He wasn't so much fat as well-endowed with ears. With big mouth and big ears, he seemed to be fashioned with intercourse in mind—the kind of talk that, even so, runs along a spectrum of refinement and perception. A small scholar, really, with little musical vibrations as fetching as picked up airs. His sallies were the delight of the house, even if he always was as puzzling as a page in an unknown language. Unconscious and irresponsible and amusing.

Of course, I refer to Eve's love child, the one she imagined she had had with Henry James. The one who reveals a Freudian twist not so uncommon in the academic world: the fantasy of having a baby with . . . an author; of having with a writer a protégé of sorts, in order to reproduce yourself as his pupil. Eve must have relished the thought to herself: my child is the child of Henry James. Often, she must have felt satisfaction in thinking their child "his pupil" in print, in knowing she had forced this adoption on an obliging bachelor (since, being dead, what could he do?). Had she channeled him? (One recalls her interest in Merrill and ghosts.) It doesn't really matter. It's enough to say what has never been said: Eve Kosofsky Sedgwick wrote Henry James' "The Pupil," then contrived to have it discovered and established in the Jamesian canon as a story he wrote and even published in 1891.

I have it on rumor (from sources deep within academic publishing) that Eve handed off her "Pupil" in a mock-Wildean fashion to Professor Michael Moon, who, I am told in an unconfirmed report, took the discovery to be in earnest.

(One wonders.) The story to date: Sedgwick told Moon she had found an uncatalogued Jamesian manuscript ("up Moon's alley") at the New York Public Library. Sedgwick would arrange to leave it for Moon, if he wished, in the cloak-room of Grand Central Station, where a gentleman of specified description would be setting a handbag on the floor; Moon was then to drop his glove (a kid glove was the sign), whereby he might retrieve the bag (in place of the kid).[1] As we know, Moon went on to write about "The Pupil"—*gants de suede* and all—in his essay from 1991, entitled: "A Small Boy and Others: Sexual Disorientation in Henry James, Kenneth Anger, and David Lynch." What few if any suspected at the time was that this version of "The Pupil" was Sedgwick's, whatever Moon himself knew or not to be the case. How it came to pass that former copies of "The Pupil" are gone without a trace—or, more ghostly, carry Eve's words in their older print (I have seen a few—I tell you that I have)—is a mystery that escapes me.

As for Eve's authorship, this was to be her most open secret—her production of this child an obvious test case for her theories. For anyone knowing her most cherished topics should have been able to spot Eve outing herself all over. Her syntax alone, its parentheticals meant to function as charming ordeals, along with her penchant for French verbal gems—vocabulary as a lapidary exercise—were not *sui generis*. They were the signs of a woman at pains to reveal her love; her love for a man's syntactical forms and the intimate surface of his words. (Eve is a fetishist of the first order; attached not to shoes—or even to gloves—but to textures of terms.) More so, her naughtiest personal essay, "A Poem is Being Written," complete with its faux-Freudian title recalling "A Child is Being Beaten," linked her own fascination with spanking, first as a child, later as a woman, to her passion for being a pupil of poetry (from the age of eight). This exploration was nothing if not a revelation that the title's implied writer-child, overseen by Eve's "I," was the Jamesian pupil: obsessed with language, rhythmic unfoldings, verbal discipline, and what it means to be "beaten" by parents. Or, to put it bluntly: Eve was revealing *how the budding intellectual* (Eve herself, you, me, the Jamesian pupil) *is a masochistic child*. This is one whose mental delights (often against parental wishes) attach themselves to thoughts of pain, and whose masochism, even more remarkably, leans on a pedagogue's whom one admires (the pupil's on the teacher's, Eve's on Henry James's).

Just below, I offer Eve's motivations (my speculations) for her perpetrated hoax, which are as telling of Eve's life-work, her academic passions, as any I know. But, first, let's remember the focus of "The Pupil." Recall for a moment the masochistic paradigm Eve could be relying upon in this tale—the sexy kind for which most readers have some kind of image (a beautiful woman, armed with a whip, delivering a blow to a willing man). As for "The Pupil," here there would be no Venus in furs; no tableaux—painterly, statuesque—assisting a dreamy young man stopping time in contemplative states, mostly nocturnal, so as to imagine a beautiful woman dressed only in furs, a woman he teaches to take up his torture, to whip him unconscious again and again, in accordance with a contract established between them.[2] Rather, in Eve's less visual tale, masochism is a distinctly mental matter (no whips, no furs), and offers a distinctly verbal pleasure. We might even say that, clearly, Eve, in stealthy manner, was taking a page from Krafft-Ebing's nineteenth-century treatise, *Psychopathia Sexualis*—that great compendium of abnormal sex. She read it, I presume, in an onanistic moment, when she had Jane Austen and masturbation on her mind.[3] (Krafft-Ebing, lest anyone should forget, was obsessed with onanistic evils.) What Eve was well placed to see in *Psychopathia*—and her essay on Austen bears this out in its playful insistence on mental masturbation—was the mental component of masochistic practice. Eve must have noticed how often Krafft-Ebing, in his remarkable range of case studies, stressed the imaginary and verbal elements of masochistic scenes:

> [Mr. Z, aged twenty-nine] recognized that flagellation was subsidiary, and that the idea of subjection to the woman's will was the important thing. . . . When he had the "thought of subjection" he was perfectly successful. At times of great excitability it was even sufficient if he told stories of such scenes to a pretty girl. He would thus have an orgasm, and usually ejaculation. (130)

In a particularly amusing version of this pattern, a masochist, attached to his torturer's "pretty shoes," must think "cruel thoughts about the shoes" in order to be potent; more specifically, "he was forced to think with delight of the death agonies of the animal from which the leather was taken" (164). In yet another case, "the mere mention of the words 'ratten cane' and 'to whip' caused . . . intense excitement" (179). Here are the seeds of Eve's idea for her Jamesian twist, allowing her to turn the physical components of masochistic tortures towards mental, and even verbal, intrigues.

Her second surprise is more stunning still. "The Pupil's" masochism weds a young man's pain to a child's. In Eve's story, a tutor makes a contract not to take on a woman, but to take on a pupil—a boy (age 11) with a weak heart but a mind so sharp that the tutor fears the child might be smarter than himself, even though the promise of the child's linguistic prowess is precisely a lure. Oddly, at the moment of the tutor's pledge to take the job, the child comes out with a puzzling cry—the narrator describes it as "the mocking, foreign ejaculation 'Oh la-la!'" (3). The boy's ejaculation over the contract (honestly, Eve) is the first indication of the child's wry sense of family secrets, especially his parents' history of making torturous contracts with his tutors which cause *him* pain. This is juicier than it sounds. For as the tale unfolds itself, the tutor is torn between his wish to escape the terms of his employment and his obvious seduction at the hands of a child, whose mouth and ears are so alluring (for all that they catch and then convey). In one of the central man/boy scenes, talk turns into and out of blushing before it ends with a playful discussion of spanking and beating.

It may not be too much to say that the text's great gag—its serious joke—is a tutor who's a masochist to his teaching contract (wink to Duke). Add to that the *pleasure* of discussing the depravity of his employers with their son (the pupil in question) and you have a recipe for an oral intercourse, one kept in motion by the teacher's masochism and the boy's verbal play. As I understand it, it is not the story's point to suggest a sexual subtext to this tutoring (making the story "about" hidden sex—wink to *New Republic*), but, truly, to assert the perverse enjoyment of talking over pain with one who aids in causing it, even if a child.[4] In this sly way, the story addresses man/boy love not in the context of sexual illegality, nor in the context of physical domination, but, by contrast, in the context of *context*: that is to say, in the context of employment, which is the context of changing positions in the public domain. For instance, in this setting, the child is both the receiver of a service (the tutor's instruction) and a representative of the employer (in this case, the family who is shafting the tutor). Of course, as one might expect in James, the boy as the tutor's conduit to torture is also being not so subtly impoverished by the parents, making boy and tutor together the sufferers of a masochistic scene. We will later see how these issues meet their end; how the family's attempt in their economic crisis to "force a constructive adoption on the obliging bachelor" (18)—the tutor, of course—changes the context of man/boy relations, changing both the contract and the masochistic pleasure, a narrative turn later accompanied by the pupil's death from a "violent" joy.

Now, however, it is time to concentrate on Eve's aspirations for "The Pupil" that she wrote. I see four rather obvious intents. To imagine a perfectly "proto-gay child," as Eve would aptly term him were she playing critic; to mother (and think of the laughs she had here) an avuncular text (especially to the point of having the family, as if they cried 'uncle', forcing their boy upon a bachelor); even more outrageously, to craft a kind of brotherly masochism shared between (and enjoyed by both) an adult and a child (wink to NAMBLA).[5] A fourth intent attaches to these. For surely it accorded with Eve's own pleasure to make it seem as if Henry James had read and transformed *Venus im Pelz* (Venus in Furs) from 1870. That is to say, I cannot but imagine that it satisfied Eve to write a novella that strongly suggested James had decided to turn Professor

Sacher-Masoch's masochistic play between men and women (replete with contracts, whips, and furs—not to mention tableaux) in a direction decidedly homosocial, possibly pedophilic, and certainly psychological. This was her icing on the Jamesian cake, her gift, in passing, to literary influence: James becomes the pupil of a Slavic masochist.

Come back now to these four intents for a closer look. It cannot be said too strongly: Eve's work, before any other work I know, and with an intelligence quite unmatched, has fostered queer kids. Recall, for starters, her remarkable essay "How to Bring Your Kids Up Gay: The War on Effeminate Boys." Part imperative, part elegy, as the title implies, Eve's essay reports on a shift shocking to any who hadn't noticed. In 1973, with fanfare, the American Psychiatric Association (APA) decided to drop from its next scheduled DSM-III (Diagnostic and Statistical Manual) the diagnostic category "homosexuality," thus removing it as a pathology. By its next appearance in 1980, the DSM-III, sleight-of-hand fashion, had added an entry: "Gender Identity Disorder of Childhood," which, Eve tells us, "appears to have attracted no outside attention . . . nor even to have been perceived as part of the same conceptual shift" (20). In essence, the DSM of the APA freed the homosexual only, then, to embattle the child, fighting the war against homosexuals on a battlefield where it could be hidden.

Why could it be hidden? Children, as children, cannot be "gay"—our culture, at least officially, presumes—a category culturally deemed too adult since it is sexual. And yet, to forbid a child this designation uncovers contradictions in the public discourse on childhood sexual orientation: the general cultural and political tendency to officially treat *all* children as straight, while continuing to deem them asexual. At this loggerheads, one tip from Eve—her continued use of the term "proto-gay"—breaks the case open.[6] From this hint, I would like to specify a fourfold theoretical spread of childhood—all of it queer, as Eve in a universalizing (*and* a historicizing) moment might proclaim it. "The Pupil" displays it.

First and foremost, with her label "proto-gay," Eve seems to know (even if she doesn't state) the gay child's strange retroactive existence.[7] Linguistic markers for its queerness arrive only later in life as a recognition of a road not taken. "I was a gay child": This is the only grammatical formulation allowed to gay childhood. That is to say, in one's teens or twenties, when (parental) plans for one's straight destination can be seen to have died, the designation "homosexual child," or even "gay kid," may finally, retrospectively, be applied. Really, it is raised as a tombstone to a death: the death of a status that confers civil rights. The phrase "gay child" is a gravestone marker for where and when a straight person died. By the time the marker is raised, however, it would seem that the "child" has died with the straight. This would truly be the most efficient means for aborting gay kids: Allow them to appear only when they can no longer exist. But there is a twist, as I think we all know. The grown homosexual *is* a child; or at least often metaphorized *as* a child. Said to be marked by sexual immaturity and arrested development, adult homosexuals in the popular political imagination are regarded as those queer children, who remain children, precisely by failing to have their own.

Two other children, of course, shadow these. In supposed contrast to the queer-child-on-linguistic-delay and the grown-homosexual-as-a-child are two other models. One might be called the child queered by Freud. This would be the not-yet-straight-child who is, in fact, a sexual child with criminal wishes — from wanting the mother to have its child, to wanting to have its father's baby, to wanting to kill its rival lover.[8] The other model is the child queered by innocence. This is the child brought to its fame by so many landmark studies of childhood and by the Romantic poets who nurtured it — that child, in whose estimation, we imagine, sex itself seems shockingly queer.[9] What do the children queered by innocence share? They all share estrangement from what they approach: the adulthood against which they must be defined. "The child," as we like to imagine we know it, is largely a creature of peculiar suspension and managed delay. Due to forms of censorship, due to a graduated school curriculum, and due to the laws that "protect" the child from its participation in market forces, the child approaches gradually, by degrees, the secrets of adult linguistic codes.[10]

Cannily, Eve endows Henry James with a threshold text that makes these distinctions among queer children converge upon each other. That is to say, in writing "The Pupil," Eve could create her own queer child. In fact, he is perfectly "proto-gay," by means of age (11–15, in this case) and, more cleverly, by his historical appearance in 1891 before the proverbial (and tiresome) starting line of the widespread entry of the word "homosexual" into English (wink to Foucault).[11] Here a child who might be "homosexual," if we could see his future unfold, is practically given over by his parents to his tutor: some kind of quasi-queer child himself, in the sense that he is fastened to the future of a child he himself has not fathered, and appears to be suspended, to put it mildly, in his own approach to normal couplehood.[12] More than that, we watch the tutor learn to love the boy for how the boy defeats the assumption of his innocence, showing, instead, a remarkably savvy sense of what is sex in James: money, family finance.[13] Only when we understand this fourfold collapse of queer child on queer child will we understand how Eve makes James queer the child before Freud, turning the screw of same-sex pedophilia in the direction of brotherly masochism.

Surely, it is odd to make the avuncular relation masochistic, as if one is wed-
ding this relation to pain as an argument against it. Such an argument would
never square with Eve. On the surface of her politics, Eve's great interest in
exploring "the avunculate," clearly stated in her piece on *The Importance of
Being Earnest,* was to take the normative family to task—really, to undermine
the nuclear nature of any family. Here she specified the range of relations,
especially the range of older men literally or euphemistically called "uncle,"
that mediate the child's relations to its parents. These are adults (and surely
tutors count) whose "intimate access to children needn't depend on their own
pairing or procreation" (63). For this reason, they may happily represent "non-
conforming or nonreproductive sexualities to children." More importantly, and
more complexly, avuncular relations thereby nurture a "less hypostatized view
of what and therefore how a child can desire." One often finds these darker
turns towards complication in Eve's lucid moments. Here, on precisely this
matter of desire, Eve swerves to pick up further entanglements, arguing that
Oedipal "accounts of the desire of any child" are "disfiguringly ritualized" (64):

> But suppose we assume for a moment the near-inevitability of any child's
> being 'seduced' in the sense of being inducted into, and more or less
> implanted with, one or more adult sexualities whose congruence with
> the child's felt desires will necessarily leave many painful gaps. . . . That
> a child, objectively very disempowered, might yet be seen as being some-
> times in a position to influence . . . *by whom s/he may be seduced*; as hav-
> ing some possible degree of choice, that is to say, about *whose* desire,
> what conscious and unconscious needs, what ruptures of self and what
> flawed resources of remediation, are henceforth to become part of her or
> his internalized sexual law: such a possibility is thinkable only in pro-
> portion as the child is seen as having intimate access to some range of
> adults, and hence of adult sexualities. (64)

Even more than by statistics ("queer teenagers . . . two to three times likelier
to attempt suicide") Sedgwick is menaced by the more protracted harms perpetrated on youth (1993b, i). Chief among them, as one sees above, is "the sys-
tematic separation of children from queer adults" (2). How fascinating, then,
that in writing "The Pupil," in taking revenge on the world of parents, Eve has
her cake and eats it, too. Namely, she makes the neglectful parents (oblivious to
needs, anxious to keep their child in the dark) strangely enabling of proto-gay
childhood and queer love. In foisting off their child on his tutor, even to the
point of "forcing . . . adoption," the parents not only obviate their non-nuclear
status but also make man/boy masochism (with its unexpected seductions and

ruptured pleasures) possible. It's as if a certain kind of pedophilia—the masochistic kind—is a tender response to parental abuse. Eve is also careful to present us with a pupil who is not an innocent. However impoverished, he is not an underling to struggles for control. Rather, with his rich linguistic store, the boy is clearly implicated in the tutor's suffering (he is the reason the tutor will not leave); he dies, moreover, not from suicide, but *from an intensity* that his parents' neglect of him has actually emboldened. It's as if his "weakness in the region of the heart" cannot find a form strong enough to hold its joy.

Here is where Eve's third intent enters in. For surely the signal Sedgwickian risk of her whole caper boils down to this: to have man and boy school each other in a pleasure that must be erected in accordance with their pain. That they suffer it at the hands of parents is almost too revealing of Eve's guiding hand; that they pleasure themselves with their endless words about it (to them it's a thrill to rehearse how they are "beaten") is Eve's clever portrait of a masochistic pleasure she knew as a child: a rhythmic, syntactical rehearsal of shame that generates aesthetic forms. Nowhere else does Eve so explicitly tip her hand as she does in "A Poem is Being Written." The title, we have said, transparently plays on Freud's famous essay "A Child is Being Beaten." Moreover, in a nod to retroactivity (the kind so typical of the queer child) Eve herself describes this essay as written "twenty-seven years late, to the extent that it represents a claim for respectful attention to the intellectual and artistic life of a nine-year-old child, Eve Kosofsky" (1993a, 177). As any reader of this essay will remember, Eve recalls her imaginative connection—almost at the level of a childish pun—between the beating of her childhood spankings and the beating, or pulsing rhythms, of her poems. "Shame," Eve writes, "was and maybe still is the mainspring of my own most characteristic motivations" (182). More than that, her essay consistently reveals the linguistic underpinnings to her view of masochism. Notice in this passage the role of certain words, how the child's linguistic control over making word connections shapes her material experience of her punishment:

> I'm struck, as they say, by the importance of French in this story. It's a problem that I sometimes don't know when I learned particular words. But while I know we were always spanked . . . 'simply' over the parental lap, the spanking in my imagination (I can only barely stop myself from saying, the spanking that *is* my imagination) has always occurred over a table, a table scaled precisely to the trunk of the child, framing it with a closeness and immobilizing exactitude that defined, for me, both the English word *truncate* and the French, of course, *tableau*. (183)

The use of tableaux, which Eve in her essay directly links to aesthetic forms (the framed look of the lyric on the page), appears as repeatedly in *Venus in Furs* as does the child's use of French in "The Pupil" ("Oh la-la").

There's another aspect to Eve's self-betrayal. Later in her essay, she extensively quotes from one of her poems, entitled "Lost Letter," calling attention to what she calls "the sadomasochistic, female-punishing tableau enacted in the poem" (188 n8). Details aside, it's enough to know that the poem's scene of masochism is a pedagogic one, in several senses. First of all, the eponymous letter is "to a former professor from an apprentice one," and makes the claim along the way: "No wonder we're uncomfortable . . . the pain of teaching being so akin / the pain of studenting, of envy and arousal / at language barely meant for our proper eyes and ears" (188, 189). The poem, as it happens, turns on the writer's (Eve's) imagination that the professor has witnessed his pupil in some kind of masochistic scene: "[He] glimpses in a waiting room a naked girl / submitting to something evidently / jazzy and frightening in the way of punishment. / He's appalled, he can't watch it, / but he's recognized her, a student he's fond of, / and, once home, writes her a hesitant note. / 'If you ever feel it would help to talk / please consider me at your disposal. . . . how long do you expect it to continue?" (189). What their mutual implication in this punishment affords both participants is, of course, the letters between them. As the teacher writes: "Your letter can bring fresh shocks of impotence, / urgency, vicarious humiliation. . . . I remain yours truly: / the fixed slave of your continuing punishment" (193). What Eve is out to illustrate she later states directly in her essay: "the aptitude of the child's body to represent, among other things, the fears, furies, appetites, and losses of the people around it, back to themselves and out to others" (199). The child is a stage for the drama of pain.

It was clever, for all of this display, that Eve used her Freudian title and slant to throw us off of the track of Gilles Deleuze. This is the last link in the chain before we turn to the story itself. I have told you from the start about the kind of masochism that does not appear in "James": men who are literally beaten by women with whom they have contractual relations. A repeated image from *Venus in Furs* has the look of tableau: A man sits dreaming of Venus as a statue or a sumptuous painting; her cold, suspended form comes to life; she holds a whip above his head, almost frozen in delay; when it cracks upon him, it marks his skin with the sign of their relation. No penetration, only surface bruising. It seems safe to say that this insistent image does not appear in James. What do appear in "The Pupil," even so, are what Deleuze (see his "Coldness and Cruelty") deems the central features of Masoch's masochism from his German novels of the 1870s. First and foremost is the masochist's *initiation* of a contract with a torturer. This is a contract he not only seeks but also, in pedagogic fashion, oversees, instructing his torturer through the contract. By being beaten according to its terms, the masochist pays up front for his attachment. He shows himself attached to delay, since he waits for a pleasure that is bound to be late, that contractually cannot follow until the pain that ensures it has been suffered. Perhaps not surprisingly, he fears the torturer cancelling the contract that guarantees repetitious beatings and delays.

What is surprising—if one buys Deleuze—is the masochist's break with all patriarchal figures, by hiding the figure of the father in himself, he who is beaten. (Eve thrills to this.) This featured break exactly reverses the Freudian model, in which the figure of the father is presumed to be "hidden" in the woman who is doing the beating. By Freud's reckoning, the masochist's self-punishment results from his guilt over his wish to usurp the father's place. Freud sees the woman as a cover for the father (in her role as punisher for this wish) because she keeps the masochist from seeming homosexual (in his wish to be beaten by a man). Woman-as-cover also allows the would-be usurper (that is to say, the masochist) to plead with his father: "You see, it is not I who wanted to take your place, it is she who hurts, castrates and beats me" (58). Deleuze takes exception to this interpretation. First of all, he argues, masochism cannot be viewed as part of an S/M whole. It is not aggression turned back upon the self. Actually, by contrast, it is *a special way of pursuing a pleasure that comes on delay*. For this important reason, the masochist does not seek relations with a sadist, whom he would be unable to instruct. Equally important, masochism is not a hidden usurpation. It does not seek to overtake the father but, rather, to humiliate the father and his law. As Deleuze writes,

> The masochist feels guilty, he asks to be beaten, he expiates, but why and for what crime? Is it not precisely the father-image in him that is thus miniaturized, beaten, ridiculed and humiliated? What the subject atones for is his resemblance to the father and the father's likeness in him. . . . Hence the father is not so much the beater as the beaten. (Deleuze, 60–61)

The result of masochism is the victim's disavowal of the world as we know it, a disavowal accomplished through highly formalized aesthetic contemplation (recall Eve's attachment to lyric tableaux). Hand in glove with this disavowal is the victim's suspension of laws by his making absurd contracts with them—especially, the sexual laws conventionally mapped for men and women. In other words, by his submission to the law, the masochist undoes it. Whipping ceases to punish erection. Rather, it produces it. Moreover, when the masochist, through his punishment, literally atones for his resemblance to the father, he seeks in its place a maternal symbolic, both nurturing and cruel.

Perhaps we can see the effect Eve achieves by making James' masochism turn around a child. To begin, it's as if the Jamesian masochist, literally a pedagogue, disavows the world not only of conventional sexual relations but also of adult relations to the child. Consenting to suffering through his contract with the parents—and behind them, the child—the tutor buys a pleasure that is wedded to delay (so fitting for his love of a protogay child). He frees a space for himself and the child in which his "beatings" do not punish the seductions he feels at the hands of a young boy. Rather, his pleasures are *the product of this contract*—to wit, a teaching contract. As this arrangement breaks the tutor's resemblance to the pupil's father ("a man of the world," detached, above the fray), the tutor's embroilment with his pupil allows him to seek a *fraternal* symbolic that would lateralize (though not equalize or equate) adult and child. Each pursues a masochism that would tilt in the direction of the other's.

These are large claims. As I rush to the story's middle scene that may support them, watch for how the novella's masochism revises the usual tropes of childhood: the child's presumed inferior grasp of literacy, education, money, sex and shame. The story's first lines:

> The poor young man [the tutor, that is] hesitated and procrastinated: it cost him such an effort to broach the subject of terms, to speak of money. . . . Yet he was unwilling to take leave . . . without some more conventional glance in that direction than he could find an opening for in the manner of the large, affable lady who sat there drawing a pair of soiled *gants de Suede* through a fat, jewelled hand and, at once gliding, repeated over and over everything but the thing he would have liked to hear. He would have liked to hear the figure of his salary; but just as he was nervously about to sound that note the little boy came back—the little boy Mrs. Moreen had sent out of the room to fetch her fan. (1)

From the first sentence, contract is the issue, and the would-be pedagogue (age twenty-six) is hung on the hook of uncertain terms. In this, the mother supplants the father, who in the initial contract scene, and in so many others, remains offstage, "a man of the world," as he's tagged repeatedly, whose banner of worldly patriarchal authority hangs over the story as a destination the boy and his tutor would jointly divert. Moreover, for all of the pupil's otherworldliness—he is a "mystic volume," "altogether different from the obvious little Anglo-Saxons who had misrepresented childhood to Pemberton" (6)—the pupil could plausibly resemble a worldly homosexual from 1891: Oscar

Wilde's Lord Henry Wotton from *The Picture of Dorian Gray*. Consider these descriptions that Eve may have tailored to correspond with Henry: The pupil is "supernaturally clever" with "a sharp spice of stoicism" (9); he has a "range of refinement and perception," making him "unconscious and irresponsible and amusing" (9–10); he is one who "liked intellectual gymnastics and who, also, as regards the behavior of mankind, had noticed more things than you might suppose" (10). At the very least, that the pupil should more closely resemble Lord Henry (one of English literature's most famous pedophiles) than he does Dorian, and that the pupil should prove to be the epigrammatic darling of his tutor, stands as a clue to the child's peculiar powers.[14] This complication of presumed dominations is only more explicit as the story engages man/boy love in the terms of employment:

> At Nice once, toward evening, as the pair sat resting in the open air after a walk, looking over the sea at the pink western lights, [the pupil] said suddenly to his companion:
> "Do you like it—you know, being with us in this intimate way?"
> "My dear fellow, why should I stay if I didn't? . . . I hope you don't mean to dismiss me."
> "I think if I did right I ought to."
> "Well, I know I'm supposed to instruct you in virtue; but in that case don't do right . . ."
> For a particular reason the words made Pemberton [the tutor] change colour. The boy noticed in an instant that he had turned red, whereupon he turned red himself and the pupil and the master exchanged a longish glance in which there was a consciousness of many more things than are usually touched upon, even tacitly, in such a relation. It produced for Pemberton an embarrassment; it raised, in a shadowy form, a question (this was the first glimpse of it), which was destined to play as singular and, as he imagined, owing to the altogether peculiar conditions, an unprecedented part in his intercourse with his little companion. Later, when he found himself talking with this small boy in a way in which few small boys could ever have been talked with, he thought of that clumsy moment on the bench in Nice as the dawn of an understanding that had broadened. What had added to the clumsiness then was that he thought it his duty to declare to Morgan that he might abuse him (Pemberton) as much as he liked, but must never abuse his parents. . . . He thought it the oddest thing to have a struggle with the child about. He wondered he didn't detest the child for launching him in such a struggle [with the parents]. . . . but to know [Morgan] was to accept him on his own odd

terms. . . . Against every interest [the tutor] had attached himself. . . .
Before they went home that evening, at Nice, the boy had said, clinging
to his arm:

"Well, at any rate, you'll hang on to the last."

"To the last?"

"Till you're fairly beaten."

"*You* ought to be fairly beaten!" cried the [tutor], drawing him closer.
(10–12)

Ending with obvious talk of beatings, the scene starts with a kind of tableau,
the aesthetic freezing that is prelude to the whip. Notice the static posture of
the pair, caught at rest in the "pink western lights"—a clear anticipation of the
surface suffusion of a mutual blush. Just as talk will color them, will make a
material mark upon the skin, talk is their suspension, and even their lash. The
pupil snaps the relation in motion, wrapped, as he is, in an intimate "us" that
ties boy and tutor together to the parents ("Do you like it . . . being with us in
this intimate way?") The tutor seems stung—perhaps only playfully ("My dear
fellow, why should I stay if I didn't?"). Whatever the tutor's tone may be, his
words voice the masochist's fear of dismissal, just as the boy's sound reluctance
to proceed. As if on cue, the tutor then plays the masochist pedagogue, fitting
the representative of the torturers to his role: "I know I'm supposed to instruct
you in virtue; but in that case, don't do right." The tutor even seems to instruct
him in blushing. Feeling the effects of their verbal play and wearing it on the
surface of his skin ("the words made Pemberton turn colour") the tutor seems
to lateral his blush to the boy, turning their prior disequivalence in the direction of mutual exchange ("pupil and master exchanged a longish glance"), one
in which the syntax lets the man and boy converge on a single verb and
object—even "a consciousness."

Entering into this mutual conveyance is the vehicle of metaphor. A phrase
such as "touched upon"—"a consciousness of many more things than are usually touched upon . . . in such a relation"—seems metaphorical (a way of saying "talked about"), but then what is talked about looks as if it has quite mate-
rially touched a face and flushed it into a red relation. Even the question that
is said to be "raised, in a shadowy form" seems plausibly material—as if this is
a gothic question, a literally haunting question that one might catch a glimpse
of. Yet, the sentence that contains it, reveals it, ends with what remains, or so
we presume, strictly metaphorical: the tutor's "intercourse with his little companion." Notice here, too, the metaphor of intercourse turns a shade material
when the secrets of adult suggestiveness seem to spill their guts in the sentence
on talking: "Later when he found himself talking with this small boy in a way

in which few small boys could ever have been talked with, he thought of that clumsy moment on the bench in Nice as the dawn of an understanding that had broadened" (11). Here the boy has gotten smaller ("this small boy"), as if Eve is throwing a dare in our face, upping the ante of pedophilic "intercourse" while she presents it as an origins tale. The first time the tutor and the small boy ever entered into this intercourse there was "the dawn of an understanding" (pink lights, pink lights). With any first intercourse, there is "clumsiness," but just when the tutor's duty enters in to make him seem older ("he thought it his duty to declare to Morgan," 11) the tutor skillfully becomes the masochist ("to declare to Morgan that he might abuse him [Pemberton] as much as he liked, but never . . . his parents," 11).

The child is the cause of the struggle with the parents; and somewhere within and beside the contract with the parents are the tutor's "odd terms with Morgan." At any rate, the last exchange is clearly, if playfully, masochistic— one in which the pupil's position as the torturer both remains ambiguous and even tilts, in lateral fashion, towards his tutor's position as the beaten. To the pupil's taunting in relation to stamina ("you'll hang on to the last": a staple in Sacher-Masoch's novels), the tutor's reply about beating the pupil reminds the reader of the tutor's position that makes his abjection before the boy so striking. The boy's ambiguous sense of beating (is it financial, psychological, or more broadly metaphorical?) is immediately rendered as a physical relation by the tutor, who is himself the target of abuse and the one who turns the talk of spanking into a pretext for their embrace. From the metaphorical-material wobblings of this passage we should be struck by how carefully Eve is transforming something like Sacher-Masoch's literal whippings into a still material masochism of linguistic relations. The fetishism so dependent on sight in Sacher-Masoch's novels (tableaux, female beauty, the nude body veiled by fur) is not in operation here. Rather, fetishistic stasis and delay are accomplished by the elegant syntactical suspensions and linguistic textures that carry Eve's (Jamesian) trademark. Here they become the tutor's drawn-out shadowy sessions of oral intercourse with a boy, an intercourse all about the family abuse of man and boy, making them "conscious," as the narrator puts it, of a "democratic brotherhood" established with each other, one in which the pupil "might pass for [the tutor's] . . . sickly little brother" (14).

Sickness, of course, is precisely the pretext for Eve's denouement. The boy's weak heart—the story's ultimate materializing metaphor—pushes the question of what forms hold what material relations. Outside of masochism, is there a form to hold boy to tutor in something other than their imagination? Actually, this question breaks the masochistic frame—which is, after all, a suspension of finality and preference for delay. Which is to say that no one is a masochist to the very end. In fact, as the tutor begins to expect the parents' impending financial crash, Eve informs us: "Pemberton [the tutor] waited in a queer confusion of yearning and alarm for the catastrophe which was held to hang over the house of Moreen, of which he certainly at moments felt the symptoms brush his cheek and as to which he wondered much in what form it would come" (43). The pupil's way of wondering takes a more aesthetic form: "He talked of their escape (recurring to it often afterwards), as if they were making up a 'boy's book' together" (41). Here is another of Eve's deft jokes. The boy's book adventure imagined by the pupil turns Joseph Conrad towards Jane Austen; man and boy, in the pupil's plan, are not going to sea but are setting up house. Moreover, the pupil's transition from a child to something much more akin to a wife is what makes the tutor fear for his pleasure:

> For the first time, in this complicated connection, Pemberton felt sore and exasperated. It was . . . *trop fort*—everything was *trop fort.* . . . He saw what the boy had in his mind; the conception that as his friend [the tutor] had had the generosity to come back to him [in his illness] he [the pupil] must show his gratitude by giving him his life. But the poor friend didn't desire the gift—what could he do with Morgan's life? (43)

Intriguingly, the changing terms of their relation are too hard (rendered in the French: *trop fort*) for the tutor's masochism. Even more pointedly, the parents giving over their son to his tutor (in something between an adoption and a marriage) officially breaks the tutoring contract and, so importantly, the grand suspension of man/boy relations in the masochistic field. Now delay and its pleasures are rushed towards a "violent emotion" that is as final as it is mysterious:

> "Do you mean that he may take me to live with him—for ever and ever?" cried the boy. "Away, away, anywhere he likes?"
> "For ever and ever? *Comme vous-yallez!*" Mr. Moreen laughed indulgently. "For as long as Mr. Pemberton may be so good. . . ."
> Morgan had turned from his father—he stood looking at Pemberton with a light in his face. His blush had died out, but something had come that was brighter and more vivid. He had a moment of boyish joy, scarcely mitigated by the reflection that, with his unexpected consecration of his hope—too sudden and too violent; the thing was a good deal less like a boy's book—the "escape" was left on their hands. The boyish

joy was there for an instant, and Pemberton was almost frightened at the revelation of gratitude and affection that shone through his humiliation. . . .

"Ah, his darling little heart!" [his mother] broke out. . . . Pemberton saw, with equal horror, by Morgan's own stricken face, that he *was* gone. . . .

"He couldn't stand it, with his infirmity," said Pemberton—"the shock, the whole scene, the violent emotion." (46–47)

Though now the surface sign of humiliation is worn by the child—he, not the tutor, wears a mark on his face, more vivid than a blush—this scene really is too violent (too hard, *trop fort*) for masochism. Eve knows this. She wants us to wonder: Is there a form to hold boyish joy at the thought of being given by one's parents to a man? Apparently not. Eve makes a wily joke, perhaps in the face of AIDS: the pupil dies from a strain of joy that has no recognized form to hold it. In fact, the parents positively cannot read it:

"But I thought he *wanted* to go to you!" wailed Mrs. Moreen.

"I *told* you he didn't, my dear," argued Mr. Moreen. He was trembling all over, and was in his way, as deeply affected as his wife. But, after the first, he took his bereavement like a man of the world. (47)

The father is more than unable to see joy—to see the "gratitude and affection that shone through his [son's] humiliation." He may be unable to see his own sorrow. This is his shame. The eccentric phrase "took his bereavement," followed by "like a man of the world," makes it sound like he takes a beating he denies with a pose (wink to Deleuze).

Such a conclusion allows something else. It lets Eve extract certain NAMBLA motifs—the child's right to design its education and its privilege to divorce its parents—without the trouble of debating pedophilia. Even the typical NAMBLA profile (described by one member) profiles the tutor: "overeducated," "underemployed," and "not [very] sexually active" (Green, 83). Such clever touches allow Eve to show (her version of) James far outreaching and outradicalizing his contemporary Edward Carpenter on "Affection in Education" (the title to a Carpenter essay from 1899). The very notion of the masochistic child as the quintessential pupil is more than rare. It is the peculiar combination of Eve and Henry James. That is to say, it is my fantasy of academic parents who have taught me that unfairness, employment, and pain are pleasures to discuss. From which I conclude:

I am Eve's pupil and, if asked, will have her child.

Notes

1. Interested readers may wish to consult *The Importance of Being Earnest*, Act I. For the record, Moon took no offense at Eve's phrase "up your alley."
2. For examples of this paradigm, see Leopold von Sacher-Masoch's *Venus in Furs*.
3. See her essay, "Jane Austen and the Masturbating Girl."
4. I presume that no one forgets the essay in the *New Republic*, with the face of Henry James on the cover, claiming that Queer Theory falsely and unhelpfully sexualizes everything. See Siegel, "The Gay Science."
5. I refer, of course, to the North American Man Boy Love Association.
6. For an example of her use of this phrasa, see "How to Bring Your Kids Up Gay," 160.
7. One hears suggestions of retroactivity in Eve's opening statements to her book *Tendencies*: "I think many adults (and I am among them) are trying, in our work, to keep faith with vividly remembered promises made to ourselves in childhood: promises to make invisible possibilities and desires visible; to make the tacit things explicit; to smuggle queer representation in where it must be smuggled and, with the relative freedom of adulthood, to challenge queer-eradicating impulses frontally where they are to be so challenged."
8. An essay such as Freud's "Femininity," insofar as it rehearses the paradigm of Oedipalization, specifies these aspects.
9. What I am calling these "landmark studies" are particularly helpful for understanding the stunning contradictions (especially with reference to class) surrounding the historical invention of Western childhood innocence. James Kincaid has most recently explored the Victorian versions of these contradictions in his indispensible *Child-Loving: The Erotic Child and Victorian Culture*. See also the earlier, famous studies by Aries, deMause, Pinchbeck, and Stone.
10. For discussion of these elements by one who greatly laments (what he sees as) the current increasing erasure of childhood, see Neil Postman.
11. Eve's appreciation of and demurs in reference to Michel Foucault can best be gleaned from her remarks in "Introduction: Axiomatic" (*Epistemology*).
12. Nowhere are the tutor's interests in women, or his marriage prospects, even mentioned. The most we learn of his circumstances (but these are monetary) are in these phrases: his "University honours had, pecuniarily speaking, remained barren" (2); "he was coming because he had to go somewhere, thanks to the collapse of his fortune at the end of a year

abroad, spent on the system of putting his tiny patrimony into a single full wave of experience. He had had his full wave, but he couldn't pay his hotel bill. Moreover, he had caught in the boy's eyes the glimpse of a far-off appeal" (4).

13. In "The Pupil," the delicate, intimate nature of money is hinted at in these lines: "When Mrs. Moreen bethought herself of this pretext for getting rid of their companion [the pupil], Pemberton supposed it was precisely to approach the delicate subject of his remuneration" (1); "he succeeded, in spite of the presence of the child, in squeezing out a phrase about the rate of payment" (2). What doesn't seem too much of a stretch to deem the closet of family finance can be seen in the pupil's later outburst: "I don't know what they live on, or how they live, or why they live! What have they got and how did they get it? Are they rich, are they poor, or have they a *modeste aisance*? Why are they always chiveying about—living one year like ambassadors and the next like paupers?" (27)

14. Any reader of Wilde's novel will remember Henry's refinement and perception; these are the qualities that seem to strike Dorian Gray after he meets Lord Henry Wotton: "[Henry's] cool, white, flower-like hands, even, had a curious charm. They moved, as he spoke, like music, and seemed to have a language of their own. . . . Why had it been left for a stranger to reveal [Dorian] to himself?" (44). In a later passage, the sense of Henry as intellectual gymnast may emerge—perhaps in response to a character's claim that "to test Reality we must see it on the tight-rope; when the Verities become acrobats we can judge them" (64). Two pages later we read: "[Lord Henry] played with the idea, and grew wilful; tossed it into the air and transformed it; let it escape and recaptured it; made it iridescent with fancy, and winged it with paradox. . . . It was an extraordinary improvisation. . . . He was brilliant, fantastic, irresponsible" (66). Unexpected hints of Henry's stoicism surface at moments in the text, especially in relation to his aging: "I am wrinkled, and worn, and yellow. . . . I have sorrows, Dorian, of my own, that even you know nothing of. The tragedy of old age is not that one is old, but that one is young. I am amazed sometimes at my own sincerity" (254–55).

Works Cited

Aries, Philippe, *Centuries of Childhood*, trans. Robert Baldrick (New York: Vintage, 1962).

Carpenter, Edward, *Selected Writings, Volume One: Sex* (London: GMP, 1984).

Deleuze, Gilles, "Coldness and Cruelty" in *Masochism*, trans. Jean McNeil (New York: Zone, 1991).

DeMause, Lloyd, ed., *The History of Childhood* (New York: The Psychohistory Press, 1974).

Freud, Sigmund, "Femininity," in *New Introductory Lectures on Psychoanalysis*, Lecture XXXIII, trans. and ed. James Strachey (London: Hogarth Press, 1974): 132.

Green, Jesse, "The Men from the Boys," *Out* (September 1994): 75–83, 128–36.

James, Henry, "The Pupil," in *The Faber Book of Gay Short Fiction*, ed. Edmund White (Boston: Faber, 1992) 1–47.

Kincaid, James R., *Child-Loving: The Erotic Child and Victorian Culture* (New York: Routledge, 1992).

Moon, Michael, "A Small Boy and Others: Sexual Disorientation in Henry James, Kenneth Anger, and David Lynch," in *A Small Boy and Others: Imitation and Initiation in American Culture from Henry James to Andy Warhol* (Durham: Duke University Press, 1998).

Pinchbeck, Ivy, and Margaret Hewitt, *Children in English Society, Volume II: From the Eighteenth Century to the Children Act of 1948* (Toronto: University of Toronto Press, 1973).

Postman, Neil, *The Disappearance of Childhood* (New York: Vintage, 1982).

Sedgwick, Eve Kosofsky, *Epistemology of the Closet* (Berkeley: University of California Press, 1990).

——. "How to Bring Your Kids Up Gay: The War on Effeminate Boys," *Social Text* 29(1991): 18–27.

——. "Jane Austen and the Masturbating Girl," *Critical Inquiry* 17.4(Summer 1991): 818–37.

——. *Tendencies* (Durham: Duke University Press, 1993).

Siegel, Lee, "The Gay Science: Queer Theory, Literature, and the Sexualization of Everything," *New Republic* (November 9, 1998): 30–42.

Stone, Lawrence, "Literacy and Education in England, 1640–1900." *Past and Present* No. 42 (February 1969).

——. *The Family, Sex, and Marriage in England, 1500–1800* (New York: Harper and Row, 1977).

von Krafft-Ebing, Richard, *Pyschopathia Sexualis: A Medico-Forensic Study* (New York: Putnam, 1965).

von Sacher-Masoch, Leopold, *Venus in Furs*, in *Masochism*, trans. Jean McNeil (New York: Zone, 1991).

Wilde, Oscar, *The Importance of Being Earnest and Other Plays* (New York: Signet, 1985).

8

Flaming Iguanas, Dalai Pandas, and Other Lesbian Bardos (A few perimeter points)

Melissa Solomon

Two different road trips between East and West: first, Erika Lopez's *Flaming Iguanas: An Illustrated All-Girl Road Novel Thing*, a series of raunchy jokes and cross-country stories about a girl biker, whose performative, self-reinventing travels are insistently and resistantly never told as a "developmental narrative," nor even necessarily as a progressive or sequential one. Her passage through Eastern and Western states astride "the smiling face" of her motorcycle reads like a bawdy alternation of the sexual/spiritual stops and starts that, for her, are only ever antinomial, various, and not (to say the very least) in binary relationship.

And second, a very different kind of East–West travel narrative in which a particular Western literary critic, Eve Kosofsky Sedgwick, turns her attention toward Asia, and especially toward Tibetan Buddhist scholarship, to learn more about the concept of the bardo, regarding the (sometimes terrifying) transitional spaces that open in and through meditative states and whose affordances reflect greatly on Sedgwick's opus of writing. My intent, in this essay, is to learn, however briefly, from the space-making projects of the Lopez novel in order to create some different angles of approach to the work of Eve Sedgwick.

Flaming Iguanas recounts the adventures of an irreverent if somewhat accident-prone Tomato Rodriguez who rides across country contemplating her own experimental sexual fantasies, including some for other women, wondering all the while whether having a lesbian affair would necessitate renarrativizing her own identity. The book is an endless stream of lewd jokes and prurient tableau that illustrate her hunger for a few particular women and yet her resistance to any of the conventional stereotypes that supposedly correspond to or describe lesbian identity. With special relish, she satirizes her own mother's unbearable, *unsexy*, "co-dependent" lesbian lover, Violet, whose "food and security issues" keep her perpetually dialing the marriage counselor for an appointment, while Tomato's fraught mother furiously reads self-help manuals in the next room, tuning out her daughter's insistent question, "Mom, when did you first know you were a lesbian?"

A mocking script that illustrates the circular lock of a particular definitional impasse when Tomato asks (and needs to ask) her own (disavowing) lesbian mother about her (disavowed) lesbian sexuality: The term "lesbian" is either situationally ridiculous or violent when applied to anything but the first-person singular, and/but the difficulty of knowing, in the absence of any applied models, how (per se) to use the term in the first person singular.[1] Contextually personal *ergo* experimental, what "lesbian" means to a lesbian mother is not necessarily what it will mean to her lesbian daughter. Because of this, the "time before"—if "time" is the right word—realizing one's own definition/s, not knowing how in the world that realization might happen,[2] is an especially difficult transition space, a "lesbian bardo." The ticklish and seeming far reach of this makes me want to ask, What are the possible meanings of those two words put together?

I. What Is a Lesbian Bardo?

Scanning the parameters and different angles of this question and offering some possible answers is much of what will preoccupy my particular approach to Lopez's novel and to several texts by Sedgwick. Preliminary definitions begin with the word "bardo," which is an "in between" state, between what has just passed and what is about to come, for instance the state between death and reincarnation in Tibetan Buddhism that determines in part what that reincarnation will be like. Other bardos include the sleep and dream states that fall between yesterday and tomorrow or, as Eve Sedgwick points out, the state of protracted illness, as with cancer, that preempts health yet precedes death.[3] For Sogyal Rinpoche, a bardo is a transition or gap between the completion of one situation and the beginning of another.[4] He writes: "What distinguishes and defines each of the bardos is that they are all gaps or periods in which the possibility of awakening is particularly present. . . . One of the central characteristics of the bardos is that they are periods of deep uncertainty" (Rinpoche, 104). His advice about finding oneself in a bardo state is, "Allow it to be a gap." Doing so deepens sensitivity and makes acute one's own alertness to the radical insights offered by gaps and transitions (106). Describing how frequently bardos occur, he further writes:

If we really examine every aspect of our life . . . we will discover how we go through, again and again, in sleep and dream, in thoughts and emotions, that same process of the bardos . . . in both life and death. . . . (346)

Attaching to "bardo" a modifying adjective (particularly an adjective as historically rich in instances of reifying definition and usage as "lesbian") might at first seem to subtract from the process precisely its definitional "in betweenness" and to suppose either that "bardo" has properties we might learn or at least a lavender-colored hue that eyes can recognize, if only extratextually. But the presumption here is not that lesbian modifies bardo, so much as that bardo, as a concept, may be useful for describing the transitional spaces between different and conflicting definitions of lesbian. As Eve Sedgwick writes, "gay identity is a convoluted and off-centering possession, if it is a possession at all" not "to be perceived or known by anyone outside of a structure of transference and countertransference" (1990, 81) and, further, lesbianism has depended for its historical meanings on contradictory models "of a universalizing discourse of acts and a minoritizing discourse of persons" (86). Sedgwick summarizes that

> both within and outside of homosexual-rights movements, the contradictory understandings of same-sex bonding and desire and of male and female gay identity have crossed and recrossed the definitional lines of gender identity with such disruptive frequency that the concepts "minority" and "gender" themselves have lost a good deal of their categorizing (though certainly not of their performative) force. (1990, 82)

These observations make the project of defining "lesbian" a usefully self-conscious and self-reflective exercise for becoming deliberately aware, in advance, of the parameters and frailties of whichever epistemology a particular definition relies upon. The concept "bardo" is in part defined by *absence* of epistemology, and so as a noun-partner to "lesbian," the word is a lexical tool for remembering that both "lesbian" and "bardo" live in the same definitional non-state and yet both concern very much what is "to come": not in an anticipatory way, but in the way that periods of deep uncertainty—for a concept whose definition is so fraught—become the condition of possibility for new change.[5] For me, the "lesbian bardo" is that Sedgwickian place (process? state? method?) I visit when I write from within the "stimulating aether of the unnamed, the lived experiment" (Sedgwick 1990, 63). For Erika Lopez, this resonantly and also deeply figural "lived experiment" involves loving, and the terror of touching, another woman for the first time: "I was a brand-new lesbian, and I still didn't know what I was doing . . . I was intimidated and I hated to be afraid of anything, especially another woman's pussy" (255). If returning to Lopez feels dizzyingly literal, or crudely vernacular, at this juncture: consider, please, the constant interface in *Flaming Iguanas* between the narrator's literal pussy hunger/terror/need (fill in any affect), and her revilement against the ways "pussy affect" gets represented in culture. This interface is a lesbian bardo.

II. Vicariating Impulses: Or, "The Use of Being Fat"

> I used to have a superstition that
> there was this use to being fat:
> no one I loved could come to harm
> enfolded in my touch.
> —Eve Kosofsky Sedgwick, "The Use of Being Fat"

Epistemology of the Closet makes a great many ground-breaking suppositions by recognizing a variety of literary-political-sexual bardo-spaces, some that have occurred and some that may yet occur. Sedgwick interpolates the latter with a creative closed-eye inner-vision that sees around and through the present-moment of contemporary events enough to know where the bardos may yet create a space in which, or a process by which, wedges of light and conscious-ness about those present moments might happen.[6] In particular, Sedgwick's opus is full of lesbian bardos, and in this essay I hope to sketch out the negative and positive spaces around a few of them and to *begin* to make some hypothe-ses about what transitions those lesbian bardo spaces mark.

Before I begin to do so, there's a need, I think, to make a kind of Sedgwick-ian personal interjection about the various reasons it might be important to begin such a project. Because Sedgwick's work is so richly and indisputably rel-evant to lesbian studies, it is surprising to me — stupefying, actually — how will-fully or vehemently that relevance has, in certain instances, been either denied or overlooked and, as a result, how little explored those riches, to this day, remain.[7] What this essay undertakes in a very nonlinear, experimental fashion, and without any pretense of mastery, is an exploration of some Sedgwickian lesbian bardos, with a little help from Erika Lopez, to open pathways in lesbian studies previously hidden or blocked. Second, working in the other direction, the concept of the lesbian bardo is, inversely, useful for thinking about Sedg-wick's work in new ways. To reach Sedgwick, I look back to Lopez's year-long road trip, a bardo space imagined as the 3,000 miles between East and West, a time *before* she ever made love with another woman and yet, symbolically, a time when the availability of pleasure in straight sex with men is only remem-bered (as "retrospective") or is transformed by her growing interest in acquir-ing what she believes to be a "lesbian imagination." Here is an example of the kind of sex she describes having during this "middle period," after heterosexuality yet before lesbianism: a time when clear meanings of the two terms "heterosexuality" and "lesbianism," as well as any suppositions about "sexual difference," seem to disappear. Spellbound, during an art class, at the sight of an exquisitely beautiful, nude female model and wanting to "bury my face between her legs" though "[I] wouldn't have known what to do once . . . there" (Lopez, 218–19), an excited but inexperienced Rodriguez further recounts:

> I just couldn't keep my hands off myself, so I masturbated all winter until I met a nice boy in the spring I could practice lesbian sex with. . . . I waited probably a week and a half to have sex with him. By then, I felt I knew him well enough to show him a lesbian sex book, so I gave it to him to take home and study. The next night, he came to my apartment with a gourmet hard-on and . . . tried to fist me just like how the book said. (Lopez, 220)

The description of "lesbian sex" in this passage is both mnemonic and palliative: it rhymes with and brings to mind a set of acts and fantasies she associates with lesbians (having read about them in a so-called "lesbian" book), and it also lubricates the difficult passage of realizing something heretofore only read about in discourse.[8] Distinguishing practice from epistemology, Sogyal Rinpoche writes, "There is a famous Tibetan saying, 'Do not mistake understanding for realization'" (126).[9] Lopez's vicariating impulse to incorporate (or crossapply?) an approximation of a newly not-quite-yet learned behavior from one kind of unfamiliar script to another more familiar one tacitly acknowledges the separation of knowing and realizing. Her practice does not necessarily privilege "realization" as an endpoint to progressive living,[10] but it does use one to learn about the other.

If it is true that "knowing" and "realizing" are often separate, it may also be true that before "realization" happens, the closest "knowing" can get to "realizing" is "vicarious knowing" (alternately, "sentimentality"[11]) and that affect may have some share in bringing about this proximity: that knowing plus yearning likely spur vicariating impulses. To Sedgwick's "friend" who acidly disliked, in chapter one of *Epistemology*, Sedgwick's explication of Queen Esther's "coming out" as a Jew to King Ahasuerus, vicariousness is both corrupted knowledge and corrupted realization; the person having had the vicariating impulse "knows nothing" and has "realized nothing" true to actual "realization," however much she might believe otherwise: "It's not [you] risking the coming out, but it's all too visibly [you] having the salvational fantasies" (153).

This problematization, and *denigration*, of anything but [one reified sort of] "realization," i.e., coming out, may in effect be the reverse of curiosity about how realization happens; at the very least, it is bardo intolerance. If "vicariating impulses" are the product of knowing plus yearning, then they indicate a willingness to tolerate bardos, transition spaces, gaps in one's understanding that yearning and the impulse to vicariate implicitly admit. Additionally, if "coming out" is a performative, then the *before* moment of "coming out" may need to be a *coming to*, a realization of one's own personal-*ergo*-experimental lesbianism, preceded by just such a bardo space, preceded (perhaps) by just such a vicariating impulse. Therefore it would be illogical, in this model of understanding, to imply—as the nameless friend seems to do—that a salvational fantasy, such as identifying with Queen Esther's story to the degree of wanting critically to explicate it, is at cross purposes to, or is the opposite of, the personal risk of "actually" coming out. It is also unnecessary to privilege or to rank any one of these placements or processes in relation to lesbian realization, since each is unique and merits expansive exploration and since each will signify differently across class, race, nationality, age, self-awareness, and context or history. The act of "coming to"—that is, what precedes it or enables it—can't coherently or stably be mapped as a progression, and for that reason it seems plausible to liken it to a particular mathematical concept: a continuous-time stochastic process.[12] I wonder, in fact, if any concept or process better self-illustrates the need for more critical breathing room than the "coming to" prior to "coming out" and the role of the bardo prior to "coming to." The way such "coming to" or "realization" happens is a complete mystery, and yet the critical response to that mystery has been less curiosity than a sort of Nike ad "Just Do It" mentality that telegraphs impatience with and intolerance for any realization that isn't always already realized. Because of this, I ask with a sense of wonder, indeed miraculous wonder: Is any book more pertinent to this set of largely ignored problematics, in both self-conscious and unselfconscious ways, than *Epistemology of the Closet*? Is any critic more committed to the "lived experiment" of her own vicariating impulses, and the life transitions they foretell, than Sedgwick?

A coda to the Queen Esther story:

Sedgwick's books are filled with the thumbprints of her mesmerized interest in (vicarious) lesbianism, in multiple and complicated ways that I hope, at least in part, to disentangle. This mesmerized interest has largely been subject to the kind of response, from lesbian critics, that Sedgwick reports her Queen Esther paragraphs earned from her nameless friend: a marriage of punishing foreclosures against and reductions of both her work and her person based on the degree to which her books are (purported to be) solely about men and for men and the degree to which Sedgwick, herself, is perceived as a straight woman whose celebratory love for certain gay male writers and friends is (purportedly) a metaphor for the limited purview and relevance of her work to lesbian studies. The (anti)intellectual evolution of this critical disregard, and the willful underreading it relies on and itself performs, merit another full-length essay altogether different from the project I attempt here.

III. Sedgwick, Lynch, Dickinson, Cather

By now, I hope the logic behind my will to discover and follow (in what may turn out to be a rather flexuous path) the "lesbian bardos" in Sedgwick's writing, and my desire to ruminate on their various functions in Sedgwick's work is beginning to seem visible. Introducing the "bardo" into this critical discourse is, among other things, a definitional challenge, since what I test here is not a developing theory of knowledge about lesbianism or a particular narration of intellectual or cultural gay/lesbian history, nor even really a reading methodology, but instead the possible uses and viability of an intersection between Buddhist ideas about transition (bardo) and contemporary Euro-American ideas about a particular identity or set of sexual acts (lesbianism) for opening new angles of approach to the work of a contemporary queer theorist. This project may not even seem to make *sense*, until one discards those aforementioned rubrics as wrong-fitting overlays, in order to see what might come about in their absence. This essay is a nascent experiment in providing lesbian studies with a different, Buddhist vocabulary (alternately, conceptual space or purchase) helpful for recognizing the bardo spaces in Sedgwick's writing pertinent to questions of lesbian realization.

Lesbian Bardo #1: "You're not a real lesbian, so what do you know?"

I return now for a final look at that moment when Sedgwick airs the aforementioned "acid" reception of her Queen Esther explication, showing the claustrophobic space it creates. The prohibition of the "friend's" implied insult, and the self-authorization behind it, could be narrativized this way, as *against* the (vicariating) interlocutory space Sedgwick occupies: "You're either not a lesbian, hence your knowledge isn't based on realization, or you're not brave enough to say that you are a lesbian." Sedgwick's airing of the complaint against her brings into focus the very phenomenon she has been describing in her critique, in *Epistemology*, of why it's so hard to discuss sentimentality without replicating the discourse one aims to deconstruct. It works, at the outermost limit of what the discourse will allow, to show that the faculties for discerning who is, or might be about to, "come out"—let's say—as a lesbian are always already shot through with the vicariating impulses the friend believes automatically distance the subject from "the real" or "the realized". Ironically, what allows the stronger possibility of "coming to" or "realizing"—let's say—a lesbian "lived experiment" is fielding that insult with the snap of a glove around a ball for the sake of how visible its delimited space and importance will then be and for the silent second that follows, in which (hopefully) the insulter will realize that "the thing she thinks she knows is a reflection of her impulse toward knowing it" (1990, 174).

Axiom #1: The space/time before "coming out" may uniquely be a vicariating one.

My use of the word "before" in that last sentence is meant only spatially, as a way of indicating, and also opening up discussion around, the bardo between knowing something and realizing something. "Before" is not used to suggest that "coming out" necessarily will happen, but instead to locate the space or time of "coming to." The definition of bardo necessitates dislinking, at every opportunity, prior intention from the path of change. As such, the *before* moments of, say, "coming out" must be talked about and explored, to the extent it is possible, as discrete moments and without positing them, to the extent that not doing so is possible, in any relation to "coming out," because in fact one cannot know in advance what sort of realization will follow from a bardo space. In other words, "coming out" cannot be privileged as the endpoint. Once this is acknowledged, a whole new space opens for talking *obliquely* if nonexpectantly about gay possibilities, in that bardo spaces can be, among other things, deeply enabling ones—though how this is so cannot be known in advance.

In this small maneuver space, I turn now to two different autobiographical moments in Sedgwick's writing: the first, from "White Glasses," an account of the seemingly obverse ability of the self "to love" coextensively with *not* "knowing" in a given instance of friendship; and the second, from "A Poem is Being Written," an account of the different and seemingly obverse abilities of the self "to know" more than "to realize" lesbianism. In each, affect catalyzes realization, either negatively or positively, and somehow pulls against what knowledge catalyzes when *lacking* affect, which seems to be, only, further knowledge. From "White Glasses":

> The day I first met Michael Lynch in New York was the day that, in Toronto, the complicated, arbitrary diagnostic process around AIDS finally caught up with Michael's ex-lover, housemate, best-loved friend, a medical researcher, Bill Lewis, who was to die suddenly the next fall . . . I have always felt, since then, that the important ways in which I *haven't* gotten to know Michael fully are somehow coextensive with my never having known Bill. The same loss, the same history of struggle and subtraction made Michael available to my identification and love, opaque to my knowledge. (1993, 253)

And from "A Poem is Being Written":

> I have spent—wasted—a long time gazing in renewed stupefaction at the stupidity and psychic expense of my failure, during [my teen years], to make the obvious swerve that would have connected my homosexual desire and identification with my need and love, as a woman, of women. The gesture would have been more a tautology even than a connection. Yet it went and has still gone unmade. (1993, 209)

Lesbian Bardo #2: "I" as heuristic device

Selecting, from the many candidates, only two examples of Sedgwick's creatively varied uses of the first-person singular "I" as an heuristic device[13] was a difficult (read: critically reductive!) but ultimately not random choice; in each, the "I" tests (vicarious) lesbianism in either oblique or frontal ways. Two terms borrowed from the visual arts,[14] figure and ground, aid my explanation: "figure" referring to positive space, that which has been drawn, and "ground" referring to background, or negative space. I hope to show that both quotations bear some relation to a particular affect (love) that vacillates in position between "figure" and "ground," as if in reverse proportion to, or in opposite but direct correlation with, how available/legible the knowledge project around that particular love is and, further, how transitive that availability is. Using some of Sedgwick's discoveries in "Privilege of Unknowing" gives me generous (creative) leeway in assuming that in this antihomophobic project, "valuing and exploring and sharing a plurality of sexual . . . knowledge . . . can be done only with every possible sophistication about the exclusionary and inflictive involvements of that knowledge" (1993, 51).

Further:

> if readers can give up the sentimental requirement of finding a unitary epistemological field in the heroine . . . then [her] politically telling, if finally unsuccessful, deployment of multiple kinds of knowledge and an associated plurality of ignorances can be read and appreciated. . . . (1993, 43)

The love I want to call "lesbian" in the passages from "White Glasses" and "A Poem is Being Written" is made visible as lesbian (and in each, *differently* visibly lesbian) because each either falls with ease or somehow cannot fall into the space of lesbian bardo that succeeds each moment: in the "Poem" quotation, *still* succeeds, for quite an extended period, that moment.

Let's start with the easier, if still oblique, "lesbian" love she describes sharing with Michael Lynch. Sedgwick writes:

> our most durable points of mutual reference are lesbian. My favorite picture of Michael was taken in Willa Cather's bed. We are both obsessed with Emily Dickinson. Tokens, readings, pilgrimages, impersonations around Cather, Dickinson, and our other lesbian ego ideals shape and punctuate our history. The first thing Michael did after my [breast cancer] diagnosis in February was to bundle into the mail to me a blanket that has often comforted me at his house—a blanket whose meaning to him is its association with the school-teacher aunt whose bed he used to lie in in childhood, sandwiched in the crack between her and her lifelong companion, wondering whether . . . it might not be this Boston marriage whose offspring he somehow really, naturally, was.
>
> If what is at work here is an identification that falls across gender, it falls no less across sexualities, across "perversions." (1993, 257)

Earlier in this essay, a passage from *Flaming Iguanas* illustrated an echoing moment in time *before* the narrator had ever touched another woman, yet a moment that, in hindsight, she understands as predating and enabling that realization in more than sequential ways: the "palliative" and "mnemonic" lesbian sex acts she tries out first with a boy. One useful, further hypothesis about that moment is that what enabled its eventual allegorical richness and performative power in other venues is the degree to which, by their admixture, *what she knows* (boys) and *what she wants* (a lesbian experiment) multiply disrupt both the tautological deadness that straight sex with a boy would bring, in which what she knows is supposed to be—but isn't—what she wants; and secondarily, the impossibility of realizing *what she wants* (a lesbian experiment) if she is frozen by a "knowledge" (of lesbianism) that didn't arrive through a painless transitive route and whose legibility may in fact be—or be underwritten by—fear in disguise. As Sedgwick teaches in "Privilege of Unknowing":

> the pressure of insistence that makes a continuous legibility called sexual knowledge emerge from and take the shape of the furrows of prohibition or of stupor is, most powerfully, *the reader's* energy of need, fear, repudiation, projection. (1993, 46)

So to condense this working theory: the way for Lopez—and, I think, for Sedgwick—to circumvent the circuits of negative affect that masquerade as (negatively preconclusive, hence delusive) sexual knowledge is to marry what she wishes momentarily and fantasmatically with what she has already realized. This particular lesbian bardo is both an autobiographical project about how to experiment with "I" as an heuristic device and an hypothesis about how knowledge and affect can either help or hurt each other, about what different enactments the two are capable of performing in tandem. For Sedgwick, it takes the shape of falling in love with Michael Lynch on the one hand and then cathecting—with Michael's love—Willa Cather and Emily Dickinson, on the other. If, in part, Sedgwick falls in love with Michael Lynch because of what she can't yet know about him (the aforementioned ignorance that makes Lynch "available to my identification and love, opaque to my knowledge") it may also be that she needs his then-transitive love to transform the "knowledge" that seems (in the "Poem" quotation) to block her love of lesbians as a lesbian, even those lesbians (such as Cather and Dickinson?) she knows she would, could, or deep down already does love in this way ("my failure . . . [to have] connected my homosexual desire and identification with my need and love, as a woman, of women"). With the examples of Lynch and Cather or Dickinson, I'm attempting to locate two different but uniquely powerful routes that begin moving toward a common destination precisely at the point where the transitivities of affect and knowledge cross, in this order: (positive) affect to "gender" and (negative) knowledge to "sexualities." When this transitivity is missing, the tautology Sedgwick describes in "A Poem is Being Written" freezes the possibility of lesbian realization, which is still "stupefied" and "stupid" in the face of even certain knowledge that hasn't any transitive potential.

Axiom #2: Of the vicariating impulses, knowledge needs love to become transitive, but love cannot ever be said to need knowledge in this way.

The sum of my project here is not, precisely, abstracting, from a few autobiographical moments in Sedgwick's writing, a theory of how knowledge and affect interact. Instead, what I've ventured to do is demonstrate the various ways that Sedgwick's critical "I" as an heuristic device is in nearly constant relation to the project, if not subject, of lesbian realization. Further, I'm positing that this underlying cartography of changing relational positions has within its power to share with lesbian studies at least a demonstration of, if not quite a teaching about, the complicated transitional, transitive, and vicariating work that seems repeatedly to characterize the spaces around, and perhaps even in, the lesbian bardo.

Notes

I wish to thank two people who, in very immediate ways, formed a circle of protection around this writing project: Barbara Herrnstein Smith for her invaluable guidance during its composition; and Stephen Barber, whose precious friendship has been, literally and figuratively, the condition of possibility for these labors. Thank you, Barbara and Stephen! Among the many gifts my mentor and friend, Jane Tompkins, has shared with me, lessons in beginning meditation were especially beneficial to the writing of this piece, in practical, intellectual, and spiritual ways. Catlin Hettel pointed me in the direction of *Flaming Iguanas* and sharpened its finer moments with some hilarious, Lopez-like jokes of her own. I am also grateful to Rabbi Steven Sager, whose explication of Psalm 62 over Yom Kippur helped me understand the concept of "bardo" from a different angle, and to my brother, Scott Solomon, for sharing ideas about mathematical probability. This essay is dedicated to Eve Kosofsky Sedgwick.

1. With this story, Lopez also undoes "lesbian" as an "objective, empirical category governed by empirical rules of evidence" (Sedgwick 1993, 9) and illustrates that, for her character, "lesbian" "seems to hinge much more radically and explicitly on a person's undertaking particular, performative acts of experimental self-perception and filiation" (9). Additionally, Sedgwick's hypothesis about usage of the term queer applies here to Lopez's destabilization of lesbian: that there are important senses in which it can signify *"only when attached to the first person"* (9).

2. There is no angle of approach to "realization" because it is preceded by a bardo. Bardo makes approach impossible because it is not a place but an in-between state (or, perhaps, a process?). Bardo frustrates the hopes and desires of the self prior to realization; additionally, the sort of realization that a bardo will make possible cannot be known until that realization has already happened, in this model of change.

3. In an artist's statement for her fiber installation, "Floating Columns/In the Bardo," at SUNY Stony Brook, Sedgwick writes: "Among the bardos specifically identified in Tibetan Buddhism are those of rebirth, living, falling asleep, dreaming, and 'the painful bardo of dying,' which occupies the space between contracting a terminal illness and death itself. With certain illnesses (cancer and HIV, for instance) and in the present state of medicine, that transitive suspension or gap, the bardo of dying, may be quite an extended one. Like other bardos, it is electric with spiritual possibility as well as with pain and loss" (Unpublished ms.).

4. "Bardo" may be likened to the space between sections "a" and "b" in a piece of Romantic music; the listener is suspended in the transitional space before the arrival of something new, whose properties s/he can't yet know or predict. Like one useful variety of writerly transition, it allows no rest.

5. "Bardo" may usefully modify the degree to which cultural studies currently rests inside the likely transitional space between contradictory, inherited

definitional models of lesbianism and lesbian identity: transitional, because after Sedgwick's *Epistemology of the Closet*, it is impossible not to face, however long it may take, the necessity of making a museum out of, rather than recirculating, those inherited models and definitions Sedgwick shows us we know.

6. For example, Sedgwick ends *Epistemology of the Closet* by stating that one project (although not *subject*) of the book is her own deep recognition of, and self-positioning within, the gender bardo between the "cynosural space" that conveys how "figures of women seem to preside . . . over both gay and homophobic constructions of male gender identity and secrecy" and, on the other hand, the anodyne possibilities (still, nevertheless, structured by the original oppression) that woman can bring a cognitive and desiring animation to the presumption that she will occupy this cynosural space "passively, fantasmatically" (251).

7. Sedgwick's handling of "lesbian" is questioned or criticized to varying extents in the following: Blakey Vermeule's essay, "Is There a Sedgwick School for Girls?" in *Qui Parle* 5:1(Fall-Winter 1991) 53–72; Terry Castle's *The Apparitional Lesbian: Female Homosexuality and Modern Culture* (New York: Columbia UP, 1993); Theresa de Lauretis's *The Practice of Love: Lesbian Sexuality and Perverse Desire* (Bloomington and Indianapolis: Indiana UP, 1994); and, more recently, Julie Abraham's review of *Novel Gazing: Queer Readings in Fiction* in *The Women's Review of Books* 15:9 (June 1998): 18.

8. This passage in *Flaming Iguanas* also questions many assumptions about whether and to what degree the selection of a [hetero] sex partner necessarily correlates to one's supposed [hetero] object-choice, and whether it is more telling, in a given instance, to privilege the gender of one's sex partner or, instead, one's choice of sex practices. For Lopez, it is initially easier to summon or bring forward her erotic interest in a particular fetishized act than it is to summon it *in relation* to another person: the book and its instructions, rather than her "lesbian" boy, being the focal point of this sexual scene. This analysis borrows from Sedgwick's essay "Queer and Now" in *Tendencies*, a text that predates *Flaming Iguanas* and sometimes seems hidden, in invisible ink, underneath quite a few of Lopez's zany fictional accounts.

9. In an artists' talk, "Come as you Are," given in November 1999 at SUNY Stony Brook, Sedgwick explores some differences between "knowing" and "realizing" (or epistemology and practice) this way:

> the only sense in which I can think of reality nowadays: reality not as *what's true* but as *what's realized*, what is or has become

real. Where is the gap between knowing something—even knowing it to be true—and realizing it, taking it as real?

Reality in this sense, as it happens, may be entirely orthogonal to the question of truth. The order of truth, after all, is propositional. The order of reality, on the other hand, while it might include people uttering or thinking propositions, isn't itself propositional. For example, there are many true propositions that would describe the room in which we're meeting this afternoon. Not even an infinite number of such true propositions, however, would exhaust or saturate this space in the order of reality.

Other characteristics that distinguish the order of reality from that of truth: the order of reality is spatial as much as temporal. (Maybe that's what makes real estate, *real* estate.) Reality, unlike truth, tends toward analog as much as or more than digital representation. And correspondingly, unlike truth, reality tends toward the non-dual.

I wonder whether it's because of this tropism toward nonduality that the psychology of realization is so much a specialty of Buddhist thought? Whatever the reason, it does seem remarkable both how much attention Buddhism pays to the gap between knowing and realizing, and retroactively, how little attention is paid to it in Western thought. To practice Buddhism, after all, is to spend all the time you can in the attempt to realize a set of understandings most of whose propositional contents are familiar to you from the beginning of your practice. The very existence, the multiplicity, the intensiveness of different Buddhist traditions testify to the centrality of the project of realization; to the sense of how normal it is for realization to lag behind knowledge by months or eons; and to a concern that any pedagogy of realization is likely to be a hit-or-miss matter haplessly dependent on the contingencies of the individual. (Unpublished ms.)

10. Though, by the end of *Flaming Iguanas*, the narrator has indeed "realized" what she has been pondering/fearing/desiring during her 3,000-mile road trip (an experience, with a woman in San Francisco, of the most intensely pleasurable sex she has ever had), Lopez makes sure to emphasize that this lesbian sex has not been the endpoint to a developmental narrative. It is not "achievement," not "progress," and not part of an evolutionary sequence. Lesbian sex, for her, is also not an allegory, or itself an

act, of politics (though *Flaming Iguanas* is not without politics); nor is it the mark of a new, stable, instantiated identity. She writes: "To my relief, the next morning I didn't feel like a member of a lesbian gang. I didn't feel this urge to subscribe to lesbian magazines, wear flannel shirts, wave DOWN WITH THE PATRIARCHY signs in the air, or watch bad lesbian movies to see myself represented. No" (Lopez, 251).

11. About the "sentimental" or "vicariating impulses" (a phrase Sedgwick invents and a theme she richly explores in *Epistemology of the Closet*), Sedgwick writes:

> The tacitness and consequent nonaccountability of the identi-fication between sufferer and sentimental spectator, at any rate, seems to be the fulcrum point between the most honorific and the most damning senses of "sentimental." For a spectator to misrepresent the quality or locus of her or his implicit partici-pation in a scene—to misrepresent, for example, desire as pity, *Schadenfreude* as sympathy, envy as disapproval—would be to enact defining instances of the worst meaning of the epithet; the defining instances, increasingly of the epithet itself. The pruri-ent; the morbid; the wishful; the snobbish; the knowing; the arch: these denote subcategories of the sentimental, to the extent that each involves a covert reason for, or extent or direc-tion of, identification through a spectatorial route. (151)

12. Although "coming to" cannot perfectly be analogized as a value, or math-ematical concept, stochastic process approximates in a different way what I am trying to describe here. From *Options, Futures, and Other Deriva-tives,* here is the definition John C. Hull provides: "Any variable whose value changes over time in an uncertain way is said to follow a stochastic process. Stochastic processes can be classified as discrete-time or continu-ous-time. A discrete-time stochastic process is one where the value of the variable can change only at certain fixed points in time, whereas a con-tinuous-time stochastic process is one where changes can take place at any time" (218).

13. About her usage of the first person, singular pronoun "I" in *Tendencies,* Sedgwick writes:

> There's a lot of first person singular in this book (and some peo-ple hate that), and it's there for different reasons in different essays; to begin with, though, I'd find it mutilating and disin-genuous to disallow a grammatical form that marks the site of such dense, accessible effects of knowledge, history, revulsion, authority, and pleasure. Perhaps it would be useful to say that the

first person throughout represents neither the sense of a simple, settled congratulatory "I," on the one hand, nor on the other a fragmented postmodernist postindividual—never mind an unreliable narrator. No, "I" is a heuristic; maybe a powerful one. (xiv)

This interest in using her "I" as a heuristic continues in Sedgwick's art work. Midway through writing this essay, I received in the mail a packet of photos documenting Sedgwick's Fall 1999 art exhibit, "Floating Columns/In the Bardo," at SUNY Stony Brook. Each photo showcases a piece of textile or fiber art, and on many of the textiles, Sedgwick has scanned computer images of her body: medical Xray and CT scan images of her spine and other interior views, as well as some exterior images of frontal nudity. For Sedgwick, who has repeatedly demonstrated how efficaciously to use the knife-edge of autobiography as one among many variously pointed, sharp, or feather-like tools of critical intervention, these photos suggest the contours of a particular bardo by showing the positive spaces around it (the body ill, the body beautiful) and letting the observer ruminate on what worlds manage *to be* (and not in any mere way), to exist between invitational closeness/medicalizing distance, pain/desire, and surface/depth, to name but a few of the possible spaces in the periperformative vicinity of her art.

14. My leverage for this move comes, in part, from Barbara Johnson's 1986 essay "Is Female to Male as Ground to Figure?" on the figure of sexual difference in psychoanalytic theory, in *The Feminist Difference: Literature, Psychoanalysis, Race, and Gender* (Cambridge: Harvard University Press, 1998) 20.

Works Cited

Hull, John C, *Options, Futures, and Other Derivatives* (Englewoods Cliff, N.J.: Prentice Hall, 1999)

Lopez, Erika, *Flaming Iguanas: An Illustrated All-Girl Road Novel Thing* (New York: Simon & Schuster, 1997)

Rinpoche, Sogyal, *The Tibetan Book of Living and Dying* (San Francisco: Harper Collins Publishers, 1993)

Sedgwick, Eve Kosofsky, *Between Men: English Literature and Male Homosocial Desire* (New York: Columbia University Press, 1985)

——. *Epistemology of the Closet* (Berkeley and Los Angeles: University of California Press, 1990)

——. *Fat Art, Thin Art* (Durham and London: Duke University Press, 1994)

——. *Tendencies* (Durham and London: Duke University Press, 1993)

Reviewing Eve

Nancy K. Miller

> Part of the motivation behind my work . . . has been a fantasy that readers or hearers would
> be variously—in anger, identification, pleasure, envy, "permission," exclusion—stimulated
> to write accounts "like" this one (whatever that means) of their own, and share those.
> —Eve Kosofsky Sedgwick, "A Poem is Being Written"

Autobiographical acts always defy death. The links between autobiography and death have become increasingly explicit over the last two decades in memoirs that practice the difficult art of revising a life when grave illness—notably AIDS and breast cancer—plays a crucial role in its design. A distinguished literary critic, a poet, a teacher, and a key founder of queer theory, Eve Kosofsky Sedgwick develops breast cancer at the age of forty. She undergoes a mastectomy, chemotherapy, and then, almost six years later, experiences a recurrence, a spinal metastasis of the cancer. Yet this isn't so much the subject of her new book as its pretext.

A Dialogue on Love is above all the remarkable account of a psychotherapy. What gives the book its distinctive shape and punch are the complicated ways these matters of illness and health, life and death, get redescribed and interwoven through the narrative of the therapy itself—entered into some eighteen months after the diagnosis. Despite the irreducible reality of the cancer, the illness per se turns out to be a down payment (albeit a hefty one) on a seductive and poignant love story about depressiveness, creativity, weight, family, friendship, poetry, erotic fantasy, S/M, masturbation, writing, weaving, therapy, an academic career, Buddhism, and, of course, the nature of love itself.

The book emerges from a collaboration, from the back and forth between therapist and patient. The therapist, Shannon Van Wey, gave Eve the notes from their sessions. His words appear in small blocks of capital letters that present in shorthand a counterpoint to her alternating authorial voices: one that re-

remembers, reconstructs conversations, muses, holds the whole structure together in standard roman font; the other, of poetry, in yet a third type face, that both condenses and expands, highlights and veils. This uncommon, seventeenth-century Japanese form of "prose interspersed with haiku," we learn near the end as Eve wonders aloud about what genre the "writing of Shannon and me" should take, is called *haibun* (1999, 194).

The design of the pages is part of what makes me say I really *enjoyed* reading this book which, among other things difficult to take in, deals with pain. The book seems to radiate the pleasure of its own form. In fact pleasure is a crucial part of the deal—and not just for us, as readers who have been invited to witness, even if we're never addressed (no more than readers of Platonic dialogues), the scene of the emotional work called therapy. This work, Shannon warns Eve, is "often *painful*." No matter. Now on the threshold of a process she hopes will leave her like Humpty-Dumpty, *not* put togetherable again—not in the same way—it seems to her "that if anything can bring me through to real change, it may only be some kind of pleasure" (1999, 8).

Opening the door to the past as the necessarily preliminary to change is never easy, but here it's not the past tense of memory that hurts the most. "No, the harder part is telling it now; choosing now to thread the viscera of the labyrinth of

> what I didn't know
> and when I didn't know it,
> and what that felt like. (1999, 15)

In a therapy memoir, as in the canonical forms of autobiography, readers are free, perhaps implicitly encouraged, to draw analogies to their lives, but as Sedgwick has also insisted elsewhere: "People are different from each other" (1990, 22).

Eve Kosofsky grew up as the middle child of a middle-class, mid-western, Jewish family.

> all with fine brown frames

> and those sparkling or
> soulful, extravagant-lashed
> eyes of chocolate

> —all but a dorkily fat, pink, boneless middle child; one of my worst nicknames is "Marshmallow." (1999, 19)

Precociously in thrall to an intense family romance, Eve Kosofsky suspects her real parents might well be "the emperor and empress of Mars" (1999, 155). How else to explain the almost crippling sense of her own exceptionality that she brings to therapy. Later in her adult life Sedgwick revisits this dilemma when she becomes "an essential, central member," as she puts it, "of a queer family." This chosen affiliation is crucial to her intellectual commitments to queer studies: "yes, I do a lot of the work of articulating, making new, making compelling to others" their ideology. And as with the Kosofsky bunch, the marshmallow among the olives, the fat among the thin, Sedgwick has wanted to convince this second family "I'm not the daughter of the king and queen of Mars" (1999, 155)—thus wishing to transform, as she comes to see in therapy, the childhood drama of loneliness and isolation into a passionate project of community. It's here that for a reader of Sedgwick's earlier books the psychic wiring behind the theoretical endeavor is finally laid bare; that the therapy memoir becomes intellectual autobiography. It's also here that for me as a teacher of her work, and for the last two years her colleague, the creative power of personal desire is most acutely brought home. The surprises of kinship—a fat woman just may not appear to resemble those with whom she identifies with the most (male homosexuals)—lie at the core of Sedgwick's body of writing and shape her role as a cultural critic. "Well, I should say that one true thing about me," she explains to Shannon early on, sketching her self-portrait, "is that my love is *with* gay men" (1999, 23).

Love, as it emerges in the dialogue with Shannon, is no small item, since the word like an umbrella shelters an array of complicated feelings. Take the formulation that comes late in the therapy with the thud of conviction as the accumulated work of the sessions sinks in:

It's true, isn't it?
I am pathetically in
love with my mother (1999, 140)

Still later, in an e-mail to her friend Tim Gould, her therapy maven, whose voice also enters the dialogue, Eve explicates what love means to her: the connection of an intimacy without which "both your soul and your whole world might subsist forever in some desert-like state of ontological impoverishment" (1999, 168). And throughout the always tricky negotiation of feeling that moves between Eve ("*Is he in love with me??*") (1999, 167) and Shannon, the therapist who takes up the challenge of leading his needy patient out of that state of hunger and dread. At stake is the very nature of the affective, transferential bond between patient and therapist. "And I love," she adds to Tim, as they continue to speculate about Shannon's feelings "that his care was not care for *me*" (1999,

219). Your therapist may love you but he doesn't love only you. That's not fun to learn. But in a kind of double pedagogy at the heart of the book, it happens.

From the start an edgy tension is set up between two professionals. Eve's "MAKING SMARTER PROJECT" includes Shannon. Is he good enough to turn her inside out?

> WED. NIGHT WAS NO SLEEP,+++ ANXIETY ABOUT GETTING MY NOTES AND HOW SADISTIC SHE CAN BE IN READING SOMEONE ELSE'S WRITING—AFRAID SHE WILL KILL ME, SPOIL ME AS SOURCE OF NURTURANCE FOR HER WITH SADISM ABOUT HOW I WRITE. HER MOTHER THE ENGLISH TEACHER. IF SHE KILLS ME FOR HERSELF SHE WILL BE KILLING HERSELF. BUT IN THE MORNING SHE RECALLS HOW RESILIENT HER SENSE OF ME FOR HER HAS BEEN SO FAR. I GIVE HER MY NOTES. (1999, 200)

Shannon often gets the dirty work—here expressing Eve's doubts about him in a typically subtle blend of their two perspectives—elsewhere reporting details of the illness, physical pain, anxiety, fear of fear of pain, and self-doubt. Has he been good enough? His increased presence on the page in the last chapters attests not only to the growth of Sedgwick's confidence in his skill, and a willingness to have his side of the story shape the denouement of their work together, but also a palpable weariness with putting words on paper. (What might be at stake for him as a therapist in this role is not explicitly addressed.)

The generic therapy plot is a journey—like haibun, "classically used for narratives of travel" (1999,194). What queers the voyage, as it were, is the hard fact that it unfolds under the pressure of another demanding protocol: how to live on, as her therapist puts it with "AN INCURABLE, NOT PRESENTLY DEBILITATING ILLNESS" (1999, 216). And yet the book is not driven by the fear of death itself. Early on Sedgwick says that the diagnosis came at a good time, right after the publication of *Epistemology of the Closet*: "It was one of those happy times when you say to yourself, Okay, this is good, this is enough; I'm ready to go now. . . . I would have been very, very content to quit while I was ahead" (1999, 4). The "wish of not living!" she avers, is an old sensation in her repertoire (1999, 5). The book, like the therapy, respects the feeling behind the wish; the words she wants to hear when she suffers are:

> That's enough. You can
> stop now.
>> *Stop*: living, that is.
>> And *enough*: hurting. (1999, 69)

This longed for permission comforts and consoles.

Almost without warning, two fresh developments emerge near the end that displace without dislodging the question of what's enough and when to stop: the craft of weaving and the practice of Buddhism. Between her apprentice-ship to the loom and to *The Tibetan Book of the Dead*, an unexpected, trans-formative kind of pleasure is born, and other desires. "I've started to elope from my school and writing, flying toward this stuff with the stealth, joy, almost the guilt of adultery" (1999, 199). As Eve works on her scarves and her dreams, there's a reluctance to return to the familiar, narrow domain of the first person. Despite the etymological links between text and texture, weaving is not writ-ing; the attention required for finishing *A Dialogue* is distracted by the rising passion for the new "crafts mania" (1999, 205). Still the book must be brought to closure, like that moment in the session when, drawing the limits of your time together, and regardless of your wishes, the therapist says "We have to stop now." (The question of if or when to stop therapy itself—to terminate in some formal manner—is never addressed. And yet there is for the reader a sense of movement, a passage to another mode of relation.) That voice of benign authority shapes the book's last paragraph, which is also the last installment of Shannon's notes and in a way, his ultimate authorization—though as always renegotiated by Eve, who as author gives him the last word.

E . . . TALKS ABOUT HAVING COME TO BE ABLE TO HEAR A VOICE LIKE MY VOICE INSIDE HERSELF WHEN IT IS QUIET THAT SHE CAN TRUST AND HAVE CONFIDENCE IN. I CAN IMAGINE THE VOICE TELLING HER SHE CAN STOP. (1999, 220)

In September 1999, the CUNY Graduate Center where Eve and I both work, moved from its perch of rented office floors with fabulous city views on 42nd Street, to "our own" space in the former B. Altman building on Fifth Avenue and 34th Street (no views). This move had been anticipated with an eagerness and anxiety appropriate only to the journey (as imagined) of the Jews to the Promised Land. "When we get to the new building," was the mantra hummed every time anything having to do with the future was discussed. Of course, the Promised Land could only disappoint—at least initially. In the spring of 2000 the lounge belonging to the English program—a space resem-bling a bus station (alternately an airport gate area)—remained a huge, bare, loft-like zone of a waiting room (waiting to become a room). The students, though, didn't seem to mind all that much since they now had computer ter-minals from which to retrieve their e-mail.

The lounge remained a dreary affair except for one brief interlude when the space was filled by Eve. Let me explain. Eve filled the space with cloth figures she had made—stuffed forms dressed in blue leggings and tunics and draped with woven cloth—and hung from the ceiling. The figures were put into context one afternoon when she read a talk and showed slides from her trip to Asia. I'm going to quote briefly in what follows from the screed Eve distributed called "In the Bardo."

First a gloss on the meaning of "bardo": "The between-state that immediately follows death. Tibetan *bar* =in between, *do* = suspended, thrown."

> The present installation offers a certain experience of the bardo of dying. The large (my size), light figures, analogous to the peaceful and wrathful deities of that other bardo, are bearers of some crucial aspects of this experience, holding them open to such psychic operations as identification, disavowal, projection, recognition, rage, or reparation. The figures' strongest representational ties are to the disorienting and radically denuding bodily sense generated by medical imaging processes and illness itself, on the one hand; and on the other, to material urges to dress, ornament, to mend, to re-cover and heal. Correspondingly, a central element of each figure is the vertebral column, which I daily experience as both physically disintegrating, yet still offering a pathway for vital energy and buoyancy. These are not opposites: in different ways both cancer and Buddhism highlight the need of coming to loving terms with what's transitory, mutable, even quite exposed and ruined, while growing better attuned to continuities of energy, idiom, and soul. . . .
>
> The pieces in this show also mean to span such productive, highly-charged, and permeable boundaries as those between craft and art; between woven fiber (cloth) and nonwoven (paper, felt, soie mariée); between feeling and meditation, or gravity and lightness; at last, between making and unmaking.

For several weeks these figures brightly constellated the zones of the English program and extended a brief reprieve from the depopulating effects of our empty interior. It also seemed to me that the suspended beings could be understood as what people in English departments fond of T. S. Eliot used to call an "objective correlative"—an object that figured otherwise unattached poetic meanings. In this case the affective structures holding together Eve's experience of illness found poetic form in the figures (her size, as she says). The cloth forms also embodied the spiritual and emotional work entailed in living with death that had gone into the writing of A *Dialogue on Love*. Put another way, as surely as the graphic signs on the page, the wordless figures invited us to meditate on the process of coming to terms with the contours and accidents that shape any given life.

The text offers the reader a way into the complicated strategies of recognition and evasion therapy demands. I wrote to Eve on e-mail after I read the book, wanting to tell her about my reading experience: "Caught in feelings of recognition, identification—and also the specificity of YOU. And learning more about you. Imagining you with long red hair, wretched at the beach." In many ways our families were alike, I thought: "My father too was Mr. Information. He'd say, making fun of me, 'don't confuse me with the facts.'" It wasn't that I didn't want to know things but I wanted to be pure, or choose my information; my father read biographies and my mother did crossword puzzles—so every minute someone was looking something up, or announcing a discovery: trivia, it always seemed to me. "I confess that I was shocked by your saying that you were 'pathetically in love' with your mother; was the war with my mother really a form of love, too?" I ended up wondering whether I had gone far enough in my therapy; I could never admit, though my therapist was keen on the theory, that I really wanted something from my mother.

I admired Eve's stubborn sense of her uniqueness, her not wanting to be "fixed"; whereas my family was addicted to fixing (not just body parts, noses, eyes, but clothing, lamps, door knobs). The problem was that no one could ever perform emotional repair. Spanking—a major Eve biographeme. "In our family, I experienced it not as care but pure rage. How could you be so stupid, was a frequent rhetorical question on these occasions." Masturbation? "My sister was the great masturbator: from the cradle, it was said. Me? Clueless." When I sent the message I started worrying about my list of "identifications": was I still seeing Eve, or had I gotten lost in my own responses, skewing the shape of her plot? Yes, I thought, the compulsion to keep working without pleasure. What sadness. But that was *my* fear for myself, not Eve's. She had found a way to move on—through her work, and self-reconstruction as a fiber artist.

A few days later, Eve answered, saying, that this kind of response was what she had wanted: "To be able to check in with other dear ones reporting back from their own worlds and corners of experience."

After receiving that message from Eve, I realized how much I wanted to review *A Dialogue on Love*. I had sworn off the activity many, many years ago as a sure way of making enemies; but after a hiatus of almost twenty years, and finding myself between projects, I thought, why not do reviews . . . occasionally? Not academic books, that desire seemed entirely dead to me, but work—probably memoirs—that moved me, or that I admired, or both. I had recently tried my hand and discovered that I enjoyed the demands of the form: word limits set by someone else, deadlines, and in the case of *The Women's Review of Books*, an audience of readers with whom I could assume to share some values and assumptions. Linda Gardiner assigned me the review.

Like the memoir, and the essay "A Poem is Being Written," the cloth figures as described by Eve in the commentary of "In the Bardo," invite both a form of identification and response. My review was grounded in identification—in broad strokes, the Kosofsky family, the Kipnis family, as a particular kind of education-driven and body anxious—middle-class Jewish family in mid-century America, Eve's therapy, my therapy, her mother, my mother, etc. But it was not built on it. By this I mean that I took as my job that of using the emotional hook of—"like me"—to fashion in writing the analysis of—please forgive the expression but it's the word I want—Eve's *mishegas* (not, I hope, mine). And my motto in this process of differentiation is an axiom of Eve's that I have quoted earlier and in other contexts: "*People are different from each other*" (1990, 22). It's one of those deceptively simple remarks that repay in all kinds of unexpected ways.

The cloth figures hanging in the depressingly undifferentiated space of the lounge hold open, Sedgwick explains, "such psychic operations as identification, disavowal, projection, recognition, rage, or reparation." These operations are at the heart of a great deal of Eve's written work. The question is what happens when the written text vanishes? What reactions are produced by the cloth figures and what sort of a response is possible?

I'm not sure I can answer my own questions or that I especially want to try. Perhaps it's not a matter of words, but rather, as in the case of one particularly sticky therapy moment, the embrace of two bodies in a hug.

I'm writing this postscript to my review in the summer of 2000, one year after reading A Dialogue on Love. When I last went to the office, the figures had come down but their polyester fiberfill insides were neatly stuffed into large trash bags lined up against the walls outside Eve's office, waiting patiently to be removed. I presume they will have been carted off by the time the new semester begins. I'm not happy about the bags. This is not how I wish to think about the figures. I'd rather remember them full and suspended, bearing signs of a journey across boundaries; beckoning to all who pass, urging us to make an effort of the imagination, or maybe the heart, that in so many ways I'm not ready for.

Works Cited

Miller, Nancy K., "Review of A *Dialogue on Love*," *Women's Review of Books* 17.2 (November 1999): 21–22.
Sedgwick, Eve Kosofsky. "A Poem is Being Written," *Tendencies* (Durham: Duke University Press, 1993) 177–214.

——. *Epistemology of the Closet* (Berkeley: University of California Press, 1990).

——. *A Dialogue on Love* (Boston: Beacon, 1999).

Envois

When Whippoorwills Call

James Kincaid

Now I know why no one in love with Eve Sedgwick (all of us) can write about her. Consider that—"write about her": We are all able to *write* and we all are inspired by *her*; it's the *about* we trip over. Who can find the distance or wants to? We all write *to* Eve or, more exactly, she writes to us. Better yet (I should have said this right off), we write with her. With Eve, it's always we. You'll be wondering why I haven't been saying "I." I haven't been saying "I" because I don't have any "I," which is not modesty but something like the reverse. Eve is the we of me.

She says this of being with her older sister:

The extravagant
Rightness of it! Intimate
Sanction for us two,

To be sealed with my
Favorite pronoun: the dear
First person plural.[1]

Like all of Eve's poetry and prose too, her lyrics are about as private as block-party orgies or her heart. It's an open invitational—come one, come all. I can be "sealed" there if I like, with the dear older sister and the younger one, uncrushed and with a crush, too. It's a seal that comes unglued at the wave of a hand or heart; and the lyric is personal but not private, shyness issuing a come-on:

> Promiscuous we!
> Me, plus anybody else.
> Permeable we!

That's something—"plus anybody else!" Anybody. So that means Eve and I are permeably sealed, which gets it just right. Here's what it is: her hugs don't hold you in place. Now, when I get hugged ordinarily (and I am very huggable), I feel often as if I am being settled down, pinned—unless, as happens just as often, I am tipping over, about to lose my balance and take my affectionate friend with me. You know what I mean. But with Eve, there is no stapling to the floor and no perilous inclining. Her hugs transport you to a just-opened (free popcorn) theater in a wild new land and hand you an admission ticket. What's more, the you that arrives is not quite the same as the you who started out in that 747 embrace. It's now a we, Eve flying the plane, servicing it, handing out the peanuts and bottled manhattans—and you too. That's what "permeable we" means. Actually, I (we) are no longer so happy with that word "permeable," especially since the postcolonialists, of whom we are none too fond, got hold of it. We now would write "ballooning we," which may suggest that the *we* Eve allows in my particular case is not her most golden-eared poetic we.

Anyhow, the problem we have in such collaborative, two-fisted writing is not where to start but how not to. It's not that we are inscribing so much as hearing, allowing Eve to blossom into our fancy, work her will, allow us to lodge with her until we are a writing we. More prosaically, we will carry on here as a kind of one voiced duet, if you follow me (and if you don't maybe you should be doing something else with your time, which isn't an insult at all). Those of you who don't grant the "we" may assume that Kincaid is simply stealing Sedgwick's words, glomming onto whole sentences, sometimes paragraphs, and pretending "we" wrote them. Don't think that way, though. If I had Aladdin's lamp for only a day, I'd make a wish and here's what I'd say.

But first a word on style. "It seems inevitable to us that the style of writing will not conform to everyone's ideal of the pellucid." That's what we wrote a while back, in a mood kittenish and wry. We were not being sarcastic or defensive. It just seemed right to give fair warning, as a friend might who tells you that you have a lovely singing voice but maybe shouldn't just yet tackle "Lucia." Our style is what it has to be, given the stakes we're playing for; and one advantage of writing with Eve, having Eve write inside you, is that you find yourself using words like "pellucid" that you didn't know were part of your accouterment.

Take this, for instance, just to get us launched. Here's what we think of structuralism and of many other moments in the past that served to catch so much energy and hope and to generate even more. Remember Robert Scholes musing that maybe structuralism would give us a kind of string-theory harmony here on earth, some way of centering a system not in power or difference but in love? That wasn't so bad, nor was structuralism simply "that mistaken thing that happened before poststructuralism but fortunately led directly to it." What it was was a "rich intellectual ecology that allowed it to mean more different and interesting things than have survived its sleek trajectory into poststructuralism." Hold onto that: *more different* is itself *more interesting*, is what makes for interest and excitement too. More different and more interesting. In order to open ourselves to the interesting, we strain to hear those odd noises from the past that at one time were intoxicating melodies. In Spain, the best upper sets do it; Lithuanians and Letts do it. Let's do it—.

Difference is a happiness. That is not, however, true if we are thinking of the difference between you and me, because there isn't any difference in essence (we speak unashamedly but not recklessly about essences, we do), especially when we're writing or dancing, and certainly when the we is Eve and I, as I've said perhaps too often. Difference need not be figured as oppositional, you know, but as an interconnected gallery of jolters to our suppositions. Some people like a lot of sex, some don't; some people like to think of sex in terms of power; others (thank Oscar) do not; some people are ironists, some comedians (and some both); some like it cold. The fun is in looking out for difference and no matter how eagle-eyed we are, wow, here it comes sneaking up around the side with a punch or a goose. It's a question of mutual generosity in the name of unanticipated pleasures.

How do we hear the past more generously? Not by trying to read it more accurately, certainly, the pursuit of accuracy being a way to bolt us more tightly to the assumptions that render the past steady and certain. Good history, in this regard, is history that conforms to what we have been able to smooth out and to disregard. It's what we might call "strong history." Weak history: that's for us, history that is not certain of its assumptions or methods, its starting place or its goals. We can only get at a more challenging and strange past by releasing ourselves from our best and most up-to-date ideas. Our first aim, Eve's and mine, is to denaturalize the present, rather than the past—in effect to "render less destructively presumable what we have come to regard as"—well, presumable.

Let me live 'neath your spell. Do do that voodoo that you do so well. Let's be specific. What do we teach our graduate students these days? Certainly a lot of good sophisticated material, engines of inquiry that are oiled and road-ready. A healthy skepticism accompanied by a keen moral sense. An ability to spot leaky arguments and, even more readily, complicit ones, arguments that might appear to be subversive but are really, when you look at them through well-trained eyes, hegemonic through and through. Graduate students must be (or we'll know the reason why) quick at learning to mimic super-cops, so alert to the activities of the secret police that they can spot them anywhere and everywhere. That's about all they can spot, maybe, but we are told it's worth it: never have academics been so super-vigilant and unbamboozled, determined not to be taken in. If this model seems to you a little too like D. A. Miller and soda, taking his paranoia and leaving behind his grace and counter-movements, a little narrow and limited, a little self-confirming, a bit never-fail—well then, you should regard yourself as obtuse, morally insensitive, a pawn of Power. The secret to the stubborn longevity of the policing model is that it not only resists but successfully condemns any questioning. Doubters must, it says, be quislings.

It's understandable that graduate students, facing a starkly Darwinian world out there, should adopt what survival tools seem ready to hand. Anyhow, what other tools are being hawked? Why are current faculty, generally well padded, so prickly, timorous, and reactionary that they (we) suppose this skittish Gothic view of things rooted in pow-pow-power is simply playing it as it lays? Why are we so jumpy that we would latch onto such a reductive and bleak system, a system that keeps us wary and distant? How about locating a model that allows us to move closer to texts, theories, ideas; to caress those things we love? Surely there are things in this world, even this world of discourse, other than traps; and there are tasks that do not involve waving minesweepers around in quest of buried horrors.

Right now we are equipping our students with "an automatic nervous system of routinized dismissal." We teach our students what to avoid, what not to explore. We murmur, without ever saying it straight out, that behind us, in the scholarly past, is only the darkness: it's all a history of error and unthinking collaboration. Whatever is worth knowing is here before us, though none of it is exactly uncontaminated either, bearing traces of the past. We are purity teachers, instilling "moralistic hygiene by which any reader of today is unchallengeably entitled to condescend to the thought of any moment in the past (maybe *especially* the recent past)." Equipping our students and ourselves "with two or three discrediting questions," we find ourselves globally armed against anything that might come from the past, as if they had nothing to send us but tanks.

Knee deep in flowers we'll stray; we'll keep the showers away. But, pestiferous as the disease is, Eve has a cure (and, naturally, so do I): Avoid the natural and easy and seek out the freakish and difficult. By that she means that we might forgo the ready pleasures of mocking what we take to be the past by taking the past to be something else. That's a start, but it's not so easy to open ourselves up to what that something else might be, since it's altogether possible we would not have the wherewithal to recognize it, much less deal with it. But *wot larx* if we can make contact with something back there or even launch a voyage of discovery, wondering what we might find, emptying our arsenal of gratuitous skepticism and trying, instead, to think, even if it takes a lot of straining to become so naive.

"How provisional, how difficult to reconstruct and how extraordinarily specialized of use, are the tools that in any given case would allow one to ask, What was it possible to think or do at a certain moment of the past, that it no longer is? And how are these possibilities to be found, unfolded, allowed to move and draw air and seek new voices and uses, in the very different disciplinary ecology of even a few decades' distance?"

After thinking it over, Eve and I have decided that this last formulation is unnecessarily formidable, asking of us more than is necessary (and certainly more than most of us have to give). For one thing, it really isn't necessary to reconstruct what was there, as if we could anyhow, as if what was there was ever there in any way that was fully present to anybody (say me, who is old) who was also there. We do not need to relocate ourselves in a past moment or somehow translate that moment into our own study. All we have to do is adopt the right attitude, develop a certain elan. In matters of grave importance, Oscar Wilde says, it is style that matters. It's the posture we assume, the air, the costume. In this case, we have to ask that wonderful question, "What was it possible to think or do at a certain moment in the past that it no longer is?" and really mean it. Like the White Queen, we have to be able to believe six impossible things before breakfast. But what we are believing we have found in the surprising past is not necessarily (is certainly not) what was *there*, whatever that means. We have heard of transference, Eve and I, and countertransference too; we know that the problem we take to the past is never the one that is solved, any more than the illness we take into analysis is the one that's treated. But that's OK. The vital thing is to open up what we take to be the past, which is all the past we have, and make it dance for us. In other words, it is vital to pump up our confidence and sense of optimistic devilment to the point of being able to believe that any trip to the past will be filled with surprises. Not just any surprises either, but surprises we can put to good use in entertaining friends and family, dazzling our colleagues, getting invited to give talks, and all else we live for. Another way to put it: You made life cheery when you called me dearie; 'twas down where the green grass grows.

The past is another country and they do things differently there, all right, but no visas are required. The past exists as difference but not as oppositional difference. At least there's nothing compelling us to think of it as oppositional. We (Eve and I) have mounted some great prose on how we might need analog models to access "difference, contingency, performative force, or the possibility of change." This is difference as a range of possibilities, not separated but connected, melting into one another. Thinking in that blessed way, we are not compelled to choose "essentialism and no essentialism. If there is a choice it is between differently structured residual essentialisms." But there's no need to place ourselves in that gloomy bind, however pleasing it may be to our current self-congratulatory Malvolioism. "Why be limited to the digital model of the choice? A repertoire of risk—a color wheel of different risks—a periodic table of the infinitely recombinable elements of the affect system—a complex, multilayered phyllo dough of the analog and the digital: these are the models" Eve and I (and, OK, Silvan Tomkins) hand over to you, no charge. Analogical and digital models can cohabit in a frisky, unstable, and dazzlingly productive arrangement—always subject to change.

The rent's unpaid, dear; we haven't a fuss. But smiles are made, dear, for people like us.

These models lead us to replay a whole pile of records from the past, and they're easy enough to lay our hands on, though not so easy to hear. Eve (me too) sets out for us a positive example of how to shop for music easily and productively in the past. That's not the hard work, but we don't hide that there is hard work. The real sweat is in making the resolution not to *know* and sticking to it. Knowingness, the spandex securities we pour ourselves into, tend to keep us always swimming in the same channels, at different speeds perhaps, but always within our lanes, pounding up against the same old walls at the end. Think of how many difficult and mysterious things we *know*: that the Victorians believed in separate spheres and were hysterical about masturbation; that men looking at women (real, print, celluloid) amounts always to objectifying; that the superior power of invisible policing is never to be doubted; that other critics are naïve/blind about police power and only imagine they are being liberatory; that we can read the past much better than we can read texts generally; that we have come to understand sexuality, the body, gender, history, language, power, the family, and bowling in ways the past simply couldn't manage. Some others I've seen might never be mean, might never be cross or try to be boss, but they wouldn't do.

Anyhow, as Eve and I said in an earlier book, "A point of this book is *not to know* how far its insights and projects are generalizable, not to be able to say in advance where the semantic specificity of these issues gives over to (or: itself structures?) the syntax of a 'broader' or more abstractable critical project. In particular, the book aims to resist in every way it can the deadening pretended knowingness by which the chisel of modern homo/herterosexual definition tends, in public discourse, to be hammered most fatally home."

Not to know in advance, which means, first, trying to remove our most familiar and reliable protections, those shields that accord us membership privileges in the radical-comfy status quo and give us the ability to churn out highly moralized, highly guarded, and highly predictable discourse. We that would gain must first lose. I'd travel through the smoke and flames; I gotta go where you are; Through the darkest night; I gotta go where you are. I'd roam through the dismal swampland, searching for you. Because if you are lost there, I want to be lost too.

Second—you remember the first?—there's a difference between not knowing and being ignorant. Blunt ignorance, in fact, operates in the world almost always in concert with knowingness and is a terrible force. Being certain that we know what we know is very much like not knowing anything at all. Ignorance, like knowingness, is filled with certainty, probably a righteous certainty; whereas not-knowing leaves certainty behind and has never had a firm grip on righteousness. Ignorance is out to get something and it knows what it wants; not-knowing has no particular destination and is glad to get (or give) what it can.

Oh the night was mighty dark so you could hardly see, for the moon refused to shine. Couple sitting underneath a willow tree, for love they pined.

One of our most crippling and unfunny certainties we share and need to shed is this: the darkest secret agent in our world and also the thing always to be spotted first, even if it is invisible, is prohibition. Of course, we must reckon on the confusing fact that power will not be saying "No" but "Yes," (Your lips tell me "No, no," but there's . . .) and making us think we are free, when the very terms of our freedom are a set of hidden prohibitions, guarded and rigorously enforced. Power operates not by prohibiting but by producing, not through easily observed external operations (laws, rules, penalties) but by implanting inside us ways of thinking and seeing. Our obedience thus seems not only voluntary but not like obedience at all; it seems like freedom. To summarize, then, power makes prohibition look like permission, more exactly, like nature; it operates through a variety of criss-crossing channels, not from a recognized center; it (and this is the hard part) does not, despite this crafty multiplicity, function through local and particular prohibitions but "through a single transcendent" one.

How could one top (or escape) this refined, exquisite paranoia? Enemies are everywhere you look and, especially, where you wouldn't think to look and couldn't see if you did. How can we, in this happy prison-house, bring ourselves to question or even recognize our habitation? How can we find the capacity even to wonder why it is we're so preoccupied with prohibition? How can we wonder why we cannot find other centers to guide us in our fun? Ask that and you are told that it's Power (unquestioned, metaphysical, ineffable) speaking through you, that you are an unwitting tool, hegemonic as the day is long. Why is Power any more convincing to us than Play or Absurdity? Why do we get our kicks from power analyses that are surely becoming by now a bit routine? What does it say about us? That we are tough-minded, on our guard, not easily fooled? Even if that characterization were apt (which it's not), who would want to claim it, wear it with pride?

It's true that Foucault, who spawned all this in a way, is a mighty thinker and a real presence amongst us. But Foucault can be read in so many ways. Why have we chosen this one? We all know texts are part of a cultural ecology of meaning-making, so the question surely is not why Foucault said this but why we want to suppose he did. It's our choice, and it's we who settle for such a nar-row-gauged construction. Anyhow, the consequences are not pretty; and as we've covered this, Eve and I, quite thoroughly in an earlier book, we'll repeat a hefty part of that here for those who missed it. Of course we'll also make some changes along the way, revisiting our own past and making it just as we like it.

Cuddle up a little closer, lovey mine. When we read Foucault in obedience to our most craven needs and niggling insecurities, we teach ourselves to believe that "The most important question to ask about any cultural manifes-tation is, *subversive or hegemonic?* Intense moralism often characterizes such readings." We'd say now that the production of that moral glow emanating from pious one-upsmanship seems to be the leading feature of this still-dominant and redundant mode, the leading feature and the leading inhibitor of the pro-liferation of more various and truly disarming models. Anyhow, back to our past wisdom: "to demonstrate (or even assert) that something is not 'natural' or not 'essential' is always to perform a powerful act." We'd now add some sarcasms about power, about power being really, really powerful and about, gee, how it is that analyses proceeding from a worship of power can produce powerful results convincing to the power faithful. But we won't indulge ourselves at this point, wanting to proceed: "To find naturalizing or essentializing points in other people's work is always politically and intellectually telling, and in self-evident ways. Every cultural manifestation must be scrutinized to determine whether, deep down, it is *really* essentialist (e.g., 'sincere'). The epistemologi-cal stress becomes infinitely insistent." We stand by this now, especially the first two sentences. Maybe we'd drop the third, since it may be a little show-offy [what's wrong with that?] and since we've been reading about string theory (reading seriously—in the newspaper and *Time*) and are not so happy with "infinitely" any more. Where bowers of flowers bloom in the sun; each morn-ing, at dawning, birdies sing and everything. A sun-kissed miss said don't be late. That's why I can hardly wait. Open up those golden gates.

In sum, "The 'subversive or hegemonic' structure of inquiry requires a wholesale reification of the status quo. One's relation to it becomes reactive, like that of a consumer, accepting or rejecting this or that manifestation of it, dramatizing extremes of compulsion and voluntarity." We just want to cheer when we read that. What prose! What a clincher! It's time to schedule the awards dinner for us, get ready the testimonials, buy the thank-you gifts. (Hint: Eve likes to weave and I like to crayon but together we're into climbing trees.) And though I'm not a great romancer, I know that you're bound to answer, when I propose: anything goes.

Yes, but what about sex? Fair enough. Eve and I (in our rare separate manifestations, Eve grants that she has learned a lot from me on this—but pshaw!) do not think we gain a lot by separating sex and sexuality and focusing entirely on the latter. We have not given up on sex. We suspect that the sex/sexuality opposition is false, that the two have the friendly relation, when all is going well (as it always does) between script and performance. Doing sex and talking about it, discourse about it (official, backstreet, generous, twaddling) and action, are not two different things but a happy coupling, or a coupling that will be happy once released from our sickly current paradigms. Sex is, even now, a whole lot of things; and it can be a whole lot more.

We don't always see that. Take Catherine MacKinnon, who is sure she knows what sex means and knows what we mean when we have it. She tells us in terms we cannot mistake what it means: "There's a whole lot of 'mean-ing' going on. MacKinnon manages to make every manifestation of sexuality mean the same thing, by making every instance of 'meaning' mean something different." Sex is not always fun and it is not always just; but sometimes it is one or the other or both. It can be understood by way of power, which gives us a good way of reckoning really bad sex: rape, coercive sex, mechanical sex. Power has nothing to say about any other kind of sex (i.e., good sex), and those so cowed by power as to think there simply is no other kind of sex—why, I hope for your deliverance.

I don't want to say exactly that sex can be what we make it, since I know what we make it is severely limited by cultural constraints we can never see or even imagine, and that, what's more, they construct not only our making but us, the very selves we imagine are thinking and writing articles, and having sex. Yeah, sure! (That "Yeah, sure!" was a sarcasm-indicator, making it clear that we were mocking the sentiments contained in the first sentence. Trouble is, nobody [friends we burdened] who read this essay seemed to catch the sarcasm, so we are adding this parenthetical clarifier, just to set you straight.) Even if there's a profitable idea in such blather, it's a thin one. Look, even if our way of thinking and doing sex is not all ways; it doesn't follow that it's one way, that we *know* it, that we can't change it, and that we need to have it or think about it always in the shadow of the pokey. Eve herself (this time without any help from me) has provided us with a cultural possibility, a whole set of possibilities that extend our range of being and give us new ways to roll in the hay. She is, you know, a part of culture. We don't need a paradigm leap or a trip to Venus to imagine our way out of Power. It's already there. Eve. Don't want to be constrained? Don't be. Gender got you down? Well, stop listening to Dr. Laura and listen to magician Eve: "Sexuality extends along so many dimensions that aren't well described in terms of the gender of object-choice at all."

In every smile that's bright and gay; I'll always think of you that way. I'll find you in the morning sun and when the day is through; I'll be looking at the moon, but I'll be seeing you.

What does it mean to see? Is seeing the same thing, necessarily, as looking? No it isn't. We have them confused. Put more clearly, we have confused seeing, which is common and empathetic, with looking, which is very rare and objectifying. (We're clearing our throat now, ready to explain.) The Gaze is another thing, please note, and don't get all tangled up with that. We're speaking here about the general talk in film and gender theory and in cultural studies and just about everywhere about seeing. Here's what Lacan says: "one leaf is sunshine, the second is rain; third is the roses that bloom in the lane." When we see somebody (or something, but let's keep it simple) we undergo a dynamic and quite wonderful set of shifts, moving at a lightning speed inside both the subject and the object position in order to register that vision. That is, we not only take the other into ourselves, but also offer ourselves up to the other, switching to the object position because we are, truly, rejecting that subject/object offensive binary. It is a melding that is both an expression of vulnerability and a declaration that there is nothing to be vulnerable about. In order to see, I need to give up the object position for a little bit, to reposition myself into the seen. Seeing you I do not distance you but deny distance, which is just the way Eve and I see one another and become we. It is electric, I can tell you; but you already know that. It's the way Whitman saw the grass, Wordsworth the child, Hardy the grave, and—you get the idea. Anyhow, it's the way we all see.

Somehow we have it confused with the sad and very uncommon, rarely occurring state of looking, looking specifically out of a fear so deep it cannot engage in the reciprocity of seeing. This is voyeurism, and it has nothing to do with seeing, not anybody's—apart from the voyeur, whom you could live several lifetimes and not run into. The voyeur is the forlorn man or woman possessed by an inescapable fear of becoming a subject. So petrified of being caught and pinned up butterfly-style in someone else's collection, the voyeur resolves never, ever to be seen, to be turned into an object, even for a microsecond. The voyeur looks so that invisibility is assured. Hiding in the bushes is not a means of hiding from the cops but of eluding the looking eyes of others. Seeing without being seen, without empathy or becoming, is the dream of the voyeur. The nightmare is that someone else is watching, can look. (This helps explain the horrifying moment in "Rear Window" when the watched [Raymond Burr] becomes the watcher, staring back through the wrong end of Jimmy Stewart's telescope and into his eyes. It also helps explain the attraction of the reductivist paranoid reading of Foucault so popular now, where all critics, though under the surveillance none of us can escape, become themselves the eager watchers, round-the-clock spotters of those deluded and dangerous souls who think they are roaming free.) Where was I?

We seize on an outlandish and pathetic state, the incomplete seeing of the voyeur, and put it in place as a cultural norm, a necessity. It's like proposing that we all were fostered by chickens or looked forward to spinning a web and eating flies. This may be true of some of us, but not all. Why not think of seeing as a generous and expansive act, a way of figuring out through experience how we might imagine other worlds and other forms of happiness. After all, seeing is switching sides; it involves entering into other states of being, into previously unthought collections of ideas and feelings. Why don't we work on that: by seeing me, you are not violating me, but getting to know me. The idea of empathetic seeing surely has a much stronger scientific and experiential base than does the notion that we are all of us sick at heart and mind. Down on your knees, up on your toes, stay after school, see how it goes!

Which brings us to feelings, to the reparative criticism we do, Eve and I, and to the search for affect and for a way to talk about it. Strange that even in the heyday of the studies of readers and what was going on inside them, little attention was given to feeling. What happens if I feel embarrassed, aroused, bored, fascinated, stunned, amused, saddened? What happens if I have a physiological response: I cry, laugh, itch, sneeze? Don't ask Stanley Fish. The reader-response criticism in this country, still some of the smartest and most intriguing we have, treated readers as calculating machines, anticipating and remembering but never suffering from affective interruption.

Another of Eve's we's, Adam Frank, got together with her for an introduction to *Shame and Its Sisters* that is so rousing it ought to be our national anthem. In that book we are shown how to listen to the past so as to hear intimately, drawing up from inside ourselves a way to think and see feelingly. The systems theorist, Silvan Tomkins, has not yet worked his way inside our practices. But he will, since he is now Eve-saturated.

I don't know if I'm in a garden, or on a crowded avenue. Here you are; here am I. Eve has for a long time been tickling and teasing the antisentimentalists,

the tough guys who devote lots of energy to detecting and denouncing whatever expressions of feeling are excessive, false, or squeam-inducing, which is
all of them. "Antisentimentalism," as we have put it elsewhere, "becomes the
very engine and expression of modern sentimental relations." It springs from a
sad insecurity and needs (oh so badly) these scapegoating exercises. What
would antisentimentalists do without Disney, Rob Reiner, and a certain few of
our best-loved poets? And, more to the point, how can they be rescued, these
pitiful Norman Mailer clones, from their need to spend so much energy wal-
lowing in what they claim to abhor? They find it everywhere and are so happy
when they do.

Takes one to know one, to be sure; and the antisentimentalists, Gore Vidal
say or his friend William Buckley, are such fine sentimentality hunters because
they are so deeply soused with cornball sentiment. Like a couple of drunks lost
in their song, they can find relief only in keeping their harmonies private, out
of the hearing of others, and blaming the noise on the radio down the hall. But
spotting and then mocking the antisentimentalists hardly seems worthwhile,
seems a version of their own game. Helping them would be more like it—more
like Eve. So she shows us how not to be afraid, how to sing on stage. She's the
karaoke master of our souls, Eve is.

Remember reader he were that good in his hart. You'll be thinking that I've
been horning in on Eve, claiming as ours what I had nothing to do with. Well,
you have a point; but she won't mind.

> "Never mind me, Joe," I said.
> "But I did mind you, Pip," he returned. "When I offered to your sister
> to keep company, and to be asked in church, at such times as she was
> willing and ready to come to the forge, I said to her, 'And bring the poor
> little child. God bless the poor little child,' I said to your sister, 'there's
> room for *him* at the forge!'"

Eve teaches us how to take all this in, *way* in. Even more kindly, she teaches
us what Pip finally learns. I don't know if he "learns" it exactly; it's rather that
wisdom seeps into his being, Joe seeps into his being. Returning to the forge to
attend his sister's funeral, he moves from thinking about how awful funerals
are, to how angry he is at his sister, to how angry he is at her murderer, to no
anger at all, as he finds himself being absorbed in a gentler memory, the sunshine and the smells, the beans and the clover:

> It was fine summer weather again, and, as I walked along, the times when
> I was a little helpless creature, and my sister did not spare me, vividly

returned. But they returned with a gentle tone upon them, and they soft-
ened even the edge of Tickler. For now, the very breath of the beans and
clover whispered to my heart that the day must come when it would be
well for my memory that others walking in the sunshine should be soft-
ened as they thought of me.

Eve stretches our mind so that we may see and feel fresh on our faces the
breath of the beans and clover. Sniff it in. None doth offend. We can be, all of
us, those others walking in the sunshine—we just have to see it, and feel it on
our skin and innards. Eve strips and softens, whispers to our hearts. In her world
there is no Tickler, unless you bring it yourself for fun and games. The most
brilliant and tough-minded among us, Eve Kosofsky Sedgwick opens her forge
to hammer us, tease us, and stroke us into smart kindness.
    Keep the love-light glowing in your eyes so blue. Let me call you sweetheart.
I'm in love with you.

Editors' Note:
James Kincaid chose to exclude all reference matter for this essay.

This Piercing Bouquet
An Interview with Eve Kosofsky Sedgwick

... the piercing bouquet of a given friend's particularity. ...
— Eve Kosofsky Sedgwick, *Epistemology of the Closet*

The following conversation between Eve Kosofsky Sedgwick, Stephen M. Barber, and David L. Clark took place in Sedgwick's apartment in Greenwich Village on the afternoon of January 8, 2000.

Q: We would like to begin with your experiences in university as a graduate student and with your early teaching. Your doctoral dissertation was published in 1980 as your first book, *The Coherence of Gothic Conventions.* In your preface to that book, added in 1986, you spell out a relation between Gothic paranoid narratives and American discourses on AIDS, and you make an argument there that would become especially familiar to readers of your next book, *Between Men,* basically about the relations between Gothic paranoid homophobia and nineteenth- and twentieth-century structures of knowledge. You were, then, in your dissertation already working through novel ways of thinking about paranoid structures of knowing and developing in your thought the formative agency of homophobia, or crises in homo/heterosexual definition, in modern culture. The latter specifically would result in your assertion, made in your third book, *Epistemology of the Closet,* that "an understanding of virtually any aspect of modern Western culture must be, not merely incomplete, but damaged in its central substance to the degree that it does not incorporate a critical analysis of modern homo/heterosexual definition" [1]. To what degree did your passions as a graduate student shape those intellectual passions that came to characterize your later work?

EKS: Let's see. I wasn't bringing a lot of passions to my dissertation. I was mostly bringing mild interest and profound depression; but yes, there were thematic preoccupations, as well as certain structural or even spatial interests, that

I had had for a long time and have kept for a long time since. It's interesting to me how seamlessly all of that could get plugged into the queer work I was doing later, but that wasn't at all where I was with it then. That said, I'm sure it's also true that the aura of perverse eroticism and sexual secrets was one of the attractions of the Gothic in the first place, and if I'd had these analyses for it back then I would greatly have relished using them.

Q: In your introduction to *Epistemology of the Closet* you recall your education "in the dark campus days of the late sixties" [55]. Dark days, no doubt, but also ones that seem to have been enlightened by training in the pleasures of possibilities of close reading. At Cornell, you point out, it was professors like Allan Bloom who exemplified a passional investment in the act of interpretation for you, and who demonstrated first-hand the riches to be found by reading against as well as with the grain of a canonical text.

EKS: Well, especially against, at that point. I was completely riveted by the performance of the closet that he enacted. The person, besides my mother, from whom I most learned really basic things about literature—which is to say, what counts as smart, as interesting, or as going somewhere—was Neil Hertz, whom I was lucky enough to have as a teacher from the time I was a freshman. I directly absorbed a whole lot of values and moves from him that would later be called deconstructive. But at that time they just felt like good close reading, and like a really unremitting impatience with dualisms. And, I guess, that Proustian sense that writing well is not only the best revenge, but a very high value in itself. All this in the context of 60s politics that were, of course, a whole lot more palatable than Bloom's.

Q: Did the intellectual and affective context change radically when you went to New Haven? You arrived as a graduate student more or less at the time when the university was coming into the period that would quickly become known, for better or for worse, as "Yale deconstruction."

EKS: Cornell kind of spoiled me for Yale. I felt as though except for Paul de Man, who was so brilliant but also way beyond me in his explicitly philosophical preoccupations, I already had a much more interesting version of deconstruction than my teachers there had. Of course, though, I was a mess at that point psychically, which made for a certain contempt for everything around me, matched only by a savagery toward myself. Yale was just such a chilling place—it couldn't have been much worse for me. I'm sure at a happier time I would have found more to learn there.

There were a few figures I was interested in, but in a spectatorial kind of way. Harold Bloom was one—funnily, he reminded me of Allan Bloom. It was encouraging to see somebody as queer, physically grotesque, unsocialized in his body and speech as Bloom be so valued, so able to make a place for himself. But I didn't want to work with him because I'd been told that he sexually harassed women students; also, his students seemed to wind up speaking and writing only to him, which looked like a dead end. But I liked his being around. I was extremely fond of Paul de Man. He was much the warmest faculty member I encountered at Yale—not that that says a great deal for the emotional ambience.

Q: What then were your resources for sustenance and succor?

EKS: I had a few very sustaining friends. Beyond that, I read Dickinson and Charlotte Brontë. The masochistic sublime was the only thing that seemed to fortify me at that time. It's still a really invigorating set of tonalities, but I don't think it would have led me to a viable way of being. The best thing I did was to leave Yale—I got my Ph.D. in four years and got away, and that helped loads.

Q: At Boston University sometime between 1981 and 1983 you taught a course on the literature of sexual triangles. Were you then thinking about *Between Men*?

EKS: Yes, but that was after two other jobs. I went to Cornell for a postdoc, which is where I started thinking about *Between Men* and then spent three years at Hamilton College, where I began writing it.

Q: Proust is so clearly akin to your ways of thinking and being. When did you start reading him? You don't mention him as a resource when you were at Yale, but so much of your later grasp on matters queer seems to indicate a long, or at least intimate, affiliation.

EKS: I didn't read Proust until right after graduate school. Those values, that intellectual idiom were a dramatic discovery of resources for me. Remembering the psychic state in which I finished my graduate work, reading Proust was a wonderful intervention in that. I think what it offered me most excitingly—rather as therapy did later, in fact—was an example of forgiving oneself enough to permit a reasonably spacious inner life, one that was allowed to be *interesting*. It was an example of what could happen if you were at home enough with yourself and your past selves to have some exploring room. I'd somehow learned to experience myself in an annihilatingly shameful and abject way, so that was a marvelous discovery. I think it's one of the things Proust demonstrates most efficiently. When I've taught Proust, I've seen my students get smarter week by week—and that's a lot of where the smartness begins.

Q: That would explain why you describe Proust as a kind of drug that you administer, as it were, to students or friends who are in crisis. You identify Proust in that same passage as a source of "truth" or "truth-telling" [1990, 240]. What is the nature of that truth, and beyond that, what might the truths of literature be for you? After all, literature is a distinctly privileged kind of writing in your own work. What is it for you that makes literature deserve that kind of distinction? Has it to do with the unsystematic resources, the nonce taxonomies that you identify in literature as the source of its power to do justice to the particularities of individuals?

EKS: Well, it doesn't interest me greatly to call it literature or not. I'm always compelled by the places where a project of writing runs into things that I just can't say—whether because there aren't good words for them, or more interestingly because they're structured in some elusive way that just isn't going to stay still to be formulated. That's the unrationalizable place that seems worth being to me, often the only place that seems worth being.

Q: Philosophical texts don't win your attention the way that literary ones clearly do. (We're still obliged for the sake of expediency to keep the name "literature.") We never see, for example, the sort of scouringly brilliant close readings of Hegel's *Phenomenology of Spirit* or Nietzsche's *Genealogy of Morals* that can characterize the work of Judith Butler. What do you think accounts for the relative nonappearance of philosophy as such and of explicitly philosophical texts in your work?

EKS: Nietzsche does fascinate me—I write about him in *Epistemology* but some might say as a writer and psychologist. I'm a terribly illiterate philosopher. It so much doesn't engage my aptitude.

Q: With the possible exception of Foucault?

EKS: I have a fascination with the first volume of *The History of Sexuality* because it seems like such a serious attempt (and a flickeringly successful one) to formulate important things that don't want to be formulated. It does seem so at cross purposes with itself, and somehow those flickering pictures are most compelling to me.

Q: You have referred to those cross-purposes as Foucault's queer performativity, which you don't see as being taken up by people who work on or with Foucault. Since so many queer thinkers are involved in Foucault's work, why this resistance or blindness to that aspect of his thought and writing?

EKS: Partly I think it's because other people who are interested in it either know their Foucault much better than I do, or have a more abiding sense of the "Foucaultian" so they have more tendency to assimilate that text to a greater overriding argument, one that might be less resistant to articulation.

Q: For that matter you've also indicated an abiding absence in critical thought of taking seriously his critique of the repressive hypothesis.

EKS: Some version of the repressive hypothesis is, I'd argue, a necessary underpinning of paranoid structures of thought. But a fascinating thing you find in that volume is the flickering glimpse that there might be radical alternatives to that—though it seems hard to absorb. It's hard to find sustainable frameworks that answer to it.

Q: It strikes us when reading your recent work on the reparative and the paranoid that you stage those structures of thought as wholly imbricated, one with the other. Is reading, then, not so much a matter of proceeding reparatively *or* in a paranoid fashion, but much rather of oscillating between these two kinds of practices, these two styles of thought?

EKS: You're right about the oscillation; I think that has to do with why Melanie Klein calls these *positions*, rather than anything more fixed. And in practice, I think people actually do read that way. Most people who are attracted to literature do read that way; it's just that what counts as an argument to make, at this juncture of critical theory, emerges from only one of the those positions, the paranoid one. One notion of what criticism, and for that matter politics, might be is paranoid, and it is that through and through, so it has almost effaced the evidences of the reparative impulse and structure. Certain kinds of reading structures have a triumphal way of exponentially expanding their own rationale and venue.

Q: You speak of attempting to do justice to "the reparative practices that infuse paranoid critical projects," and to the "paranoid exigencies that are often necessary for non-paranoid knowing" [1997, 8]. Such justice would presumably not *need* to be done, if it weren't for the fact that the two projects get so tightly bound up, one with the other; more, if it weren't for the fact that the positional and reparative seems more readily to get displaced or at least effaced by a hermeneutic that is more recognizably "paranoid" and suspicious. I am thinking that perhaps all positions are reparative, but some have forgotten themselves to be reparative. If you will bear with me for a moment, I am wondering, for instance, about the difference between, *on the one hand*, what is rightly made of Lacan, by you, and by others, and, indeed, what Lacan is capable of making of himself, in terms of his work being an exemplary instance of the suspicious hermeneutic, and, *on the other hand*, a certain disruptively reparative undercurrent in seminars like the "Rome Discourse," where Lacan attempts— maybe to no avail, and with clearly deeply mixed motivations, given the Freudian context—to stage the psychoanalytic relation as a much more improvisational, open-ended and nonteleological enterprise, irreducibly intersubjective in character, in which something like the analysand's self-perceptions and filiations, her "knowledge" of herself, is always rendered purely contingent and experimental by the fact that the analyst can only ever be "presumed" to know. Lacan had himself once described this process in precisely performative and reiterative terms as one in which "imaginary servitude" gets repeatedly undone or severed by "love"—presumably, never completely to be undone. It would seem, though, that paranoid structures so quickly overwhelm whatever reparative impulses are also at work in any given project—this, to the point, as you suggest, that criticism is itself now virtually coextensive with this paranoia.

EKS: I think you're right that it's the self-misrecognitions that happen in the name of the hermeneutic of suspicion that not only perpetuate but expand the field of paranoia. So that the moment of transmission to another generation of people who may use the ideas — it's moments like that that permanently institute such misrecognitions. They get taken up and are given a more authoritative currency, and they take over the conditions of possibility of the original text. Also, though, as Silvan Tomkins points out from a systems theory point of view, the paranoid styles of thought expand their field of application just insofar as they're unsuccessful. And when they have the need and make the claim of predicting the future and thus warding off surprise, such failure is almost guaranteed.

Q: Why do you think this seemingly irresistible foreclosure of the reparative occurs in criticism, theory, politics? But we remain curious about the nature of the relationships that obtain between paranoid and reparative practices. Is it a case of parasitism? Of being blindnesses to each other's insights?

EKS: Yeah. That's at the heart of so many methodological and theoretical issues: the interpretive proceedings that make certain kinds of perceptions or articulations easy will inevitably make others more difficult. That doesn't itself describe their value. But to try to recover or retain the sense that another angle might make something else visible, well, it's hard to do. To go back to Tomkins' terms, what he calls "weak theory" has an advantage in this respect over "strong theory," which is more likely to spread uncontrollably and to obscure the ground of its possibility.

Q: To return now to the truth effects in Proust, what relation between paranoid and reparative positions do you see operative here that in effect produce these effects?

EKS: In this respect, I'll admit to having at the moment a very over-simple schematization of Proust, that anyone can deconstruct who wants to. It's very over-simple but nonetheless, for now, carries me with it. On the one hand, there's a current of epistemological pressure that in Proust gets presented as heterosexual desire per se (indeed as sexual desire per se) and which is interminable and paranoid. Take the Odette/Albertine plot as a prototype of that — where the question of "what is she really?" (which somehow always gets dichotomized as virgin or whore) takes over the landscape of the subject's consciousness and tries to shape everything to its violent dichotomies.

And then there's another current, completely different — that of happiness — which has nothing to do with epistemology or even with the question of "what's the truth?" Now this latter current isn't absent from the cross-sex relationships any more than the same-sex ones, but neither does it have any privileged relation to heterosexual desire, or even to sexual desire. The happiness topic emerges in, for example, Charlus' long relationship with Jupien, or at *moments* between Swann and Odette or the narrator and Albertine—but it emerges just as much in relations to landscape, or music, or grandmothers, or all kinds of other moments. And in relation to writing particularly. As I say, it's way over-simple just to see the happiness current as the "right" one (though I sort of want to)—there's more a systemic choreography of those two currents than a direct competition between them. But I could emphasize that the moments of hap-piness tend to represent "weak theory" in that they don't have an aptitude for taking the book over; they're affectively expansive, but not cognitively or strate-gically so. You might talk about a happiness "plot," but it doesn't constitute plot in the same way, with the same forceful impetus, that the epistemology plot does. It's difficult to move the happiness moments anywhere near the realm of reductive generalization—much as the book in fact wants to. While the cur-rent of paranoid, jealous desire, with its intense epistemological stress, is a pro-totypically inexorable "strong theory" plot.

Q: Could you tell us more about the one object of possible object relations that is perhaps most satisfying to you right now, namely *textiles*? "Big pleasures with-out big goals" [203], the making of textiles is called in *A Dialogue on Love*; and yet you don't hesitate also to link this making to a kind of impulse to document and reconceive yourself at this "new juncture" in your life, the juncture that has seen your cancer reappear. It is hard for me, though, to imagine a bigger goal than the carrying out of such a project, not least because it can instantly render so small the sorts of goals that conventionally are imagined to quicken and loom large in our lives. The textiles are, as you write, "so *not* writing," which is to say, *not* made up of the gossamer fabric that many of us are much more used to fin-gering on our keyboards. In the same context, you've also evoked the possibility of a "texture book" whose attraction is that it "wouldn't need to have a first per-son at all, any more than weaving does" [1999, 207]. No need for a first person? I need to say here that the prospect of that future comes as a bit of a shock for someone, like myself, who feels like he is just beginning to get a feel for the warp and woof of your writing, writing for which the phrase "first person" hardly begins to describe its sense of queer particularity, its irrepressible quality of being the person "Kosofsky." This relatively recent "mania for making unspeaking objects" [1999, 207], how does that nevertheless speak to your writing, the writ-ing that so palpably performs the first person, or perhaps first persons? What cur-rently joins and separates your writing and non-writing impulses? You once said (in *Epistemology*) that the erasure of the first-person was always "mutilating" and "disingenuous," but clearly, under the present circumstances, that erasure has come to possess new possibilities for you.

EKS: Well, it's mutilating to rule the first person out in advance, I mean to forbid it—erasure in that repressed or repressive sense. I'm thinking here of an old, stylized way of writing: "One cringes, does one not?" or "Here we feel that the poet has not earned his pathos." That arrogant, disciplined, transparent avoidance of the first person, seeming to place such a low value on any overt introspection and self-relation.

But that's different from working in areas where there just isn't a first person because the things involved are nonverbal to begin with. Objects don't have a first person because they don't utter. So restful and refreshing! An artifact does not have syntax, thus doesn't insist on invoking that subject/object relation that Nietzsche, like Buddhism, deprecates as a serious distortion of mental process. Things are so different from propositions; if they can't be more true than propositions, at least they can be more real.

But there are also psychological motivations, no doubt, behind this wish to do without the first person. One of them—a fairly recent one, I guess—has to do with the consciousness of mortality that's gotten so sharp. I have an intense wish to be assured that the people and communities I'm leaving behind can take care of themselves—that they don't need "me," my thought, my labor of regenerating a first person to keep them going. Obviously that corresponds to an insanely grandiose fantasy about my importance to others' lives!—You know, that if there isn't Mrs. Ramsay the dinner can't go on. So the thing you say in kindness about this persona, also rather makes my heart sink.

For me that realm of self-construction is also closely tied to a lifelong mix of extreme shyness with a funny exhibitionism. Really it's surprising I didn't arrive earlier at the artisanal combination of silence with productivity and display. Being the object of a lot of attention is excruciatingly uncomfortable for me, even as it does organize some very durable, even quite productive fantasies and articulations. It's a complicated field of desires and fears; also of attempts to find ways to speak truthfully. There being the one pronoun for it all, just "I," is absurdly difficult. I don't understand why other people don't talk about experiencing these sorts of things—it seems so unlikely that others don't wrestle with them too.

Q: Part of your own queer performativity lies in or is generated by a notion you've described more than once: "being available to be identified with." In *Tendencies* you write, for example, of how much "transformative political work [there is] to be done just by being available to be identified with in the very grain of one's illness" [261]. This particular formulation comes from "White Glasses," your obituary-essay on Michael Lynch (a version of which, happily, he heard before his death in 1991 from AIDS). In a more recent and as of yet unpublished essay you describe the bardo of dying as constitutive of some of the energies that helped congeal ACT UP! I'm wondering, now, how you think about—if you do—a relationship between a self who avails herself to be identified with and the first-person "in" the bardo of dying. I'm asking this because it seems like there is a complicated but manifest relation between your availability-self and your bardo-self, given their respective attachments to, among other matters, what's going on around HIV, AIDS, and cancer. Maybe another way to broach this—but I hear in advance how far away it sounds from my question, and yet, I promise you, it's related; or I think so—is how do you conceive of the person that produces the textiles? What is "her" relationship to the earlier texts? And to the earlier self-performativities? And what are the diacritical marks between the relationships on the one hand of the writing "I" to her texts, and on the other of the weaving "I" to her texts?

EKS: I think you're asking about a very floating set of relations with a lot of micro-variations. Somewhere in *Tendencies* I say: "'I' is a heuristic," and that still makes sense to me. It's a trying something out to see what happens around it, even to make new things happen around it. And it works in really different ways from one paragraph, setting, or situation to the next. You know, what my "I" means to a hopeful listener like you, and what it means to somebody who just can't believe that anybody could be so Gothic or so self-involved, are really different. There are also lots of people who can't wrap their minds around the notion that somebody could use the first person singular without trying to appear as attractive or exemplary as possible—that's a disability for them in profiting from my work. They seemingly have less ability to surface with a certain pleasure, a curiosity, a childish sadism about themselves than I sometimes have, so they don't respond to that mode of learning.

Q: Someone who did surface (first in a class and then more abidingly albeit all too fleetingly in your life) with just such pleasures, curiosities, and—well, yes—passionate S/M ties was Gary Fisher. All of these qualities appear in the book that you edited and saw through to publication in 1996, *Gary in Your Pocket: Stories and Notebooks of Gary Fisher*. What has its reception been like?

EKS: It's barely been received at all, yet. I keep being told that people are writing about it, but I haven't seen that writing yet. I can't wait. There's a review by Arthur Frank of Gary's book and Gillian Rose's book [*Love's Work*] together, about how both of them push back against the sort of unitary "I" that autobiographies of sick people are supposed to aim at reconstructing. I thought it a very interesting and moving essay because he really, viscerally recoiled at the racialized S/M in Gary's book. He hated it, but he could tell that Gary was trying to do something intensely interesting in his self-relation through that sexuality, so Frank was struggling with it and really did make some progress with it. That felt like a good kind of response, but aside from that I haven't seen a lot.

Q: In *A Dialogue on Love* you speak of having been perceived as "the wrong person to be promoting this material" [179], an "error" so to speak, that you identify positively with a larger pattern of professional misdeeds.

EKS: At conferences where I've presented Gary's writing, there's been some very predictable stuff about "You're a white woman," for instance.

Q: How did you respond to such takes?

EKS: Well, you know, more or less forthcomingly and patiently depending on what I could manage.

Q: So these weren't venues in which you thought you could unpack the complicated modeling of your relationship with Gary and the notebooks?

EKS: I did as much as I could, and sometimes did get very helpful or interesting interlocution about it. But you know, there are frameworks of thought where you probably just aren't going to encounter a lot of new ideas. One black critic is quoted somewhere as saying something like, the only question is whether I'm playing Gary for a sucker with this book, or he's playing me for one.

Q: This was reported to you?

EKS: It was published, I can't remember where. To me it seems a pretty stylized view of a complicated relationship that, I think, Gary and I were both glad to have. Not that I suppose using and being used are such bad things. If people use my work I feel that I've done what I've wanted. Speculation about motives is kind of a noxious byproduct.

Q: What was it like for you when you were bringing it together for publication?

EKS: It was emotionally pretty wracking, although in some ways lovely to be taking responsibility for somebody's writing that I loved so much. There were many moments when I felt, how fabulous to be able to present this writing, which I could never have produced myself. A hard thing, though: when Gary wrote something that I didn't get, or I wouldn't have done it that way, or it just felt unmatured, I had a responsibility to put it forward just as it was. But also I was making a claim for people's best attention to Gary's writing, so I always wanted it to be as good as I could make it—but it wasn't I who was making it.

Q: We are now starting the third decade of the AIDS epidemic, and, notwithstanding certain mournfully triumphalist declarations, the crisis is far from over. In a certain, irreducible way, it will never have been over. It is not something that we can have done with, neither all at once nor all in the same way. That is to say, nothing, no future imagined "technological" masterstroke (for example) will ever wipe out the significance—the significances—of what has happened, *what is happening*. One of the many, many chastening things about the AIDS epidemic is that it now has been with us long enough that it *has* a history, or rather *histories*, some much more palpably fantasmatic, careless, and willfully nonknowing than others. Media discourse about HIV and AIDS may be said to be changing, although certainly not necessarily in any way that does justice to the epidemic, whether here in North America or anywhere else in the world. But we presently have a growing and highly variegated body of biographical and autobiographical narratives that differently witness, scour, illuminate, and explore particular lives and deaths in the age of the epidemic, and that can differently be described as AIDS activist. Amy Hoffman's *Hospital Time* or your own edited collection of Gary Fisher's stories and notebooks come to mind as examples of this powerful kind of writing, a writing, that, in its own way, is also constituting a history of the epidemic. Do these texts speak to and out of the epidemic in ways that are importantly distinct from autobiographical narratives from a decade ago?

EKS: I wish I felt there was an active discourse now about AIDS—I don't see one; and it horrifies me and frightens me. Mainstream–North American gay culture is resolutely amnesing AIDS in the present and as much as it can in the past, so that AIDS issues are nowhere in the political programs of mainstream gay organizations. Marriage is, the military is, but AIDS isn't there. It really frightens me. The mainstream gay and lesbian culture resembles and is led by mainstream culture in general; they act as though they really believe the epidemic is over.

Q: Do you see this amnesia as part of a larger amnesiac impulse or as symptomatic to mainstream gay culture?

EKS: I'm sure that in some ways it's specific—queer people have been so battered by loss and mourning that there hasn't been time to work through. But the covert permission to just forget it is getting seized on more avidly than is good for any of us. The silence about AIDS probably means different things in the *New York Times* than in the *Advocate*. It seems very bad to me in either venue: dangerous for people's health in the first place, but it also seems to be wantonly throwing away a whole history of reflection, politics, experience that shouldn't be erased.

Q: Given the scenario that you've described it's astonishing that any of these books should appear. They are acts of counter-memory that resist that amnesia.

EKS: That's the wonderful thing about the printed word—it can't be updated instantly. It's allowed to remain anachronistic in relation to the culture of the moment.

Q: You have linked the emergence of queer thought or queer theory to the emergency of AIDS. Given that the latter is being amnesed, how do you see queer thought as presently faring?

EKS: I don't know how to map queer thought, but it certainly seems to me that gay and lesbian culture—mainstream gay and lesbian culture, which mostly means white gay male culture—has gotten a lot less queer and way less interesting. There are lots of things I'm not reading anymore, but gay mainstream publishing is high on the list.

Q: Someone whose work you've introduced me to is Kiki, who is about as far away from mainstream gay culture as I can imagine. How do Kiki and Herb figure in the queer performative course you recently taught?

EKS: As presiding deities. I asked everybody to go see Kiki and Herb early on in the semester because I wanted people to have a real powerful jolt of queer performativity. Also I wanted to do an end run around a notion of drag performance as parody and "subversion." That seems to me relatively unproductive at this point—and I don't think anybody who's experienced the huge, cathartic rapture of Kiki and Herb will be tempted to recognize them in such programmatic analyses.

Q: Unwarranted claims to the contrary, you've written a lot about women's eroticism, especially in *Tendencies*. There the set of categories you develop in *Epistemology* don't appear quite in that form; instead, issues revolve around auto- and allo-eroticism, or else, as you've said elsewhere, between the sexual and the unsexual. Given that "sexual difference" as a concept or category for thinking is repulsive to you, what critical lexicon appeals here? ("Here": but you're denying such a "place" for sexual difference, so there may be no "replacement" of terms.) Does your lexicon stand in and arise out of opposition to theories of sexual difference, or is it not in that kind of relationship? Perhaps in *Between Men* there is more recourse, however unnamed, to (the concerns of) theories of sexual difference, given its study of literature during the years, approximately, from 1750 to 1850, which predate the power structure of the twentieth century that you call "the Name of the Family—that is, the name Family" [1993, 72]. In the essay on Wilde from which this phrase is taken, you indicate your impatience (a "certain" impatience!) with the Name of the Father [72]. Perhaps the movement from, even if we fictionalize here, the Name of the Father to the name (of the) Family suggests a move from theories of sexual difference to queer theories?

EKS: I want a question about fairies, not about sexual difference! I just don't seem able to identify with those concerns. I used to, didn't I? Did I? Maybe you have to go through the experience of having all the estrogen removed from your system by drugs to grasp how much I don't identify with this question. [laughs] I really don't.

[Momentary break during which Eve shows David and Stephen textiles on which are imprinted her X rays. David says it looks like a shroud, Eve says it's her fantasy of a security blanket, to take with you if you go to the hospital to hold onto. She talks about the dye process, and that she's intending to make a quilt of one particular piece.]

Q: Are you still writing the advice column for *MAMM*? How does the magazine correspond, or not, to the shape of cancer politics now?

EKS: [laughs] Nominally it's an advice column, but I make up all the letters. I wish people would write and ask for my advice. I have to try and guess what might be helpful to people at different stages of dealing with cancer.

I'm very proud of what *MAMM* is doing now. The people involved are doing a wonderful job at making a space for serious, critical discussion of cancer issues—which no mass-market journalism has done before. "Cancer politics" may be a bit premature as a label, compared to, say, AIDS politics (and note that *MAMM* began to publish under the aegis of *POZ*, a magazine about AIDS).

Cancer offers so many important similarities to and differences from AIDS—the most obvious difference being that there isn't much of a stigma attached to having cancer. Historically there's certainly been stigma, but even so, it was nothing compared to that attaching to AIDS. A more important difference, probably, is that treatment issues and prevention issues in cancer are so very separate in their sites. I really think it's true that serious prevention in cancer, for most cancers, means environmental activism and nothing else. So the prevention issues are not identity-based in any way, as they often are with AIDS, and there isn't really a specific community that has an interest in environmental activism—at least not an obvious, pointed interest. It's everybody's business, which can often leave it as nobody's business.

Treatment issues are awfully interesting, too, and there's a lot to be done there. There's so much seemingly that could be being learned from AIDS treatment activism, from the analyses that led to and surrounded that activism, which I don't see getting discussed enough in cancer activism. How, for example, research should be structured, what the trade-offs are in the design of protocols. I don't think there are obvious lessons on such matters to be directly extracted from AIDS activism, but certainly these are conversations that have been going on for quite a while now. How do traditional and alternative medical options relate to each other—including in testing? How do you balance thorough testing of drugs against the need to get new drugs into sick people quickly? How do you define "side-effect," and how do you measure side-effects in relation to quality of life? For that matter, how do you conceptualize and measure quality of life? How do you conceptualize *cure*, and what is meant by chronic *disease* when that is held up as a goal of treatment? How can drugs be distributed in an affordable way? I don't see these conversations going on enough between AIDS people and cancer people, and I think they may be more important than adopting ACT UP! modes of activism per se.

It's very worrying that a lot of the public pressure around issues like breast cancer is aimed at goals that just aren't worth a lot. Events and legislation get organized around demands like earlier mammograms; coverage for bone marrow transplants; longer postmastectomy hospital stays; frightening more women into breast self-examination. To the best of my knowledge, none of these strategies has a significant life-saving effect. Or the activism gets couched in terms of more money for this cancer as opposed to that cancer, or more money for cancer as opposed to AIDS, or more clinical trials of the same old chemotherapy drugs—which also are not going to get any of us anywhere. Then there's the ever-popular question: How do you get enough people eating low-fat diets?—which is pointless until you figure out what's getting into animal fat that is so dangerous to people in the first place. But the latter is not a question that's popular.

To me, the quality of political analysis is the first place where change needs to happen. There are a few people and groups doing wonderful work in this area—and then there's a whole lot of noisy, politically more popular misinformation.

Q: How does the notion of the bardo resonate for you here—that is to say, is there "politics" in or of the bardo?

EKS: They sound mutually exclusive, because the question of what can happen to your soul in the bardo of dying doesn't, ideally, seem to involve mobilizing rage or grievance. Or I guess it does involve anger, but mostly in the sense of finding other things to do than project outward to a vision of a hostile world, an analysis of the world's hostility.

But if you define the bardo of dying as the space between diagnosis and physical death, I think just the recognition of it as a distinct place that many people spend a fair amount of time in, out of which they can speak directly to others as well as to themselves—I think that recognition affords its own opportunities, its own tasks and also anxieties. I do think it was one of the big discoveries that potentiated AIDS activism. It is full of potential for activism as well as reflection around other slow-acting diseases.

Q: When it comes to speaking about your complex relationships with your various families, you have been known to figure yourself as a sister from another planet. I'm thinking here, for example, of what you say in your poem, "Not": "I didn't put in for a transfer to this planet, / I can assure you" [1994, 36]. And in a telling moment of anagnorisis in A Dialogue on Love, you speak about the other project operating behind the "gay-lesbian scene" that you helped create: I'm "trying to convince this family," you say, that "I'm not the daughter of the king and queen of Mars" [155]. Maybe because one of us happens right now to be writing about Kant's unlikely fascination with what he calls "nonterrestrial rational beings," I've got to ask: Are you an alien?

EKS: Do any of us know? It's certainly been a big motivation for me—to go back to the first person question—a lot of the reason why I use the first person so much is wanting to check in with people and figure this out. You know, does everybody really feel this way, does it work this way for other people? (Whatever "this way" is in a particular instance.) I would love it if other people would report back just as candidly about what it's like for them—maybe we could figure out what it would mean to *be* from the same planet. Is thinking the same for many or all of us? Does what counts as sexuality mean similarly for people? Do you find that your memory works as wackily as mine does? I am really, really curious about other people's minds. That seems like a fairly primordial motive—I can't convince myself others don't share it. It's a lot of why I read novels, no doubt.

Q: In "A Poem is Being Written" you claim as one of your motivations the desire to have other people start writing experimentally. Are they in a way that is satisfactory to that desire?

EKS: Some are. But not a lot. I don't understand why not.

Q: Perhaps for many this has to do with a sense that to engage publicly in truth-telling—about one's illness, for example—is to risk professional security?

EKS: I'm so grateful when people get to the point and just say what seems to them like the truth. A great thing about communicating with other people with life-threatening illnesses: people don't have time to bullshit. They have a sense of urgency about wanting to be truthful and to hear truth told, and often feel like sort of a first audience for each other.

Q: What form is your therapy currently taking?

EKS: Informally; by phone. At this point it's not therapy but shmoozing, though with a fun, mutual-therapy edge. But it's also, for me, keeping a channel open in case of need—becoming very sick or just being too depressed again.

Q: Has the therapy influenced your teaching? And how has teaching changed for you these last years?

EKS: Teaching hasn't changed much with the move to New York, except that my class load is smaller. So I get to bring more to my classes and hence enjoy them more. My institutional situation has changed more. I came here being very candid about my health and the consequent limitations of time and energy. It's the first time in my career that I've not invested a lot in institutional identification, not brought all my utopian fantasies to bear on the institution, and that's very relaxing.

The specific effect therapy had on my teaching was very strong and almost immediate. It made me so much of a better teacher. I think my students are finding it much more feasible to achieve that very relaxed, yet very alert and focused form of relation that seems to characterize both hypnosis and good pedagogy. That's where I am in class, too—enjoying my students, relatively straightforwardly, without worrying as I used to "Am I smart enough?" "Do I deserve to be in front of a classroom?" "Are these people mad at me?" "Are they disappointed?" It's become quite a pleasure to discuss books in such a setting.

Q: Queer activism has been integral to your relations with students in the past. What's it like now?

EKS: It feels a little more peripheral. That is to say the space in which I continue relating to graduate students feels more peripheral to the rest of the world than it used to. There are several reasons for that. One is a retreat into (relative) privacy that I've consciously made since the spread of this cancer. Another is that activism is harder to find. A third is that the profession itself is so catastrophically situated now: There are fewer straightforward narratives of empowering students, moving them into an ongoing profession, helping them in turn pass along the good stuff to the young ones. Careers don't tend to get shaped predictably like that.

It feels more, nowadays, as though we snatch what enlightenment we can from each other, hollowing out and nesting in the most provisional spaces; and people use these resources as best they can.

Q: Eve, you have written recently, based in part on your rereading of Melanie Klein, about what fruitfully reparative critical conversations, knowledges, and practices might come from speaking *less* in terms of "theoretical ideologies" where the object is to clamour to demonstrate who possesses a certain "paranoid" competence or awareness, and *more* in terms analogous to Klein's notion of the psychic life of "positions," or what you call "changing and heterogeneous relational stances" [1997, 8]. These stances, *as* stances, more subtly register the limitations and expectations of, as it were, the local psychic and social ecologies in which a person might live and breathe and have her being. Now, the conversation or conversations that you record and reflect upon in *A Dialogue on Love* would seem to embody that notion of a nonparanoid, reparative work, and represent a case of you *showing* us what you mean by this kind of non- or at least other-than-theorizable labor. Would this be a fair description of that book?

EKS: Yes, at least it records some ambitions I had for it.

Q: We wonder too about the contingent relational stance whose name is "Buddhism" in your most recent work, which, arguably, you stage as a kind of zero-degree paranoiac condition of thought and action. Is this one stance among many, or is it fair to say that it forms a more deeply felt attachment than provisional terms like "stance" or "position" might imply?

EKS: It probably shouldn't be surprising that the more I learn about Buddhism, the less stable is my sense of what it represents and for whom. The learning curve is steep for someone who's been so ignorant about Asia, and I've been reading a lot of work recently that problematizes, in quite a sobering way, the terms of accessibility of Buddhist traditions in the west. It feels currently as though the result of these past three years' immersion in Buddhist thought is oddly bifurcated for me.

On the one hand, I've a far stronger sense of the claims, the gravity, the direction and potential, of a certain sense of spiritual reality. Some important terms in describing it would include nondualism, spaciousness, an intimate and nonlinear relation to mortality, an alert pedagogical relationality free of projection, an emptying of the concept of self, and at the same time a primary emphasis on happiness. The Buddhist tradition is rich in resources on all these matters, maybe uniquely so. Most of them represent lifelong biases for me, though, as well (biases in the sense that that's how my cloth seems to be cut). Though of course I recognize them rather differently, in the context of this Buddhist tradition—differently and, it seems, better.

On the other hand, I guess I'm further than before from having a reified or even a negotiable sense of what constitutes Buddhism as an entity. Increasingly I'm fascinated, respectful, yet rather baffled in relation to a very complex history and set of practices that I've barely any tools for navigating. But bracketing that complex history off from something *else* called "Buddhism"—"Western Buddhism," say—would be claustrophobic and tautological, as well as politically rather violent.

Q: Regarding your recent work around Buddhism and textiles, what connections and discontinuities obtain around their relation to your earlier work? You suggest, for example, a recognition of the bardo of dying as a mobilization for so much queer life and politics around the time of ACT UP! And in your thinking about *The Tibetan Book of Living and Dying*, a *kind* of queer performativity therein has been mobilizing for you, it seems, in many directions. It may be, though, that you are as interested, maybe even more so, in the irreducibility of your forays into thought about "realization" to your preceding work. How do you see or chart this?

EKS: Irreducibility is quite a magnet for me in itself. One of the big attractions of Buddhist thought is a prospective dispensation from ceaselessly generating and revising these narratives of self. What if you could stop revising your c.v.— what if it didn't have to be up to date, or even coherent?

Q: In the supplementary "Note on 'The Warm Decembers'" you speak about how "part of [your] . . . motive as a poet was that the most writerly writing I could do, and the most thinkerly thinking, be shown *not* to be generically alien to each other" [160]. Not alien, then, but, as you go on to suggest, decidedly not identical either, joined and divided as the fields are by "ontological thresholds not to be denied or dissolved." We're wondering if it is fair to say that your writing has always occupied that irresistible and irreducible no-man's land. And if it has, how have the features of that interzone changed for you, in what ways have you differently inhabited it?

EKS: It's funny how electric the energy of generic crossing, generic juxtaposition and deformation, remains for me, even when the content of the terms changes—going as far as, say, "weaverly weaving"!

Q: The relevance of childhood to your writings has always deeply impressed us, whether you are writing of your own or that of other queer kids. Given your sense of a broad cultural amnesia around AIDS, how do you view the kinds of struggles facing queer youth today?

EKS: Truthfully, I feel awe of anyone who is making a go of or even surviving childhood; queer childhood most of all. Such awe is probably, usually, more of a hindrance than a help in actually connecting with people, but there it is.

Q: Your intellectual relationship with psychoanalysis is clearly a complex and, we would say, pressingly vexed and vexing one, for the perhaps obvious reason that it is disfigured, at the start, by carceral and denuding heterosexist and homophobic premises. But we wonder too if part of the "problem"—and a productive "problem" it is—is that for you, as for others, there may be no "psychoanalysis" as such, and that whatever plural things it is, it has possessed different valences for you at different points in your life as a thinker and writer, valences we might give particular names: Freud, Lacan, Klein, and so forth. If you don't actually come out and say *"Forget Freud!"* (as if one could!), you do exclaim, twice in *Tendencies*, that we should at the very least try to "Forget the Name of the Father!" As a self-declared "oedipal conscientious objector" (as you put it in *A Dialogue on Love*), you nevertheless note that psychoanalysis has "not become dispensable as an interpretive tool for any project involving sexual representation" [1993, 74]. We appreciate your careful phrasing here, *"not become dispensable,"* evoking as it does the possibility of a future in which psychoanalysis would or could be something that one could take or leave. What might that future look like? Or is it the case, as Foucault says of Hegel, that just when we think we might have put Freud behind us (and an interesting place that is for him to be), he is there before us, waiting?

EKS: The best strategy I can come up with for dealing with "Freud" is not to try and go mano-y-mano with him as a gigantically singular, protean, transferential figure; that seems like a mug's game, in the sense that the theorist's own propulsions lead circularly, inexorably to an endless reinstitution of Freud's terms and problematics. Lots of critics undertake that rigorous struggle, but what's the point? To me, I guess it seems more promising and interesting to figure a plurality of psychologies, allowing them to converse with each other and various other texts, to explore what gets opened up or foreclosed in each instance. For sure, Freud's own writings are diverse enough in their assumptions to occupy several different chairs around this table—a fact that's sometimes repressed in "psychoanalytic" theory—but there are other powerful interlocutors, too. In terms of the structure of psychological thought it does make sense to me that opening out this transferential space could only be a happy thing.

Q: In 1995, you brought to publication *Shame and Its Sister: A Silvan Tomkins Reader* for a whole series of reasons that you address in yours and Adam Frank's introduction to the book. To what degree has his work altered the recourse that critical thought implicitly or explicitly takes to psychoanalysis? How has his work figured in your own recent thinking about queer performativity?

EKS: It's no simpler to envision a single "applied Tomkins" mode of reading than a single "applied Freud" one, but since publishing that book I've found— I think Adam Frank has had a similar experience—that Tomkins' writing has only continued to work its way closer to the center of my own. I've continued to find his dislinkage between drive and affect extraordinarily helpful, and wish a lot more people were willing to engage with it. His sense of the autotelic nature of several important affects seems to have become a ground of my aesthetics, such as they are. One of Tomkins' useful divergences from Freud is his simultaneous refusal to privilege childhood as the determinant, *or* "maturity" as the telos, of psychic life—that's a key move, it seems to me. Then, Tomkins is sensitive to the seeking of positive affect as one strong, continuing motive and the avoidance of negative affect as a distinct, sometimes conflicting one; this articulation makes it possible to follow into adulthood a lot of dynamics that tend to get smothered under the "reality principle" in Freud. I could go on singing! Tomkins offers so many kinds of useful leverage—I feel I'm only beginning to learn how to use him. It would be great to have more company, too.

Q: You have done so much to create a culture of pleasure in critical writing. These days, what counts as pleasure for you? What are your intense pleasures?

EKS: Usually not writing, these days. Not sure why not: I speculate that some combination of effects of chemotherapy, hormone therapy, and the cancer itself has occasioned cognitive changes that make it much harder to take pleasure in writing. The word-hoard is intact, I think, but the search engine has become painfully laborious. It turns out this isn't unusual in cancer patients, but it's been a big change for me.

Whether or not as a result, visual and sensuous beauty loom much larger for me than before. Also, between the fascination of textiles and of Buddhism, I'm intensely drawn toward Asia and Asian travel. Craft learning—new techniques, new materials and imaginative possibilities—are a tremendous recent pleasure.

Works Cited

Sedgwick, Eve Kosofsky, *A Dialogue of Love* (Boston: Beacon Press, 1999).

——. *Epistemology of the Closet* (Berkeley: University of California Press, 1990).

——. *Fat Art, Thin Art* (Durham: Duke University Press, 1994).

——. "Paranoid and Reparative Reading; or, You're So Paranoid, You Probably Think This Introduction Is about You," in *Novel Gazing: Queer Readings in Fiction*, ed. E. K. Sedgwick (Durham: Duke University Press, 1997) 1–37.

——. *Tendencies* (Durham: Duke University Press, 1993).

SELECTED BIBLIOGRAPHY OF
TEXTS BY EVE KOSOFSKY SEDGWICK

Books, Authored

——. *A Dialogue on Love* (Boston: Beacon Press, 1999).

——. *Fat Art, Thin Art* (Durham: Duke University Press, 1994).

——. *Tendencies* (Series Q) (Durham: Duke University Press, 1993).

——. *Epistemology of the Closet* (Berkeley: University of California Press, 1990).

——. *Between Men: English Literature and Male Homosocial Desire* (New York: Columbia University Press, 1985). (With a New Preface, 1992.)

——. *The Coherence of Gothic Conventions* (New York: Arno Press, 1980). (Rpt. New York: Methuen & Co., 1986.)

Edited

Sedgwick, Eve Kosofsky, ed, *Novel Gazing: Queer Readings in Fiction.* (Series Q) (Durham: Duke University Press, 1997). (Includes "Paranoid Reading and Reparative Reading; or, You're So Paranoid, You Probably Think This Introduction Is about You." 1–37.)

Fisher, Gary, *Gary in Your Pocket: Stories and Notebooks of Gary Fisher*, ed. E. K. Sedgwick (Series Q) (Durham: Duke University Press, 1996).

Frank, Adam, and Eve Kosofsky Sedgwick, eds., *Shame and its Sisters: A Silvan Tomkins Reader* (Durham: Duke University Press, 1995).

Parker, Andrew, and Eve Kosofsky Sedgwick, eds., *Performativity and Performance* (New York: Routledge, 1995).

Journal, Special Issue

Sedgwick, Eve Kosofsky, ed., "Introduction: Queerer than Fiction," *Studies in the Novel* 28.3 (Fall 1996): 277–80.

Columns

——. "Friendship 101: How to be Good Company in Bad Times," *MAMM Magazine* (February/March 1999): 26.

From "Off My Chest," Column for **MAMM** Magazine

Sedgwick, Eve Kosofsky, "Fond Farewells: Why Time Together Surpasses The Perfect Goodbye," *MAMM Magazine* (June 2001): 20, 57.

——. "Living with Advanced Breast Cancer: The ABC's," *MAMM Magazine* (May 2001): 26, 32.

——. "Advanced Degree: School Yourself in Resilience to Beat DePion," *MAMM Magazine* (September 2000): 24.

——. "Your Results May Vary: Know the Limitations of Current Survival Statistics," *MAMM Magazine* (June 2000): 18.

——. "The Guy Factor in BC Support Groups," *MAMM Magazine* (April, 2000): 31.

——. "Dealing with Recurrence," *MAMM Magazine* (January, 2000): 24.

——. "Hair and Now," *MAMM Magazine* (November/December 1999): 28.

——. "The Punitive Phantom: Getting a Better Handle on Self Blame," *MAMM Magazine* (June 1999): 35.

——. "Treatment on Terra: Confronting a Confusing Diagnosis," *MAMM Magazine* (April 1999): 24.

——. "Comfort Cushion: Softening Pain with Perspective," *MAMM Magazine* (December/January 1999): 24.

——. "I Got it Good . . . and that ain't bad," *MAMM Magazine* (October/November 1999): 24.

——. "A Voice for Choice: It's Your Treatment after All," *MAMM Magazine* (August/September 1998): 33.

——. "A Scar Is Just a Scar: Approaching that First Postmastectomy Tryst." *MAMM Magazine* (June/July 1998): 27.

——. "The Happiness Trap: Sometimes You Just Got to be Down." *MAMM Magazine* (April/May 1998): 34.

Articles

Sedgwick, Eve Kosofsky, "Pedagogy," in *Critical Terms for the Study of Buddhism*, ed. Donald S. Lopez, Jr. (Chicago: University of Chicago Press, forthcoming, 2002).

——. "A Dialogue on Love," *Critical Inquiry* 24.2(Winter 1998): 611–31.

——. "Teaching 'Experimental Critical Writing,'" in *The Ends of Performance*, eds. Jill Lane and Peggy Phelan (New York: New York University Press, 1998) 105–115.

Moon, Michael, and Eve Kosofsky Sedgwick, "Confusion of Tongues: Louisa

Van Velsor Whitman and Walt Whitman," in *Breaking Bounds: Whitman and American Cultural Studies*, eds., Betsy Erkkila and Jay Grossman (New York: Oxford University Press, 1996) 23–29.

———. "Warhol's Shyness, Warhol's Whiteness," in *Pop Out: Queer Warhol*, ed. Jennifer Doyle, et al. (Durham: Duke University Press, 1996).

———. "Gosh, Boy George, You Must be Awfully Secure in your Masculinity," in *Constructing Masculinity*, eds. Maurice Berger, et al. (New York: Routledge, 1995) 11–19.

Frank, Adam, and Eve Kosofsky Sedgwick, "Shame in the Cybernetic Fold: Reading Silvan Tomkins," *Critical Inquiry* 21(Winter 1995): 496–522.

———. "Shame and Performativity: Henry James's New York Edition Prefaces," in *Henry James's New York Edition: The Construction of Authorship*, ed. David McWhirter, (Stanford: Stanford University Press, 1995) 206–39.

———. "Inside Henry James: Toward a Lexicon for The Art of the Novel," in *Negotiating Lesbian and Gay Subjects*, eds. Monica Dorenkamp and Richard Henke (New York: Routledge, 1995) 131–46.

———. "Breast Cancer: Issues and Resources," *Lesbian and Gay Studies Newsletter* 22.3(Fall 1995): 10–15.

———. "Against Epistemology," in *Questions of Evidence: Proof, Practice, and Persusasion Across the Disciplines*, eds. James Chandler, et al. (Chicago: University of Chicago Press, 1994) 132–36.

———. With Michael Moon. "Queers in (Single-Family) Space," *Assemblage: A Critical Journal of Architecture and Design Culture* 24(August 1994): 30–37.

———. "Queer Performativity: Henry James's The Art of the Novel," *GLQ* 1.1(1993): 1–16.

———. "Queer & Now," in *Trotsky and Wild Orchids: Messages from American Universities*, ed. Mark Edmundson (New York: Penguin Books, 1993) 237–66.

———. "White Glasses," *Yale Journal of Criticism* 5.3(Fall 1992): 193–208.

———. "Gender Criticism," in *Redrawing the Boundaries of Literary Study in English*, eds. Stephen Greenblatt and Giles Gunn (New York: Modern Language Association, 1993) 271–302.

———. "Socratic Raptures, Socratic Ruptures: Notes Toward Queer Performativity," in *English Inside and Out: The Places of Literary Criticism (Essays from the 50th Anniversary of the English Institute)*, eds. Susan Gubar and Jonathan Kamholtz (New York: Routledge, 1993) 122–36.

———. "Nationalisms and Sexualities in the Age of Wilde," in *Nationalisms and Sexualities*, eds. Andrew Parker, et al. (New York: Routledge, 1991) 235–45.

——. "Epidemics of the Will," in *Incorporations*, eds. Jonathan Crary and Sanford Kwinter (New York: Zone, 1992) 582–95.

——. "How To Bring Your Kids Up Gay," *Social Text* 29.9:4 (1991): 18–27.

——. "Writing, Gay Studies, and Affection [Memorial for Michael Lynch]," *Lesbian and Gay Studies Newsletter* 18.3(November 1991): 8–13.

——. "Jane Austen and the Masturbating Girl," *Critical Inquiry* 17.4(Summer 1991): 818–37.

Moon, Michael, and Eve Kosofsky Sedgwick, "Divinity: A Dossier, A Performance Piece, A Little-Understood Emotion," *Discourse: A Journal for Theoretical Studies in Media and Culture* 13.1(Fall–Winter 1990–91): 12–39.

——. "Pedagogy in the Context of an Antihomophobic Project," *South Atlantic Quarterly* 89.1(Winter 1989): 139–56.

——. "Review of Sandra Gilbert and Susan Gubar, *No Man's Land, Vol. 1: The War of the Words*," *English Language Notes* 28.1 (September 1990): 73–77.

——. "Tide and Trust," *Critical Inquiry* 15:4(Summer 1989): 745–57.

——. "Across Gender, Across Sexuality: Willa Cather and Others," *South Atlantic Quarterly* 88.1(Winter 1989): 53–72. (Rpt. in *Displacing Homophobia: Gay Male Perspectives in Literature and Culture*, eds. Ronald R. Butters, et al. [Durham: Duke University Press, 1990] 53–72.)

——. "Epistemology of the Closet(I)," *Raritan* 7.4 (Spring 1988): 39–69.

——. "Epistemology of the Closet(II)," *Raritan* 8.1(Summer, 1988): 102–30.

——. "Privilege of Unknowing: Epistemology and Lesbianism in Diderot," *Genders* 1.1(Spring 1988): 102–24.

——. "A Poem is Being Written," *Representations* 17 (Winter 1987): 110–143.

——. "The Beast in the Closet: James and the Writing of Homosexual Panic," in *Sex, Politics, and Science in the Nineteenth-Century: Selected Papers from the English Institute (1983–84)*, ed. Ruth Bernard Yeazell (Baltimore: Johns Hopkins University Press, 1986) 148–86.

——. "Sabrina Doesn't Live Here Anymore," *Amherst Student* (Winter 1985).

——. "Sexualism and the Citizen of the World: Wycherley, Sterne, and Male Homosocial Desire," *Critical Inquiry* 11.2(December 1984): 226–45.

——. "Whitman's Transatlantic Context: Class, Gender, and Male Homosexual Desire," *Delta: Revue du Centre d'Etudes et de Recherche sur les Ecrivains du Sud aux Etats Unis* 16 (May 1983): 111–24.

——. "Homophobia, Misogyny, and Capital: The Example of Our Mutual Friend," *Raritan* 2.3(Winter 1983): 126–51.

——. "Review of David Punter, *The Literature of Terror: A History of Gothic Fictions from 1765 to The Present Day*," *Studies in Romanticism* 21.2(Summer 1982): 243–53.

——. "The Vibrant Politics of Josephine Miles," *Epoch* 31.1 (Fall–Winter 1982): 68–76.

——. "The Character in the Veil: Imagery of the Surface in the Gothic Novel," *PMLA* 96.2(March 1981): 255–270.

Interviews

Williams, Jeffrey, "Sedgwick Unplugged (An Interview with Eve Kosofsky Sedgwick)," *Minnesota Review: A Journal of Committed Writing* 40(Spring–Summer 1993): 52–64.

Kerr, Mark and Kristen O'Rourke, "Sedgwick Sense and Sensibility: An Interview with Eve Kosofsky Sedgwick." http://www.smpcollege.com/litlinks/critical/sedgwick.htm.

Poetry

Sedgwick, Eve Kosofsky, "Pandas in Trees," *Women and Performance* 8.2 (1996): 175–83.

——. "Penn Central: New Haven Line," *Los Angeles Times Book Review*, Oct. 2, 1994.

——. "Our," *Raleigh News and Observer*, Sept. 25, 1994.

——. "Selections from 'The Warm Decembers,'" *Raritan* 6.2(Fall 1986): 51–62.

——. "Sestina Lente," *The Massachusetts Review* 25.4(Winter 1984): 576–78.

——. "Trace at 46," *Diacritics* 10.1 (Spring 1980): 3–20.

——. "Sexual Hum," *Salmagundi* 14.3 (Winter 1979): 102.

——. "Ring of Fire," "When, in Minute Script," and "An Essay on the Picture Plane," *Poetry Miscellany* 5, (1975).

——. "Explicit" and "The Palimpsest," *Epoch* 24.2 (Winter, 1975): 112–13.

——. "A Death by Water" and "Artery," *Epoch* 23.3 (Fall 1973): 78–79.

Chapters and Articles Anthologized after Initial Publication

From **Tendencies**

Sedgwick, Eve Kosofsky, "Jane Austen and the Masturbating Girl," rpt. in *Questions of Evidence*, ed. James Chandler et al. (Chicago: University of

Chicago Press, 1994); rpt. in *Psychoanalysis and Cultural Studies*, ed. E.
Ann Kaplan (London: Edward Elgar, 1995); rpt. in *Solitary Pleasures: The
Historical, Literary, and Artistic Discourses of Autoeroticism*, eds. Paula
Bennett and Vernon A. Rosario (New York: Routledge, 1995) 133–53.

——. "How To Bring Your Kids Up Gay," rpt. in *Fear of a Queer Planet: Queer
Politics and Social Theory*, ed. Michael Warner (Minneapolis: University
of Minnesota Press, 1993) 69–81; rpt. *The Children's Culture Reader*, ed.
Henry Jenkins (New York: New York University Press, 1998) 231–40.

Moon, Michael, and Eve Kosofsky Sedgwick, "Divinity: A Dossier, A Performance Piece, A Little-Understood Emotion," rpt. in *Staging Public Out-
rage*, ed. Stephen Tifft (Ithaca: Cornell University Press, 1994).

——. "Tales of the Avunculate: The Importance of Being Earnest," rpt. *Pro-
fessions of Desire: Lesbian and Gay Theory, Criticism and Pedagogy*, eds.
George Haggerty and Bonnie Zimmerman (New York: Modern Language
Association, 1995) 191–209.

From **Epistemology of the Closet**

——. "Axiomatic," rpt. in *The Cultural Studies Reader*, ed. Simon During
(London: Routledge, 1993) 244–68.

——. "Pedagogy in the Context of an Anti-Homophobic Project," rpt. in *The
Politics of Liberal Education*, eds. Darryl J. Gless and Barbara Herrnstein
Smith (Durham: Duke University Press, 1992) 145–62.

——. "Axiom 6: The Relation of Gay Studies to Debates on the Literary
Canon Is, and Had Best Be, Tortuous," rpt. in *Falling into Theory: Conflicting Views on Reading Literature*, ed. David H. Richter (Boston: Bed-
ford Books of St. Martin's Press, 1994) 181–86.

——. "Epistemology of the Closet," rpt. in *The Lesbian and Gay Studies
Reader*, eds. Henry Abelove, et al. (New York: Routledge, 1993) 45–66.

——. "Billy Budd: After the Homosexual," rpt. in *Herman Melville: A
Collection of Critical Essays*, ed. Myra Jehlen (Englewood Cliffs, N.J.:
Prentice-Hall, 1994) 217–34.

——. "The Beast in the Closet: James and the Writing of Homosexual Panic,"
rpt. in *American Literature American Culture*, ed. Gordon Hutner (New
York: Oxford University Press, 1995); rpt. in *New Century Views: Henry
James*, ed. Ruth Bernard Yeazell (New York: Prentice-Hall, 1994); rpt. as
"Das Tier in der Kammer: Henry James und das Schreiben homosexueller
Angst," in *Deckonstrucktiver Femininismus: Literaturwissenschaft in
Amerika*, ed. Barbara Vinken, and trans. Hans Dieter Gondek (Frankfurt:
Suhrkamp, 1992) 247–78; rpt. *Homosexual Themes in Literary Studies*,
eds. Wayne R. Dynes and Stephen Donaldson (New York: Garland, 1992)

300–38; rpt. in *Speaking of Gender*, ed. Elaine Showalter (New York: Routledge, 1989) 243–68.

——. "Wilde, Nietzsche, and the Sentimental Relations of the Male Body,"
rpt. in *Oscar Wilde: A Collection of Critical Essays*, ed. Jonathan Freed-
man (Upper Saddle River, N.J.: Prentice-Hall, 1996) 193–233.

From Between Men: English Literature and Male Homosocial Desire

——. "Introduction" and "Gender Asymmetry and Erotic Triangles," rpt. in
Feminisms: Gender and Literary Studies, eds. Robyn Warhol and Diane
Price Herndl (New Brunswick: Rutgers University Press, 1991) 507–23
and 524–31, respectively.

——. "Homophobia, Misogyny, Capital: The Example of Our Mutual
Friend," rpt. in *Raritan Reading*, ed. Richard Poirier (New Brunswick:
Rutgers University Press, 1990) 329–50; rpt. in *Modern Critical Views:
Charles Dickens*, ed. Harold Bloom (New Haven: Chelsea House, 1987);
rpt. in *Charles Dickens*, ed. Steven Connor (London: Longman, 1996)
178–96.

——. "Adam Bede and Henry Esmond: Homosocial Desire and the His-
toricity of the Female." rpt. in *The New Historicism Reader*, ed. H. Aram
Veeder (New York: Routledge, 1994) 270–94.

——. "Tennyson's Princess: One Bride for Seven Brothers," rpt. in *Critical
Essays on Alfred Lord Tennyson*, ed. Herbert F. Tucker (New York: G. K.
Hall, 1993) 125–35; rpt. in *Tennyson*, ed. Rebecca Stott (London: Long-
man, 1996) 181–96.

——. "Murder Incorporated: James Hogg's Confessions of a Justified Sinner,"
rpt. in *Romanticism: A Critical Reader*, ed. Duncun Wu (Oxford: Blackwell's, 1995) 359–77.

Stephen M. Barber is Assistant Professor of English at the University of Rhode Island. He has published on 1930s British and European culture, Virginia Woolf, Michel Foucault, and Gilles Deleuze.

Lauren Berlant is Professor of English and the Director of the Center for Gender Studies at the University of Chicago. She teaches and writes about cultural studies, sexuality theory, the novel (especially the historical novel and the romance), popular and mass culture, U.S. minority literatures, and nation formation. She has written over two dozen articles in journals such as *Social Text* and *Feminist Studies*, and is the co-editor of *Critical Inquiry* and *Public Culture*. Author of two books, *The Anatomy of National Fantasy: Hawthorne, Utopia, and Everyday Life*, and *The Queen of America Goes to Washington City: Essays on Sex and Citizenship*, she is also editor of *Intimacy* and co-editor (with Lisa Duggan) of *Our Monica, Ourselves: The Clinton Affair and the Public Interest*.

Deborah P. Britzman is a Professor of Education, Social and Political Thought, and Women's Studies at York University, Toronto. She is author of *Lost Subjects, Contested Objects: Toward a Psychoanalytic Inquiry of Learning* and *After-Education: Anna Freud, Melanie Klein and Psychoanalytic Histories of Learning*.

Judith Butler is Maxine Elliot Professor in the Departments of Rhetoric and Comparative Literature at the University of California, Berkeley. She is the author of *Subjects of Desire: Hegelian Reflections in Twentieth-Century France, Gender Trouble: Feminism and the Subversion of Identity, Bodies That Matter: On the Discursive Limits of "Sex," The Psychic Life of Power: Theories of Subjection, Excitable Speech*, as well as numerous articles and contributions on philosophy, feminist and queer theory. Her most recent work on Antigone and the politics of kinship is entitled *Antigone's Claim: Kinship Between Life and Death*. Her new project is a critique of ethical violence that works with modernist philosophical and literary texts.

Ross Chambers is the Marvin Felheim Distinguished University Professor of French and Comparative Literature at the University of Michigan, Ann Arbor. His current research, for a book to be entitled *Untimely Interventions*, concerns the rhetoric of testimonial writing in Australia, France, and North America in the twentieth century. It refers to the writing of the 1914–18 war, the Holocaust, and especially AIDS.

David L. Clark is Professor in the Department of English at McMaster University, Hamilton, Canada, where he teaches critical theory, continental philosophy, and courses in the discourses of HIV/AIDS. He has twice been Visiting Professor at the Center for the Study of Theory and Criticism at the University of Western Ontario. His published work ranges in subject matter from philosophical conceptions of animality, to structures of addiction in Heidegger and Schelling, to the question of the surgical separation of conjoined twins. Co-editor of *Intersections: Nineteenth-Century Philosophy and Contemporary Theory* and *New Romanticisms: Theory and Critical Practice*, he is completing projects on the work of mourning in Schelling and on desire and disavowal in Kant's late texts.

Douglas Crimp is a Professor of Visual and Cultural Studies at the University of Rochester. He is a recipient of the College Art Association's Frank Jewett Mather Award for distinction in art criticism and twice recipient of the Critics Fellowship from the National Endowment for the Arts. He is the author of *On the Museum's Ruins*, and *AIDS Demo Graphics*, and editor of *AIDS: Cultural Analysis/Cultural Activism*. A collection of his writings on AIDS and sexual politics, *Melancholia and Moralism*, is forthcoming from MIT Press in 2002. He is currently writing a book on the films of Andy Warhol.

Paul Kelleher is a doctoral candidate in English at Princeton University. His dissertation, "Feeling Queer: Sentimentalism, Sexuality, and the Ethical Life in English Literature," rereads the history of sexuality through the literature and philosophy of sentimentalism. He is also the author of forthcoming essays on perverse childhood in Freud, Klein, and Foucault, and queer forms of affect and social relation in Enlightenment and contemporary philosophy.

James Kincaid is Aerol Arnold Professor of English at the University of Southern California and author of, most recently, *Erotic Innocence: The Culture of Child Molesting, Annoying the Victorians*, and *Child Loving: The Erotic Child and Victorian Culture*.

Nancy K. Miller is Distinguished Professor of English and Comparative Literature at the Graduate Center, CUNY. Her recent books include: *Getting Personal: Feminist Occasions and Other Autobiographical Acts* and *Bequest and Betrayal: Memoirs of a Parent's Death*. A co-edited collection, *Extremities: Trauma, Testimony, and Community*, will appear in 2002, as well as her personal essays, *But Enough about Me*.

Melissa Solomon is a Ph.D. candidate in the department of English at Duke University. Her research interests include race, gender, and sexuality studies and nineteenth- and twentieth-century American literature. She has published an essay on Henry James in *Novel Gazing: Queer Readings in Fiction*, edited by Eve Kosofsky Sedgwick, and is the co-author, with Christopher Newfield, of "Few of our seeds ever came up at all: A Dialogue on Hawthorne, Delany, and the Work of Affect in Visionary Utopias," an essay in the forthcoming Duke University Press collection, *No More Separate Spheres!*, edited by Cathy N. Davidson and Jessamyn Hatcher. In addition, Solomon is the managing editor of the *Lesbian and Gay Studies Newsletter*, published by the gay and lesbian caucus of the Modern Language Association. She is writing a dissertation titled "Queer American Ladies and Friends" on lesbian allegory and affect in turn-of-the-century American Literature.

Kathryn Bond Stockton, Associate Professor of English at the University of Utah, is the author of *God Between Their Lips: Desire Between Women in Irigaray, Brontë and Eliot*. Her articles have appeared in, among other places, *boundary 2*, *Novel*, and *Cultural Critique*. She is currently finishing a book on debasement that engages queer connections to anal economics, miscegenation, stone butch wounds, and the brain's prophylactic relations with the dead. A third book, under way, is tentatively titled *The Queer Child*.

INDEX

Mackenzie, Henry, 154
The Man of Feeling, 154
MacKinnon, Catherine, 237
Maddox, Everette, 49
Mailer, Norman, 240
male paranoid plot, 6
See also under male (paranoid Gothic)
Mallarmé, Stéphane, 40
MAMM Magazine, 255
Marx, Karl, 111
masochism, 42, 43, 182–83, 186–91, 194–96
See also masochist pedagogue; S/M
Masochism: Coldness and Cruelty; Venus in Furs" (Gilles Deleuze), 189
masochist pedagogue, 193
masochist sublime, 245
McKeon, Michael, 159n.12
The Origins of the English Novel, 159n.12
Melville, Herman, 177–78
Merrill, James, 181
Mill, John Stuart, 73, 144
Autobiography, 73
Miller, D. A., 24, 47, 148, 232
"Secret Subjects, Open Secrets," 148
Miller, Nancy K., 24, 45, 46
minoritizing/universalizing (views of homo/heterosexual identity), 40, 116–17, 124, 150, 166–78, 203
See also essentialist-constructivist debate; homo/heterosexual definition(s)
misrecognition, 32, 71, 72, 75, 81, 86, 89, 102, 104, 126
poetics of, 71, 72, 104
Mitchell, Juliet, 124
modernity, 74, 146
attitude of, in Foucault, 8
epistemology of, 117
in Frances Barker, 31
Moon, Michael, 14, 43, 118, 181, 182
"A Small Boy and Others: Sexual Disorientation in Henry James, Kenneth Anger, and David Lynch," 182

Nabokov, Vladimir, 102
NAMBLA (North American Man Boy Love Association), 184, 196
negation, 72, 81, 84, 91, 104
denegation, 87, 88
Freud on, 131
in Klein, 135
New Republic, 184
New York Times, 63, 64, 253

Nietzsche, Friedrich, 36, 150, 176, 177, 246, 250
Genealogy of Morals, 246
umwertung, 176
normativity, 40, 151–52, 174
The Norton Anthology of Theory and Criticism, 41

open secret, 148, 149, 175, 182
optimism, 71–72, 74, 75, 81, 84
compulsion to repeat 85, 87, 89, 90, 92–94, 102–4
O'Rourke, Kristen, 1, 41
Owens, Craig, 16

Pale Fire (Vladimir Nabokov), 76
paranoid Gothic, 22, 147–49, 243
male, 144, 146, 151, 152, 157
See also Gothic, the; male paranoid plot
paranoid reading, 24, 39, 46, 149, 239
See also reparative reading
paranoid-schizoid position: Sedgwick's use of, 37
Klein on, 125, 130, 132, 135, 138n.5, 139n.7
See also depressive position
Parker, Andrew, 9, 15
Performativity and Performance, 9, 16
performance/performativity studies, 9
performative acts, 8
performative utterances, 9
performativity, 2, 9, 26–27
and the transformation of shame, 65
of Warhol's performers, 67
operative in *Gender Trouble*, 64
Peter Pan, 79, 89
Petot, Jean-Michel, 134
phantasy: Klein on, 38, 122–25, 127–31, 133–36
Phenomenology of Spirit (Georg Wilhelm Friedrich Hegel), 28, 111, 246
Phillips, Adam, 91–92, 133
"On Composure," 91
Pierce, Kimberley, 35, 36
Boys Don't Cry (film), 35–36, 114–16
Plimpton, George, 62
Edie: American Girl, with Jean Stein, 62–63
The Political Unconscious (Frederic Jameson), 75
Pontalis, J. B., 134, 137n.2
Popism (Andy Warhol), 58, 59, 62
POZ (magazine), 255
See also MAMM Magazine